Beckett's Words

The Promise of Happiness in a Time of Mourning

Also available from Bloomsbury

Damned to Fame: The Life of Samuel Beckett, James Knowlson
Samuel Beckett: A Curated Life, Judith Wilkinson
The Dramatic Works of Samuel Beckett, Charles A. Carpenter

Beckett's Words

The Promise of Happiness in a Time of Mourning

DAVID KLEINBERG-LEVIN

Bloomsbury Academic
An imprint of Bloomsbury Publishing Plc

B L O O M S B U R Y
LONDON · NEW DELHI · NEW YORK · SYDNEY

Bloomsbury Academic

An imprint of Bloomsbury Publishing Plc

50 Bedford Square	1385 Broadway
London	New York
WC1B 3DP	NY 10018
UK	USA

www.bloomsbury.com

BLOOMSBURY and the Diana logo are trademarks of Bloomsbury Publishing Plc

First published 2015

© David Kleinberg-Levin, 2015

British Library Cataloguing-in-Publication Data

A catalogue record for this book is available from the British Library.

ISBN:	HB:	978-1-47421-685-2
	PB:	978-1-47421-683-8
	ePDF:	978-1-47421-686-9
	ePub:	978-1-47421-688-3

Library of Congress Cataloging-in-Publication Data

A catalog record for this book is available from the Library of Congress.

Typeset by RefineCatch Limited, Bungay, Suffolk
Printed and bound in India

The dog believes that his master is at the door. But can he also believe that his master will come the day after tomorrow? Can someone have hope only if able to talk? —Only someone who has mastered the use of language. Situations of hoping are instances of this complicated form of life.

—*Ludwig Wittgenstein*, Philosophical Investigations

CONTENTS

ACKNOWLEDGEMENTS

I would like here to remember and acknowledge, with heartfelt thanks, a few friends with whom, since I began to contemplate writing something on Beckett, I have enjoyed conversations that have contributed in significant ways to making this present work a much better undertaking than it otherwise would have been. Hoping that my increasingly weak memory is not failing me, I wish in particular to thank Jay Bernstein, Gerald Bruns, Seamus Carey, William J. Earle, Doris Gahler, Robert Hullot-Kentor, Michael McGillen, Gregg Horowitz, John S. Rockwell, and David C. Wood. It should of course be understood that I alone am responsible for the words in this book.

I thank the Samuel Beckett Estate, Grove Atlantic, and Faber & Faber for permission to use textual material from Beckett's published works. See the permissions page at the end of this volume.

For the cover image of *Et in Arcadia Ego* (1618–1622) by Giovanni Francesco Barbieri (Il Guercino), I thank the Soprintendenza Speciale per il Patrimonio Storico, Artistico ed Etnoantropologico e per il Polo Museale della Città di Roma. This lovely painting, which I am very fond of, is on exhibit in the Galleria Nazionale d'Arte Antica, Palazzo Barberini, Rome.

The book's cover

Only a part of the painting is shown on the cover of this volume. Not shown is the second, younger shepherd, whose gentle visage is lit up by the sun shining into the clearing. Also not shown is an owl, Minerva's delegate, perched on the branch of a tree overlooking the skull. The skull that the two astonished shepherds encounter, evoking the lonely soliloquies of Beckett's prose "skullscapes," should remind us that, even in paradise, it is Death that writes the last sentence. The lower tree branch, gesturing on the right, minatory and ominous, suggests Death's bony fingers, extending the justice of the word.

ABBREVIATIONS

AT   Theodor Adorno, *Aesthetic Theory*, trans. Robert Hullot-Kentor (Minneapolis: University of Minnesota Press, 1997).

C   Samuel Beckett, *Company*, in *Nowhere On: Company, Ill Seen Ill Said, Worstward Ho* (New York: Grove Press, 1996).

H   Samuel Beckett, *How It Is* (New York: Grove Press, 1964).

IS   Samuel Beckett, *Il Seen Ill Said*, in *Nohow On*, ed. S. E. Gontarski (New York: Grove Press, 1996).

MD   Samuel Beckett, *Malone Dies*, in *Samuel Beckett, Three Novels: Molloy, Malone Dies, The Unnamable* (New York: Grove Press, n.d.).

MO   Samuel Beckett, *Molloy*, in *Samuel Beckett, Three Novels: Molloy, Malone Dies, The Unnamable* (New York: Grove Press, n.d.).

TN   Samuel Beckett, *Texts for Nothing*, in *Stories and Texts for Nothing*, trans. Samuel Beckett (New York: Grove Press, 1967).

UN   Samuel Beckett, *The Unnamable*, in *Samuel Beckett, Three Novels: Molloy, Malone Dies, The Unnamable* (New York: Grove Press, n.d.).

WG   Samuel Beckett, *Waiting for Godot* (New York: Grove Press, 1954).

WH   Samuel Beckett, *Worstward Ho*, in *Nohow On*, ed. S. E. Gontarski (New York: Grove Press, 1996).

WP   Friedrich Nietzsche, *The Will to Power*, trans. Walter Kaufmann (New York: Random House Vintage, 1967).

PROLOGUE

Nothing ... But Words: Words and Tears

*And you have seen their fruitless longing, a longing
that should have been fulfilled, but was given
them [instead] for their eternal mourning.*

DANTE ALIGHIERI, *Purgatorio*[1]

"Our age," says Kierkegaard, "will remind one of the dissolution of the Greek city-state: everything goes on as usual, and yet there is no longer anyone who believes in it. The invisible spiritual bond which gave it validity no longer exists, and so the whole age is at once comic and tragic—tragic because it is perishing, comic because it goes on."[2] Beckett's works, at once tragic and comic in just this sense, are indeed works of and for our time.

In writing about Nietzsche's words proclaiming that "God is dead," Heidegger reflects that, "When God dies as the metaphysical ground and orientation of all reality, [...] then human beings no longer know where they are and where they are going."[3] And he urged us to find our way by listening to language, observing that we are human "only because of what is granted [*Zuspruch*] by language."[4] What language grants, as Derrida has argued, is the promise: "The promise is the basic element of language."[5] Indeed, as we shall learn, what language grants is the promise *in* the promise.

In an important reference to Beckett, Theodor Adorno also invokes the promise—that is, the promise of happiness, although he does not relate it explicitly, here, to the bearing of language as such:

> Beckett's *ecce homo* [dismantling the subject] is what has become of human beings. They look mutely out from his sentences as though with eyes whose tears have dried up. The spell they cast and under which they stand is broken by being reflected in them. The *minimal promise*

of happiness which they contain, which refuses to be traded for any consolation, was to be had only at the price of a thoroughgoing articulation, to the point of worldlessness.[6]

Adorno had little hope for the future; but the little that he could permit himself was what he could draw, above all, from true works of art. "All that art is capable of," however, "is to grieve for the sacrifice it makes and which it itself, in its powerlessness, is."[7] True art, for him, is the preserve of the imagination in its struggle against all the forces of repression and inhumanity. Hence he argues, with implications for an understanding of the uncanny element of comedy even in Beckett's darkest works, that, "The more profoundly society fails to deliver the reconciliation that the bourgeois spirit promised as the enlightenment of myth, the more irresistibly humour is pulled down into the netherworld, and laughter, once the image of humanness, becomes a regression to inhumanity."[8]

But of course, art alone cannot redeem the world. Nor can philosophical thought. But there is, nevertheless, a need for philosophical thought, which must assume its proper responsibility—a responsibility that, in part, calls for it to sustain the promise of reconciliation borne by the work of art:

> The only philosophy which can be responsibly practiced in face of despair is the attempt to contemplate all things as they would present themselves from the standpoint of redemption. Knowledge has no light but that shed on the world by redemption [. . .]. Perspectives must be fashioned that displace and estrange the world, reveal it to be, with its rifts and crevices, as indigent and distorted as it will appear one day in the messianic light. To gain such perspectives without velleity or violence, entirely from felt contact with its objects—this alone is the task of thought.[9]

In writing this present volume of philosophical criticism on Beckett's literary works, I am attempting, in keeping with Adorno's persistent exhortations, to continue the articulation of this urgent undertaking. My claim is that, with just one exception, namely *The Lost Ones*, a horrifying evocation of the gas chambers in Auschwitz-Birkenau, even in the darkest of Beckett's plays and stories, the light of this redemption, weak though it is, can occasionally be glimpsed.

§1

How can literature's words bear the promise of happiness for the spirit of our time, a time of immeasurable loss and mourning? Mourning: not only over the death of God with all that means for our moral, spiritual and epistemic confidence, consolation, reassurance, and peace of mind, but also over the remoteness, still, even now, of a justice worthy of humanity. Beckett eloquently expresses this spirit of the time when, in *How It Is*, his narrator says: "I keep dying in a dying age."[10]

There is a phrase in *The Unnamable* (1949–1953) that expresses in sublimely condensed form what I think compelled Beckett to write: "the little murmur of unconsenting man, to murmur what it is their humanity stifles."[11] This gets at the very heart of Beckett's commitment to writing. It expresses his imperative. Beckett is one of the greatest storytellers of the twentieth century, a keenly perceptive witness to the human condition in our time, radically transforming the storytelling art he inherited. I resolved to write this volume not only to explain my admiration for his art—an art whose time Benjamin, for reasons somewhat different from Hegel's, once believed to be past—but also as a way to attain a deeper and richer understanding of the philosophical significance of the stories he tells. But of equal importance for me is the hermeneutics and phenomenology of language, which I shall be approaching in large measure from the perspectives that figure in the writings of Benjamin and Adorno. Drawing on their contributions, I shall situate Beckett's storytelling in the context of modernist aesthetics, literary innovation, and the phenomenology of language; and I will show, taking us into the realm of political theology, how Beckett's ways of using words relate to questions of faith and hope in the *terrestrial* fulfillment of the promise of justice essential for the sharing of happiness in ethical life.

In his "Theologico-Political Fragment" (1920–1921), Benjamin argued that the secular world "should be erected on the idea of happiness."[12] By this, he meant a *universal* happiness impossible without the achievement of justice. In his later 1940 reflections "On the Concept of History," he asserted that "our image of happiness is so indissolubly bound up with the image of redemption that the former may be said to carry the latter as an abiding resonance."[13] Moreover: "The same applies to the idea of the past, which is the concern of history. The past carries within it a secret index by which it is referred to redemption." He also said, in the "Fragment," that this image is "thoroughly coloured by the time to which the course of our own existence has assigned us." It is in keeping with this third proposition that we find Beckett's themes of happiness and justice cast in the word-images of a world that must now survive without the manifest presence of God. This world into which his characters are thrown is bleak and gray, colored by a sense of loss. It is a time of mourning. And yet, there *is* this "secret index." In "Commitment," his essay on the question of a politically committed literature, Adorno recognizes in Beckett just such a "secret index." He insists that it is always possible to detect, even in the grimmest of Beckett's stories, at least some hints of a "minimal promise of happiness." It is those intermittent hints, those occasional traces or echoes of a promise, omens and auguries, about which I want us to think, bearing in mind, however, that, as Jacques Rancière mischievously observed, leaving "construction" open to interpretation, "discourse on fiction is always itself a construction of fiction."[14]

*

After attending recently a performance of some extremely short Beckett plays, a fragment of an imagined conversation erupted into consciousness from the depths of my mind, just as I was crossing into sleep:

"It's not easy being human."
"Don't worry. You'll get over it!"

What does my natural consciousness seem to know that I do not? What could justify such faith—if that is what those words ultimately mean? But if, in the world through which we briefly pass, one does not shut one's eyes and turn a deaf ear, how easy is it, really, to go on? Staying close to events, what one sees is enough to make one weep. Viewing this world from a distance, as in Beckett's theater, one might be overcome by laughter. But the laughter would likely have come only to make the unbearable bearable. A bitter laugh, never removed far enough from the misery of the world to become entirely pure or god-like.[15]

Beckett's "comedies" work as "morality plays," simultaneously generating social critique and utopian imagination; however, although they provide moments of superficial amusement, relief from the assault on our defenses, they ultimately leave us without, in Adorno's words, any comfortably secure "place of reconciliation from which one could laugh."[16] Yet laughter in Beckett is not a cynical expression of nihilism, nor is it disdain for the world, but far rather, as Gilles Deleuze says, comparing Beckett to the painter Francis Bacon, an intensely compelling response to the ontological and existential conditions of life: "In the very act of 'representing' horror, mutilation, prosthesis, fall, or failure, they have erected indomitable figures, indomitable through both their insistence and their presence. They have given life a new and extremely direct power of laughter."[17] In *Aesthetic Theory*, what Adorno said about the connection between comedy and the sublime, no doubt with Beckett in mind, suggests how we might understand that subsequent remark by Deleuze. For Adorno: "The legacy of the sublime is unassuaged negativity, as stark and illusionless as was once promised by the semblance of the sublime. This is at the same time the legacy of the comic" (AT 199).

In *The Will to Power*, Nietzsche opines that perhaps he knows best why man alone laughs: "he alone suffers so deeply that he had to invent laughter. The unhappiest and most melancholy animal is, as fitting, the most cheerful."[18] It is the laughter of protest and resistance, refusing to accept the unacceptable. At a certain point in Beckett's *Endgame* (1955–1957), Nell says: "Nothing is funnier than unhappiness. . . . It's like the funny story we have heard too often, we still find it funny but we don't laugh any more."[19] Stanley Cavell comments on this:

As it is, we've heard it all, seen it all too often, heard the promises, seen the suffering repeated in the same words and gestures, and they are like any words which have been gone over so much that they are worn strange. We don't laugh, we don't cry; and we don't laugh that we don't cry, and we obviously can't cry about it. Now that's funny.[20]

The world that Beckett (1906–1989) depicts, especially in his early work and the works written soon after the Second World War, is a world of physical, moral, and spiritual devastation in which people, painfully estranged from one another, emotionally isolated and reduced to the minimum conditions necessary for survival, are hungry for meaning and desperately seeking to find refuge in the chattering of words, afraid of the silence that words empty of meaning fall into. But even when the dominant mood is dark, there is vaudeville comedy in the works for the stage and moments of wit, humor and wordplay in the stories for reading. What happiness is possible in that world—*our* world?

Contemplating the entirety of Beckett's works, when all is said and done, I cannot associate him, despite the moments of comedy and laughter, with the existential absurdity of Gide, Camus, and Sartre. The predominant mood he leaves me with can be expressed only by a traumatized shudder at all the horrors this planet has borne.

Of Beckett's works, Adorno observes that "everyone shrinks from them in horror, and yet none can deny that these eccentric novels and plays are about things everyone knows and no one wants to talk about." "Philosophical apologists," he says,

> may find it convenient to view Beckett's oeuvre as an anthropological sketch, but in fact it deals with an extremely concrete historical state of affairs: the dismantling of the subject. Beckett's *ecce homo* is what has become of human beings. They look mutely out from his sentences as though with eyes whose tears have dried up. The spell they cast and under which they stand is broken by being reflected in them. The minimal promise of happiness [*Glücksversprechen*] that they contain, which refuses to be traded for any consolation, was to be had only at the price of a thoroughgoing articulation, to the point of worldlessness. All commitment to the world has to be cancelled if the idea of the committed work of art is to be fulfilled. [. . .] Kafka's prose and Beckett's plays, and his genuinely colossal novel *The Unnamable*, have an effect in comparison to which official works of committed art [such as Sartre's plays and novels] look like children's games—they actually arouse the anxiety that existentialism only talks about. In dismantling illusion they explode art from the inside [. . .].[21]

*

This book is the third volume in a trilogy giving thought to how language, in literature, might bear the promise of happiness.[22] What in this volume I want to claim is at stake for Beckett concerns the prospect, occasionally glimpsed, occasionally worded, of a morally, spiritually transformed world, a more humane world, its haunting *absence* remembered in this book using the figure, or trope, of the utopian or messianic "promise of happiness." In Beckett's stories, as we shall see, traces of this promise are redeemed for our memory— but only by a distressed use of language, words wrought as fault and failure. But in reading *How It Is*, we shall find that for Beckett, as for Benjamin and Adorno, the redeeming of this promise is ultimately not possible without the conditions of justice—a justice free of theology.

In the years following the Second World War, Beckett, feeling increasingly obsessed by an indeclinable "imperative" to write, abandoned his Joycean experiments with fiction-writing, as he began to formulate in clearer terms what kind of writing he thought the second half of the twentieth century required of him. If language is ever to redeem something of its sublime promise to make the world more humane, it must first be redeemed itself. But what "economy" of writing might undertake such redeeming? The answer that Beckett gradually found compelling was inherently paradoxical: only a language of destitution; only a language manifesting the "destitution" of the most sublime.[23] When the words fail to come or fail to do their work, as he knows they must, Beckett now says: "Fail again. Fail better."[24] His failures, as I shall argue, are inevitable, because the time of the traditional art of storytelling has irrevocably passed. But that untimeliness only makes the failures all the more urgent and timely. In Beckett's later stories and works for the stage, we are confronted with the emotional demands of this impoverished, denuded language, only occasionally permitted to shift from the "banality" of words bearing disavowed truth to the lyrical eloquence of "poetic" sentiment, recalling spirit's unbearable loss in the very expression of hope.

The terms of the project undertaken here in this volume require at once some explanation, even if at this point it is only in very brief hints. As we proceed, further definition will emerge, since the meaning of words emerges in their contexts of usage. By "utopia" I shall mean here, in an initial formulation, that ideal condition of a society, a world, in which the promise of happiness is grounded in—or say is a function or consequence of—the achievement of a time of reconciliation, such that all the historical antagonisms, diremptions, and contradictions, and all the malevolence—all the things responsible for avoidable forms of misery and suffering—are overcome and forever banished. However, as Adorno has argued, this would be the achievement of a movement in the direction of a justice befitting our humanity: "The reconciled condition would not be the philosophical imperialism of annexing the foreign. Instead, its happiness would lie in the fact that the foreign, in the proximity it is granted, remains what is distant and different [. . .]."[25] This same theme, which I take to imply a certain conception of social justice, was articulated in *Minima Moralia*, where he said

> Only by the recognition of distance in our neighbor is strangeness alleviated: accepted into consciousness. The presumption of undiminished

nearnesss present from the first, however, the flat denial of strangeness, does the other supreme injustice, virtually negates him as a particular human being and therefore the humanity in him, "counts him in," incorporates him in the inventory of property.[26]

This conception implies that my happiness is impossible without justice for all: "justice" broadly understood as ethical life, characterizing the right ways for human beings to live and dwell with one another. And if, as Heidegger says in "Building Dwelling Thinking," "mortals must ever search anew for the right way of dwelling, since they are still needing to learn what it means for mortals to dwell,"[27] then learning how to live with others who are "foreign," "alien," "strange," and different from us must be essential to our learning the way of dwelling.

Heidegger's words imply the need for "thinking": without mindfulness of the immeasurable and the unnamable illuminating the nature of our passage through life, he argues, building and dwelling will be abandoned to the nihilism of meaningless activity. For Adorno, however, what building and dwelling need first and foremost is a thinking that is capable of being a force of critical resistance, heightening consciousness in regard to the conditions and causes of suffering, but overcoming the temptations of resignation and cynicism. As he says, only such thinking "has the element of the universal." His argument concludes, defining the "happiness" with which, in our reading of Beckett, we shall be concerned:

> The happiness that dawns in the eye of the thinking person is the happiness of humanity. [. . .] Thought is happiness, even where it defines unhappiness by enunciating it. By this alone, happiness reaches into the universal unhappiness. Whoever does not let it atrophy has not capitulated to resignation.[28]

It might seem an unbelievably vain audacity, certainly a misreading too far-fetched, too counter-intuitive, for serious consideration, to undertake a reading of Beckett's works intent on showing their ways of signifying, or giving expression to, this promise of happiness. After all, his works are so massively gray and grim. But for a rigorously careful reading, there are, as I hope to show, surprising traces, rewarding glimpses, although most of them appear only dialectically, by way of negation, through a syntax of pain, figures of loss and absence, and expressions of almost hopeless longing.[29]

Beckett never forgot the thought, the dream, of happiness. Nor therefore would he ever forget justice—justice free of theodicy, though still an end in the distance. Even the very words he uses to negate it undo the negation, for they preserve it in memory and longing. Although tempted by resignation and despair, he never completely lost touch with the utopian dream, for we find that, even when his stories and images take us into the very depths of cruelty, suffering, despair, and deadness, the representation of our existential condition as an object for self-reflection summons into consciousness the longing for a finer humanity, keeping alive the promise of happiness. No doubt with Milton's poetic work in mind, Proust, whom Beckett read with admiration and insight, remarked that, "the true paradises are the paradises we have lost."[30] Paradoxically, it is in the mourning over what we have lost and in the nihilism of despair that the longing and the hope for happiness are most compellingly sustained. But in Beckett, this mourning is also filled with longing for a paradise that has never taken place: a *future* paradise to come, "*à venir.*" At stake for Beckett as writer, as storyteller, is—drawing, here, on the grammar of both the subjective and the objective senses of the genitive—language as the language *of* justice. Language holds the promise of happiness—holds it, however, in a structure of withholding. In Beckett, therefore, this promise can only be the name, and the enactment, of an absence almost lost in silence—the object of endless longing and mourning. In *Watt* (1945), he writes of the "nothingness" that "words enclose."[31] In *Happy Days* (1961), it is all about happiness, and the tone of his words can seem quite different—but they still enclose nothingness.

*

In the summer of 1930, Beckett was reading Schopenhauer. Writing a letter to his friend, Thomas MacGreevy, he expressed admiration for that philosopher's paradoxical "intellectual justification of unhappiness."[32] In his essay "On the Suffering of the World," Schopenhauer had argued that, if only we could see others as kindred sufferers, that experience might "remind us of what are the most necessary of all things: tolerance, patience, forbearance and charity," qualities of character which, he thought, "each of us needs and each of us therefore owes."[33] In other words, the dialectical "justification" of unhappiness, of suffering, modeled after Kant's equally paradoxical "justification" of war, consists in the assumption of the fact that our misery causes us to become aware of what is ethically required of us to overcome it. It would accordingly be reasonable to infer, I think, that these "most necessary of all things" are what would constitute, for him, the core of happiness—insofar as happiness is at all possible. And it should be noted, before we leave this thought, that, when we reflect on the four "necessary" factors, we can only conclude that the philosopher implicitly stakes the possibility of happiness on a humane response, oriented by the claims of justice, to the misery and suffering that seemingly constitute, for Beckett, the almost unbearable fate of the human condition.

In the context of this volume, I shall take this to mean that, if only for the sake of a negative critique of the present, it should make any sense at all to contemplate the utopia of happiness, we must imagine happiness to be inseparable from the gestures of ethical life, the gestures of justice, that would represent the "perfection" of our humanity, our capacity to acknowledge the other—above all, the *suffering* of the other. And this means, as Beckett's early experimental tale *Dante and the Lobster* (1932) poignantly reveals, responding not only to the suffering of human beings, but also to that of the other animals with which we share the planet— even the lobsters, who are very much alive when thrown into pots of boiling water. And as A. Alvarez points out, interpreting the allegorical meaning of that tale, "real agonies are [often] expressed by displacement and disguise."[34]

In keeping with Schopenhauer's dark vision, Beckett shows us much misery and suffering. But we should not hasten to infer that Beckett's works must exclude all traces of a utopian or messianic promise. Although the persistence of hope, the affirmation of that promise in the text and texture of his stories, frequently seems like the cruelest of jokes, for the most part appearing indirectly through negative images, as the narrated events defy meaning and the needed words fail to come, it will be the task of this volume to call attention to those hauntingly hopeful word-traces, allegorical figures, metaphors and allusions, no matter how ambiguous or questionable they may be, that suddenly appear within the narration of so much unjustifiable cruelty, misery, and suffering. Just as Beckett's character Watt searches for traces of the presence of the elusive Mr. Knott, his employer, who might, for all he knows, be the God of his faith, we shall search through Beckett's words for traces and echoes of the promise of happiness—"happiness" understood, here, as an issue of justice, the most humane way for us to be with others: what critical social theory, drawing on Hegel and Marx, represents by the concept of "reconciliation." Our profane redemption: a justified happiness—without the God of our fathers.

*

In 1857, Marie-Henri Beyle, Stendahl as he is commonly known, wrote in his essay "On Beauty" that, "beauty is only the *promise* of happiness." "La beauté," he declared, "n'est que la *promessse* de bonheur." A century later, Theodor Adorno would reformulate in a negative dialectic the skepticism weakening that dictum, making art the subject and arguing, accordingly, that what is true in art is something nonexistent—a time of happiness (AT 131). Moreover, he argued, amending Stendahl's assertion, that "Art is the ever broken promise of happiness" (AT 136, 311). Art will always *break* its promise, will always betray it, because art is only fiction, only aesthetic semblance. But at the same time that Adorno asserts that the promise to transform the world will always be broken, he nevertheless holds on to the conviction that art can still, to some extent, keep the promise, keep it alive, keep it going on, as the expression of a mimetic anticipation of the possible: what Ernst Bloch called an "anticipatory illumination," a "*Vor-Schein.*" However, even when it does this, it cannot *fulfill* the promise if it is to remain faithful to the dialectical logic of the utopian idea it bears. Paradoxically, it can accomplish this fidelity only by not fulfilling it, not keeping it, in order to keep the happiness that it promises as a critical incitement to ever-renewed efforts, something never to be finally achieved, free of fatal compromises. This, therefore, constitutes a second reason why art will always break the promise of happiness.

But how is the promise kept—kept, for example, in the art of literature? And what can we learn about the hermeneutical phenomenology of language from Beckett's stories and plays? How might *language* bear and impart intimations of the promise of happiness? In our reading of Beckett's works, we shall examine his word-constructions and inventions, narrative metaphors, allegorical figures and allusions, taking note of where and how this hopeful promise is manifest, where and how it appears.

In defending the free play of the imagination that figures in the language of surrealism, Georges Bataille argued, appropriating Kant, that the fiction surrealism has produced can expose readers to a novel experience of freedom, since words no longer bound to practical usefulness "set themselves free and so unleash the image of free existence."[35] He is right to call attention to the connections between aesthetic play, freedom, and utopian happiness. Adorno, however, accuses surrealism of frivolously "betraying" the promise of happiness, sacrificing "to the [mere] appearance of happiness transmitted by any integral form, concern for its truth."[36] But what is happiness? What is at stake in the claim that, in the realm of life as in art, happiness—happiness here on earth—can be no more than a *promise* of paradise? What is the justice that brings happiness? Why must earthbound justice free itself from the divine dispensations of justice in theodicy? And how does the very existence of language—language as such—bear and sustain, in its challenge to theodicy, that promise of happiness? Finally, taking Adorno's argument about art into the language of literature, I want to ask: How does that promise figure, how and where is it carried and imparted, in the storytelling language of literature? I would like these questions to serve as an indication of what, in the pages to follow, we shall be taking up for thought.

I now want to venture a connection between Adorno's claim about art and something that Wittgenstein remarked about language in a Cambridge "Lecture on Ethics": "I am tempted to say," he observed, "that the right expression in language for the miracle of the existence of the world, though it is not any proposition in language, is the very existence of language itself."[37] Bringing Adorno's and Wittgenstein's thoughts together, the principal claim I wish to explore in reading Beckett is: that language, as such, is the bearer, or metaphor, if only in the form of ciphers and traces, of the utopian or messianic promise of happiness. This promise, I want to say, is a structural feature of all language: an "arche-writing,"[38] if you will, that remains in effect but without determinate content, open accordingly to all communicative engagements. Thus, how it is engaged and set in motion—how, and in what institutional forms, it is made determinate—will be different in different political cultures and correspondingly different formations of language. Here, of course, our attention will be concentrated on how Beckett's distinctive appropriation of this structure operates in the writing of his fictional stories. Language may be full of promise, but its signifying power has irrevocably exposed us to nothingness.

*

Another way of rendering my principal claim here is to say: language bears a utopian or messianic promise that, like a transcendental condition, grounds the concealed inception of another history. But language does not merely "bear" this promise, does not merely "announce" it: Creatively, proleptically, struggling against the nihilism that perpetually haunts it, it *founds* the utopian, or messianic time of faith and hope. At stake, as will soon enough be evident, is a promise that I propose to interpret here as a question of justice—but justice in a sense more broadly conceived than is customary, namely, as concerned with the humanity of our relations with one another.

In "How to Avoid Speaking," a text engaging with theological questions provoked by his readings of Levinas, Benjamin, and others, Derrida wrote:

> The experience of negative theology perhaps holds to a promise, that of the other [. . .], not of this or that promise but of that which [. . .] inscribes us by its trace in language—before language.[39]

However, he warns, the "promise" which is at stake "will always have escaped the demand of presence," for it is that which "renders possible every present discourse."[40] What I want accordingly to argue is that the promise through which we are, as it were, "inscribed" is the utopian or messianic promise of happiness: a promise that indeed belongs to a past that has never yet been present; a promise, moreover, that in its appeal to our humanity, implies a new order of justice. (It should be recalled that, in his *Nichomachean Ethics*, Aristotle defined happiness, which he understood to be essentially related to the good, as the *telos* of political life.) This phrase, "promise of happiness," which has resounded for years in the discourse of critical social theory, will, in this book, therefore, be given something of a new meaning—a new vocation, connecting it to the workings of language—the language, in particular, that is operative in works of literature, such as the stories that Beckett has told in writing.

If, as Maurice Blanchot maintains in "Literature and the Right to Death,"[41] literature begins at the moment when it becomes a question, a question addressed to language, by language that has become literature, Beckett's works must be regarded as exemplary, for they are nothing if not works of literature in which language questions itself—questions, above all, its capacity to bear, to carry and bring forth, the promise of happiness, without suppressing the nihilism that, given the nature of language, words can always express.

If language can bear or metaphor this promise, that is because language, understood as communication, *is* the way to justice, a justice without which the happiness here at issue would be impossible. Language uniquely offers individuals and communities the hospitality, the generosity, the justice—in brief, a sharing of our humanity—which talking things over with one another expresses and makes possible.[42] And language bears traces and echoes of this promise by giving expression to the grievances that cry out for the justice in its recognition—and, correspondingly, by giving expression to sympathy and solidarity, keeping hopeful indications of profane redemption alive in the community of remembrance and imagination.[43] For, as Hölderlin says in his hymn "Celebration of Peace," there is hope for a better world, "since we have been a conversation and have heard from one another [. . .]."[44]

Language is the promise of reconciliation. And, as those words of verse show he knew, in the poetic use of language, a design that manifests the miraculous power of language to create something out of nothing, there is encouragement for the creative realization of that promise, that gift of treasure, in a time of reconciliation. But the dream, a dream of paradise, an achieved humanity worthy of pride, means nothing unless it is brought into the mortality, the sufferings and joyfulness, of time.

*

Before we continue our study of Beckett's ways of using of language in relation to the promise of happiness, it would, I think, be helpful briefly to have in mind the three ways in which the possibility in this promise is carried by language, namely: carried in poetry, carried in prose fiction, and carried in our everyday forms of dialogue. Our attention in the present work will of course concentrate on how the promise is borne and kept by Beckett's appropriation of language in his works of prose fiction.

[1] *Poetry*. In his *Aesthetics: Lectures on Fine Arts*, Hegel virtually breaks into song to praise the speculative treasures present in the German language, calling attention to words such as "*Sinn*": "'Sense,'" he declares, "is this wonderful word that is used in two opposite meanings. On the one hand it means the organ of immediate apprehension, but on the other hand we mean by it the sense, the significance, the thought, the universal that underlies the thing."[45] Words that originally signified only something sensuous are sometimes "carried over into the spiritual sphere," and our memory of their metaphorical derivation "gradually vanishes."[46] Poetry is what takes place in the event that reveals the creation of meaning. Poetry is the form of language that celebrates, and plays with, the emergence of intelligible sense from the originality of the sensible sense. It thus exhibits, contrary to Platonism, Cartesianism, and empiricism, a sense of "sense" in which the two types of sense, the intelligible and the sensible, are not sundered and in opposition, but are operating wholly together as one in the music of a creative movement. As poetry, therefore, language expresses, and promises to satisfy, at least in aesthetic semblance, the longing for the *reconciliation* of the two senses of "sense." In other words, in poetry, language shows that, whether in harmony or in dissonance and tension, those two senses can work together to set in motion certain desired aesthetic effects, indicating

in that way the possibility of overcoming the pathology in our cultural dissociations: the dualisms separating the sensuous and the ideal, mind and body, flesh and spirit, feeling and reason, sensibility and thought, nature and freedom, action and contemplation, dimensions of our being as "rational animals" which, since ancient times, have been separated by imaginary, culturally constructed, but nonetheless debilitating, dualisms, appreciating the one, repressing the other. In the reconciliation of the sensuous sense and the intelligible or cognitive sense that takes place especially in the language of poetry, we are given the chance to experience what the end of the dualisms—and the theodicies—that have served a culture of renunciation and repression might mean: the end, namely, of what I have characterized, in writing about Nietzsche, as our "civilized cruelty."[47] So, in the beauty of poetry, and in the freedom of its play with sound and sense, its language at once sensuous yet intensely disciplined, rich in meaning yet no longer subordinated to, or completely determined by, the presentation of a spiritual content, the cognitive sense, we can get an inkling of a utopian possibility emerging from the determinate negation of the ancient repression of human nature, sacrificed over centuries for the sake of mastery, the will to power. And if, as Kant suggests in his third *Critique*, the aesthetic experience of beauty can symbolically reveal, or bring out, the promise, the prospect, of a *sensus communis*, then the experience of language in poetry, where the two senses of "sense" are working creatively together, might bring out, or reveal, something that the promise of an as yet unapproachable utopia of happiness is pledging. Although poetry can speak only in the mode of aesthetic semblance, in the reconciliation between sensible sense and intelligible sense, the language of poetry becomes a mimetic *anticipation* of the longed-for wholeness, essential condition for genuine happiness.

However, besides being only aesthetic semblance, even this reconciliation, limited as it is to the language of poetry, can never be complete, final, or perfectly stabilized. We are thus reminded that the happiness language promises remains elusive, never entirely released from the questioning of its possibility. Thus a certain melancholy inevitably affects even the most genuinely joyous poetry, as we find ourselves compelled to acknowledge our distance from the possible in a perpetually compromised happiness—a lost present. And, as Adorno says in an essay on Eichendorff, "only mourning for the lost moment has preserved what the living moment [in poetry] continues, even today, to miss."[48]

[2] *Fiction*. As prose in the fiction of literature, language might be found to bear the promise of happiness in that it is an aesthetic mimesis or repetition of divine creation, the *creatio ex nihilo*, a spontaneous and productive power of origination; it expresses, and promises to satisfy, the longing for the fulfillment of creativity in life; it is the desire to originate *ex nihilo*, using the imagination to create alternative realities that dispute old assumptions; it is the desire to reveal what things conceal about themselves from ordinary, untutored apprehension. Thus, in literature, language figures in the desire

to retrieve and thereby redeem still unrecognized possibilities, making surprising things happen in the fictional worlds of aesthetic semblance. Once again, the very essence of language as a medium of creative transfiguration seems to be manifest, silently, implicitly sustaining in memory the utopian or redemptive promise.

[3] *Dialogue.* The promise of happiness is also to be found in everyday forms of communication, carried by virtue of the fact that the very existence of language promises, despite countless occasions for misunderstanding and failures of intelligibility, something more than and other than the continuation of a history that has been one long condition of unjustified suffering, namely, the emergence of a form of sociability within which communities respectful of differences—the pluralism of singularities—might be built. (Adorno strongly disparages what he calls "communicative language," by which he means reified and reifying language, forms of language in the service of cruelty, injustice, hatred, and ideology, merely supporting the status quo. That, of course, is a sense of "communication" which I do not intend. Adorno's aversion to that terminology, however, is a useful reminder, warning against philosophical projects which assume that dialogue necessarily bears the promise without distorting or otherwise damaging it.) As the primary medium for everyday forms of communication, language is social-political "originality," the poetically political power that Hölderlin invoked with the word "founding," "stiften," and that Hannah Arendt called "natality," the power to bring people together, to create, without sacrifice to singularity and plurality, a certain commonality, a gathering of understanding, if not also of action. These two allegorically powerful words not only express the longing for an ideal form of community; in an exemplary way, I think, they also show that, and how, language bears the promise of happiness. Because universal happiness depends on enlightened processes of dialogue, gathering mortals into relationships that adumbrate the founding of a world where ethical life might finally flourish. As Kant argued in his third *Critique*, when we members of the human species received the gift of language, marking us as "creatures intended for society", we also received the transcendental idea of universal communicability, the imperative beginning of civilization, bearing the prospect of a society formed through its communal sense and sustained by the art of a reciprocal communication of ideas.[49] Insofar as language bears within it the promise of happiness, language would bespeak, however obliquely, however indistinctly, the empirical desire—what Kant wanted to call a certain "enthusiasm"—for the creation of a more perfect world. Whatever else communication communicates, it always communicates the promise or possibility of a new, radically enlightened form of community—hence, again, the promise of universal happiness.[50]

In these three ways, and in every instantiation—in poetry, the prose of fiction, and dialogue, language bears a promise, constitutive of its very essence, that calls and summons us—and lays claim to our thought.

*

In *How It Is* (1961), the subject of Part Three in this present volume, Beckett's narrator speaks of "refreshing alternations of history prophecy and latest news" (H 129). I want to relate this to a note on "The Dialectical Image" that Benjamin composed for his *Arcades Project*: a note in which he introduces the "Idea" of an "integral prose," a storyteller's prose, corresponding, he says, to "the messianic Idea of universal history, ['a world of complete and integral actuality'] that can be understood by all mankind, just as the language of the birds can be understood by children born on Sunday."[51] If Beckett's shockingly new form of storytelling prose can be understood by all mankind, as I think it can, might that be because it bears, in the purgatory of language, and in unappeasable longing, "the messianic Idea of universal history," the impossible Idea of a world in which the ideals constitutive of our humanity, hence justice and its promise of happiness, would be realized?

Although Beckett's prose takes us into the darkest, coldest, emptiest recesses of the human "soul," shows the wretchedness of the human condition, and challenges the inhumanity at work in theodicy in all its different historical versions, and is thus critical of the providential justice it promises for a time beyond death, forsaking thereby the cause of justice and its utopia of happiness here on earth, his prose is kept radically open, nevertheless, to traces and echoes of the felt presence of the paradisiacal in the world as we experience it, fragmentary reminders, uncomfortable like splinters in the flesh, entering our world in various ways and allegorical figures, keeping in the life of words the promise of happiness they bear.

Thus I also want to consider, shifting to a more specifically literary dimension of interpretation, the related proposition that language in literature can bear, or metaphor, this promise in *five* distinct but interactive textual dimensions: the sensuous material, the syntactical or grammatical style of the prose, the semantic constitution of the prose, the structure of the narrative, and of course the narrative content, or story. Reading Beckett, we shall see that literature can make language manifest the bearing of the promise in all these dimensions, even shaping the physiognomy of the material stratum—as when the poetic lyricism of the writing "animates" the sensuous material in what Merleau-Ponty would call the "ontological rehabilitation of the sensible," hence the literary *reconciliation* of the antinomy that for centuries has controlled the two senses of "sense."[52] I am referring here to Beckett's ways of "resolving" the antinomy of the sensible and the intelligible, as when, for example, his prose suddenly turns lyrical and dithyrambic, and significant utopian meaning, an intensely felt, often elegiac sense, accrues from the sensuous beauty and sublime longing inherent in the words—even though such a reconciliation, by itself, is of course fated to be irremediably transient, incomplete and profoundly unstable.

Overcoming the temptation to embrace skepticism, it is my conviction, and the principal claim at stake in this book, that the very existence of language—language "as such," Benjamin would say—represents the utopian, or redemptive "promesse de bonheur," even though its mere existence cannot, as such, realize and fulfill the promise. But the promise that the language of literature seems to bear, vouchsafe and transmit takes place, as already noted, only in the realm of semblance: it is powerless, as such, immediately to alter the world. Nevertheless, the promise functions, I believe, somewhat like an anticipatory mimetic semblance of the possible redemption of the world which language can serve; and perhaps it can, in serving that way, even approach its own redemption as a potent medium of creation and revelation reminiscent of the mythic language of paradise.

*

So then, inspired in part by Benjamin's early writings on language and by Adorno's practice of criticism, the chapters in the present book are philosophical reflections on language as it figures in Beckett's literary works, arguing for an interpretation that discerns, sometimes despite almost impenetrable obscurities, compelling phenomenological evidence, often no more than hermeneutical traces or echoes, of a utopian or messianic "*promesse de bonheur*" allegorically conveyed by his stories and plays. Our reflections will consequently also take up for the questioning of thought the further argument that language is, as such, a message of hope and faith, a bene-diction, the bearer of this metaphysical promise, *despite* the damage to language in its reification and impoverishment—and *despite* the use of language in cruelty and violence: processes that have been taking place since the very beginning of history.

But what can we actually hope for from words, from language? From the very beginning, the creative, almost magical power of language has been subject to abuse. Today, it seems that, as never before, language is undergoing irremediable corruption and damage, compelled to submit to the conditions of "life": standardization, commercialization, and other types of reification, decay and impoverishment, the loss of etymological roots.[53] What chance is there for the promise of happiness—for that message—as long as language is bound, as Beckett's stories never cease to remind us, to the cruelty, inhumanity and nihilism that prevail in the material conditions of its possibility?[54] Moreover, as Heidegger argues in his meditations on Hölderlin, language is the most dangerous of gifts, because it exposes us to the nothingness of being. And how might the promise of happiness be kept when every word in the discourse of the social project of moral enlightenment—*freedom*, *justice*, *equality*, *peace*, *friend*, *community*, *education*, *humanity*, and even *spirit*, a seemingly innocent word—suffers from reverberations that register an essential, hence interminable duplicity, an inherent complicity with the forces of oppression and malevolence—or with the unscrupulous commercialism that exploits words like "freedom" for their profit? Each of these evocative words can be used to say something morally repugnant. Each of these words is riddled with internal contradictions that reflect and perpetuate contradictions in our social-political economy.

I am reminded of a television commercial that especially distressed me: "Everyone loves liberty! Liberty Mutual Insurance!" Are no words safe from plunder and exploitation?

Even when language in the literary works we shall be considering seems, perhaps, to remember its promise, or to impart it in the allegorical register of a narrative, it does so in a mood that will not spare even its momentary evocations of happiness, its moments of wit and vaudeville humor, from the shadows of an inconsolable sadness. For, first of all, these moments of happiness are taking place only in the realm of aesthetic semblance. Secondly, they are invariably ephemeral. Moreover, thirdly, the deferment of the promised fulfillment must be endless and its concrete determinate form must be left open, if it is to avoid reduction to a compromised positivity; but every instant that defers the promise of happiness, or leaves the structure of actualization open, as it must, to the contingency of events, is an unjustifiable perpetuation of misery—and a skeptical, guilt-burdened rebuke to the redemptive assumption. Thus, the indeterminate content of the promise, the very openness that protects its futurity from compromises with prevailing reality, casts it at the same time in an aporetic structure, constantly vulnerable to betrayal.[55]

Today, it seems, the promise in language—the promise of language—can be kept, maintained in its interminable deferment, only in an experience of despair and longing. And we who care about the fate of language must mourn its damaged condition even as we, for whom religious faith and the traditions of ritual that have sustained the promise seem no longer able to offer the consolations of transcendence, nevertheless mourn a world bereft of its old horizon of faith and hope, a world in which the promise of happiness, the promise that would bring us to our humanity, being perpetually deferred, risks becoming a merely speculative and ideological fantasy—or perhaps nothing but entertainment, the ultimate realization in the production of instant gratification. But we are, paradoxically, lamenting the loss of something we have never actually received from the past—or received so far only in fragments.

Ultimately, the keeping of the promise becomes a question of the responsibility that we must acknowledge and learn to bear for the words we use and abuse.[56] The existence of language as such cannot guarantee the actualization of the universal happiness it offers; the promise remains conditional, is, we might say, only an offering—the gift of an Idea, which the very existence of language grants, and which it is in our power to accept, actualize, refuse, deny, or betray. So whatever the "redemption" of language might be supposed to mean, in the context of the present work it will not be something vouchsafed by any teleological or eschatological economy. Nor will it be assured by any material historical determinism. Theodicy and all its avatars in materialism can enjoy no credibility in the modern world. Its words are exhausted. As W. G. Sebald, a writer strongly influenced by Beckett, remarks:

The theocratic props collapsed a long time ago; henceforth, we must take comfort in the recognition that, as mortal individuals, we are part of a greater process, which in a very reassuring way follows its course. But the transcendence [offered by theology] no longer provides a stable grounding.[57]

And yet, he says, as he watches the world fall ever more rapidly into a catastrophic state, he finds himself feeling ever more keenly the need for a responsible literature—and a language capable of redeeming the things that ultimately matter. There is no God to save us. But there is, he believes, a solemn calling for the writer. For, the writer can watch and bear witness, summoning the past in memory and calling attention to what is presently happening—because the present is already our future.[58]

Is there, in this "present," the "gift" of a utopian or messianic promise, a promise not only *conveyed* in language but also, as Wittgenstein suggests or implies, *constitutive* of language? We will recall that, in "A Certain Impossible Possibility of Saying the Event," Derrida declared that, "The promise is the basic element of language."[59] For Derrida, the promise is an "impossible act, therefore the only one worthy of its name."[60] The promise is impossible because it always and only promises an unknowable future; moreover, a promise is not a promise if what it promises is guaranteed, is calculable and predictable. It must be open to the future. But that means, as Derrida says, that a promise must be able not to be kept: "it must risk not being kept or even becoming a threat to be promised."[61]

Language necessarily enters into and is engaged by a temporal succession; but this sets language in a double bind, the *aporia* that binds every promise; because, although the meanings that words bear belong to the past we inherited, what those words *might* mean is always open, always still to come, available for further interpretation, retroactively altering the earlier meaning: the meaning of the beginning always comes later, and sometimes too late. Although what is said is said and done, the meaning or sense of what is said can never be final; it is perpetually exposed, possibly even threatened by what is to come—conceivably threatened as a consequence of the words said or the event of enunciation. The promise of language is not only a threat to the community that inhabits, and is formed by, that language; it is even a possible threat to language itself. Manifest especially in a time of crisis, the promise is always both opportunity and threat: a small, uncertain chance for reconciliation and happiness.

In "Faith and Knowledge," Derrida remarks that "The promise promises *itself*, it is *already* promised, that is the sworn faith, the given word [. . .]. *Religio* begins there."[62] And he explains thus his invocation of the "religious" dimension of the promise: "No to-come without some sort of messianic memory and promise, of a messianicity not only older than religion, and more originary than every messianism, but also released from all the doctrines and dogmas that make messianism dangerous. No discourse or address of the other without the possibility of an elementary promise."[63] In a formulation plainly influenced by Benjamin, Derrida states that the messianic names "the opening to the future or to the coming of the other as the advent of justice, but without horizon of expectation and without prophetic prefiguration."[64] It is, he says, "a general structure of experience."[65] What is promised is only the promise as such. Carried in memory by language, messianicity is that structure which *opens the possibility* for every singular actualizing messianic event; consequently, it *exceeds* all messianisms. As Michael Naas summarizes it:

> It is the name of a time or of an awaiting where that which is always beyond our horizon of expectations, where the radically unexpected and indeterminate, can come at any moment, at any moment "in" history but also, insofar as the unexpected cannot be understood from within the horizon *of* history, as an interruption of history.[66]

For Derrida, as for Benjamin, although what transformation the messianic might bring is indeterminate, it "always takes the phenomenal form of peace or of justice."[67] In our context here, what Derrida will call "the invincible desire for justice,"[68] for a "democracy still to come,"[69] is represented by faith in the promise of happiness. "This justice," he argues, "inscribes itself in advance in the promise, in the act of faith or in the appeal to faith that inhabits every act of language and every address to the other."[70] Moreover, this promise, as Naas notes, is "not for this or that conception of justice, but is justice itself."[71] Such will be the modernist conception of the messianic that, in thinking about language and its promise of happiness, we will engage.

How, then, in the context of this book, might we conceive what is involved in seeking to reclaim for immanence, for worldly interpretation, the "redemption" of the promise of happiness that language, as I believe, inherently recalls? Following Derrida, John Caputo has proposed an audaciously "modernist" way to think about language, literature and our world as the light of transcendence, figured here as the God of theology, fades away:

> The name of God is the name of a promise—and a promise cannot be made safe from a threat without being turned into a sure thing, a guarantee. [. . .] The promise that transpires under the name of God is the promise of the world itself, so that to invoke the name of God is in the end a way of calling upon something embedded within the world, embedded within ourselves [. . .]. What classical theology was searching for under the figure of the "transcendence" of God is here refigured as provocation [. . .]. The figures of transcendence, which readily assume the form of literature or mythology, of dreams or desires, are ways of retracing the lines of immanence in imaginative form, ways of reclaiming immanence in all its richness and intensity.

Therefore, the name of God is, he says, in words reminiscent of Benjamin, "the name of an event that breaks open the present."[72] In his *Diaries*,

Gershom Scholem wrote, taking the name metaphorically, of course, and with a touch of humour: "The Messiah will be the last—and the first—philosopher of language."[73] It is language that bears the event.

Can reading works of literature, attentive to the operations of language, reclaim the promise of happiness for a worldly redemption? Can we find in the language of literature indications of the promise in its immanence? My claim is that the stories and plays of Beckett have in remarkably original ways preserved their inheritance of an expressive potential, a redemptive potential, greatly weakened but not yet lost, that Benjamin thought of as "prophetic" and "messianic," inclining the world towards its political and spiritual ideal of perfection—but without ever attaining that end.

*

In Adorno's *Negative Dialectics*, the utopian promise of happiness appears in terms of the concept of reconciliation: the resolution or dissolution of all the antagonisms, contradictions, and diremptions that persist in our world as eliminable sources of misery, suffering, and injustice. Adorno argues in this work for something of a "Gnostic" reading of the question of reconciliation in Beckett, an essentially cosmological or metaphysical interpretation, to supplement or displace the earlier existentialist interpretation:

> To Beckett, as to the Gnostics, the created world is radically evil, and its negation is the chance of another world that is not yet. As long as the world is as it is, all images of reconciliation, peace, and quiet resemble the image of death. The slightest difference between nothingness and coming to rest would be the haven of hope, the no man's land between the border posts of being and nothingness. [. . .] The true nihilists are the ones who oppose nihilism with their more and more faded positivities, the ones who are thus conspiring with all extant malice, and eventually with the destructive principle itself. Thought honors itself by defending what is damned as nihilism.[74]

Beckett engages nihilism in order to subvert and defeat it. This analysis is very compelling, although, except for the story in *The Lost Ones,* I can find only questionable grounds for the "Gnostic" attribution of "radical evil."[75] Nothing confirms that reading, although Beckett does borrow, for his own purposes, especially in *How It Is*, some of the Gnostic metaphorics.[76] And whilst Beckett's works are saturated with Christian theological references and allusions and show, with the most generous sympathy, his understanding of the dire need that compels shelter in religion, it is impossible to read his works as *encouraging* a theological perspective on creaturely life. The theological references and allusions are merely necessary literary devices; they are required because the life-world about which and for which he is writing has been decisively formed by the Christian religion and its Judeo-Christian theology. In any event, however, what I think that Beckett's works compellingly demonstrate is articulated by Adorno's assertion that the negative image of our world can create a dialectic through which "the chance of another world that is not yet" might break forth into view. We will return in due course to the question of Beckett's proximity to nihilism. First, however, we need to think some more about happiness and the justice in its promise.

*

David Hume, writing at the very beginning of an industrial revolution that would challenge all the traditional concepts and institutions on which the social order had been based, thinks of "liberty and laws as the source of human happiness."[77] Benjamin, in his "Theologico-Political Fragment," refers, with something at once much more material and much more spiritual in mind, to a longing for the "happiness of a free humanity": against all odds, "das Glücksuchen der freien Menschheit."[78] Against all odds: for, ironically and indeed paradoxically, as Adorno argues in his early essay on "The Idea of Natural History," reconciliation "is above all there where the world most presents itself as semblance: that is where the promise of reconciliation is most thoroughly given." But, he adds, reminding us of the dialectical aporia which virtually erases all traces and echoes of that promise, that aesthetic semblance is also precisely "where at the same time the world is most thickly walled off from all 'meaning'."[79] Walled off, that is, from the force of the aesthetic imagination—from art's potential to influence revolutionary transformations of the world. What, in that case, can the use that literature makes of language realistically promise? What would be its authority? What claim would it be entitled, then, to make? Questions to ponder, addressed only obliquely, however, in the reflections that will follow on Beckett's contributions to literature. In Part Three, on the theme of justice in Beckett's *How It Is*, we shall return to the idea of a "free humanity."

*

In the "Introduction" to his *Philosophy of History*, Hegel observed that, "The history of the world is not the theater of happiness. Periods of happiness are blank pages in it, for they are periods of harmony—periods when the antithesis is in abeyance."[80] Today, I think, it would be even more difficult, straining credibility, to make a claim for such happiness. We no longer can enjoy Hegel's faith in the operations of a dialectic represented by the rational, providential interpretation of history. We are living in a time of extreme disenchantment—indeed, a disenchantment so thorough that it has enabled the phantasmagoria of capitalism to fill the vacuum with its false promises. The Enlightenment project of universal happiness in a "reconciled," cosmopolitan world of freedom, social justice, and peace—happiness in a culture no longer requiring the pathologizing existential dualisms of the past—seems just as remote, just as outlandish, as it seemed in earlier centuries, if not even more unapproachable today. For even those old cherished values, and the words that have named them, are in jeopardy, abused and twisted by cynical politics and unscrupulous corporate interests. The wasteland of nihilism continues, it seems, to grow.

In the absence of any transcendent authority, where might we turn to find the normative grounds of human sociability and justice? What Beckett's works show, I think, is that, whenever words are used, there is an implicit address to the other, and an acknowledgement of the humanity of that other. The normative grounds of sociability and justice are to be found in language, where even in this time of mourning there still beckons, in Beckett's engaging phrase, "a chance of happiness," the ideal, universal happiness imagined in the prophecies of ancient thought. In Beckett's stories and plays, it is always possible—despite the wretched circumstances of the characters, despite their destitution, despite their poverty of words—to detect the redeeming of that chance shimmering faintly in the very existence of their words. To the extent that, in struggling to redeem our damaged and corrupted words, restoring or renewing their revelatory power, their capacity to say something singularly meaningful for our time, Beckett accomplished that intention, to that extent his words have, I think, redeemed with the beauty of their justice, their truth-content, the promise of happiness they bear.

Since there has been much debate in recent years surrounding various so-called "redemptive" readings of modernist literature, I want, before we proceed any farther, to clarify a little more, if possible, what will be meant in this volume by the invocation of "redemption."[81] Taking the "redeeming" engaged by the "aesthetics of redemption" to refer to the claim that, in Martin Hägglund's words, "a certain type of repetition of experience in art can repair inherently damaged or valueless experience,"[82] I want, whilst advancing this claim, to insist, first of all, that no "repairing," no "rescuing," can ever attain completeness, perfection, or finality; and, secondly, that it is not at all a question of anything otherworldly. The redeeming of the redemptive power of language—the power of language to "redeem" what its words invoke, and thus the redeeming of our historically bound experience and the world in which we live—takes place entirely within our world: here and nowhere else.

Beckett greatly admired Nabokov; but the sentiment with which his stories leave us is even more remote from, and even perhaps more at odds with the otherworldly, if that is possible, than that of John Shade, the character in Nabokov's *Pale Fire*, who declared in his poem that he would "turn down eternity," unless all the things that make up our world down here can also be "found in Heaven": "The melancholy and the tenderness/ Of mortal life; the passion and the pain; [. . .] the train of silver slime/ Snails leave on flagstones; [. . .] this slender rubber band/ Which always forms, when dropped, an ampersand [. . .]."[83] Van Veen, in Nabokov's *Ada*, follows John Shade, arguing that the "paradise" we want is not to be found in an afterlife, but only, if at all, in a life coming *after* the utopian transformation of this, our present historical world. The "paradise" offered by religion is nothing but "a shabby trick of feigned restitution."[84] As Nabokov explains:

Van pointed out that here was the rub—one is free to imagine any type of hereafter, of course: the generalized paradise promised by Oriental prophets and poets, or an individual combination; but the work of fancy is handicapped—to a quite hopeless extent—by a logical ban: you cannot bring your friends along—or your enemies for that matter—to the party. The transposition of all our remembered relationships into an Elysian life inevitably turns it into a second-rate continuation of our marvelous mortality.[85]

What we want is not an afterlife, but a continuation of creaturely life, mortal life, right here on earth—but a *better* life, a *new* life, one that is possible only *after* our work has created here the conditions necessary to realize the dream of happiness that language contingently promises.

Even when Beckett's characters lament and mourn living in a god-forsaken world and express in the familiar language of the Christian and Judaic religions their longing for a meaningful existential story, Beckett's late short story, *Ill Seen Ill Said* (1981–1982), suggests that it would be a mistake to interpret such expressions as implying that the old theological stories could still—now, today—be somehow resurrected and redeemed unchanged, compelling faith and sustaining trust as once they did. Understanding that "sentimental" reality, Beckett makes powerful emotional and allegorical *use* of the old stories, but he weaves them into *new* stories: stories that give to our historical situation voices and words eloquent in their very poverty.

*

The possibility of a radical, revolutionary transformation of the world, affecting even the smallest, most insignificant matters, allegorically expressed in the poetic language of a theology, has always been an elusive conceit, difficult to express, withdrawing from the word into its reserve, its self-concealment. But it is only in our time that this story has been felt to conceal the nothingness into which our words, sent on their way, soon fall. The starless night of nihilism, increasingly visible, as Beckett's stories and plays exemplify, in the spaces or breaks between our words, is threatening to extinguish the already fading enlightenment of the sun. As Giorgio Agamben has argued in "The Idea of Language," drawing a connection between theology, nihilism and language:

Contemporary thought has approached a limit beyond which a new epochal-religious unveiling of the word no longer seems possible. The primordial character of the word is now completely revealed, and no new figure of the divine, no new historical destiny can lift itself out of language. The fulfilled revelation of language would be a word completely abandoned by God. And human beings are thrown into language without having a voice or a divine word to guarantee them a possibility of escape from the infinite play of meaningful propositions. Thus, we finally find ourselves today alone with our words; for the first time we are truly alone with language, abandoned without any final foundation. [. . .] For the first time, what preceding generations called God, Being, spirit, and the unconscious appear to us as what they are: names for genres of discourse. [. . .] The veils that theology, ontology, anthropology and psychology cast over [language] have now been torn away [. . .]. We now look upon language without its veils, [. . .] wholly revealed [. . .].[86]

Is the nature of language, even today, totally revealed, or totally exposed? Could it ever be? Beckett certainly makes us intensely conscious of this "veiling"—and the abandonment of language, bereft of its old divine authority. But why is this final stage in our appropriation of language to be described as "nihilism"? In a 1937 letter written in German to his friend Axel Kaun, Beckett confides his struggles with language:

And more and more my own language appears to me like a veil that must be torn apart in order to get at the things (or the nothingness) lying behind it.[87]

What Merleau-Ponty says about the philosopher could also be said of Beckett: "[The philosopher] writes in order to express his contact with being; but he did not say it, and could not have said it, since it is silence. So he recommences."[88] Writing about his struggles as a new type of storyteller, Beckett says that the storyteller's truth must somehow register its damage, its loss, in and as its form of expression. What he takes this truthfulness to require of him as a storyteller, is the confession of a profound anxiety, the desperate worry that, for our world,

there is nothing to express, nothing with which to express, nothing from which to express, no power to express, no desire to express, together with the obligation to express.[89]

We need to hear, reverberating in these words, the shockwaves of the modernist crisis of skepticism regarding the continuing repetition, in literature, of an entire regime of sense-making—thus, indeed, skepticism regarding the very possibility of a literature capable of communicating in shared meaning. To remain rigorously faithful to this aporetic experience with language, saying it and showing it, accordingly becomes the storyteller's first and foremost obligation. Regardless of the cost, regardless of the sacrifice. This aesthetic logic led Beckett to a style of increasingly expressionless minimalism—or, to use his own word, "lessness."[90] What Adorno says of Beethoven's late style might thus in fact be said with equal insight about Beckett's own late works:

The power of subjectivity in the late works of art is the irascible gesture with which it takes leave of the works themselves. It breaks their bonds, not in order to express itself, but in order, expressionless, to cast off the appearance of art. Of the works themselves, it leaves only fragments behind, and communicates itself, like a cipher, only through the blank spaces from which it has disengaged itself. Touched by death, the hand of the master sets free the masses of material that he used to form; its tears and fissures, witnesses to the finite powerlessness of the "I confronted with Being," are its final work.[91]

Perhaps recalling Hamann's fear and foreboding, raising questions about how there could be any resurrection, any redemption if our language is left with nothing but "dead letters,"[92] and complaining, in *Texts for Nothing*, of having to write with "nothing ever but lifeless words" (TN 135), Beckett cursed the English language, cursed, too, the writer's calling; but we have to believe, nevertheless, that he passionately loved the language, since he never ceased to struggle with it, forcing it in the most violent ways to say without compromise what he felt he needed to say, and we have to believe that, although writing under a certain compulsion, as if haunted by the relentless urgings of the categorical imperative, he loved the story-teller's literary calling, since he resolutely chose it despite repeated frustrations and dead-ends, submitting to its impossible demands the entirety of his life.

As if commenting on this confession by Beckett, and differing from Agamben, Adorno affirms what one might call the enigmatic sublimity of such language, going on despite its traumatic history, despite its damage, destitution, and helplessness:

That it is spoken, that distance is thus won from the trapped immediacy of suffering, transforms suffering just as screaming diminishes unbearable pain. Expression that has been objectivated as language endures; what has once been said never fades away completely, neither the evil nor the good, neither the slogan of "The Final Solution" nor the hope of reconciliation [*Versöhnung*]. What accedes to language enters the movement of a humanness that does not yet exist; it is compelled towards language and alive only by virtue of its helplessness. (AT 117)

This "movement toward humanness" that is possible because we enter into the "conversation," the language of a community, is precisely what Hölderlin celebrates in his poem, "Celebration of Peace." And it is, I suggest, an essential key to understanding Beckett. In the gift of language, he believes, there is promise, there is hope, for a future humanity, despite the reification, commodification, and corruption into which it has fallen in the course of a brutal history. That hope, that promise, has for the most part retreated into allegory, the safety of almost illegible ciphers. It lives on, however, in many of the old bedtime stories for children; for, as Emerson noted, "infancy is the perpetual Messiah."[93] But in Beckett's stories and plays, the truth in expressions of suffering still unredeemed breaks through their semblance-character, which sometimes is only faintly disguised and rendered bearable by vaudeville comedy and dry laughter.

The promise of happiness demands, as I have already suggested, the utopian transformation of society, ending by reconciliation the injustices, antagonisms, and contradictions that are the cause of unnecessary misery and suffering. Art could have a role to play in this reconciliation. Beckett, I believe, thought it could. How so? "Art," says Adorno, "is not reconciliation in the classical sense. Reconciliation [Versöhnung] is the comportment of artworks by which they become conscious of the non-identical" (AT 134). In terms of Beckett's works, that means that they must engage in the dialectics of negation, refusing to be reconciled with any smug, premature reconciliation, any promotion of complacency, consolation, resignation, or indifference. It means, moreover, that the *language* in his literary works must in some material way, whether by sound or rhythm or grammatical form, mimetically perform, and make present thereby, that of which it would speak.[94] Beckett's prose creates word-fissures, word-cracks that at once interrupt the narrative physiognomy, frustrating the habitual assumption of a smoothly flowing teleological and eschatological continuum, and at the same time also open the narrative or the dialogue to the felt sense of a radically disruptive event—perhaps the eventuality of a justice, an earthly redemption, to come. In Beckett's artful use of language, the continuously sweeping flow of words is repeatedly disrupted, mimetically expressing—and choreographing—the breakdown and disintegration of the religious teleologies and eschatologies that, for centuries, ruled over our world.

Whilst insisting that authentic art must somehow bear witness to the promise of reconciliation, keeping revolutionary faith and hope alive, Adorno also argues, with equal vehemence, against any art that presents reconciliation in an affirmative way: "For the sake of reconciliation, authentic works must blot out every trace of reconciliation in [the positivism of ordinary] memory" (AT 234). According to Adorno, Beckett exemplifies in this regard the scrupulous honesty of the storyteller: "Art can be reconciled with its existence only by exposing its own semblance, its internal emptiness" (AT 250). Thus, to the extent that Beckett's fiction is able to claim our conviction, it must relinquish the total self-absorption, the illusionism, of the traditional literary work, opening and exposing itself, exposing its struggles—but without any "theatricality," any obsession with effects, that would negate that claim. It would be a mistake, therefore, to call the "internal emptiness," which appears so persistently in Beckett's stories and works for the stage, evidence of his nihilism. Beckett pictures our world in the madness of nihilism—but this heightening of our shared self-consciousness and self-understanding proffers the hope, as he surely knew, that the machinations of that nihilism might be subverted. As reading Hegel would have taught him, the spirit is only spirit when it is the negative of a negative. The promise in that negative of the negative, though easy to overlook, trivialize or denigrate, will show up again and again in Beckett's stories: the darker the story, the more sublimely its restrained illumination can assume its legibility.

*

Alain Badiou argues, convincingly I think, that, in Beckett's art, "not even twists of irony can abolish 'happiness'."[95] And, he contends, implicitly drawing on Heidegger's enigmatic invocations of an "Ereignis," a singular inceptive event breaking into history, and on Derrida's cautious references to a "messianicity without messianism," the language in Beckett's work time and time again creates openings that make his narratives and dialogues seem receptive to apocalyptic events, chance events of earth-shaking significance, promising breaches in "being"—or in Adorno's words, breaches in an ontology controlled by the oppressive logic of identity. "We ask," says Badiou: 'Is something happening?' And more precisely: 'Can we name an emergence, an incalculable advent which detotalizes being and wrenches the subject from the predestination of its identity?'"[96] His answer is that, at least in the post-war middle period works, *Waiting for Godot, Endgame*, and the trilogy (*Molloy, Malone Dies*, and *The Unnamable*), it seems that "in the end nothing happens. Godot will never come; he is nothing but the promise of his coming": "a promise," moreover, "that cannot be kept." We must of course agree that no apocalyptic event, nothing messianic, takes place.[97] There is no prophetic, messianic event interrupting the tragic course of history, no Pauline *kairos* bringing to an end the destitution that Beckett shows us, at least in those two plays and three novels. But I submit that, even in these despairing, so-called "middle period" works (1945–1957), there *are* small epiphanies, hints and intimations, tiny traces, tiny openings, easily overlooked, where something of significance, something we might call "promising," is actually taking place. In this regard, what Adorno argues is worth noting:

> The appearance of the nonexistent as if it existed motivates the question as to the truth of art. By its form alone art promises what is not; it registers objectively, however refractedly, the claim that because the nonexistent appears, it must indeed be possible. The unstillable longing in the face of beauty [. . .] is the longing for the fulfillment of what was promised.

And he observes, importantly, that:

> Idealist aesthetics fails by its inability to do justice to art's *promesse de bonheur*. It reduces the artwork to what it in theoretical terms symbolizes and thus trespasses against the spirit in that artwork. It is what *spirit* promises, and not the sensual pleasure of the observer, that is the locus of the sensuous element in art.[98]

In other words, the sensuous dimension—Beckett's sudden shifts into a certain lyricism in phrasing, for instance—may be partially understood in relation to what spirit promises, namely, the happiness of a utopia, the perfection of society. Even if immediately followed by ridicule, irony or sarcasm, his lyricism cannot be entirely erased: it is not only an intimation or anticipation of that promise; but by virtue of its "ontological rehabilitation of the sensible," it is already, in fact, its glorious incarnation in a moment of poetic reconciliation, when the two senses of "sense," namely the sensuous and the cognitive, which since Platonism our Western culture has kept estranged in antagonistic, irreconcilable, irreducible dualism, coalesce to express a meaning that only their reverberating reciprocity could have made possible. In that meaning, something of the sense of paradise seems to offer itself for our recognition.

§2

At the heart of the promise of happiness is, as already indicated, redeeming the universal hope for justice: justice in a much broader sense than is customary, designating necessary conditions for the possibility of ethical life, a way of being with others, in its entirety. But happiness also engages, for Beckett, what might be called an "existential" or "ontological" justice. Justice in this sense would assume a profound transformation, redeeming the meaningfulness of life and death in the way we live and die. This does not require the coming of a new god or the return of the ancient one, but mortals learning how to live a full life within the meaningfulness of their mortality. How, then, does language bear something of this promise in literature—and more specifically, in the construction of Beckett's stories?

In the chapters that follow, I shall undertake a reading of Beckett's stories and plays, attempting to vindicate my claims regarding language, literature, and the promise of happiness in relation to his work.[99] Beckett's stories and plays do not preach, do not prescribe; they present powerfully engaging interpretations of our world and leave it for us to draw out the ethical, moral, and political implications. They show us to ourselves; yet the intelligibility and truth they claim cannot fit the traditional requirements for realism in representation. We might take this to indicate Beckett's conviction that conventional realism could not reach into the depths of our reality, a reality in which it is not only the dimensions of transcendence that have been lost, but also even the fundamental—though ultimately uncanny— human sense of being "at home" in the world: "Modernism as the forsaking of realism is hence the record of the sorrow of the world, its lack of human worldliness."[100] In showing us how life endures in "our world," in bearing witness to "our situation," Beckett's works provoke us to think and question, putting us in touch with disavowed emotions and abandoned dreams and hopes—and perhaps setting in motion the redemption of the promise for which he thinks our words have been secretly longing.

What does it mean to live without theodicy, without the justifications and consolations that require a dimension of transcendence, whilst continuing to have hope for a more perfect future, faith in a more enlightened humanity, believing still in a history somehow oriented toward the eventual redemption of earthly justice, believing in a history exposed, therefore, to interruption, to the possibility that something might happen to end century after century of tyranny, war, and cruelties of unimaginable horror? Whatever else it means, living without theodicy surely means that justice, and all the other conditions required for an enlightened humanity, the achievement of which is at the very heart of the utopian promise of happiness, are now entirely in our own hands. We must accomplish by ourselves, right here on earth, the justice that theodicy was supposed to provide. Living without theodicy ultimately means, therefore, achieving a radically new understanding of our being human.[101] But can we mortals live without theodicy? Is there no existential meaning in suffering? Why must a theological interpretation of suffering be the only possible form of meaning? Why, indeed, must suffering neglect the little moments of meaningfulness in daily life, seeking instead some grandiose consoling justification?

And why is there still, in a world that has passed through centuries of "civilizing," centuries of "culture," so much meanness of spirit—so much barbarism, so much "civilized" cruelty?[102] Taking into account all the horrors of the twentieth century, counting all the acts of cruelty, and all the individual, everyday acts of coldness and meanness, what happiness, what earthly semblance of an enlightened world, utopia or paradise, is even possible for the human species? And what is literature to make, in a time of extreme disenchantment, of the promise of happiness, versions of which first appeared in the texts of faith that formed our culture? How can literature redeem the promise with its weak and paltry words? These are philosophically motivated questions that Beckett's works daringly explore, questions that he, as a writer of fictional works, turned into the lives of his characters—his "delegates," as he once liked to call them—and struggled with through them.[103]

§3

Beckett often felt he could not talk—could not find the right words, or the right way, to talk about our experience of living in a time bereft, without a god, without the justifications and consolations of theodicy, and without any absolute grounding. A dog's life? Beckett was not without words; even in stories he thought of as failures, failing to express our experience of the present, experience that sometimes seemed inexpressible, he was able, nevertheless, to give expression to our sentiments, the darkest recesses of our consciousness, giving body and voice, if only in broken words and halting speech, and in gestures barely discernible, to what, in this time of destitution, we have urgent need to hear and see expressed. Uncompromising in his commitment to truth, bearing witness to his time, Beckett shows us to ourselves in all our strangeness, our uncanny, estranged familiarity, causing a disquieting moment of recognition not easy to acknowledge.

In *Dream of Fair to Middling Women* (1932), the first of Beckett's novels, not published, however, until 1992, Belacqua (named after a Florentine lute maker whom Dante assigns to sit in Purgatory and brood bent over on his sins) is given these words to write:

> The experience of my reader shall be between the phrases, in the silence, communicated by the intervals, not the terms, of the statement, between the flowers that cannot coexist, at the antithetical (nothing so simple as antithetical) seasons of words, his experience shall be the menace, the miracle, the memory, of an unspeakable trajectory.[104]

I think it fair to state that, throughout half a century of experiments with the writing of prose fiction, Beckett remained rigorously faithful to this project. But in his later years of writing fiction, the unspeakable, the inexpressible, haunting his words from within the looming silence between them, became ever more significant. His reference to "flowers that cannot coexist" recalls Stéphane Mallarmé's observation in "Crisis in Poetry" regarding the separation of the signifying word, the name, from the thing named or signified—a separation that implies the eventual absence, death or destruction of the signified.[105] Nothing therefore can be named by language without, in effect, sentencing the named to the fate of eventual absence or annihilation. Words are messengers of fate, foretokens of doom. Even a flowering life is bound by its signifier to a time of death. Beckett's reference also recalls Hölderlin's poetic evocations of words as like flowers of the mouth. As such, it would convey Beckett's morbid reflection on the poet's experience with words.[106]

It should not be surprising that a writer of Beckett's integrity and honesty found the calling of writing—writing fiction—to demand an incessant struggle with words. In the 1970s and 1980s, he was haunted by doubts that seemed to become more intense and more threatening the more his earlier works, especially his plays *Waiting for Godot* and *Endgame*, were receiving critical acclaim. But in one of his last prose works, *Worstward Ho* (1983), written when he was in his seventy-seventh year of life, he lucidly recalls that struggle and finds a way to express his determination to persist, to continue despite feeling bereft of inspiration, bereft of words:

> On. Say on. Be said on. Somehow on. Till nohow on. Said nohow on. [. . .] All of old. Nothing else ever. Ever tried. Ever failed. No matter. Try again. Fail again. Fail better.[107]

"Thought-breaths," Northrop Frye calls these sentences.[108] There is peaceful resignation in these words, but also a youthful spirit of faith and hope, dissipating despair. Words matter. Writing may be "a sin against speechlessness," but what would silence be, what meaning could it have, if there were no interruptions in its reign and no words to name and evoke it?

Beckett's words struggle against a silence they nevertheless long for, fighting it in order, finally, to fall into its depths and learn there its secret— or perhaps the secret of its allure.[109] Philosophers have also sought to learn the "truth" held in silence; but the silence their words assume is nothing but an artifice of thought. In a text from the last years of his life, Merleau-Ponty, pursuing his phenomenological reflections on language, succinctly describes the experience with language that ultimately compels philosophical thought to abandon its longing for a silence it had imagined to reign as its absolute origin:

> The philosopher speaks; but this would be a weakness in him, and an inexplicable weakness: ·[consistent with the grandiose dream of metaphysics,] he should keep silent, coincide with silence, and rejoin in Being a philosophy that is there ready-made. But yet everything comes to pass as though he wished to put into words a certain silence he hearkens to within himself. His entire "work" is this absurd effort. He wrote in order to state his contact with Being; he was not able to say it and could not have said it, since it is silence. Then he recommences. . . .[110]

It is from felt silence that our words come; and like the philosopher, Beckett struggles time and again to bring that enigmatically creative silence into words.[111] But, as he painfully knows, words conceal it. And yet, confiding his chronic weakness and his irrepressible faith, he recommences after every failed attempt to express the inexpressible. Molloy: "From where did I get this access of vigour? From my weakness perhaps" (MO 79). However, unlike the philosopher, Beckett was writing prose fiction and works for the stage. And by the time he wrote the dialogues in *Waiting for Godot* (1948– 1952) he had learned how to use and interrupt words to create, or yield to, deep and intricately meaningful silences that would say, at times, limitlessly more than any words could possibly say. And paradoxically, the more he reduced his words, subtracting and impoverishing expression, condensing and compressing, as in the later prose fiction and works for the stage, the more the words that remained were able, precisely in their uncanny "weakness," to give expression to the inexpressible haunting of a silence charged with meaning. And silently imparted, always, even in the greatest weakness, even where only shadows are dusting the page and ghostly voices are echoing, there is something of the promise of happiness, the utopian or messianic ideal of hospitality and justice he never lost faith in, because, despite having to struggle against its ruination, he never entirely lost faith in the testimony of language.

Language as such is testimony, always silently bearing witness to the promise of happiness. As Derrida declares in *Monolingualism of the Other*:

> Each time that I open my mouth, each time that I speak or write, I am imparting a promise. [. . .] And this promising announces the unicity of a language still to come. It is [. . .] the promising of a language that at the same time precedes all the languages, a claim that recalls all words and already belongs to each of the [different] languages as to each and every word.[112]

The language still to come, which language is promising, is the language that, with its creative, revelatory, and metaphorical power redeemed, would keep alive for remembrance and imagination the prophetic promise, gathering the world into the beginning of a time that reconciles and redeems. Genuine prophecy is not prediction, but words that fearlessly speak the unbearable truth, words that summon to the courage of a future-oriented questing and questioning: words that belong to what beckons.

In the twentieth century, such words of promise will not come easily to the writer, will not yield their treasure without demanding an epic struggle. Why, and how, does literature such as Beckett's seem nevertheless to *redeem* damaged language, so that, keeping the promise of happiness it bears and bears witness to, despite its damage, and transfiguring our sense of the world, revealing possibilities in the midst of desolation, precisely there where nihilism prevails, language might become a "prophetic" medium for the utopian or messianic redemption of our world? What faith in language is necessary for that to happen? At least in *Krapp's Last Tape* (1958), we will be denied what we imagine to be a revelatory event in Krapp's life. Several times, each time with unnerving symbolism, he abruptly stops the tape recorder's words immediately before the moment we are expecting to receive the little revelation they seemed to promise.

In *The End* (1946), the narrator, homeless and forlorn, concludes the long story he has told, telling us:

> The memory came faint and cold of the story I might have told, a story in the likeness of my life, I mean without the courage to end or the strength to go on.[113]

The narrator's regrets were two: not only wanting to have had a different story to tell, but also wanting to have had the words with which to bring that untold story, full, we suppose, of important meaning, to expression. In *Enough*, a much later story (1965), the storyteller's plight has not essentially changed. Now the narrator says:

> All that goes before forget. Too much at a time is too much. That gives the pen time to note. I don't see it but I hear it behind me. Such is the

silence. When the pen stops I go on. Sometimes it refuses. When it refuses I go on. Too much silence is too much. Or it's my voice too weak at times. The one that comes out of me. So much for the art and craft.[114]

§4

Almost from the beginning, the very earliest years of his life as a storyteller, and into his last years, Beckett struggled to find the words and the literary form that would enable him to express, and reflect on, the experience of crisis—we might call it a crisis of meaning, though it is also a crisis in the nature of our experience and consequently in the art of storytelling—that he took to be somehow distinctive of our time, our historical moment.

From poets and fiction writers of the last decades of the nineteenth century and the early years of the twentieth, Beckett inherited a compelling sense that the old ways of representing reality and giving expression to experience could no longer claim authenticity. Events had exposed the literary forms of the past to a reality the experience of which they were unable to express or represent with any degree of credibility, validity, and legitimacy. Eventually, by the time the First World War had ended, the recognition of this situation constituted for many artists something like a compelling sense of existential urgency and crisis, and it involved calling into question both the content and the form of representation; hence, for many writers, the problematic nature of language could not be ignored, and new ways to express what people were experiencing had to be invented. The crisis presented a challenge, of course—but also an opportunity. Every crisis, every emergency, becomes an occasion to imagine the possible emergence of something startlingly new.

Indicative of the urgent sense of crisis is Robert Musil's lament that the character of modern life is so radically different from what it had been in the past that it could not be narrated—it had become, he said, thinking in terms of the nineteenth-century novel, "*unerzählbar*." But as we know, he did in fact make the challenge in this situation an opportunity to experiment with fictional narration, attempting to write a novel of and for his time: a novel, however, that, with its alternative versions of reality, ultimately escaped his authorial control and accordingly could never be completed. Published nevertheless in its fragmentary condition, *The Man Without Qualities* (1930) showed new possibilities for the fictional novel.

In *The Theory of the Novel*, Georg Lukács proposed to define the novel as "the epic of an age in which the extensive totality of life is no longer directly given, in which the immanence of meaning in life has become a problem, yet which still thinks in terms of totality."[115] It is "the epic of a world that has been abandoned by God."[116] A certain "daemonic" psychology accordingly compels its characters, for they, reflecting their authors, inhabit a world conscious not only that it is bereft of meaning, bereft of faith and hope, but also that, without meaning, without prospect, their reality loses its intelligibility and "disintegrates into nothingness."[117] I think that the stories and novels about which we will be reflecting here confirm this diagnosis. However, the present situation is actually worse than Lukács believed, because language is suffering much more today than it was in the past: constantly threatened by etymological forgetfulness, overcome by commodification, reduced to one-dimensional tonality, and enduring other types of reification; consequently, it has lost much of its power to express this devastation with compelling conviction, using—unchanged—the inherited forms and conventions of literature. Moreover, the overwhelming power, today, of a paradigm of knowledge, truth and reality that recognizes only what can be quantified, mechanically reproduced and exchanged, devalues and delegitimates individual experience. And yet, there is also, in twentieth-century literature, fierce resistance to this damage—a resistance in language by language that bears witness to its weakness but struggles to find truth within that very weakness: a new expressive power, redeeming something, even if that something is almost nothing, of its utopian promise. Such engagement of writing in the fate of language is what Beckett calls his "syntax of weakness."[118]

In "The Storyteller," an essay fragment written sometime in 1935 or 1936, years still suffering the traumatic afterlife of the war, Benjamin, an admiring reader of Kafka and Musil, reflected on the fate of storytelling in the modern world, and called attention to the disintegration and atrophy of experience, experience understood as "*Erfahrung*," as journey and venture, increasingly forgotten in the shocking rush of experiences, "*Erlebnisse*," atomic, fragmented moments of *reduced* experience, bereft of memory, history, and meaningful venture:

> With the [First] World War, a process began to become apparent which has not ceased since then. Was it not noticeable at the end of the war that men returned from the battlefield grown silent—not richer, but poorer in communicable experience [*Erfahrung*]? What ten years later was poured out in a flood of war books was anything but experience that goes from mouth to mouth. And there was nothing remarkable about that. For never has experience been contradicted more thoroughly than strategic experience by tactical warfare, economic experience by inflation, bodily experience by mechanical warfare, moral experience by those in power. A generation that had gone to school on a horse-drawn streetcar now stood under the open sky in a countryside in which nothing remained unchanged but the clouds, and beneath these clouds, in a field of force of destructive torrents and explosions, was the tiny, fragile human body.[119]

Benjamin thus believed that, with the disintegration of authentic experience, the art of storytelling was finally reaching its end, "because the epic side of truth, of wisdom, was dying out."[120] In a time of sensationalism, writers are compelled to struggle to sustain a narratively thick sense of experience.

In a sense, Beckett thought his literary projects were from the very beginning doomed to fault and failure, not only because of what had happened to language, but also because, in a time when the subjectivity of the subject, especially in its reflective capacity, had been eviscerated and experience had lost its voice, reduced to sensations, its claim to bear meaning and truth, the art of storytelling—Beckett's art—could no longer satisfy the inherited conventions and fulfill its historical role. The loss of existential experience, of reflective subjectivity, bringing to an end centuries of storytelling, thus became that art's only historically true substance. So, for Beckett, literature's appropriation of its inevitable failings, its condition of destitution—melancholy consequence of the work's belatedness—became the only possible claim to authenticity and legitimacy that it could make. Success must consist in sucessfully failing. Beckett's stories accordingly redeem this claim by showing their failings in a language of enduring stress, and in a fiction bereft of *fiction*—fiction's traditional ways of producing literary enchantment—as the very condition of their possibility.

However, just as there are philosophers who think that the problems philosophers struggle with are nothing but the phantastical creations of a peculiar philosophical madness, so there are writers who encounter no troubles at all telling a story and no difficulties at all finding in the inherited language the words they want to use. For them, the inherited language of quotidian use is perfect just as it is: the language we use is in need of no radical improvement or reconstruction. And in fact, don't we all have stories drawn from the events of our daily lives to tell? Aren't these stories of ours, recounting some experience, occasionally memorable, more often banal, the very substance of social life? And aren't they imparted without undue difficulty, accepting and appropriating the words our language provides? Why, then, are writers such as Beckett unable to express what they mean using the potential inherent in the language they inherited? Why are they unable to continue the narrative tradition of representationism? Are these struggles by Beckett—and other poetic spirits—to overcome the limits of inherited language, these lamentations over the damage and mortification of language, and these struggles to tell a story for our time, nothing but theatricality, a glorification of failure—or an excuse *avant la lettre*, a circuitous apology for the writer's shortcomings, or perhaps a self-serving rationalization of failure turned into a new plot, a novel subject for narrative? Or are they instead, as I am wont to believe, telling expressions of a truth about our world, signs and symptoms of a crisis that others somehow cannot perceive—or prefer to ignore?

*

There can be no doubt, I think, that, in the context of severe economic stress and political discontent, the traumatic experience of the First World

War brought renewed attention to the inflammatory writings of Friedrich Nietzsche, whose unprecedented critique of European culture, religion, social forms, and political institutions encouraged acknowledgement of a grave crisis in reason—a crisis from which language, as our primary medium of expression, experience, and truth, could not possibly escape. Emboldened, perhaps, by the extremely audacious writings on language by the early German Romantics (I am thinking, in particular, of J. G. Hamann's 1762 "Aesthetica in nuce" and Novalis's 1797 "Monologue"), and by the "language critique" in Herder's 1799 "Language and Reason," challenging Kant's naïve assumption that there is no need for transcendental thought to reflect on the common language in which such thought is expressed,[121] Nietzsche undertook his own critique of language, writing "On Truth and Lies in a Nonmoral Sense" (1873), in which he claimed that language, the language in which philosophical thought finds truth, is nothing more than a "mobile army of metaphors, metonyms, and anthropomorphisms":

> In short, a sum of human relations, which have been enhanced, transposed, and embellished poetically and rhetorically, and which eventually, after long use, seem to be firm, canonical, and obligatory: truths are illusions about which one has forgotten that this is what they are; metaphors which are worn out and without [creative] sensuous power; coins which have lost their pictures and now matter only as metal, no longer as coins.[122]

After arguing, in *Beyond Good and Evil* (1886), against our common habit of projecting the contingent, ultimately groundless grammatical features of our native language, whatever that tongue happens to be, onto the world we inhabit and taking our disavowed projections to represent ontological or metaphysical truth, Nietzsche wrote: "I shall repeat a hundred times: we really must free ourselves from the seduction of words!"[123] Not only the concept of "truth," but also all our other philosophical concepts, such as "cause" and "effect," "freedom," "justice," and "reason," are ultimately nothing but mythologies, "conventional fictions for the purpose of designation and communication."[124]

This revolutionary critique of language that Nietzsche set in motion did not fade into oblivion. In fact, at the turn of the century, various intellectual circles in Vienna, hospitable city of residence at one time or another for, among others, Karl Kraus, Fritz Mauthner, Hugo von Hofmannsthal, Moritz Schlick, Rudolf Carnap, Ludwig Wittgenstein, and of course Sigmund Freud, resumed the reflections on language inherited from their German predecessors and began debating the question of a thoroughgoing critique; some even ventured projects designed to reform or reconstruct the language. Kraus, a fanatical grammarian whose passion for language was such that he would agonize for days over the placement or misplacement of a comma, dedicated his life to defending language against its corruption and abuse, firmly believing that careless language is careless thought. In

1896, he and von Hofmannsthal became acquainted with one another as members of a youthful social-intellectual club called "Jung Wien," where "*Sprachkritik*" was the subject of much heated conversation. In 1901, the first of Mauthner's magisterial three-volume *Contributions to a Critique of Language* appeared in print, received with much acclaim and debate. The third volume came out in 1903. And, beginning in 1910, the first parts of his *Dictionary of Philosophy* (1910–1911, 1923–1924) were published, attempting to give philosophical terms a precision they had never before enjoyed. Terms that could not be so favored were accordingly to be rejected, cast out and forever banished from legitimate philosophical thought. This rigorous *operational* positivism set the stage for ambitious experiments in *logical* positivism to carry out that programme.

Mauthner's *Critique of Language* soon aroused the curiosity of James Joyce, who, because of failing eyesight, requested a much younger Samuel Beckett to read that work aloud for him.[125] Intense discussions between them ensued. If that study accomplished nothing else, at the very least it encouraged Beckett to experiment, in his writing, with ways to say the seemingly unsayable even in damaged words, somehow breaking them open to a world of great suffering, a world in which, as one of his anonymous surrogate narrators was moved to say, speaking in a voice reminiscent of the Baroque spirit that figures in Benjamin's *Trauerspiel* study, we must learn to accept "fleeting joys and sorrows of empires that are born and die." (H 12).

Mauthner's work was an important inspiration for Moritz Schlick, who founded the "Vienna Circle" in 1926 and published, among other works, a *General Theory of Knowledge* (1918–1925), in which he argued, more radically than had Kant, against metaphysical speculation; and, in keeping with the austere empiricism behind that argument, he encouraged the view that, since the discourses of ethics and aesthetics are capable neither of the kind of rigorous definition possible in mathematics nor the kind of objective verification possible in physics, they must be considered meaningless. Carnap, intensely interested in working through what he perceived to be a crisis in the sciences related to the looseness of language, joined Schlick and his colleagues in the "Vienna Circle," and in 1928 he published *The Logical Construction of the World*, in which he undertook to construct out of a phenomenalist language, and according to the strict laws of logic, all the terms required by the physical sciences. The publication of this work followed by just a few years Wittgenstein's *Tractatus Logico-Philosophicus* (1922), a wildly bold attempt, inspired by Mauthner's project, to reconstruct language, rendering it in the purity and transparency of logical form. Both Wittgenstein and Carnap failed in their respective attempts; and whilst Carnap simply abandoned the fantasy of a logically transparent language to ground the terms needed in the discourse of physics, Wittgenstein soon repudiated the very idea of such a language, celebrating instead the perfection of ordinary language. Language, he insisted, in an excess of conservative fervour, is perfect just as it is.

During these same years, we know, Sigmund Freud was also a resident of Vienna; and during his student years at the university there, he undertook studies in epistemology and metaphysics with the philosopher Franz Brentano, an important figure for Edmund Husserl, whose *Logical Investigations* (1901), studies essentially concerned with the formation of concepts in language, prepared for his subsequent contributions to phenomenology.[126] Turning from philosophy, however, and pursuing a course of studies that led him eventually into the practice of psychiatry, Freud found himself increasingly fascinated by the nature of language. Approaching language from a perspective totally different from the one that would emerge from logical positivism of the "Vienna Circle," he sought to reveal and interpret the encrypted, unconscious undercurrents operating in language. His *Interpretation of Dreams* was published in 1899; and just two years later, in 1901, he published *The Psychopathology of Everyday Life*, soon followed by *Jokes and their Relation to the Unconscious* (1905).

Hugo von Hofmannsthal was another of Vienna's illustrious intellectuals, a poet and writer of novels, essays, and libretti for some of Richard Strauss's operas. And he too became obsessed with language. But obsessed in ways quite different from Husserl, who never abandoned his hopes for transcendental intuitionism, and from the philosophers committed to logical positivism, with its ideal of a standardized, referentially perspicuous system of language; for, much closer in spirit to Mauthner and Kraus, and decades before Joyce and Beckett, von Hofmannsthal was deeply distressed by a crisis in language that he experienced as affecting the very possibility for him to say and impart anything at all really meaningful. Thus, in 1902, just one year after Mauthner's *Critique of Language*, in a formulation of the crisis that has become a key to understanding "modernism," he expressed his despair in a fictional letter written by a certain Lord Chandos to his friend, Francis Bacon. In this last of his letters, Philipp speaks of a crisis he passed through, in which

> The abstract words that the tongue must enlist as a matter of course in order to bring out an opinion disintegrated in my mouth like rotten mushrooms.[127]

First, he lost his natural fluency; then he found that he could not use words— he calls them the "grand words"—such as "spirit," "soul," or "body," without experiencing "an inexplicable uneasiness." And this affliction, he averred,

> Gradually broadened, like spreading rust. Even in simple, informal conversation, all the opinions which are ordinarily offered casually and with the sureness of a sleepwalker became so fraught with difficulties that I had to cease participating entirely in these conversations.[128]

"I felt," he said, undoubtedly mindful of the bitter irony in his allusion to paradise, "like someone locked in a garden full of eyeless statuary, and

I rushed to get out again."[129] So whilst he experienced some marvelous moments enjoying the mere presence of ordinary things, moments indeed of little Proustian "revelations," his happiness was threatened because what he felt in such moments of illumination "had no name and is not namable." Moreover, very much like Beckett, the words he felt he needed in order to communicate the experience of failure failed to come. His sense of loss could not have been greater. He found himself left to recall in languishment the transience of "a sublime and deeply moving aura which words seem too weak to describe."[130]

This fictional "Letter," exhibiting a radically new form of subjectivism, was a powerful and influential expression of a self-consciousness for which failure—the failing of words, the failing of meaning—had become the principal experience that the writer felt compelled to convey.[131] Insofar as Beckett's use of language in his storytelling has brought rescue and redemption, redeeming both the words themselves and the things that the words mark and remark, name and signify, those words will have accomplished this ambition only by maintaining their openness and exposure to the perpetually threatening possibility of their "most splendid failures."[132]

This failure is the theme of "The Word," a poem by Stefan George that first appeared in 1919. In 1928, it was published in a book of verse bearing the title *Das Neue Reich*. The poem, just seven short strophes, ends with these words:

> So lernt ich traurig den verzicht:
> Kein ding sei wo das wort gebricht.
> [So it was with sadness that I learned renunciation:
> No thing may be where the word breaks off.][133]

One should note that the final line lends itself to a double reading: according to one reading, it expresses a crisis in ontology—Heidegger would say a crisis in the modern experience of being; in another reading, however, it expresses a crisis in language, a crisis in its capacity to speak of that which is—or speak of it without reiterating old, shop-worn words.[134]

Recapitulating Adorno's argument, Martin Jay noted that, for Adorno, "genuine experience, experience worth rescuing from the damaged variety of modern life, is closely tied to the memory of happiness, whose faint promise to return is what art is able to offer."[135] The Chandos "Letter" confirms that interpretation in the surprise of a dialectical oscillation, pressured by despair and melancholy, that shows us words seemingly too weak to bring into the world even a glimmer of redemption somehow able, nevertheless, to continue bearing the eternity of the promise.

*

"The corruption of man," Emerson observed, "is followed by the corruption of language."[136] In 1897, thus five years before Mauthner's *Kritik* and six before von Hofmannsthal's "Letter," Rilke penned a poem in which he lamented the condition of language:

> I am so afraid of people's words,
> They say everything so clearly:
> And this is called *dog* and that is called *house*,
> and here is the beginning and there is the end.[137]

The vagaries and indeterminacies of meaning were not at all what he was lamenting. On the contrary, what distressed him was precisely the fixity of meaning, the rigid determinism of meaning, an excess of clarity in words used so frequently, so thoughtlessly, and with such comfortable certainty, that nothing about them was left to the free play of poetic imagination. The people use words in ways that deny in the things they designate all their wonder and mystery, their secret potential for surprising, enigmatic turns.

What, today, can "paradise" possibly mean? Have we not lost the meaning of that word? Can it have any meaning in our secular world? It is, said Wallace Stevens, evoking Hölderlin's words, "As if the paradise of meaning ceased/ To be paradise, it is this to be destitute."[138] In this, our time, it seems, the mindless damaging of language—destruction inseparable from its capacity for destructiveness and malevolence—has been taking place with ever-diminishing resistance. Can language, subject moreover to endless contingencies fatal to meaning and transmissibility, show nevertheless that it bears, or metaphors, a redemptive promise? Would bearing such a promise require that, in the continuum of historical time, language actually keep it?

*

The sense of a crisis in literature, above all in regard to its expressive exhaustion and limitation, was not restricted to the European continent. It also figured in the poetry of T. S. Eliot, with whose work, of course, Beckett was familiar. In "East Coker" (1940), a poem, Eliot confided his anxieties as a writer of poetry, struggling to learn how he might use inherited words to say something new and, in the writing itself, acknowledge his starts, stops, and failures.[139]

Even into his later years, and even after much favorable acclaim, Beckett would acknowledge suffering such feelings of frustration, anxiety, and failure. But he persisted, ceaselessly experimenting with new forms of expression. He inherited, from the Germans, from Eliot, but especially from Joyce, a keen understanding of the crisis of meaning as a critical problem both for aesthetics and for the production of literature; but he also inherited, especially, once again, from Joyce, a sense of possibilities for renewing or reanimating in literature a commodified, worn-out language. Gradually, however, he abandoned his youthful enthusiasm for the exotic, extravagant esotericism that Joyce had inspired. Despite everything, he believed in what language promises. Thus, over the course of many years, he experimented with styles and narrative structures, different ways of telling a story and different forms of expression. And this is what constitutes what I want to call his "reflexive modernism," using a term for which we are indebted to Clement Greenberg and Michael Fried, art critics of exceptional erudition and discernment. "Reflexive modernism" is, and should accordingly be recognized as, a *distinct version* of modernism.

As I propose to interpret it, *reflexive modernism* translates Kant's so-called "Copernican revolution" into the realm of art, so that, instead of being solely or primarily concerned with mimesis, representations of reality, and references to reality, the work of art becomes radically reflexive, or "transcendental": solely or primarily concerned with the presentation or exhibition of its own conditions of possibility, exploring and examining those conditions, testing and contesting them, generating questions and provoking reflections. For modernist literature, this reflexivity means that the telling of a story becomes an opportunity for the story to explore and raise questions about, or at least call attention to, its own terms of possibility.[140] What are the constitutive conditions of a literary work of art? How is language engaged in its creation, its artifice, its semblance and pleasure? How does language reflect the multiplicity of ways by which it can express and also at the same time reflexively exhibit—recognize, state, question, negate, conceal or reveal—the beings it engages and our relationships to them? Why are the means of expression that we inherited in literature no longer working? How can literature acknowledge writing as social *praxis* and acknowledge the materiality of its medium? How can literature acknowledge, express, and accommodate the crisis of meaning whilst telling a story?

There are many ways for this Kantian reflexivity to function within the literary work. Sterne's *Tristram Shandy* and Cervantes' *Don Quixote* might perhaps be recognized as early precursors; but their occasional moments of reflexivity, calling attention, say, to the print, the fictional artifice, or the reader's expectations, are designed purely for entertainment and amusement; they neither register nor provoke questions disturbing the prevailing literary conventions. Things could not be more different in the literature that is claimed by our time. Stéphane Mallarmé's daring "reductions" showed the way.[141] And of course Joyce, Beckett's modernist mentor, boldly experimented with numerous reflexive operations. Vladimir Nabokov's novels—the ones he wrote in English—are also exemplary works in this regard, inheriting Mallarmé's experiments—and Joyce's, too.[142] Interrupting the narrative in all kinds of ways to reveal its underlying *material conditions* of possibility—ink, paper, a flat white surface for writing—as well as its *grammatological* conditions, such as punctuation, sentence structure, and spelling, and indeed also *what the work undergoes* in the editorial stages of its publication, Nabokov's reductions and deconstructions repeatedly call our attention to questions of meaning and representation only to turn them into opportunities for creating, in the very recognition of an inherited crisis, an enjoyable and memorable experience of reading a work of fiction. These modernist experiments in reflexivity are attempts to redeem the power of language in literature, rescuing the promise in words.

§5

In 1937, Beckett, who read German literature in the original language, wrote a letter to a German friend, lamenting the difficulty he was having in his efforts to break free of the paralyzing structures of the English language. Finding the way to a redeeming appropriation of the crisis of meaning became a challenge that would engage him throughout the years of his writing:

> Let us hope the time will come, thank God, that in certain circles it has already come, when language is most efficiently used where it is most efficiently misused. As we cannot eliminate language all at once, we should at least leave nothing undone that might contribute to its falling into disrepute. To bore one hole after another in it, until what lurks behind it—be it something or nothing—begins to seep through; I cannot imagine a higher goal for a writer today.[143]

Already at this time, Beckett was contemplating "an assault against words in the name of beauty," somehow creating a "literature of the nonword," sacrificing what can be said for the sake of the unsaid and renouncing what can be named for the sake of the unnamable—somewhat like the poet Hölderlin before him.[144]

Also like that poet, Beckett sought to renew his native language by approaching it in a detour, not, however, through the Greek of the ancient tragedies, but through contemporary French language. And, again following the example of Hölderlin's shockingly concrete translations, rendering the Greek without the genteel discretion of euphemisms, he sought that renewal in a certain precise literalism: a minimum of words, as concrete, blunt, and immediate as possible: using "a zone of stones," for example, to refer to a cemetery. Thus, in a sense, as Cavell points out, Beckett shared with the Vienna positivists the wish to reduce the language he would use to "the directly verifiable, the isolated and perfect present."[145] A kind of "purification" or "purgatory": "lessness." However, unlike the positivists, his intention was not to create literature in a language of logical transparency; nor was it to preserve or reinforce the "normal" meanings of words. Indeed, his use of words frequently *defeats* the normal meaning, or he finds ways to play with it, and maybe make fun of it.[146]

But must we say what we mean and mean what we say? How might we understand the frequent insertion of the words "my God," used in the narrative of *How It Is* in a flat, neutral way, not as an exclamation or curse, nor indeed as any other typical type of locution, such as would be used to convey an attitude or disposition? (H 24, 33, 34, 42, 88) I suggest that these interpolations function to desacralize, to neutralize the sacred, removing from the word "God" the last few remaining traces of awe and aura. Creating uncanny effects in the tension between a certain liveliness of spirit and an appalling deadness, Beckett's prose can suddenly shift from an emotionally flat, lifeless tone of voice into a voice of the most sublime lyricism—and return, just as abruptly, to a tone bereft of all expressivity. And sometimes the elegiac poetic mood will take over, only to be interrupted and disavowed by words of derision, a tone of sarcasm, or a turn to frivolity, calling into question the sincerity and seriousness of the lyrical sentiment. (I am reminded of Rilke's words in the first of his *Duino Elegies*: "And it's hard, being dead, and full of retrieving, until one gradually gets a small trace of eternity": "Und das Totsein is mühsam/ und voller Nachholn, daß man allmählich ein wenig/ Ewigkeit spürt." Can we be certain that there is, in Beckett, no longing to retrieve that trace?)

Much like the lyric poets as Adorno characterizes them, thinking, among others, of Stéphane Mallarmé and Stefan George, Beckett always sought to "hear his own language as though it were a foreign tongue." The lyric poet, says Adorno, "overcomes its alienation, which is an alienation of use, by intensifying it until it becomes the alienation of a language no longer actually spoken, even an imaginary language, and in that imaginary language he perceives what would be possible, but never took place, in its composition."[147] Beckett's experiments with the language of literature make crucial norms, norms necessary for communication in everyday living, problematic, even at times defeating their operation, as a way to compel attention to how words work and open them to adventures in interpretation. As Jean-François Lyotard notes, "the power of a literary or pictorial expression [lies] in that which holds and maintains open and 'free' the field of words, lines, colors, and values so that truth can 'figure' itself therein."[148] For the ordinary purposes of life, ordinary language may be, as the later Wittgenstein maintained, perfectly adequate as it is; but for the literature that Beckett felt beckoned to write, it needed to undergo processes of deformation that would make it unfamiliar, strange, and unsettling. He forced his prose to undergo subtraction and fracture, intensified its syntactic corruption, its grammatical trauma, and, at the same time, rendered it with uncompromising concreteness, compelling respect for the truth in literalism. Only in this way, he thought, could the shocking, disruptive, revelatory power of language be renewed and redeemed. As in Hölderlin's translations from the Greek, Beckett's experiments in reductionism, literalism, and traumatism present the familiar and the ordinary in revelations of astonishing and sometimes shocking beauty and pathos. I am thinking here, for instance, of his description, profoundly poignant, in *Worstward Ho* (1983), evoking the image of an old man and a child, one shade, another shade, plodding on, hand in hand. In these moments, he left far behind him the century's accommodations to the crisis of meaning.[149]

For Beckett, the crisis of meaning—the crisis of language and storytelling—certainly represented a haunting challenge: the impossibility of meaning had somehow to be turned into the form and content of a meaningful story. But this required that the writer resort to the most extreme measures: destroying meaning, destroying the means of expression, to make the expression of something meaningful possible.[150] In this time of abandonment and disenchantment, Beckett understood that his words must not only *impart* our overwhelming sense of loss; they must compellingly *constitute* that sense in the evidence of their failings: stammering and stuttering, unable to master the meaning they bear, breaking off and falling shattered into abysses of silence.

In 1943, Maurice Blanchot reflected, in *Faux Pas*, that: "The writer finds himself in the increasingly ridiculous situation of having nothing to write, having no means with which to write it, and being constrained by the extreme necessity of always writing it."[151] Some years later, Beckett would appropriate this thought to describe his own aporetic situation as a writer. Recalling Beckett's words from December 1977 in her Beckett memoir, Ann Atik reports his struggle with the impossible:

> All writing is a sin against speechlessness. Trying to find a form for that silence. Only a few, Yeats, Goethe, those who lived for a long time, could go on to do it, but they had recourse to known forms and fictions. So one finds oneself [today] going back to *vielles compétences* [know-how, as opposed to the creative act]—how to escape that. One can never get over the fact, never rid oneself of the old dream of giving form to speechlessness.[152]

And yet, in *From an Abandoned Work* (1957), Beckett's surrogate narrator would confide that, "I love the word, words have been my only loves, not many."[153] Beckett will at times vehemently curse words, curse language; but he knows that language is the only possible way to break the spell of that curse. So, despite the struggles, he does not altogether lose his faith in the possibility of redeeming language.[154] The principal nameless voice in *The Unnamable* (1953) thus acknowledges, with what seems to be a degree of serenity, resigned but without regret, that:

> When all goes silent, and comes to an end, it will be because the words have been said, those it behoved to say, no need to know which, no means of knowing which, they'll be there somehow, in the heap, in the torrent, not necessarily the last [. . .]. [UN 363]

In his essay on Beckett's *Endgame*, Stanley Cavell resists commentary on the challenges to eschatology that the play suggests in order to concentrate on how the playwright negotiates the crisis of meaning.[155] According to Cavell,

Beckett's characters suffer the curse of meaning; longing to be released from that curse, the flood of old, worn-out meaning, they seek the meaningless realm of silence. Better to suffer in silence than betray suffering by misrepresenting it in old words with dead meanings. But all their efforts to escape meaning nevertheless carry meaning. So, for Cavell, Beckett's crisis is not that his words fail to mean, but rather that he cannot wrest the words away from the meanings they have accumulated, the unbearable meanings they persist in bearing.

In *The Unnamable*, the narrating voice complains: "these voices are not mine, nor these thoughts, but the voices and thoughts of the devils who beset me" (UN 341). Shortly thereafter, the voice says: "Ah if I could only find a voice of my own in all this babble [. . .]." Later, the voice laments: "I'm in words, made of words, others' words, what others, the place too, the air, the walls, the floor, the ceiling, all words [. . .] I'm all these words, all these strangers [. . .]" (UN 379–380). And, later still, after concluding a little story, the narrator remarks, "that's the way it is this morning." But reflecting on these words, the voice tell us: "Morning, I call that morning, [. . .] I haven't many words, I haven't much choice, I don't choose, the word came. [. . .]" Eventually, however, the narrator does find, or receive, a new word: "it's the dayspring, but it doesn't last, I know it, I call that the dayspring, if you could only see it" (UN 394).

Calling God "the unmakable" and calling the narrator "a devised deviser" are two among many examples of Beckett's way of turning old signifiers into new ones. These new words carry subtle, and by no means insignificant, shifts in meaning. But Beckett has other ways of creating meanings. His prose, especially in the stories without punctuation, often creates a vague beckoning of words before which the reader must find a way to some meaning that is obscurely expressed or expressed to suggest other equally compelling meanings. As Sartre says of Giacometti's paintings, "emptiness seeps in everywhere."[156] It is as if Beckett were carefully following Kant's distinction between [1] the determinate judgment operative in the formation of knowledge, where the unifying conceptual principle is given and [2] the reflective judgment operative in the realm of the aesthetic, where the conceptual principle is not given but therefore must be found. For what he creates, especially in his late works, involves indeterminate atmospherics of words, what in "Quant au livre" Mallarmé will describe as "centers of vibratory suspense,"[157] words without any punctuation that require the reader's hermeneutical engagement in the construction of meaning. Approaching that construction beginning from the words, which words might be gathered together to form meaningful unities? Or, approaching the construction beginning with one or more interpretations, what interpretations might be selected to organize the words? Consider, for example, this:

A kind of air circulates, I must have said so, and when all goes still I hear it beating against the walls and being beaten back by them. (MD 47)

We may organize the words in two different ways, yielding several different meanings (in [1], either immobility or silence, in [2] temporal continuity):

> [1] *When all goes still/ I hear it beating* and [2] *When all goes/ still I hear it beating*

(The French, less pliant, leaves us no such ambiguity: "et quand tout se tait je l'entends.") Readers are called upon to experience and exercise their freedom in the interpretation of Beckett's words, making of them, in effect, a convincing story of their own. There is a certain affinity between this beckoning to freedom by way of ambiguity and antithetical sense and the challenge to the freedom of Reason in Hegel's "speculative proposition," in which the very same word bears opposite meanings. The German word "*aufheben*," for instance, can mean both to preserve and to leave behind; and in English as in German, "sense," or "*Sinn*," can mean either a sensuous sense or a cognitive sense, two senses of "sense" that, in the long history of Western thought and culture, have always been regarded as irremediably opposed to one another. And, as Nabokov shows us in *Ada, or Ardor*, "husked" can mean either covered or uncovered.[158] Beckett's intention is no doubt much closer to Nabokov's word-play than to Hegel's dialectic of Reason, namely: to call attention to the operations of language as such and draw us as readers into the process of making—or failing to make—his words into a meaningful construction.

In discussing Beckett's literary texts, Adorno astutely observes that what we get from Beckett is seldom more than a "suggestion of meaning in the midst of meaninglessness" (AT 154). In some ways, Beckett's prose fiction calls for a phenomenology of reading that is like the way one must look at a traditional oil painting—say a painting by Greuze, Constable, or Vuillard. As we know, when one ventures very near such paintings, the illusion, the aesthetic semblance, instantly vanishes; everything composing its recognizable world disintegrates, dissolving into crude brush strokes and masses of colored pigment. Likewise, especially with Beckett's later prose, it can be difficult to discern determinate shapes of meaning when struggling to read closely in the customary way; whereas, when one moves away, as it were, letting go of one's tight semantic and syntactic demands, permitting a looser, felt sense of meaning to become visible and legible, the prose will suddenly begin to reveal configurations of meaning one had not been able to recognize.

In *The Key*, a book of aphorisms, Edmond Jabès broods on these matters, conscious of a crisis of meaning that, for him, required above all a hermeneutically radical rethinking of the words that figure in the religious texts of Judaism: "The meaning of a word is perhaps only its openness to meaning. The word God *has* no meaning. Not several either. It *is* meaning: the adventure and ruin of meaning."[159] This interpretation of "God," however, would be, like Scholem's use of the name "Messiah," the ruination of eschatology and the final judgment demanded by theodicy. The invocation of "God" immediately abolishes all limits to meaning: there is no end to the possibilities. For Jabès, and I believe for Beckett too, it is possible to write—to tell stories—in a way that keeps the words endlessly open to interpretive adventures: the hospitality and justice in deconstructions. On the ruins of meaning, meanings inevitably arise. That is what, through many painful trials, many experimental "failures," Beckett gradually realized. At a certain moment in the telling of his long story about surviving in what I want to call "a state of nature," the nameless narrator in *How It Is* says: "it comes the word we're talking of words I have some still" (H 26). Words come.

§6

Beckett's language is, as Thomas Altizer notes, "a language that is the very opposite of everything given us as a common language, and opposite because it is the language of an apocalyptic humanity, or the language of a truly new world."[160] More controversially, he argues that it is "an apocalyptic, theological language," struggling against the present world and against its "enslaving language." This is a thought-provoking claim; but can its validity be sustained? We must first understand, though, how vehemently Beckett repudiated the substance of Judeo-Christian theology, theodicy, and eschatology whilst acknowledging at the same time the profound spiritual needs and longings to which, for centuries, these systems have been meaningfully responsive. Thus we encounter theological words throughout his works; but it is crucial to notice that they are functioning in new and subversive ways. If Beckett's language is theological, it is so only in order to appropriate the substance of theology for a radically subversive intention, rescuing or salvaging the *experience* that theological language has appropriated from the oppressive, life-denying interpretations that that language has imposed. But Beckett understood that this was a difficult and treacherous undertaking.

Altizer is certainly right, though, in pointing out that the crisis in language is also a crisis in ethics and ethical language. "Our only ethical language," he says, "is a common language [. . .]."[161] But this raises an urgent question for us, no less urgent for writers who want to be storytellers for their time:

> If our common ethical language is finally incapable of being an ethical language for us, is this not a summons to a radical new quest, and a summons inseparable from a radical and even absolute ethical crisis?

Pursuing this question leads him to the thought that, "It is becoming increasingly manifest that nothing is more difficult for us than an actual ethical language or an ethical language that could now be a truly *liberating* language, or a language actually opposing and reversing those dark and alien powers that are now engulfing us."[162] The present "crisis," a crisis he discerns in our ethical life and language, is, he argues, a consequence of the "death of God":

> A crisis that the deepest expressions of full modernity have known as a consequence of the death of God, a death of God that is not simply the eclipse of God, but the dissolution of all actual transcendence, or the transformation of transcendence itself into an absolute immanence. But thereby the ultimate ground of every established ethics collapses [. . .]."[163]

This, of course, is exactly what Nietzsche could see already taking place in his time. Altizer continues his analysis and argument:

> Now, in this situation, to attempt to practice ethics is finally to move in a circle, a circle in which we can never move beyond our given condition, can never actually do the good, or never actually do anything at all. And this is because now there can be no good or no goal beyond our immediate condition, or no such goal and no such good that can be anything more than fantasy or illusion, because now all actual transcendence has disappeared or has been wholly transformed into a new and final immanence. (Ibid.)

This situation is confirmed by the immobility or, at times, by the barely perceptible movement that Beckett will impose on many of his characters. It is also confirmed by the vertiginous circularity that frequently disrupts the logic of their dialogues: for example, those in *Waiting for Godot* that take place between Vladimir and Estragon and those in *Endgame* between Hamm and Clov.

Beckett would concur, I think, with Altizer's essentially Nietzschean way of overcoming despair:

> We need not necessarily despair at our new condition, as it could make possible a new world or a new life for us, but only insofar as we lose every illusion about our condition, and above all surrender that illusion of ethics which appears to be so necessary for us.[164]

This argument continues:

> If Nietzsche could unveil ethics as our deepest and purest illusion, or as our most destructive and self-destructive ground, this nonetheless has made possible a radically new ethics, but a new ethics that is unknowable and unnamable as ethics.[165]

Intent on showing the breakdown of our ethical life, bearing witness above all to its inhumanity, Beckett does not attempt to represent any new, unnamable form that might follow in its wake. But he does occasionally show us our ethical life in what might be called a redemptive perspective or light, a light, however, that is always faint and quickly passing, leaving barely a trace.

Like Nietzsche, Altizer is reluctant to speculate about a utopian form of ethical life, preferring to concentrate on the necessary moment of deconstruction:

> Any ethics that could be an ethics for us will inevitably be a nihilistic ethics, at the very least an ethics directed to a nihilistic condition, hence an ethics employing a nihilistic language, one already present in the revolutionary imaginative languages of late modernity, languages which themselves are ultimately ethical, even if their meaning can only be called forth by a radical hermeneutics.[166]

To return us to ourselves, Beckett's language increasingly manifested this "nihilism," this broken condition. But, for the patient and attentive hermeneutical reader, his storytelling writings occasionally yield echoes and traces of the redeeming promise, except in *The Lost Ones*, the only story in which hope seems absolutely impossible.[167] In this respect, it must be said that his language, his fiction, is engaged in a ceaseless struggle *against* nihilism: what Altizer is calling Beckett's "nihilism" is, in truth, this struggle to find a *way out* of nihilism.

In keeping with his interpretation, Altizer's ruminations conclude with a dialectical thought that finds hope precisely in the negative:

> Could it be that the deepest ethical way is wholly concealed as an ethical way, or wholly unreal in everything that we can recognize or know as ethics, or wholly unspeakable in everything that is possible as an ethical language?

"Perhaps," he suggests, "such an unnamability is a real hope for us, and if our ethical language is the most actual source of our ethical illusion, then the seeming impossibility of a genuinely ethical language for us could be a decisive sign of a truly new possibility, and as such one wholly absent from all of our horizons." Without an apocalyptic event, the new language can only emerge from the old. But old words can in fact be used in new ways to say something radically new. In the course of his experiments, working persistently toward "lessness," Beckett demonstrates this possibility. Language needs to pass through a kind of purgatory, if its power to redeem is to be redeemed; but Beckett's uncanny genius found expression in his understanding that, in literature, language is itself a kind of purgatory, at once a medium in which and through which every word must justify its truth, its authenticity, and also a medium in which and through which everything its words conjure into presence, or into the semblance of presence, must pass, compelled to justify the signification it bears. Thus, the unnamable continued to summon his writing, haunting the silences where words come and words fail. He grumbled and raged, struggling with words; but he never abandoned the telling of stories and never relinquished all hope in the promise that words must bear. And it is for the sake of the transmissibility of this promise that he gave the unnamable so many different voices.

§7

Altizer affirms his faith in the promise of a "New Jerusalem," but holds that the fulfillment of this dream is possible "only when we have finally made our adieu to God."[168] This would be, he says, "the dawning of an absolute immanence."[169] However, he also believes that, "If an absolute transfiguration is happening right now, it could only occur through darkness and emptiness, a truly annihilating emptiness and darkness."[170] Our liberation from the oppressiveness of the old religions is possible only by way of nihilism, a prolonged process of annihilation, tearing down the construct of beliefs under which, in return for its paltry benefits and graces, we have been deeply suffering. This thought evokes what Paul of Tarsus says in Corinthians (1 Cor 7: 27–28): "God chose what is weak in the world to shame the strong. God chose what is low and despised in the world, even things that are not, to bring to nothing the things that are." The so-called "nihilism" in Beckett's plays and stories is revolutionary, I suggest, in just that way, haunting us with what is not, the return of the repressed and disavowed, the unacknowledged and denied, and bringing to nothing that in our world which is terribly "out of joint." It is a "nihilism" for the sake of a redeeming hope.

This is the sense in which Beckett's stories, showing us the human species in various conditions of impoverishment, are affirmations of nihilism. But are they expressing his disdain for the world? This question is asking about Beckett's "world-view," his reflectively sifted experience of the time he inherits and inhabits, which, needless to say, is a matter that must be separated into [1] Beckett's own thoughts and feelings, especially in regard to the art of storytelling, and [2] the nihilism expressed by his characters and manifest in the conditions of their lives.

In "This Strange Institution Called Literature," an interview, Derrida comments regarding Beckett that,

> A certain nihilism is both interior to metaphysics (the final fulfillment of metaphysics, Heidegger would say) and then, already, beyond. With Beckett in particular, the two possibilities are in the greatest possible proximity and competition. He is nihilist and he is not nihilist.[171]

Alain Badiou seems to deny any ambiguity, any undecidability: "Beckett," he avers, without any shading, "was never a nihilist!"[172] And he justifies this reading, arguing that the only support for what critics interpret as Beckett's nihilism is his repeated lament that his "writing has nothing to assert." He will argue, though, that there is nevertheless something like a "negative theology" in Beckett's prose fiction and works for the stage. But this is not nihilism, he says, because, as in the hypothetical Cartesian reduction, "there is always *something* that cannot be reduced to the being of the inexistent, and that is reflection as such, the cogito, [. . .] the one for whom there is always at least the black-grey and unsayable presence."[173] This "something," this "presence," certainly makes what he is arguing true in a narrowly literal sense. But his argument, I think, misses all the intricacies and ambiguities, which Derrida's interpretation is intended to register. Sandra Wynands, undoubtedly influenced by Adorno as well as by Derrida, likewise denies that Beckett supports nihilism: "In his works, as in the most rigorous negative theologies, a dialectical process of negation operates to negate not only affirmation, but also its presumed polar opposite, negation, and thus to enter a space of undecidability whose discursive manifestation is the trace."[174]

We must not confuse the nihilism that Beckett's stories *show* us with Beckett's own attitude regarding life. His writings are, to be sure, strongly iconoclast; but that is not the same as *advocating* nihilism; nor is it the same as *accepting* nihilism as the fateful condition of our time. Iconoclasm is not disdain for the world. On the contrary, as I shall argue, Beckett's stories always bear, at the very least, prophetic traces and echoes of something hopeful; and they always remain open, if only by the tiniest of fissures, to what we might think of as redemptive possibilities. Because, as I believe, Beckett himself, Beckett the "deviser" of stories, is not committed to nihilism, the stories he devises never fail to sustain, there where the deepest despair prevails, in the midst of our wreckage, some glimmer of hope. Hope that is meaningful only in, and because of, its struggle, its resistance—its inseparability from the negative.

To get a better sense of Beckett's own world-view, and of the world-view that he presents in his stories, I suggest that it might be useful first, to consider Nietzsche's thoughts in *The Will to Power* (1883–1888), wherein he formulates his conception of nihilism. As I read Beckett, Nietzsche's distinction between active nihilism and passive nihilism serves well to illuminate not only the world-view he presents in his stories, but also features of his own world-view—features that enter in various ways into both the form and the content of his stories.

According to Nietzsche, "nihilism represents the ultimate logical conclusion of our great values and ideals. . . ."[175] But it is not only the skeptical weakening or destruction of these traditional values and ideals. It also weakens or destroys our experience, the "subjective" resources for creating new values. But that, he says, requires an understanding of what it is that nihilism has taken away from us. So he adds, significantly, that, "we must experience nihilism before we can find out what value these 'values' really had" (WP 4).

Is it not precisely *this* experience—the experience of our present historical time—that Beckett is attempting to understand and interpret? But must such an attempt to *show* us the nihilism of our time—this endgame for metaphysics and theology, when the transcendental world-view loses its authority and its consolations are no longer consoling—necessarily fall into a nihilistic despair, abandoning all hope? "What," Nietzsche asks, "does nihilism mean?" Answering his own question, he says: "That the highest values devalue themselves. The aim is lacking: the 'why?' finds no answer" (WP 9). But there are two forms of nihilism. The term, he says, is ambiguous:

A.   Nihilism as a sign of increased power of the spirit: as *active* nihilism

B.   Nihilism as decline and recession of the power of spirit: as *passive* nihilism (WP 17)

"Passive nihilism" is the nihilism we suffer and endure. It is the destruction of spirit, our loss of what Nietzsche calls, implicitly drawing on Spinoza's ethics, "the will to power," namely the capacity and the courage to affirm life, affirm the values of a flourishing life. "Active nihilism" attempts to destroy everything inimical to the affirmation of life; it is the will to power *affirming* the values of life. It is a *liberating* nihilism: nihilism engaged to defeat nihilism. Thus it is also, in fact, a robust "humanism": "The most universal sign of the modern age: to an incredible extent, man has lost *dignity* in his own eyes" (WP 16). Is Nietzsche committed to nihilism? "On the whole," he observes, defeating at least one of the charges of nihilism, "a tremendous quantum of *humanness* has been attained in present-day mankind. That this is not felt generally is itself a proof: we have become so sensitive concerning small states of distress that we unjustly ignore what has been attained" (WP 42). "In my own way," he avers, no doubt indicating his difference from Hegel's providential theodicy, "I attempt a justification of history" (WP 43). So, then:

> Overall insight. Actually, every major event of growth involves tremendous crumbling and passing away: suffering, manifesting the symptoms of decline, belongs in the times of great advances; every fruitful and powerful movement of humanity has also created at the same time a nihilistic movement. It could be the sign of a crucial and most essential growth, of the transition to new conditions of existence: that the most extreme form of pessimism, genuine nihilism, has come into the world. *This I have comprehended.* (WP 69)

Nietzsche plainly was engaged in the liberating iconoclasm of "active nihilism," attempting to complete the destruction of a passively suffered nihilism and all its destructive, life-denying conditions: all the social practices and institutions inimical to the affirmation of life—and that includes everything involved in what I have named, with a twist of irony, "civilized cruelty."[176] For Nietzsche, the Judeo-Christian culture of shame and guilt, especially its repressiveness in relation to the body and its sexuality, is a culture of cruelty, of nihilism, masquerading as necessary for "civilizing" the human "beast." We must therefore, he argued, end that culture, end that interpretation of "civilization." And, despite the emotional impact of living at last in a world without the transcendental dimension—suffering from chronic depression, Nietzsche experienced the symptoms of that loss himself—we must, as he never tired of insisting, go beyond active nihilism, turning this time of transition into a time of self-creation. A crisis is not merely an emergency; it is also a moment when, out of the experience of nihilism, new possibilities might emerge, affirming the meaningfulness of mortal life.

Like Nietzsche, Beckett observed a world suffering in the abjection of passive nihilism; that is the world that he wanted to understand, express, and show us. And as a storyteller, Beckett's only "obligation" was to *bear witness* to this historical moment.[177] The "truth" in his art as a witness of—and for—his time emerges from the forcefield operating in the tension between fact and fiction. Also much like Nietzsche. However, whereas the philosopher was deliberately engaged in destroying the social practices and institutions responsible for our plight by using essentially "rational" discourse—description, explanation, argument—and, now and then, the rhetoric of exhortation, to make us comprehend what he had comprehended, Beckett was not writing to *compel assent* to any interpretation of our historical moment; nor was he writing social critique, a critical diagnosis of our experience; he was simply writing, rather, to record, to express, or find a way to express, by way of fictional stories and plays for the stage, the *experience* of our time. His art works like a mirror, reflecting our time, showing us what we hide from ourselves, and encouraging our capacity for self-reflection.

That what calls for reflection and expression in Beckett's stories is our experience of living in a time in which all our trusted values, ideals, and institutions seem to be founded on nothing, and that this sense of loss and privation is the experience which Beckett's literary works represent, *shows* us a world suffering the death of God, suffering in nihilism; but it cannot commit him to nihilism. He is the "deviser" of stories, not to be confused with the characters and situations he devises. He is merely witness and messenger, struggling to find some way to tell stories drawn from the depths of his own historical experience. And it is ultimately in this struggle with words that he learns what suffering nihilism means. Addressing us from out of that anguish and suffering, what he gives words and voice to—what he shows us—including his own painful struggles with language, stammering and stuttering, and sometimes broken off, reduced to silence, faithfully and compellingly reflects our shared experience, our world bereft, longing for new authentic sources of meaning. Through his words, we "see" the ravages of nihilism: desolate, barren landscapes; empty, yet claustrophobic spaces, grimly gray; lost souls, discarded as if nothing but trash, searching and waiting, killing time. And through his words, we get in touch with our mourning, sustaining both our sense of loss and, as inseparable from that consciousness of loss, our longing for a meaningfulness we can believe in.

As in the German Baroque *Trauerspiel* that Benjamin interprets, we "see" the transience and ephemerality of all the things in our world; we "see" all that we have valued in decay, being finally reduced to fragments and ashes—nothingness. Everything we have counted on suddenly appears without any foundation: beneath the world that we have built there is nothing but an abyss. And we experience, through Beckett's tormented structures of expression, the damaged inheritance of words. Moreover, because that experience, bleak and sorrowful, is expressed and reflected with the compelling lucidity of great literature, we undergo an experience of our time as it takes the uncanny shape of nihilism: a profound, inhuman emptiness inhabited by shadows and ghostly voices. But that cannot make Beckett himself a nihilist, if we take this word to mean someone resigned in despair to the destruction of our values, ideals, and institutions—our way of life. As a storyteller and playwright, Beckett's concern is not to judge but to tell and show: to bear witness, as honestly as he can, to the end of the metaphysical, theological world-view; to preserve in cultural memory, through unforgettable stories, our loss of an absolute authority, or an absolute foundation, for all our most fundamental values, ideals, and institutions; and to tell of our despair and longing, as we confront the abyss, the ultimate nothingness of our civilization. Nihilism haunts his stories, stalking the lives of his characters. That is how it is. But that is not how it must be, how it must remain. And that is what, carefully disguised, Beckett's occasional "interventions" in his stories seem devised to tell us.

*

The first sentence in *Murphy* (1938), an early novel, tells us that, "The sun shone, having no alternative, on nothing new." But how serious is this? The narrator mockingly evokes "the Nothing," blasphemously distorting St. Anselm's formulation of his argument for the existence of God, describing it as that "than which in the guffaw of the Abderite [Democritus] naught is more real."[178] Nihilism here, in fact, seems to be not a threat but a blessing: "Not the numb peace of their own suspension, but the positive peace that comes when the somethings give way, or perhaps simply add up, to the Nothing [. . .]." Years later, in *The Unnamable* (1953), a narrative voice likewise evokes that nothingness, but in a surprising way, perhaps recognizing it as granting a time for the emergence of new possibilities: "a blessed place to be," it says, but then it adds, vanquishing that optimism: "where one feels nothing, hears nothing, knows nothing, says nothing, is nothing" (UN 367–368). There is, however, no denying the suffering that comes with freedom from transcendental tyranny: "it's too difficult, too difficult, for one bereft of purpose, not to look forward to his end, and bereft of all reason to exist, back to a time he did not" (UN 378).

In Beckett's Sartrian *Watt* (1953), Watt experiences the nothingness of existence when he describes the "soul-landscape" in which he lives. In Mr. Knott's house, where Watt assumes the duties of a servant, the meaning of his life evaporates because nothing ever happens there. He is waiting for something "significant" to happen; but nothing happens—unless we count an encounter with nothingness:

> What distressed Watt in this incident of the Galls father and son [. . .] was not so much that he did not know what had happened, for he did not care what had happened, as that nothing had happened, that a thing that was nothing had happened, with the utmost formal distinctness, and that it continued to happen, in his mind, he supposed, though he did not know exactly what that meant. . . . Yes, Watt could not accept [. . .] that nothing had happened, with all the clarity and solidity of something [. . .] a nothing had happened.[179]

But, unbearable though that is, Watt makes his situation worse by turning that experience of "nothing happening" into a mysterious substance or being, saying "a nothing had happened." His reification of the grammatical form, an error that Nietzsche and later Wittgenstein warned against, creates a dreadful, ghostly presence, making the experience of nihilism that much harder to escape or vanquish.[180] We, though, could regard his experience as nothing but a consequence of taking a philosophical pun much too seriously, missing the joke.

Pozzo, in *Waiting for Godot* (1952), gives lucid expression to nihilism as a world-view, bringing out its existential or ontological significance, its bearing on one's experience of life:

> One day we were born, one day we shall die [. . .]. They give birth astride of a grave, the light gleams an instant, then it's night once more.[181]

This ontological experience of mortality was very common in the mediaeval world, with its death's heads, dancing skeletons, and gruesome scenes of the crucifixion represented everywhere. And it was prevalent, also, during the troubled, war-weary years of the Baroque, poignantly expressed in Dutch and Flemish still-life paintings, objects created to remind their wealthy owners of the ephemerality and vanity of all earthly pleasures. But when evoked in our own time, this experience of mortality, of existential or ontological vulnerability, takes on the singular meaning of meaninglessness, which could not be more at odds with the earlier historical experience, heavy as it was with dimensions of existential or ontological meaningfulness.

*

Having briefly argued that, although Beckett is not himself committed to nihilism, the world he shows us is indeed a world experiencing the reduction to nothingness of its traditional values, ideals, and institutions, we will take up the question of nihilism in Beckett as a matter of "form" or "style," the art of expression, telling stories in writing. To begin this interpretive reading, however, I wish first to recall Schiller's *Letters on the Aesthetic Education of Man*, in which he declared:

> However sublime and comprehensive it may be, the *content* always has a restrictive action upon the spirit, and only from the *form* is true aesthetic freedom to be expected. Therefore, the real artistic secret of the master consists in his *annihilating the material by means of the form*.[182]

But in Beckett's works, what is form and what is material? And what if truth demands that the form—say the narrative structure, the communicative success of the dialogue, the grammar of the prose, and the logical coherence of meaning—must also be as if "annihilated"? In another *Letter*, Schiller argues against an exclusive formalism, insisting that art should not neglect the truth content—what he calls "reality."[183] However, this "not neglecting" does not mean a naïve or slavish reproduction of "reality": indeed, in yet another *Letter,* he states that the artist "is to eradicate in himself everything that is merely world," transforming the material truth of the world into a form of art.[184] Taking these *Letters* into account, I think it might be argued that there is, in Schiller's conception of art, a decisive moment of negation. But the art that he had in mind was pictorial art, not literature.

In Beckett's fiction and works for the stage, the "factual" truth about the world is of course reduced to its "truth content," revealing what he sees as its reality; and the material of language, in these works, exposing its brokenness, its damage, is accordingly constitutive of both form and truth content. Taking our cue from Schiller's surprising invocation of a process of annihilation, we might perhaps characterize Beckett's "style" using the term "nihilism," since he submits both language as form and language as material content to processes of extreme de-formation and disintegration, seeking expressive potentials in the radical disruption of the inherited literary conventions.

This conception is elaborated in Benjamin's interpretation of the work of art. It is an interpretation that will cast a singularly illuminating light on Beckett's art, which not only redeems *language* as a compelling medium for the revelation of the ordinary but redeems *literature* as a language of truth—exposing the truth content through negation and through subtraction, a way of writing, sometimes painful in its lucidity, that he would in later years call "lessness."[185]

In a brief fragment on the imagination—"Fantasie"—written sometime in 1920 or 1921, Benjamin argued that the figures of fantasy are de-formations of what has already been formed.[186] The work of imagination, he declared, is the dissolution of existing forms, making way for new forms to appear:

Its supreme law is that, while imagination de-forms, it never destroys. Genuine fantasy is unconstructive, purely de-formative—or, from the standpoint of the subject, purely negative.

But the first thing to note, he says, is that, like the free play of aesthetic experience in Kant's *Critique of Judgment*, it is "without compulsion." Second, he says, departing in the most extreme way from Kant,

> It never leads to death, but immortalizes the doom it brings about in an unending series of transitions. [...] Thus, all de-formation of the world will imagine a world without pain that is nevertheless permeated by a rich flow of events. This de-formation shows further [...] a world caught up in the process of unending dissolution; and this means eternal ephemerality. It is like the sun setting over the abandoned theater of the world with its deciphered ruins. It is the unending dissolution of the purified appearance of beauty, freed from all seduction. However, the purity of this appearance in its dissolution is matched by the purity of its birth. It appears different at dawn and at dusk, but not less authentic. Thus, there is a pure appearance [...] at the dawn of the world. This is the radiance that surrounds the objects in Paradise.

Finally, he says, there is "a third pure appearance": "the reduced, extinguished, or muted one. It is the gray Elysium," evoking scenes of longing and mourning. The fragment ends with this remarkable claim, rightly repudiating any misleading notion of the prophetic:

> The exact opposite of fantasy or imagination is prophetic vision. Pure prophetic vision cannot form the basis of a work, yet such vision enters into every great work of art. Prophetic vision is the ability to perceive the forms of the future; imagination or fantasy is the awareness of the de-formations of the future. Prophecy is the genius for premonition; fantasy is the genius for forgetting.

Fantasy is "the genius for forgetting" in the sense that it releases us from the determinate conditions imposed by "reality" and its past. Although some of Benjamin's assertions here are obdurately enigmatic, much of what he says can nevertheless make sense of Beckett's approach, including in particular the question of his supposed "nihilism." In Benjamin's terms, Beckett's works engage a dialectic in which they undertake *both* fantasy and prophetic vision. But the "prophetic," in Beckett, is not the false type, the swindle which is prediction: it belongs to the courage in speaking out, encouraging a power of critical reflection to free itself from the past and open itself to futural possibilities. For, unquestionably, as Badiou has argued, Beckett's prose, whether in stories or in dialogues for the stage, is subjected to deconstructions that defy the rhetorical conventions of semantics and syntax, sometimes even sacrificing immediate comprehensibility; but these deconstructions permit breaches and openings for something like pure prophetic vision to take place: *caesurae* making it seem possible beyond all reason that, like an astonishing, miraculous *event*, the radiance of paradise, and "premonitions" of the future happiness it promises, might, if only for the briefest of moments, be granted to our experience. As in *Ill Seen Ill Said* (1981), one of Beckett's last prose fictions, where, amidst so much greyness, so much haze, obscuring what the fantasies of the imagination struggle to envision, a sudden radiance will make its prophetic appearance.

*

I want at this point to read a set of texts by Beckett that bear on the imagination in relation to the question of nihilism. In each of these texts, Beckett is rigorously exploring the ways that words work to create images for the play and prophecy of the imagination. In *Company* (1980), Beckett's solitary narrator, himself a creation of the imagination, is engaged in "the conjuring of something out of nothing."[187] The text begins with the words: "A voice comes to one in the dark. Imagine." And, in a time such as ours, it seems that, for Beckett, this power enigmatically invested in words can be not only a wonderful consolation but also an extraordinary source of hope or faith. Might we not identify this power with the "weak messianic force" that Benjamin evokes in his reflections "On the Concept of History"? Perhaps that is not as far-fetched as one might at first suppose. Fifteen years before the publication of *Company*, Beckett wrote a short experimental tale, *Imagination Dead Imagine* (1965), in which he imagined a nameless narrator surveying and describing a "white rotunda," a "white speck" almost invisible at first, lost in the "white void." Inside this rotunda, there are two white bodies lying down back to back, "each in a semicircle." These creatures, motionless and white, are barely breathing. The story that the narrator tells begins with these words:

> No trace anywhere of life, you say, pah, no difficulty there, imagination not dead yet, yes dead, good, imagination dead imagine.[188]

Is the imagination dead? The imagination can, after all, imagine a world in which the imagination is dead! But the imagination that produces that image necessarily survives the image. Beckett's experiment reveals the paradox, the aporetic logic from which there is no escape. The narrator can invite us to imagine the death of the imagination. The imagination has amazing powers to conjure into presence and annihilate whatever it invokes. There is no way, however, that the writer can absolutely annihilate the imagination. Nihilism is defeated. Imagine that!

Following that conclusion, the narrator begins to imagine a scene, a seascape in fact, conjuring into imaginary existence what, with a single word, he cancels as easily as he brought it into that imaginary existence, hoping that, if he can make the seascape vanish, what will remain before the imagination is all whiteness, nothing remaining visible:

> Islands, waters, azure, verdure, one glimpse and vanished, endlessly, omit. Till all white in the whiteness of the rotunda. No way in, go in, measure [. . .].

But, despite that forbidding whiteness, Beckett's narrator is determined to go into it and take numerous measurements—as if the gathering of such quantitative information, satisfying the objectivity required by the empiricist's paradigm of knowledge, truth, and reality, could make the imaginary tale more credible. In fact, it has the opposite effect, just as too much protesting confirms the suspicion that a truth is being denied. The tale ends with the narrator telling us that,

> It is clear however, from a thousand little signs too long to imagine, that they [the two human bodies] are not sleeping. Only murmur ah, no more, in this silence, and at the same instant for the eye of prey the infinitesimal shudder instantly suppressed. Leave them there, sweating and icy, there is better elsewhere.

"No," the narrator continues,

> life ends and no, there is nothing elsewhere, and no question now of ever finding again that white speck lost in whiteness, to see if they still lie still in the stress of that storm, or of a worse storm, or in the black dark for good, or the great whiteness unchanging, and if not what they are doing.

There is "no question now of ever finding again that white speck," because Beckett, in a style far from "*Sturm und Drang*," is bringing the story to an end. But instead of providing an ending to satisfy conventional expectations, he gives us alternative versions, leaving the ending to our own imagination. In literature, the imagination is a joint venture—in the company of words. Faulty words that fail in their redeeming mission. Yet, in the way they impart that failure, these words—as if by some miracle—redeem their bearing.

In *Enough* (1967), published two years later, the narrator tells us a story about himself as a child, walking with an older man, presumably his father or grandfather, through flower-covered fields and hills—fields and hills that evoke the Elysian, an earthly paradise. Beckett brings his tale to an end, saying:

> Now I'll wipe out everything but the flowers. No more rain. No more mounds. Nothing but the two of us dragging through the flowers.[189]

This is not an affirmation of nihilism, but in fact a vigorous, unequivocal assertion—call it a redemption—of the astonishing power of language and the magic of semblance in the art of writing. Hence, too, it is a redeeming of the promise language carries in so many metaphors. The narrator's mood seems triumphant; he is enjoying that power, that magic, which he has mastered. This power is as much the power to create as it is a power to negate. But, although it is confined within the conditions of fiction, hence a power over only the semblance of truth, Beckett's modernist reflexivity makes his words also exhibit the truth of this semblance. And in the allegorical survival of the flowers, following the gesture by Beckett's surrogate that metaphors nihilism, the promise of happiness continues to be carried by language. The flowers of hope remain. The promise of happiness is "dragged," in effect, through the flowers.

The final text I want to consider in this context is *Worstward Ho* (1983), a very late prose work in which every attempt to lessen or worsen language only generates more language. And again, the narrator exercises his power to annihilate what his words have made present. But the ultimate effect, as in *Enough* and *Ill Seen Ill Said*, is to confirm, against nihilism, the sovereign power of the writer's imagination. Through his narrator Beckett tells us what he has learned from his experiment with words in storytelling: the endeavor to make his words go "worstward" cannot, after all is said and done, lead him into the nothingness of nihilism:

> Say child gone. As good as gone. From the void. From the stare. [. . .] Say old man gone. Old woman gone. As good as gone. (WH 113)

In a work of fiction, to say is to accomplish. This was, according to biblical scriptures, a signifying power that, at the beginning, only God enjoyed. But the mortal's power turns out to be limited: the narrator's words cannot entirely create a void: "Void most when almost. Worst when almost." The writer, or narrator, can easily invoke a boy, a man, a woman, and, as soon as they are declared all gone, they will indeed vanish from the story; but there will still be a void after the void is declared gone. Something always remains, preserving truth, in the dust of words. So, in a paradoxical way, no matter how many words mean to obliterate the void, the presence of a void cannot be avoided. And yet, the presence of the void defies representation; it is the limiting condition, we might say, against which the creative power of language is decisively shattered and, with equal measure, decisively settled. The magic of language can neither create nor annihilate nothingness; hence it cannot represent an encounter with absolute nihilism. But it can indeed expose us to the nothingness of being: this is the strangest, cruelest gift, a gift that only language can give us.

Beckett's exhibition of the supreme power of authorial dictation recalls Husserl's equally hubristic, equally paradoxical claim for his phenomenological reduction, formulated in the first volume of his 1913 work *Ideas: General Introduction to Pure Phenomenology*. In a section of that work, invoking the "nullifying" (*Vernichtung*) of the world, which Beckett almost certainly read, Husserl argued that the world is nothing more than, nothing other than, a correlate of our consciousness:

> The whole spatio-temporal world [. . .] is according to its own meaning mere intentional being, a being therefore which has the merely secondary, relative sense of a being for consciousness. It is a being which consciousness in its own experiences posits, and is, in principle, intuitable and determinable only as the element common to the (harmoniously) motivated manifolds of phenomena, but over and beyond this is just nothing at all.[190]

Repeating the phenomenological *Vernichtung*, he adds: "Reality is not in itself something absolute, binding itself to another only in a secondary way; it is, absolutely speaking, nothing at all [. . .]." Although claiming to appropriate the Cartesian method of doubt as only a "device of method," he assumes "our perfect freedom" and makes the doubt into an annihilating machine, obliterating "anything and everything" in order to reveal the consciousness that remains.[191] "The reflections in which we have been indulging," he says, continuing to press questionable assumptions, "make clear that no proofs drawn from the empirical consideration of the world can be conceived which could assure us with absolute certainty of the world's existence." And, as if to reassure us that he is not really mad, he hastens to tell us:

> The world is not doubtful in the sense that there are rational grounds which might be pitted against the tremendous force of unanimous experiences, but in the sense that a doubt is *thinkable*, and this is because the possibility of non-being is in principle never excluded.[192]

One might conclude, however, that if there are no *rational grounds* whatsoever for doubting our experience, or doubting the existence of the world, then doubting, or even feigning doubt in a philosophical speculation, is sheer madness. But he is determined to impose his speculative hypothesis, a hypothesis that, in the final analysis, silently obliterates the phenomenological difference between perception and imagination, or fantasy: No "real thing," he argues, nothing that "consciously presents and manifests itself through appearances," could therefore ever be "necessary for the being of consciousness." So, once we have supposedly "nullified" the world of our mere "belief," consciousness—the consciousness that performed the obliteration—remains in its absolute purity and sovereignty.[193] After this philosophical arrogance and insolence, he is ready to tackle the transcendence of God: God, too, must be subjected to "reduction" or "suspension."[194] With this final, brazen move, Husserl certainly shows that he is, at the very least, attuned to the time!

Beckett's strategy is unquestionably to use negation in various ways. He turns narrative and dialogical traditions against themselves; and using devices such as distortion, exaggeration, interruption, fragmentation, reflexivity, and literalism, he appropriates "exhausted" literary forms and practices, and, as in literalism, even our social conventions of meaning, reinventing and reanimating them with astonishing new sense. This is negation used *against* the pressures of nihilism.

§8

In *Aesthetic Theory*, Adorno makes this important comment on negation in relation to the promised utopia of happiness:

> The new is the longing for the new, not the new itself. That is what everything new suffers from. What takes itself to be utopia remains the negation of what exists and is obedient to it. At the center of contemporary antinomies is that art must be and wants to be utopia, and the more utopia is blocked by the real functional order, the more this is true; yet at the same time art must not be utopia in order not to betray it by providing semblance and consolation. If the utopia of art were fulfilled, it would be art's temporal end. (AT 32)

In the light of Adorno's critical commentary on Beckett, Jay Bernstein formulates two questions we must consider as we read and think about Beckett's art:

- How can art in general, and Beckett's art in particular, make a promise that is not complicit with what has undone all promises?

- How can a storyteller like Beckett sustain the promise through determinate negation?[195]

Succinctly stated, the answer to the first question is that, although a certain degree of complicity cannot be avoided, the writer has many ways of acknowledging this complicity and keeping it in a critical consciousness. A brief answer to the second question is more difficult; but first of all, we must *see* that the primary way to sustain the promise is, paradoxically, through repeated forms of determinate negation—words, for example, that evoke images of catastrophe and ignite long-suppressed passions. The more intensely the negation is pressed, the more intensely the hope borne by the promise is remembered and felt. Here, answering both questions, is what Adorno will argue:

> Through the irreconcilable renunciation of the semblance of reconciliation, art holds fast to the promise of reconciliation in the midst

of the unreconciled: This is the true consciousness of an age in which the real possibility of utopia [. . .] converges with the possibility of total catastrophe. In the image of catastrophe, an image that is not a copy of the event but the cipher of its potential, the magical trace of art's most distant pre-history reappears under the total spell, as if art wanted to prevent the catastrophe by conjuring up its image. (AT 32–33)

Beckett intuitively understood this; but if one does not recognize the operation of this dialectic, and does not grasp its aesthetic necessity, one will be tempted to take the stories he tells to register, straightforwardly, an outlook that can only be described as nihilism. In fact, however, the determinate negation of utopia, ventured through the image of catastrophe and made manifest in language that fails its end, is precisely what rescues the promise of happiness from betrayal.

*

But from the letters in which a young Beckett confided his tormented struggles with language, we learn that they involved an essentially impossible pursuit, defying Husserlian phenomenology: to find words that would take us beyond themselves to a reality independent of subjectivity and its language: words that would somehow vanish in the very act of signifying, leaving what they have conjured to claim an absolute objective reality.[196] But such an undertaking is as doomed to failure as the attempt to possess real knowledge of the thing-in-itself, an attempt that Kant struggled to renounce, accusing it of mysticism. An older Beckett abandoned that dream, although the longing remained with him. In the fifth of his *Fizzles* (1973–1975), he wrote: "There is nothing but what is said. Beyond what is said there is nothing."[197] Is this true? Is this invocation of nothingness suggesting a version of nihilism? Not necessarily. At any particular time, the limits of our language at that time are the limits of *our* world. But *the world* always exceeds the limits of our language. After Kant, we are pressed to concede that there can be no object of *experience* exceeding our modes of representation. Nothingness would accordingly be merely an illusory projection of the grammar of our language: without the word, what would we experience?

Although it is not certain what of Nietzsche and Heidegger Beckett read, it is apparent that he takes very seriously the historical *experience* described by Nietzsche in *The Genealogy of Morals* and *The Will to Power* (1887), by Heidegger in *Being and Time* (1929), and by Sartre in *Nausea* (1938), and indeed faithfully shows the *reality* of existential or ontological suffering in the "ruinstrewn land"[198] that we find ourselves inhabiting once our cultural consciousness has realized the metaphysical groundlessness of all our beliefs and given up on a benevolent, all-powerful God. So he enables us to reflect on the proposition that the frightening specter of "nothingness" that his characters claim to encounter might merely be, or be nothing but, a metaphysical or transcendental illusion dependent on an abuse of language. Our existential suffering, our experience of loss, deprivation and abandonment, our mourning and apathy, are for Beckett a terrible reality, as are the anomie, alienation, and intense despair. This experience of our time is not an illusion, not merely something that language enables us to imagine. And yet, the ironic reflexivity in his stories regarding language provokes us to imagine the grain of truth in nominalism: What freedom might we enjoy, and what justice, if we were to suppose that the abyss, the dreaded image of the nothingness that *denies* us all possible foundations, all possible absolutes, all reassuring authority for our beliefs, the image that tells us there is nothing, no ultimate thing, to ground our experience of the things we encounter in our world, is in truth as much a projection of language as the language-transcending absolutes we feel we have lost? The voice in *The Unnamable* declares:

> But it seems impossible to speak and yet say nothing, you think you have succeeded, but you always overlook something, a little yes, a little no, enough to exterminate a regiment of dragoons. (UN 305)

If nothingness is dependent on language, that belies its claim to be absolute nothingness. The nothingness that "nihilism" attempts to name remains, however, a profoundly challenging situation, even resisting and eluding all our names.[199] Naming, Nietzsche would say, is always the enactment of the will to power.[200] When authors name their characters, they assume that control—lending their support to the paradigm of absolute knowledge, absolutely sovereign authority. Beckett would not want to encourage such claims.

In "Letter on Humanism" (1946), published seven years before Beckett's *The Unnamable*, Heidegger urged us to consider: if we are to venture the redeeming fulfillment of our finest potentialities as human beings, "we must first learn to exist in the nameless."[201] In Beckett's 1953 story, we are indeed thrown into an uncanny world of unnamable voices, unnamable characters. And in this world, where the words that are needed fail to come or fail to mean, we must learn to exist with nothingness. There are no words that can conjure away the evidence of negativity. We are bereft of words, but words nevertheless remain. But within these words that remain, is there borne still a promise and hope? Just a little?

§9

Because, for Beckett the storyteller, nihilism is inseparable from the crisis of meaning, we take hold, now, of certain threads of interpretation that we left, in order to give further thought to Beckett's lifetime obsession, as a writer and storyteller, with new ways to engage and appropriate the crisis of meaning—the crisis of language—that, like many other writers since the late nineteenth century, he regarded as distinctive of the modern experience. His post-war play calls attention to the challenge. *Endgame* (1957):

HAMM: What is happening?
CLOV: Something is taking its course.
HAMM: Clov!
CLOV: What is it?
HAMM: We're not beginning to . . . to . . . mean something?
CLOV: Mean something! You and I, mean something! Ah that's a good one![202]

In times such as ours—times, in Adorno's words, of "damaged life," meaning is also damaged. With biblical stories in mind, Beckett alludes to the "corruption" of language. The obstacles he encounters as a writer are not only a consequence of his "weakness," a "weakness" that I would like to think about in relation to Benjamin's invocation of a "weak messianic force"; they are difficulties intrinsic to the "crisis of meaning" that figures in the literature and the aesthetics of modernism. Be that as it may, according to the biblical story, allusions to which abound in Beckett's own stories and plays, language has been undergoing corruption since the mythic time of the Fall. But in our time, it seems, the corruption, the damage, has made authentic meaning and expression much more difficult. We should notice that both Hamm and Clov register whatever is happening in their chatter, whether or not it be meaning— as an event: something "happening," "taking its course."

Alain Badiou maintains that, after *Endgame*, and beginning with *Krapp's Last Tape* (1958) and *How It Is* (1960), Beckett ceased to work out his struggle with language in terms of a "hermeneutics of meaning," an esotericism he tried out in his early years when under the influence of James Joyce, increasingly experimenting, instead, with other ways of reanimating or reinventing language. This change, which Badiou calls a "poetics of naming," was an attempt to release meaning from the reifications that settle its "being," exposing it to the radically other—an "event" bursting into language that would be beyond the control of inherited networks of meaning.[203] Badiou's reading in this regard is very illuminating. And his chronological interpretation, neatly charting Beckett's moments of change, is suggestive; but in the final analysis, his tracking of Beckett's evolution is, I think, too cut-and-dried. All Beckett's stories, at least all those belonging to the post-war period, and not only the later stories post-1960s, were open and exposed to fictional correlates of apocalyptic or otherwise disruptive "events" of meaning. I would argue that in the post-war stories, *The Expelled*, *The Calmative*, and *The End*, published around 1945; in the plays *Waiting for Godot* (1948–1949) and *Endgame* (1957); and in his trilogy of novels, *Molloy* (1947), *Malone Dies* (1948), and *The Unnamable* (1949), in other words—contrary to what Badiou seems to be claiming—long before the 1960s, Beckett was *already* writing in ways that created, in the language, irresolvable ambiguities, extreme indeterminacies of meaning and other deformations in sense and syntax; *already* writing in ways that cracked open and exposed this language to possibilities "beyond being," chance events of meaning and startling illuminations. Thus, however, Beckett's "poetics" would increasingly force language into the eradication or destruction of its expressive resources, making meaning emerge, as Badiou says, "from the void itself of what happens."[204] The event in which the word bears new meaning accordingly becomes, in Beckett's stories, an event that, as in St. Paul's *Letters*, which were written in terms of the Hebraic conception of time and history, breaks into historical time to bear the dialectical image of a wholly new futurity.[205] Beckett is not only attempting a renewal or reinvention of the creative energies of language; he also wants to illuminate our experience of the world, which we inhabit with too little attention and too little caring. The word, in Beckett, is an event that summons to moral vigilance and lucidity.

Writing, in *Aesthetic Theory*, about the historical relevance and meaningfulness of *Endgame*, Adorno states that Beckett's "determinate negation" of meaningfulness in expression needs to be understood in relation to a severe "crisis of meaning" in the modernity created by the Western bourgeoisie and the capitalism ruling its political economy.[206] More specifically, his negativity needs to be understood as "putting meaning on trial." This is not resistance to the expression of meaning as such, but resistance to the commodity-driven demand for fullness and totality of meaning, and also resistance to the ideological obfuscations, distortions, and deceptions taking place within the operations of language under the rule of late capitalism:

> Beckett's plays are absurd not because of the absence of meaning, for then they would be simply irrelevant, but because they put meaning on trial; they unfold its history. His work is ruled as much by an obsession with positive nothingness as by the obsession with a meaninglessness that has developed historically and is thus in a sense merited, though this meritedness in no way allows any positive meaning to be reclaimed. (AT 153–154)

The argument continues:

> Artworks that divest themselves of any semblance of meaning do not thereby forfeit their similitude to language. They enunciate their meaninglessness with the same determinacy as traditional artworks enunciate their positive meaning.

"Today," he declares, "this is the capacity of art":

> Through the consistent negation of meaning it does justice to the postulates that once constituted the meaning of artworks. Works of

the highest level of form that are meaningless or alien to meaning are therefore more than simply meaningless because they gain their truth content through the negation of meaning.

"Beckett's oeuvre," he observes,

> already presupposes this experience of the destruction of meaning as self-evident, yet it also pushes it beyond meaning's abstract negation, in that his plays force the traditional categories of art to undergo this experience, concretely suspend them, and extrapolate others out of the nothingness. The *dialectical reversal* that occurs is obviously not a derivative of theology, which always heaves a sigh of relief whenever its concerns are treated in any way, no matter that the verdict, as if at the end of the tunnel of metaphysical meaninglessness—the presentation of the world as hell—a light glimmers. (Ibid. Italics added)

Nevertheless, in all of Beckett's works, a light does sometimes glimmer. We have already encountered that dialectical reversal in Beckett's handling of the imagination, reversing the destructive Cartesian act that Husserl's phenomenological reductions repeated, creating in the very process of destroying. One might even suggest that, in his use of words, Beckett undertakes the breakdown and disintegration of language, effects which express and reflect the character of our existential experience of the present,[207] in order to make cracks in our defenses—cracks through which, as an unforeseeable event, the promise of happiness, that light of redemption, coming, as it were, from paradise, might perhaps shine and glimmer.

§10

In the course of a dialogue with Georges Duthuit, Beckett spoke of what he called his "fidelity to failure."[208] For Badiou, it is precisely this failure that makes possible fidelity to the possibility of "an event."[209] This point nicely fits Adorno's interpretation. But Badiou refrains from saying more about this enigmatic "event," although one might conjecture that it is somehow supposed to evoke Heidegger's equally enigmatic invocations of an "Ereignis," or perhaps, following Derrida's Benjaminian reflections, it is supposed to evoke the inception of a time of messianicity. In any case, he is right in remarking the places in Beckett's prose stories and works for the stage where there are "*ruptures événementielles*," interruptions or breaks, or pauses or silences, that *open* the dialogue or the narrative to the possibility of some incredible event, perhaps an event of world-historical significance, that could never have been anticipated. And, like Adorno, he rightly calls attention to Beckett's increasing "restraint," his increasingly rigorous subjection of the language he uses to "lessness," "*noir grise*," a process of subtraction, reduction and impoverishment.[210] (Corresponding to this "lessness" in the prose, a kind of purgatory, Beckett's works for the stage increasingly restrict bodily action, reducing it to stillness or to movements that become virtually imperceptible. Likewise, Beckett's stages and narrative settings are increasingly emptied and rendered more and more abstract, more disorienting, but in consequence they make the meaning more allegorical and universal.) The point of the experiment is to see what sense, what meaning, if anything, remains. Especially in Beckett's later prose works, however, one of which is actually called *Lessness* (1969), the austere "lessness" that he achieves with an aesthetics of reduction, an aesthetics of "failure," in no way seems to diminish the immediate richness of meaning. Indeed, quite the contrary seems to happen, as in, for example, the ending of *Ill Seen Ill Said* (1981), a text we shall be reading fairly closely. The reduction of language to its bare minimum still seems to leave its promise of happiness intact—and even, as in that wonderful late work, to let its presence somehow be seen and felt, even perhaps more intensely, if only for the briefest of moments.

*

In Shakespeare's *King Lear* (IV.1, 29–30), Edgar tries to find some consolation and hope in the worst:

> The worst is not
> so long as we can say 'This is the worst.'

Even when the expressive power of language to represent, to say and mean, is reduced, damaged, stripped bare, it can still say and show just that very condition. And that, though very little, almost nothing, is not nothing.

Edgar's discovery of hope in giving words to adversity is remembered in Beckett's *Worstward Ho* (1983). In this very late prose work, suggesting in its title, for the hermeneutically attuned ear, "west-ward," "worst-ward," and "worst word," that is to say, a writing headed westward, towards the setting of the sun, and worstward, towards the worst word, the word ill said, the word "missaid," the writer nevertheless continues to write, stubbornly perseveres, going on. We are to see an old man and child, holding hands: "Plod on as one." "At rest plodding on" (WH 93–94). No words could conceive a more poignant, heart-wrenching image. But now, in our time, writing means going on without theology, the divinity of words, and without any divine plot of meaning, or theodicy; writing therefore undergoes both impoverishment and liberation. So there is, inescapably, endless longing, vain longing, but also, kept in that longing, a faint hope (WH 109). And since new, authentic words for this experience, words with the compelling character of truth, have been lacking, or have failed, there is an intense, unappeasable longing for the right words to come. But what words? And to say what? The old words are useless; they no longer carry conviction, authentic truth content. Language must be stripped bare, radically reduced to its essentials. But the longing persists. And then what? "What when words gone? None for what then. [. . .] What words for what then? None for what then. No words for what then when words gone" (WH 104). But are there really no words left at all? Is there no way to go on, no way to write about this situation? "No once. No once in pastless now" (WH 110). We can no longer rely on words bearing a mythic past, prophetic "imaginings of the head." And we can no longer count on support from the fairytale "once upon a time." Our time—and our language, our words: it all *seems* bereft of any promise. "Blanks for no-how on" (WH 105). And yet, "blanks" is still a word, even if "Said nohow on" (WH 116). And so, there is still, in the end, something to say and something said. Said with compelling truth. Is there no promise still in the least word, the worst word?

Adorno will remind us, however, warning that the genuinely new appears only in "the longing for the new, not in the new itself," insofar as what we take to be "the new" invariably is a continuation of the old. It is better, therefore, to remain with the longing, dissatisfied with what-is than to accept the old in the guise of the new. But that uncompromising utopianism is not nihilism:

> That is what everything new suffers from. What takes itself to be utopia remains the negation of what exists and is obedient to it. At the center of contemporary antinomies is that art must be and want to be utopia; and the more utopia is blocked by the real functional order, the more this is true; yet at the same time, art must not be utopia, in order not to betray it by providing semblance and consolation. If the utopia of art were fulfilled, it would be art's temporal end. Hegel was the first to realize that the end of art is implicit in its concept. [. . .] But Hegel betrayed utopia by construing the existing as if it were the utopia of the absolute Idea. [. . .] Only by virtue of the absolute negativity of collapse does art enunciate the unspeakable: utopia. In this image of collapse all the stigmata of the repulsive and loathsome in modern art are gathered. *Through the irreconcilable renunciation of the semblance of reconciliation, art holds fast to the promise of reconciliation in the midst of the unreconciled*: This is the true course of an age in which the real possibility of utopia—that given the level of productive forces the earth could here and now be *paradise*—converges with the possibility of total catastrophe. (AT 32–33. Italics added)

I maintain that what is taken to be Beckett's "nihilism" is precisely his uncompromising renunciation, by way of subtraction—what he later calls "lessness"—of every semblance of reconciliation: a renunciation, a dialectics of negation, that is not advocating nihilism, but precisely holding fast, in faithful longing, to the *promise* of reconciliation, the *promise* of happiness—and the astonishing triumph of the weakest possible meaning, despite the crisis—in the midst of an unredeemed world.

§11

But ambiguities and tensions will necessarily persist. And the obligation to follow the exigencies of the negative dialectic, the *via negativa*, cannot be completely discharged. So can we still claim that there is a redemptive schema in Beckett's literary works? More specifically: Is there a redemptive schema regarding justice? How might the history of divine justice bear on the restitution of the profane, secular, earthly justice and the promise of existential happiness that his writings implicitly demand?[211]

In a prose that can take us from unfathomable depths of pathos, expressed in passages of incomparable lyrical beauty, through scenes of wild, irresistible hilarity and bawdy humour to exalted heights of poetic imagination and back again to an anguish excruciating almost beyond words, Beckett's stories, novels, and works for the theater are peppered with words referring, either directly or indirectly, to matters of importance in the realm of theology and theodicy. And besides all these words, there are also countless metaphors, symbols and words allegorically charged, enigmatically alluding to an imagined utopia, paradise, and some event of resurrection and redemption. But so what? What do all these invocations, these allusions, prove? What is their point? Do they appear only as occasions for irony and sarcasm?

Why does Beckett repeatedly insert words that invoke or allude to matters that solely belong to the religious life, in particular to Christianity, when, we suppose, neither he nor his fictional characters continue to live with God in their lives? My suggestion is that that supposition is not entirely right. I think Beckett understood that skeptics, and even atheists and nihilists, are still compelled to come to terms with matters of faith; understood that, even in a time such as ours, a time when faith is weakening, the role of religious institutions is declining, and the horrors of war and genocide seem to be telling us that God has abandoned us to work out our own fate, no one can escape the terms of a history shaped over the centuries by religion and its theology, no one can entirely break away from the influence of the spirit that prevails in the culture. There is no "immunity," even for the most ardent advocates of atheism. Speaking to, but also out of, what he recognizes as the deepest, most intense emotional investments of our time, Beckett tells stories that move us to question these investments. His allusions and invocations erupt like splinters into the weave of his stories, reminding us of longings and other emotional investments that we are trying to forget, either because their disappointment is unbearable or because their persistence belies a claim of freedom from the weight of history. Erupting like splinters, creating jarring incongruities, ambiguities, and contradictions, these religious and theological references disrupt our assumptions and challenge us to defend our convictions.

Beckett's use of so many religious and theological words provokes another constellation of questions. Does language play a role in the redeeming of our world? How could that be possible, when, as we are compelled, I believe, to acknowledge, our language, which Plato (*Phaedrus* 276d) once called a "garden of letters," has been badly damaged, becoming the bearer, the metaphor, of a promise that has always already compromised itself, deferring its fulfillment in order to journey through a world where its meanings cannot avoid shades of duplicity? How might we expect such language to serve our hope for the utopian perfection and redemption of the world?

The three parts in this volume will accordingly reflect, as the title implies, on what Beckett is saying about divine and profane justice—theodicy and its secular counterpart—in the modern world. In question, therefore, are the chances for realizing a utopian or messianic promise of happiness—not only the promise of justice, but also the promise of a heightened sense of life and death—that Beckett's lifelong struggle with language seems, even in its moments of deepest despair, to suppose and open to. Can language as such, in its very existence, really bear the message of a promise of happiness despite the inevitable compromise and treachery?

Because of the natural connection between beauty and pleasure, it seems that, even when despair and hopelessness are what Beckett's words are *saying*, the restrained lyricism of his prose, intermittent and always astonishing in its austere beauty, can at least *give tonal expression*, if only in the negative, to a certain utopian hope—or a certain melancholy longing—for a world of happiness.

Indeed, we have already noted that in Beckett's style of writing, with its rhythms and rhymes, its patterns of alliteration, echoes and resonances, there is what Merleau-Ponty would recognize as an "ontological rehabilitation of the sensible," and we have argued that this moves his writing towards the reconciliation of the sensible and the intelligible, the two senses of "sense." Thus I suggest that we should think of this reconciliation as a modest anticipation, a proleptic "mimesis," of the promise of happiness—that more comprehensive utopian or messianic reconciliation which seems to beckon even in his most downcast words.

*

It is time, perhaps, for a brief orientation. In Part One of this present book, we shall pursue the question of happiness and the prospect of utopian reconciliation, examining *the representation of theodicy* in Beckett's stories and drawing out the connections between Nietzsche's scathing critique and his own no less compelling representation. I shall argue that, with as much fervour as Nietzsche had, Beckett shows us characters caught up in the injustices of the world: injustices that countless theodicies have sought to explain, justify, and make bearable. We shall be led in this way to reflect on Beckett's Nietzschean depiction of the pathological effects and after-effects of theodicy, vividly showing its attacks on life in the "profane" world.

In Part Two, we shall reflect on the configurations and illuminations of experience—hope and despair, longing and waiting, remembering and forgetting—through which, in the language of Beckett's stories, the promise of happiness speaks to us.

Then, in Part Three, we shall undertake a reading of *How It Is* (*Comment c'est* in the original French), in which Beckett imagines his characters in a Hobbesian state of nature; and we shall concentrate on Beckett's *representation of justice in social relations*, which he casts in terms of the Hegelian dialectic of recognition and acknowledgement.[212] And bearing in mind the pronunciation of the French title, we shall follow his search for words that might spell the justice of a way out of the state of nature with its brutal dialectic, and configure, in recording the journey through an allegorical Purgatory, the possible commencement of a more humane world: a world in which there might be a real chance of universal happiness. Assuming, to borrow and alter in this context the sense of Dante's words, that "the course of judgment is not halted."[213]

*

In "Cello-Entry," a poem published in 1967 that Beckett might have read, Paul Celan explores what comes from "lessness":

> everything is less than
> as it is
> everything is more.[214]

Such might be said of ashes. And of the dust in which Beckett's remaining words struggle to appear. . . .[215]

Like the poet Hölderlin that Benjamin describes in "The Task of the Translator," Beckett shows us—in the impoverishment of a prose finally reduced to the plainest possible expression, and, of words, the absolute minimum necessary for the emergence of meaning—a world without metaphysical grounding, in which "meaning falls from abyss to abyss until it threatens to lose itself in the bottomless depths of language."[216] But there are moments, nevertheless, when his words suddenly ignite and break free of their despair and pain, taking shape in the poignant beauty of an austere yet joyous lyricism and showing that, after all, meaning is still possible. And it is most of all, I think, in just such moments that something attesting the promise of happiness appears, its gloriously incandescent traces breaking through the ashen gray of hopeless creaturely life. But language and revelation will always be, for us, in the greatest, most extreme tension— not in mystical union, as they were, perhaps, for the experience behind the Holy Scriptures.

Our world has fallen into a time of destitution and mourning. This is the world into which Beckett casts us. Writing within, and for, a world bereft, acutely conscious of losing not only its traditional sources and dimensions of meaning, both religious and secular, but also the words to express and sustain our sense of that loss, Beckett struggled to wrest from language—a weakened, damaged language, reduced to service as a commodity and a standardized instrument for the exchange of information and the ideological control of consciousness—new possibilities for meaning and its expression. His life as a writer was consumed in a ceaseless search for ways to resurrect dead or dying words, and redeem their power to reveal and actualize those possibilities of meaning for a world in spiritual crisis. Such is, I believe, his redemptive schema. However, at the same time that he sought to find, or create, ways to express meaningful life within this world, he also sought to resist the illusory consolations and theodicies that have offered to make sense of the world and compensate for its injustices, but only—as Nietzsche's accusation argued—by sacrificing the humanity in human nature in order to absolve the guilt and punishment it perversely invented for that very nature. Thus, in the three parts that follow this Prologue, we shall give thought to Beckett's representations of divine injustice and the journey towards an earth-bound world redeemed by the light of a truly humane institution of justice.

§12

In *Remnants of Auschwitz: The Witness and the Archive*, Giorgio Agamben observes, with Primo Levi's testimony in mind, that "there is no voice for the disappearance of voice."[217] Here is where I shall again quote Beckett's words, the ones that figure as an epigram for this volume as a whole, and that represent in the most unequivocal way his understanding of the storyteller's vocation he felt compelled to make his own. His words challenge Agamben's claim: "the little murmur of unconsenting man, to murmur what it is their humanity stifles [...]" (UN 319). In "Molloy's Silence," Georges Bataille supports this interpretation of Beckett's voice and vocation, arguing that what his stories show us in anguish and protest is "reality at its most indigent and inevitable."[218] As John Calder notes, Beckett sought "to make us face, head-on, the realities of the human condition," hoping that we would confront them "with courage and dignity."[219]

Beckett's struggle with words was not only the struggle of a storyteller to say something that would speak in a meaningful way to the needs of his time. It was also the struggle of a storyteller to serve his time as a *witness* morally committed, regardless of the necessary aesthetic sacrifices, to the need for truth. His surrogate voices in *The Unnamable*

advert more than once to the witness's—or storyteller's—sense of an
obligation to write. But there are many obstacles to overcome. Among
those obstacles, there is this: "I shall have to speak of things of which I
cannot speak. [. . .] I am obliged to speak. I shall never be silent. Never"
(UN 285). But how to tell the truth through stories that are fictional?
And indeed, as Derrida points out in "Demeure: Fiction and Testimony":
"There is no testimony [no witnessing] that does not structurally imply
in itself the possibility of fiction, simulacra, dissimulation, lie and perjury
[. . .]."[220] Fictionality will always disrupt the referential relation in language
between storyteller and reader. How to assume the obligations of a witness?
In Beckett's stories, questions about witnessing and questions about
testimony arise more frequently than one might have surmised.[221] In *Watt*,
for example, a question arises about Watt's qualifications as a witness in
consequence of his conjectures about what Mr. Knott seems not to need.
"For except, one, not to need, and, two, a witness to his not needing, Knott
needed nothing, as far as Watt could see":

> But what kind of witness was Watt, weak now of eye, hard of hearing,
> and with even the more intimate senses greatly below par?
> A needy witness, an imperfect witness.
> The better to witness, the worse to witness.
> That with his need he might witness its absence.
> That imperfect he might witness it ill.[222]

For a writer such as Beckett, witness of and for his time, the question
of witness reliability in the context of fiction is a serious and knotty one;
but here he playfully acknowledges cause for skepticism, multiplying the
ambiguities.

Critics who either praise or condemn Beckett for his supposed "nihilism"
are failing to recognize and understand his historical position as a
storyteller—the position, namely, of witness. The characters that he creates
are his surrogates; their assignment is to bear witness in some exemplary
way to something essential in their experience of our historical moment. He
calls them "delegates."

In the twelfth of his *Texts for Nothing*, one of Beckett's surrogate
voices asks, challenging the old institutions of theodicy: Do we still need
a god to be the "unwitnessed witness of witnesses?" (TN 135). Beckett's
appropriation of the writer's vocation gives us an unequivocal answer. The
writer, the storyteller, must assume that role. There are limits to that role,
however, as Celan must remind us, for there could be no witnesses for the
absolute horror, experienced only by those who died in the gas chambers of
Auschwitz-Birkenau.[223]

But for much that takes place in our world, the storyteller can be a
compelling witness. With a wry, double-edged twist, in the fifth of his *Texts
for Nothing*, Beckett's narrator assumes the role:

I'm the clerk, I'm the scribe, at the hearings of what cause I know not.
[. . .] To be judge and party, witness and advocate, and he, attentive,
indifferent, who sits and notes. (TN 95)

"It's an image," he assures us!

In *How It Is*, the narrator tells us, "all I hear is that a witness I'd need a
witness" (H 18). His story calls for a reliable witness and a reliable scribe.
And "he would need good eyes the witness if there were a witness good
eyes a good lamp [. . .]" (H 44). But the testimony of the witness must of
course be credible; it cannot be full of contradictions: "to the scribe sitting
aloof he'd announce midnight no two in the morning three in the morning
[. . .]" (ibid.). Krim and Kram cannot, however, be counted on: they lose
most of what the narrator tells them. Moreover, paradoxically, in a way that
is reminiscent of Kafka's *The Trial*, he denies them independent existence,
calling them mere inventions in the story he wants to tell, and postulates
infinite generations of witnesses (H 80–84).[224]

In Beckett's late work, *Ill Seen Ill Said* (1981), the moral and epistemological
position of the witness, Beckett's surrogate storyteller, constitutes the very
structure and content of the narrative. There are, as always, many plausible
interpretations of this work. One that I wish to suggest here reads it not only
as telling a story about the Resurrection, but as also telling a story about the
logic of the promise as such. Derrida ruminates on this very logic in *Avances*,
where, as he concludes his reflections on the doctrines of faith at the heart
of the Christian religion, and in particular, the doctrine of resurrection, he
stresses all the uncertainties and perplexities surrounding the promise
cryptically given in the mysterious event at the tomb where Christ's body
was buried.[225]

Over the course of many days, many seasons, the narrator-witness, on
a lonely vigil, relentlessly follows from a distance the movements of an old
woman living alone in a tiny cabin in the countryside and making frequent
visits to a tomb in a "zone of stone." She is often not visible: "Nor by the eye
of flesh nor by the other" (IS 56). But when she is, she invariably appears in
the "immaculately black" cloth of mourning (IS 68). Despite recording some
very precise details, ambiguities proliferate. If, at first, we are encouraged to
believe that the seeing and the seen are supposed to be taking place in the
real world, the story soon seems to be something conjured up with great
difficulty by the "relentless" eye of the imagination: "Imagination at wit's
end spreads its sad wings" (IS 56). It is a struggle by the imagination to
become an imaginary witness, to "see" the Crucifixion and Resurrection and
the mother's mourning, events that have become, for many, an unlikely, no
longer deeply moving story. So the narrator undertakes to "bear witness"
to those events by imagining and retelling the ancient story, but in a way
that stresses, in scrupulous reflexivity, the difficulty imagining and retelling
it, leaving epistemological and historical skepticism intact. There is, we are
told, a haze like a shroud, making visibility especially difficult: "Shroud of

radiant haze. Where to melt into paradise" (IS 64). But miraculously, that haze appears radiant, indicating some proximity to paradise. The narrator occasionally overcomes adversities, imagining a glorious scene and recording it in a "deposition" (IS 84): "The silence merges into music infinitely far and as unbroken as silence. Ceaseless celestial winds in unison. [. . .] The stones gleam faintly afar and the cabin walls seen white at last" (IS 74). But the clarity and sureness do not last:

> She is vanishing. With the rest. The already ill seen bedimmed and ill seen again annulled. The mind betrays the treacherous eyes and the treacherous word their treacheries. Haze sole certitude. [. . .] The eye will close in vain. To see but haze. Not even. Be itself but haze. How can it ever be said? (IS 78)

The stones' gleam of hope, an event that might encourage faith in the promise, turns out to be nothing but a fiction, a mirage, and a mockery of that faith.

How is truth possible, when perception is fallible, memory weak, claims to knowledge vulnerable to doubt and endless revision, events inevitably shadowed by belatedness, and all words treacherous? Once again, troubling questions with which Beckett himself was struggling in his role as a storyteller obliged, as he thought, to bear witness to the truth about his time. And even, as in this powerfully moving story, to revive—as if by a miracle of memory woven into the imagination, and witnessing, impossibly, what is claimed by the past—one of the greatest stories of all time.

But is there, in his words, the promise of happiness? Here is the ambiguous ending of the story, in potently compressed syntax and the plainest of words, rich in its suggestions of meaning:

> Farewell to farewell. Then in that perfect dark foreknell darling sound pip for end begun. First last moment. Grant only enough remain to devour all. Moment by glutton moment. Sky earth the whole kit and boodle. Not another crumb of carrion left. Lick chops and basta. No. One moment more. One last. Grace to breathe that void. Know happiness.

Beckett's French version says "*Connaître bonheur.*" But the sounding of the English word is equivocal, raising doubts: No happiness? And yet, even so, does not the play of words as such, confirming by their freedom the creative potential in language, still bear the promise? And is there not at least a trace, a tasting of happiness in the amusing evocation of Khronos, "Father Time," who succeeded, according to myth, in greedily devouring five of his children—all but one—to secure his eternal rule?

§13

There have always been storytellers, writers, to bear witness to life in earlier historical periods. But of all the periods past, I can think of none with so many similarities to Beckett's interpretation of our own than the Baroque period in Germany as it was interpreted by Benjamin in its misery, decadence and disorientation and brought to vivid expression in the German-language mourning plays.

It will be recalled that both the first and the second acts of *Waiting for Godot* end after this exchange between Vladimir and Estragon:

> Well? Shall we go?
> Yes, let's go.

Beckett's directions for staging follow immediately: *They do not move.* A strange immobility! But let us recall the Apostle Paul's counsel (1 Corinthians 7:17), urging people to live in the present "messianically," or *hos me*, "as if not," suspending every movement, act of life, in its time of execution.[226] Might Beckett be recalling this messianic suspension? Perhaps. But if so, would the stage directions in parentheses—the playwright's intervention and, in effect, his commentary—suggest a messianic moment, or would they suggest instead the rejection or negation of any hopeful movement, any faith in the future? Didi and Gogo do not move: their intended movement is suspended. Beckett's stage directions ensure that the resolution of our question will itself remain in suspension, leaving the characters suspended between the redemption of hope and the destitution of abandonment. They seem to be playing out Benjamin's notion of dialectics at a standstill. And like the absolute sovereign in the German Baroque *Trauerspiel*, or "mourning play," these characters are indecisive and unable to act. Their inaction symbolizes, moreover, the historically disastrous separation of action from reason, leaving moral reason impotent and action, especially political action, irrational and barbaric. Such was how, in the *Trauerspiel*, historical life during the German Baroque appeared; such, too, is how historical life in the twentieth century appears in Beckett's plays and works of prose fiction. The affinities are significant.

The somber, ash-grey of light and color that appears in Benjamin's dissertation on the German Baroque mourning play also enters into some of Beckett's works—most intensely, perhaps, in *Lessness* (1969). About his *Trauerspiel* study, written to define and interpret the profound differences between Greek tragedy and its historical transformation in the form of the German Baroque *Trauerspiel*, Benjamin wrote that, "The German mourning play is taken up entirely with the hopelessness of the earthly condition." It is consequently a genre bearing witness to "the total disappearance of eschatology, and is an attempt to find in the reversion to the bare state of creation, consolation for a renunciation of the state of grace."[227] Beckett's world, like the world depicted in the German Baroque theater, is a world that has undergone horrendous historical catastrophes and shocks to its spirit. Not only devastating wars, famines, poverty, and homelessness, but also moral corruption and spiritual emptiness. Such was—and for Beckett still is—our creaturely condition. We of today are living in a world struggling to find meaning in a time of mourning. Of all the animals inhabiting this earth, we are, despite, or perhaps because of, our consciousness, the most vulnerable—but also, without question, the most cruel. Nevertheless, according to Benjamin's interpretation, despite confirming an overwhelming sense that God has abandoned the world to the daemonic forces of fate, the Baroque *Trauerspiel* encouraged the persistence of hope that "the light of grace is still reflected from the state of creation." Although, he added, "it is mirrored in the swamp of Adam's guilt."[228] As if representing this very condition, Beckett's novel, *How It Is*, compels us to confront questions of justice, justice social and existential, casting his characters, burdened with unspecifiable guilt, into a muddy swamp faintly illuminated by light coming from the world above—or perhaps from an even more remote place of surmised redemption.

And there is another curiously striking similarity between Beckett's world and the world of the German Baroque theater: as in the latter, so in the world that Beckett presents, language fails to attain any closure or fulfillment of meaning. Thus, not surprisingly, what emerges from this repeated failure or breakdown in communication, and the consequent sense of metaphysical isolation and abandonment, is a feeling of inconsolable sorrow—a sorrow, in fact, that is even denied the possibility of receiving meaningful expression in language. Though supposedly bearing, when it comes, the promise of happiness, language fails to come. As in allegory, according to Benjamin's definition, Beckett's characters are cast into the destitution of creaturely life, coping with a disenchanted world that has been transformed by some apocalyptic catastrophic events, making almost impossible the fulfillment, in history, of any human endeavor to create an enlightened world order. Indeed, in Beckett's world, even the slightest gestures, the smallest movements, the most minimal expressiveness, can seem too difficult, too pointless, too exhausting. Creaturely life bereft of individual and historical purposiveness. "This," Benjamin observes, "is the heart of the allegorical way of seeing, of the Baroque, secular explanation of history as the Passion of the world; its importance resides solely in the stations of its decline."[229]

Thought-provoking indeed, these similarities and affinities between the Baroque world represented in the *Trauerspiel* and our contemporary world, compellingly represented in Beckett's contributions to literature and theater. But whatever one concludes from this fact, one must nevertheless at least recognize that Beckett refuses to identify our contemporary historical situation with what might be described as the "eternal creaturely condition." And in that respect, his depiction of the world, less hopeless though still without fulfilling resolution, could not be more at odds with the representation of the Baroque world that figures in the German *Trauerspiel*. Whereas our world, like the Baroque world in Benjamin's *Trauerspiel* interpretation, appears emptied of ultimate meaning, the latter is felt to be an irrevocably *closed* world, closed to any supervenient event, any metaphysical dimension of transcendence, whilst ours, even when claustrophobically closed off, as in *How It Is* and many of Beckett's later works, somehow remains susceptible of a breaching eventuality—an openness to something that might possibly expose the creaturely life going on within its immanence, its closed space, to a frightening infinity, drawing us into the abyss of an origin and an end for the comprehension of which no science has the words. But that event of opening could instead permit us to glimpse a new beginning, the possibility of a renewed, redeemed humanity, completing the meaning of "happiness."

A world in which one can exist only by being guilty is an archaic, mythic world ruled by fate, a world under a spell, a curse. Is there a way out of the history of endless guilt? Would it be sufficient to escape the old theodicies and their eschatologies? Is there a way out of the closed world-space into which theodicy has imprisoned us? In concluding the ninth of Beckett's *Texts for Nothing*, the narrative voice evokes "a way out" of our present world, dreaming of the beauty of the skies and the stars of the night; but despite the beauty of the allegorical image that his words created, an image of the time of redemption reminiscent of the one that Kant constructed in his second *Critique*, he continues to lament that the rescuing words, the redeemed and redeeming words, have not yet come.

But how is it possible even to think of the redeeming enlightenment of this world, if language, the very medium of thought, has been severely damaged, reified, commodified, and reduced to an instrument of domination? How can words so massively compromised still bear a promise of happiness, and still play a role in the redeeming of our world?

§14

In his essay "On Language as Such and on the Language of Man," Benjamin proposed an interpretation of the theological story about the expulsion of Adam and Eve from the Garden of Eden and the story of the building and destruction of the Tower of Babel, arguing for the convergence of the theory of language and the theory of justice:

> The enslavement of things in foolishness follows the enslavement of language in chatter [. . .]. In this turning away [from the original experience of things], which was enslavement, there arose the plan for the Tower of Babel [. . .].[230]

In *Totality and Infinity*, Emmanuel Levinas declared, in a characteristically lapidary and enigmatic formulation: "language is justice."[231] I take it that he intended to say that language, as communication, as address to the other, is a responsive acknowledgement of the kindred humanity of the other and an invitation to the other that opens a dialogue in which grievances and different conceptions of the good life might be expressed, discussed, and sometimes resolved. In other words, one's entrance into the language of one's community is at the same time, *ipso facto*, a commitment, or pledge, to justice—justice, indeed, for the other. [232] And giving promise to hope, to a chance for happiness.

Now, what I want to suggest is that the thought in those three words— "language is justice"—points towards a hermeneutical phenomenology of language, for the significance of which I shall be arguing in the chapters that follow, namely, that the very existence of language—language as such— constitutes, or represents, the promise of happiness, a chance of happiness, because of the corresponding potentiality for a time of justice. A time of justice, I mean, after the collapse of all the archaic, mythical theodicies that have shaped our civilization and its cultural life. All the versions of theodicy we in world history have known—acknowledging the existence of different versions, I will in future refer to them in the plural—imposed as vengeance the justice that is supposed to correspond to an irreversible order of guilt. However, as Benjamin observed: "The order of the profane is to be erected in relation to the idea of happiness."[233] That, and only that, a transformation in the human condition, hence in the existential, or ontological meaning of living and dying, must be the measure of justice and peace in this earth-bound world.

§15

In *The Death of Empedokles*, fragment of a tragedy that Friedrich Hölderlin never completed, the philosopher-poet laments the fate of poetizing words, words that, if only they were to be heeded, might found a happier world of justice and peace:

> Always the impatient word rushes ahead of mortals
> And will not let the hour of accomplishment
> Mature unhurried.[234]

But without denying this disappointment, nor forgetting the struggle to express his experience of life in words that would reflect his time, Beckett will nevertheless pledge his words, solemnly addressing us in an oath, or promise, that evokes an essential moment in the accomplishment of justice, the decisive moment, namely, of acknowledgement: "*I give you my word.*"[235]

As Horkheimer argued in a major essay, written in 1943, even as the

Holocaust was turning Europe into a factory of death—of genocide—we must have faith in the redeeming word:

> [The] psychic fetters under which people suffer today burst open when *the telling word* is sounded, for this word can to a great extent dissolve the tremendous isolation of human beings from one another that is peculiar to the current era. This force is inherent in truth, although truth not only rejects all ideological consolation, but is also intent upon destroying it.[236]

There is no alternative, it seems, to faith in the promise that language brings—other than capitulation to the forces of fate. In *Endgame*, Clov says: "I ask the words that remain—sleeping, waking, morning, evening. They have nothing to say." And yet, they say that, conveying a truth that remains even as it is dialectically contested.[237] Beckett's art shows that literature bears in this regard a singular responsibility. And it is a question, in part, of arousing our cultural memory—"so that a sign borne through darkness might be maintained":

> daß bewahrt sei
> ein durchs Dunkel
> getragenes Zeichen [. . .][238]

What does Beckett as a storyteller do, after all, if he is not patiently *giving us* his words, bearing "the telling word" through the darkness of our time?

Regarding Celan's experience of the "death of language" in the Holocaust and the question that his poetry raises regarding the possible "resurrection of language," Derrida remarks:

> There is another death in the mere banalization, the trivialization of language [. . .]. And then there is yet another death, the death that comes over language because of what language is: repetition, lethargy, mechanization. The poetic act therefore constitutes a sort of resurrection: the poet is someone permanently engaged with a dying language that he resuscitates, not by giving back to it a triumphant line, but by sometimes bringing it back [to life], like a revenant or phantom. He wakes up language, and in order to experience the awakening, the return to life of language, [. . .] he must first be very close to its corpse. He needs to be as close as possible to its remnants, its remains.[239]

The promise of happiness depends on remembering and reviving these remnants of an earlier language—whatever has been imparted, whatever we have inherited. But, as Benjamin argued, in his major essay on language: "Language is not simply the imparting of the impartable [*Mitteilung des Mitteilbaren*]; it is also symbolic of that which *cannot* be [immediately and fully] imparted."[240] Here is an example, taken from *Endgame*:

HAMM: And the horizon? Nothing on the horizon?
CLOV: What in God's name could there be on the horizon?

These questions remain unanswered; and in fact, they leave us with more questions. And yet, paradoxically, with that invocation of an event beyond the horizon, do the words not keep their promise after all? To be sure, Clov responds by asking another question, not making an assertion. But even as questions, a future beyond the present is brought into words. And in words, even words irremediably corrupted, there is hope. Hope, perhaps, for freedom from the curse of theology, the curse, namely, of God's word. For in Clov's question, the words that would normally express impatience and anger in the form of a curse are rendered matter-of-factly, without that sense. One is inclined, of course, to understand that dialogue as giving expression to questions that lead to skepticism. And no doubt, Beckett wanted to suggest that interpretation. However, departing from that way of understanding Clov's question, we might take him to be asking a Wittgensteinian question about how the *word* "God" is working in our Judeo-Christian "language game." Or, more specifically: How does possessing and invoking the word, the name "God," open up the horizon for us, and keep it open? Challenging questions for thought, but not necessarily nihilistic or even skeptical. However, once such questions are raised and the adventures of critical thought commence, there is *no telling* where one will end up. The course of genuinely critical reflection must be without end, without teleology.

In the chapters that follow, I shall be taking Benjamin's argument to imply that, inherent within the communicative structure of language, as what alone remains indestructible, the promise in its heart, remnant recalling paradise, is repeatedly imparted, though its presence is often difficult to recognize. Thus, it depends on the art of the poet and the storyteller to make its presence felt. Could there be a more poignant, more deeply moving evocation of this promise than Moran's redemption of Kant's cosmological sense of law and justice in the chronicle of his journey in search of Molloy? Surveying the plain below where he was standing and the city that lay at some distance, Moran tells us, "I gave thanks for evening that brings out the lights, the stars in the sky and on earth the brave little lights of men" (MO 153).[241] The existence of language is not only justice and the promise of justice; it is also the way to thankfulness, the giving of thanks, and the happiness that promises. Despite the impoverishment of our words. Despite the perpetual threat of distortion and destruction.

More conscious than earlier generations had cause to be that we are absolutely alone on this planet, dwelling here as if orphaned, as if abandoned, compelled in any event to assume responsibility for working out the terms of our own destiny, we turn in a time of mourning to the greatest of our storytellers, hoping for words that might help us remember the promise of happiness that language is perpetually offering. But what storytellers like

Beckett are telling us is that the story of this promise can no longer be told as it was before. For, although language itself, language as such, bears that promise in virtue of its infinitely patient communicative sympathies, what Benjamin refers to as our "fallen language" has today, reduced as it increasingly is to one-dimensionality, virtually lost the power to impart the utopian promise.

"The corruption of man," as we noted Emerson to have observed, "is followed by the corruption of language."[242] Our language, the language we use, this gift we have taken for granted and abused, is now damaged, alienated, estranged from itself. In its turn, however, the corruption of language makes the redeeming of our humanity in justice and peace, and the meaningfulness in living and dying, all the more difficult. If it is to speak to and for its time, literature is accordingly obliged to register this catastrophe in the very way it uses language, telling stories that are somehow able to sustain, through the unfathomable intrigues of mourning, a compelling sense of what has been damaged and lost, whilst preserving, or restoring, at least a weak sense of the concealed promise, resisting in the design of their aesthetic form the power of death that, because of our thoughtless abuse, is ceaselessly threatening to take total possession of our words. How, then, might the last word be given to justice?

"*I give you my word*": these particular words constitute a "performative" utterance that, like a promise, simultaneously accomplishes the act it designates.[243] They are also words in the very form of which the utopian dream of happiness, the promise of language, staking its inherent relation to justice, is silently imparted—imparted with seemingly infinite patience, for it cannot be reduced to presence. "My words are my tears," one of Beckett's surrogates will say.[244] I take him to mean "tears" in both senses of that spelling, for his words are not passive, not expressions of helplessness, but the linguistic substance of an aesthetic form of resistance, tearing down the shibboleths, the illusions that oppress us. Evoking the allegorical image of a heaven on earth in a dialectical confrontation with these illusions, and with all the injustices of theodicies, Beckett says: "I have high hopes, a little story, with living creatures coming and going on a habitable earth crammed with the dead, a brief story, with night and day coming and going above, if they stretch that far, the words that remain, and I've high hopes, I give you my word" (TN 105). Perhaps one of Beckett's most significant sentences, this oath, this gift, of words that are tears, figures in not one but two of his *Texts for Nothing* and is repeated in *Molloy*, its words putting themselves at risk, compelled to struggle even against themselves for the sake of a future society formed by trust, ending the past and beginning anew.[245]

In Beckett's stories, we are witnesses to this struggle in a prose the very structure of which reflects an almost hopeless longing and gives form to the expression of despair. Though failing to redeem completely what had been ruined or destroyed, his prose aspires at least to sustain a keen sense of loss, preserving in language some stirrings of remembrance, and resisting

the vanishing of the promise and the sublime possibility of its redemption—
even if only by respecting the emptiness, the silence of death, into which his
breathless words abruptly fall.[246] Perhaps, in a time such as ours, it will be—
must be—mostly in signs and traces of damage, weakness, and suffering that
writing, redeeming at least its own fidelity to truth, though not its power, can
bear witness to the forever unfulfilled promise of happiness—the dream of a
reconciled, redeemed world where, even with imperfections all too human,
the inhuman, at least, is no more.

Happy days? Not yet! And in any case, not the happy days envisioned
by Jeff Koons, providing aesthetic distractions and indulging to his profit
the self-satisfaction and insouciance of the nouvelle bourgeoisie. But if, as
Adorno said in his work on Kierkegaard, no doubt recalling "Celebration
of Peace," Hölderlin's great hymn, "the sole organ of reconciliation is
the word,"[247] then I would like to suggest that the utopian promise of
happiness—although its redemption is no more than a chance, a chance
maintained by the very existence of language, a chance, however slight, for
the emergence of a new, more just society—reverberates and echoes through
the social bond of recognition actualized in these incomparably powerful
words, the plainspoken oath, the profane, worldly origin of justice, and the
storyteller's gift: Beckett's "I give you my word."[248] What could be more
telling than the truth, or the plea for trust and faith, in that testimony, that
oath, that promise—expressed in his works of fiction, but paradoxically and
aporetically, as we now must acknowledge?[249] Expressed in stories written
with words set in motion by the sublime rhythms of a slow but inevitable
reduction to dust and ash.

PART ONE

No Theodicy: A Chance of Happiness?

CHAPTER ONE

Negative Dialectics

In *Negative Dialectics*, Adorno sharply defines the methodology he considers to be imperative for all philosophical attempts to interpret the world in which we are living: "Dialectics is the consistent consciousness of non-identity. It does not begin by taking a standpoint. Thought is driven to it by its own inevitable insufficiency, its guilt in relation to what is thought."[1]

Hence, as Marcuse has argued, truth will be "preserved better in human misery and suffering, and in the struggle to overcome them, than in the forms and concepts of pure thought."[2] Hence, too, in Adorno's words, even "the legacy of the sublime," the dream of a redeemed humanity, "is unassuaged negativity, as stark and illusionless as was once promised by the semblance of the sublime."[3] And, as he notes there, negative dialectics is also the only way to inherit and transmit "the legacy of the comic" without betraying its immanent promise.

*

My principal claim in this chapter is that Beckett's negativity is profoundly dialectical, and that, therefore, what is often described as his existential or ontological "nihilism" must be interpreted accordingly. Thus, for instance, there is a dialectical pressure at work when he writes, in one of his letters, that "Nothing will ever be sufficiently against for me, not even pain [*pas même la douleur*]. . . ."[4]

In *Waiting for Godot*, which Beckett described as a "tragicomedy in two acts," the play ends leaving the two main characters on stage, in what Adorno interprets, borrowing a concept from Benjamin, as a dialectical moment, a moment of maximum ambiguity and tension, when the action is arrested, and everything stands still:

VLADIMIR: Well? Shall we go?
ESTRAGON: Yes, let's go.

The stage instructions simply say: "*They do not move.*" Seemingly incapable of moving, of going on with their lives, they remain on stage as the curtain closes. Why do they stand still? Might they be refusing to let the curtain put an end, a period, to what took place on the stage, enclosing its existential threat, its abyss of meaning, in the security of theatrical illusion? In any case, I say they are metaphorically disputing eschatologies—suspending the ending. It is not only acedia, or bereftness of purpose.

*

Beckett's literary work is always, like the lyric genre as Adorno defines it, "the subjective expression of a social antagonism."[5] It reflects this condition—our broken world, our destitute time—in a writing profoundly at odds with itself, failing even to fail, despite his stubborn conviction that literature, story-telling, the tradition of literary expression and representation, is no longer possible. However, if we assume the common interpretation of "nihilism" as the will to nothingness, it would be a grotesque distortion of his undertaking to read as nihilism his aesthetic resistance to society as it exists. We must recall Christ's apostle Paul, for whom the more the world decays into nihilism, the closer it gets to the end-time of redemption. If the world that Beckett shows us appears in the figure of nihilism, the world in its abandonment and destitution, that is because, for him, nihilism operates within a dialectic that arouses hopes for redemption. But for Beckett, diverging from Paul's announcement of hope, this redemption is tragically problematic, appearing only in fragmentary traces and fading echoes of longing and disappointed hopes. These are not nothing! So Beckett's "nihilism," as some feel compelled to call it, is, like Nietzsche's, actually a struggle *against* despair of achieving a happiness worthy of our humanity and *against* nihilistic fantasies of vengeance. As Cavell points out, repeating Nietzsche's argument in *The Will to Power*: "world-destroying revenge is a kind of despair caused by an illusory hope, or an illusory way of hoping—a radical process of disappointment with existence as a whole, a last glad chance for getting even with life."[6]

Strange as it may seem, what Adorno says about lyric poetry holds true as well for Beckett's distinctive form of resistance, often expressed by a presumably male narrator, often without a name, telling his tale in an unstable first-person singular: Resistance

> is not something absolutely individual; the artistic forces in that resistance, which operate in and through the individual and its spontaneity, are objective forces that impel a constricted and constricting social condition to transcend itself and become worthy of human beings; forces, that is, that are part of the constitution of the whole and not merely forces of a rigid individuality blindly opposed to society.[7]

Following Friedrich Nietzsche's distinction between *passive nihilism* (suffering the adversities of life in a life-destroying resignation or complacent acquiescence) and *active nihilism* (destroying, or negating, whatever is inimical to life), Adorno defends Beckett's so-called "nihilism," arguing, in his post-Holocaust book, *Negative Dialectics*:

> The slightest difference between nothingness and coming to rest would be the haven of hope, the no man's land between the border posts of being and nothingness. Rather than overcome that zone, consciousness would have to extricate from it what is not in the power of the alternative. The true nihilists are the ones who oppose nihilism with their more and more faded positivities, the ones who are thus conspiring with all extant malice, and eventually with the destructive principle itself.

"Thought honours itself," he concludes, "by *defending* what is damned as nihilism."[8]

Adorno argues, moreover, with Beckett's post-war novels and theatre still in mind, that, after Auschwitz, "there is no word tinged from on high, not even a theological one, that has any right unless it has undergone transformation."[9] And, whilst he acknowledged, in the light of Paul Celan's poetry, that, "it might have been wrong to say [as he in fact had said in an earlier text] that after Auschwitz, one could no longer write poetry," he insisted that "it is not wrong to raise the less narrowly cultural question how, after Auschwitz, one can go on living."[10]

It is not accidental that Beckett's words have a way of leaving us with after-images: images that repeatedly withdraw from presence without vanishing into the finality of absolute absence; images that will persist, haunting us with the memories they awaken and the hopes for a future whose passing they already mourn. How to go on living? That is a question Beckett's writings raise again and again. Not only as a question about going on *after* the Holocaust, but also as existential questions about going on *living after* the failure of Enlightenment rationality, the "death" of God, the collapse of all theodicies, and indeed after the emptiness of traditional culture. For him as a writer, moreover, in question is also how to go on writing and telling stories *after* the damage that language has suffered in the twentieth century and when the traditional techniques of representation can no longer serve the truth. What life is possible, now that moral experience has lost its absolute grounding in the will and word of God? What life is possible, now that divine justice—consolations, punishments, rewards— with all the language, all the words, bound up with it, is no longer, as it once was, compelling, or even convincing? What life is possible, now that its metaphysical dimension of meaning is no longer credible? What ends, if any, are worth living and dying for? What is the end of life? And *after* we have put aside all the trivia of daily life, what if anything remains? Is there—for us, or for a future humanity we might sacrifice ourselves for—in Beckett's dialectically wrought words, "a chance of happiness"?[11]

In *Mercier and Camier* (1946), written right after the war, Beckett's two characters repeatedly attempt to leave their city, a thinly disguised version of

Dublin, only to abandon their journey and return. Read allegorically, these two characters are going in an endlessly repeated circle, returning again and again to Purgatory. The story that would tell of the end of life's tortured journey, the story that theodicy required them to live through, has somehow been halted, foreclosing the way to redemption. This certainly seems like a world of irredeemable nihilism. In Dante's story, paradise is at least a possible end to trials and punishments. But Beckett's subsequent stories cast our world into nihilism. They will *show* that, but only in order to raise consciousness above it. And, paradoxically, for such is the way negative dialectics works, the more truthfully Beckett's stories exploit their world-disclosive potential, showing things as they are for a consciousness that does not yet prevail, but in a nihilism that seems to exclude the very possibility of a genuinely humane world, the more compellingly disruptive and critical the stories become, empowered by their inflection of that truthfulness to encourage the hope that can survive only in a critical reflective consciousness. Because, as Jay Bernstein has argued in "Melancholy as Form," "only in what fails the ideal is the authentic hope of the ideal to be found."[12]

According to Benjamin, because our experience of life is now a journey without the mythic dimensions of purpose and meaning, the time of the story-teller has irrevocably passed. Thus, into the metaphysical and theological problematic, ultimately a challenge for ethical life, Beckett repeatedly felt it necessary to interpolate the questions that a late modern story-teller must confront and struggle with: How, and why, commence? How, and why, go on?[13] How tell the truth today in a fictional story? How redeem the revelatory power, the justice, of words?

What might be the connection between the existential questions and the questions for the writer, the story-teller? Both, I suggest, express anxieties concerning the possibility of meaningful engagements in the life of the world. Beckett's surrogate characters declare that they cannot go on; however, they know that they must, and despite their lassitude, their apathy, their despair, they in fact not only go on, but also entrust that resolve to words, making meaningful a condition that had seemed to be bereft of meaning. There is meaning in suffering—only not the metaphysical interpretations that the theodicies projected. So I will accordingly argue, in concordance with Adorno, that, in the stories that Beckett tells, we are shown a world in which, although nihilism seems to prevail in the bleakest, most desperate destitution, there are, nevertheless, even now, even here, persistent demonstrations of resistance to despair and hopelessness emerging by way of a negative dialectic from the truthful, unblinking representation of this reality.

In keeping with Nietzsche's critique of passive nihilism in its life-denying forms, Beckett's stories operate on two fronts: on the one, they unmask, by satire, by parody, by irony and sarcasm, the nihilism of the theodicies, teleologies of fate, and apocalyptic eschatologies, showing the ways in which they have oppressed us, haunting, blaming, and marking us with unverifiable accusations of guilt, whilst on the other front, they refuse to capitulate to a nihilism that, still captivated by theodicy, or too weak to renounce its fatal temptations, assumes that life without God and theodicy can only be meaningless and worthless. In *The Will to Power*, Nietzsche observed: "One interpretation has collapsed; but because it was considered the *only* interpretation, it now seems as if there were *no* meaning at all in existence, as if everything were in vain" (WP 35). Thus, he argued, the disillusionment or disenchantment that is an essential moment in the project of Enlightenment, unmasking as mere assumptions and projections the stories which for centuries had served as rationalizations and consolations for suffering, provides no grounds for "devaluating the universe" (WP 13). In no sense does the end of theodicy compel the nihilism of despair. On the contrary, it could create an unprecedented time of promise: "There is an element of decay in everything that characterizes modern man; but close beside this sickness stand signs of an untested force and powerfulness of soul." Hence his "insight": "the *ambiguous* character of our modern world: the very same symptoms could point to decline and to strength." Indeed, the promise that language bears is inherently, irreducibly contingent, for what may come of it could turn out to be either a happy chance or a dreadful danger: every expression of the promise implies the possibility of both alternatives. Echoing "Becoming in Dissolution,"[14] a fragmentary text in which Hölderlin reflected on the spirit of revolution that was stirring young German intellectuals of his time, Nietzsche pointed out that,

> every major growth is accompanied by a tremendous crumbling and passing away: suffering the symptoms of decline belong in the times of tremendous advances; every fruitful and powerful movement of humanity has also created at the same time a nihilistic movement. It could be the sign of a crucial and essential time of growth, a sign of the transition to new conditions of existence, that an extreme form of pessimism, genuine nihilism, should arise in the world. (WP, §112, 69)

But the "ambiguity" that Nietzsche has referred to is in the *aporetic structure* of the promise, inasmuch as the present decay could instead be the sign, the harbinger of much worse still to come.

Nietzsche's attack on theodicies was never metaphysical, never authorized by anything absolute; it was always empirical and historical in its logic. He does not reject the world, but indicts theological justifications for misery and suffering. And he rejects other-worldly consolations, reconciliations, and solutions. Moreover, he willingly acknowledged that there was a time, many centuries ago, in the early years of civilization, when theodicies were life-affirming, not only because they offered consolation, but also because they provided the best possible explanation of the way things were, making the experience of life and death not only comprehensible but also meaningful. However, in the modern world, these theodicies, no longer compelling as consolations and explanations, have instead become life-denying, hence, in a word, nihilistic.

In *Stages on Life's Way*, Kierkegaard, like Nietzsche an important figure in Beckett's representations of religion, casts himself into the hopelessness of a baroque dialectic, insisting that:

> Everyone is asleep; only the dead rise at this hour from the grave revived. But I, I am not dead, so I cannot be revived; and if I were dead, I could not be revived, for indeed I have never lived.[15]

Malone Dies begins with Malone, dying or perhaps already dead, mumbling to himself words that, as if by sheer coincidence, form an intricate allusion to Kierkegaard's words of speculation:

> I shall soon be quite dead at last in spite of all. Perhaps next month. Then it will be the month of April or of May. For the year is still young, a thousand little signs tell me so. Perhaps I am wrong, perhaps I shall survive Saint John the Baptist's Day and even the Fourteenth of July, festival of freedom. Indeed I would not put it past me to pant on to the Transfiguration, not to speak of the Assumption. But I do not think so, I do not think I am wrong in saying that these rejoicings will take place in my absence, this year. I have that feeling [. . .].

And then, invoking the hidden judge behind Christian theodicy, he imagines finally getting "repaid" for all he suffering in the course of living his life (MD 173–174). But what is it for us mortals to be living? The nameless voice in *The Unnamable* seems to believe that, in the world determined according to the Christian religion, our lives are lived as if we were already dead. But for him, that living death is not the despair that, for Kierkegaard, is a sickness unto death. Rather, it is religion and theodicy that negate life; and anyone whom the happenstance of life throws under the influence of that institution will suffer a living death, for that influence is inimical to life. Theologians promise resurrection and redemption, but do not permit people to live a full, rich life before they die. Thus, an unnamable voice, the principal one in Beckett's novel, again alluding to Kierkegaard, reflects, sardonically, on life and death within the law of the Church:

> But say I succeed in dying, to adopt the most comforting hypothesis, without having been able to believe I ever lived, I know to my cost it is not that [i.e., robust worldly life] that they wish for me. For it has happened to me many times already, without their having granted me as much as a brief sick-leave among the worms, before resurrecting me. But who knows, this time, what the future holds in store. (UN 335)

What can death and the promise of resurrection mean to one whom religious laws and doctrines have never allowed to enjoy a full, rich, and robust life? Malone tells us: "The truth is, if I didn't *feel* myself dying, I could well believe myself already dead, expiating my sins, or in one of heaven's mansions" (MD 177). With the rack just behind it, the old Church offered redemption in Heaven. Not surprisingly, the unnamable voice decisively rejects this temptation. One can almost hear the mockery and see the contemptuous sneer:

> I am he who will never be caught, never delivered, who crawls between the thwarts, towards the new day that promises to be glorious, festooned with life belts, praying for rack and ruin. The third line falls plumb from the skies, it's for her majesty my soul, I'd have hooked her on it long ago if I knew where to find her. (UN 332–333)

What if the religious institutions worked to make the redemption that theodicy offers take place right here on earth, turning social life into a new paradise?

In a poem that evokes the Nazi extermination camps, where God's justice is absent, Celan states the Nietzschean argument in the strongest possible way: "Eternity grows old [. . .] they ladle soup into all beds and camps."[16] Eternity, the dimension that has always been regarded as a metaphysical, supernatural, world-transcendent source of redemption, must no longer be isolated from world-historical events: the old conception of eternity has aged; having failed to redeem the world from which, in the idolatry of our imagination, it was separated, and indeed having failed to stop the exterminations, the genocides, its promised time of justice has irrevocably passed. Whatever redemption there may be for us can now come only from *within* the world of time that our deeds and activities have created. The enchantments of religion must be dispelled. But are the new enchantments our technology makes possible less destructive, less deadening, less inimical to life?

I have been arguing that both Nietzsche and Beckett have been misunderstood: neither is an advocate for nihilism as it is commonly defined, namely, as life-denying, denying the possibility of meaningful life and denying, also, that there are any values worth living and striving for. Neither nurses some perverse wish for Hell to extend its reign on earth, reducing life to a brutal, miserable, meaningless subsistence. Hoping to raise consciousness, salvaging the human dream of a chance for happiness, Beckett's stories bear witness to the suffering that marks his time; they are allegorical representations that show us to ourselves in the clearest, most truthful way, penetrating our disguises and revealing our darkest, innermost secrets. They are also attestations of a tragic heroism: they preserve a fragmented memory of what, in our commitment to modernity, we have lost or abandoned, whilst sustaining, even in the material and spiritual destitution of our creaturely life, an unshakable sense of our sublime humanity, an indestructible dignity in the face of suffering. What lies behind Beckett's consistently bleak depictions of the human condition is the hope that, by raising consciousness regarding the damage that theodicies continue to induce, he might weaken their spell and serve the cause of our emancipation, giving us just a little more of a chance for happiness—the happiness, namely, that, as I said in the Prologue, would bring humanity to itself. But his works also demonstrate the undying *strength* of the old metaphysics, the old theological stories, again and again interrupting *his* story, the story *he* wants to tell, with invocations and evocations of the old theology, as a way of noting how difficult it is for us—even today— to abandon the emotionally compelling stories that religion tells, despite realizing the destructiveness theodicy causes, when there is no new story of equal explanatory and consolatory power—and above all, no life-affirming story—to replace it. So temptations to fall back on the old stories—on their promises of salvation and redemption—repeatedly find expression in the midst of the devastation theodicy has not redeemed, making life seem meaningful once more and encouraging hope for a happy ending. Beckett does want, after all, to keep hope—and the promise of happiness—alive. But what can language do? What good are words?

With the rise to power of the modern ego and its will to power, the nihilism that has increasingly determined the modern world was set in motion. According to Nietzsche's diagnosis, this will to power, which dominates and destroys by reducing everything it encounters to an object subject to its will, must eventually, when all subjectivity except itself has been turned to stone, turn on itself in a final self-destructive fury. The paradigm of objectivity that the ego in its rise to power imposed on everything finally denies the ego its remaining vestiges of interiority, leaving the once powerful ego, the ego that once challenged God, empty and dead. The God of the Judeo-Christian world, whose transcendent, metaphysical independence this will to power could not tolerate, was only its penultimate victim. But the death of God that Nietzsche proclaimed, merely registering the signs and symptoms of an abandonment he recognized as already present in his time, was not necessarily, he thought, the irreparable loss, the absolute disaster that many in his time—and in ours—have felt it, or understood it, to be. For, it has also meant our liberation, our repudiation, at long last, of centuries of servitude and self-abasement, the abjection of a life denying itself life. It has also been our own empowerment, a stage of advancement in our maturity, the assumption, at long last, of full responsibility for the suffering of injustices and the amelioration of the human condition. Instead of leaving the work of justice on earth to God—or, in effect, to the forces of fate, we must finally be committed to undertaking it ourselves.

Thus I want to argue that what Beckett gives us, what he represents in his stories and on the stage, showing us to ourselves with the redemptive power of painful honesty, is not the fanciful world of a possible future, not our world as if already redeemed, but our world revealed, exposed in all its nakedness and destitution, drifting in the most extreme existential anguish between two equally miserable conditions, either suffering under the tyranny and torments of an implacable theodicy or else shrouded in mourning over the loss of the divine dimension, surviving that loss as spiritless orphans of abandonment, the garbage of a dying civilization.

I want to argue, moreover, that Beckett, despite struggling against, and showing, the damage language has endured in our time, and despite often feeling bereft of words, nevertheless persists in his faith in language—in language as bearing vestiges of the utopian promise of happiness. Words not yet corrupted or lost, "the words that remain" (UN 406), often mere word-fragments suggestive of the light of redemption, images of paradise, of love, tenderness and happiness, break into his texts from time to time, indicating that theology lingers on in the collective memory and imagination, but only in a confusing mixture of fear and trembling, guilt and punishment, remorse and atonement, desire and longing, doubt and despair. Might we read Beckett's stories as negative theology? We should recall here what, in "How to Avoid Speaking," Derrida thought to suggest:

> The experience of negative theology perhaps holds to a promise, that of the other [. . .] not of this or that promise but of that which [. . .] inscribes us by its trace in language—before language.[17]

At stake is "a promise" that "will have always escaped the demand of presence ... [but which] renders possible every present discourse."[18] We shall be reading Beckett in search of the traces of that promise, a promise of happiness—only a chance—that might redeem earthly life without the torments of theodicy. But Beckett's fictional works are not philosophical treatises; what he wants to say is accordingly said using numerous surrogate characters, often nameless ghostly voices, and the thoughts he ventures, experimenting with the possibilities of language, are frequently expressed only in negations, fragments, metaphors, and shy, oblique allusions. We must pursue the intimations, the fragmentary traces, even the faintest of fading echoes, "the faint sign for us of a change some day nay even of an end in all honour and justice" (H 135).

In this regard, Adorno's conception of authentic art nicely illuminates Beckett's art, an art which is uncompromisingly truthful in its *mimesis*, no matter how much the world it represents seems to have fallen into nihilism, and increasingly rigorous—rigorous to the point of itself seeming nihilistic—in stripping his prose of everything even slightly *auratic*. As Hullot-Kentor states it: what is crucial in authentic art is

> the relation between aura—that [meaning or truth-content] which is more than what is factually present in an art work—and mimesis: just by its internal mimesis of what is untrue [or wrong] in the world,

the radically anti-auratic art work becomes the negative figure of what would be other than the given; and therefore, [the work] once again becomes auratic.[19]

It is in this commitment to negative dialectics, both as style and as narrative structure, that Beckett's art gives the auratic a chance—a faint chance—to appear.

So how might we read the undecidable dialectical ambiguities, existential riddles, taking place in his stories—*Watt*, for instance, where words are telling us that, when all is said and done, his tales will,

nothingness
in words enclose?

Is nothingness, then, a word's invention? Do words hold it in their power? Does sense—or say hope—not hinge, here, on the word that bears our stress? In the end, a tale gets told. And words have come to be. Haven't they?

CHAPTER TWO

In the Secret of Guilt: Punishment as Meaning

In *The Origin of German Tragic Drama*, Benjamin reflects on the barbarism inherent in the moral-theological construction of our "civilization." "Fate," he argues,

> is not a purely natural occurrence—no more than it is purely historical. Fate, whatever guise it may wear in pagan or mythological contexts, is meaningful only as a category of natural history [where] it is the elemental force of nature in historical events, which are not themselves entirely nature, because the light of grace is still reflected from the state of creation. But it is mirrored in the bottomless swamp of Adam's guilt.[1]

In Beckett's story, *How It Is*, this swamp becomes a realm in which there is a struggle against fate, against the elemental force of nature—against the unjust nature of its justice. In other stories, Beckett's characters struggle to break free of the persistent oppressiveness of theodicy, continuing its fateful legacy in a theater of guilt and punishment.

*

With immense compassion, but without the slightest sentimentality, Beckett observes the depths of suffering consuming the world. Through the characters in his stories, we see ourselves lost in a time of mourning, having abandoned the many gods and the one God, or feeling that they—the one or the many—abandoned us to the fate of our own making. Thus we see that, despite the irrevocable vanishing of the dimension of transcendence, we are still longing for a miraculous transformation of our hearts and minds, redeeming the earth's promise. But we also see how our suffering has been appropriated and mystified by theological interpretations. Beckett alludes to this when he has his narrator in *The Unnamable* pondering the meaning of suffering that figures in Judeo-Christian theodicy: "Is not a uniform suffering preferable to one that, by its ups and downs, is liable at certain moments to encourage the view that perhaps after all it is not eternal?"[2]

The stories that, for centuries, theodicy has been telling have created their own types of guilt, suffering and justice: they have given our suffering meaning, but that meaning has imposed a terrible guilt in its justification of the suffering. There is something dreadfully wrong in our world when even hope *requires* suffering. In *The Unnamable*, one Beckett's characters remarks: "As long as he suffers, there's hope" (UN 360). Hope for what? If the suffering must be "without hope of diminution, without hope of dissolution," then the hope in question is not hope for the ending of earth-bound suffering but hope for the future of theodicy (UN 360–361). In the twisted logic Beckett's irony reveals here, *we* must remain *without* hope for our life here on earth, if the "justice" served by theodicy is to seem like a way out of our endless misery and destitution of spirit.

Whilst showing us lives of wretched existential and ontological suffering that we are afraid to acknowledge, Beckett's stories question the stories of theology, giving at the same time the most poignant expression to the phenomenology of that suffering, encouraging our hope through allegorical word-images that occasionally break into his narratives and inflect his linguistic structures. To connect to our experience in its historical context, these images are often drawn from the religious iconography we in the Western world have inherited. At the same time, however, Beckett's way of using them is invariably their undoing, setting in motion a liberation from their force.

*

In *Endgame*, Beckett puts these words in Clov's mouth: "I say to myself—sometimes, Clov, you must learn to suffer better than that if you want them to weary of punishing you. . . ."[3]

In "Postmodernity and Guilt," a chapter in *The Call to Radical Theology*, Thomas Altizer argues that "Late modernity has been a primary site of ultimate guilt; only in this time is such guilt called forth philosophically, as in Nietzsche and Heidegger, only then does it pass into the purest language, as in Kafka and Beckett."[4] The argument continues, connecting this deeply existential guilt—an ontological guilt, really, since it concerns our very being—to the death of God, an "apocalyptic explosion" of the prevailing structure of existentially fundamental beliefs:

> Postmodernity is a consequence of that explosion, as now a truly new humanity and new world has been born, but a new world impossible apart from the apocalyptic explosion of modernity itself, one not only ending modernity but also realizing a postmodernity that is a metamorphosis of the most negative expressions of modernity, and expressions that

here pass into their very opposite. So it is that the devastating guilt of a late modernity passes into a new innocence, but a new innocence that, just because it is a metamorphosis of that guilt, is a new and ultimate impotence, an impotence freezing everything that once was life, and issuing in an infinite series of simulacra of life itself. [. . .]

"Is this," he asks, "a humanity truly liberated from guilt, and thereby liberated from all deep and ultimate illusion [. . .]? Or is it far rather the most enslaved humanity that has yet come forth, one most truly and comprehensively impotent, and one most profoundly closed to the possibility of transfiguration?"[5]

*

In any event, the world is out of joint. Again and again, Beckett, like Kafka, tells us stories showing, as operative in Judeo-Christian theodicy, the *objective* disconnections between guilt and punishment, suffering and guilt: disconnections that theodicy attempts to validate in a tormented *subjectivity*—"as if there existed a relation between that which suffers and that which causes to suffer."[6] Were there a discernible connection or correspondence, perhaps a Leibnizian, pre-established harmony, all things manifestly hanging together, as in a transparently rational world order, human suffering, if it could still happen, might at least be tolerable. But Beckett's protagonists can discover no compelling reason, not even a recognizable empirical cause, for the peculiar type of suffering that theodicy tries to justify. As long as our suffering calls for, needs, a story, what matters is that it be a story which makes the meaning of the suffering compelling. Perhaps some day, humankind will be strong enough to live without any theodicy; but would it not be a sad day when the stories that science tells are so overwhelming that there is no more appreciation of fiction, no more desire to imagine other dimensions of meaning? What the different versions of theodicy give us, instead of science, are "all the old noes dangling in the dark and swaying like a ladder of smoke" (TN 131). Theodicy promises heaven for those who surrender to the punishments of its judgment; but the ladder it erects for the climb out of suffering turns out to be nothing but smoke.

Beckett's stories are provocations to question the mysterious connections that theodicy claims. To be born and go on living: Is there a debt to be repaid for this? Is one's living in some way a "usurpation" of the rights of the other? Are we guilty simply for being? Guilty for going on? For merely consenting to play our part on the stage?

A voice in the ninth of Beckett's *Texts* expresses the wish that all the old theological stories might be silenced, for there is already too much misery without the added burden of original sin and guilt. And yet, this voice, despite its apparent rejection of the word, is still calling for the telling of a story. A better story:

Let there be no more talk of any creature, nor of a world to leave, nor of a world to reach, in order to have done, with worlds, with creatures, with words, with misery, misery. [. . .] If only I could say, There's a way out there, there's a way out somewhere, then all would be said, it would be the first step on a long travelable road, destination tomb, to be trod without a word. [. . .] (TN 118)

The words we have been given, inherited in the old theological stories, perpetually sentence us to unnecessary suffering.

In his doctoral dissertation on Kierkegaard, Adorno emphasized what theodicy depends on, namely, the torments of an inescapable and originally unconscious guilt, a guilt that can be forgiven only when it is wholeheartedly avowed in symbolic self-sacrifice:

Reconciliation is the imperceptible gesture in which guilty nature renews itself historically as created nature; without reconciliation, it remains obsessed with its greatest gesture, that of sacrifice.[7]

It is not surprising that, in his early essay on Proust, Beckett refers to "the double-headed monster of damnation and salvation": "double-headed," because it is one and the same theological system that first damns and then offers to save us from the punishments it threatens to impose. This extortion by torment is what Winnie, in *Happy Days*, is evoking when she quotes a verse from Milton's *Paradise Lost* (10, ll. 741–742): "O fleeting joys/ Of Paradise, dear bought with everlasting woes." Our history is a story of guilt induced by a theodicy that, holding history hostage, burdens human beings with the accusation of an original indebtedness, a mythic guilt borne in the very substance of our nature, crypt of the flesh. Again and again, Beckett shows us characters in mortal distress, guilty of nothing: their only offense is their very existence. And through them, he shows us to ourselves. Guilt is inseparable, as Benjamin says, from theodicy.[8]

*

Expelled, one of the short stories Beckett wrote in the 1950s, a poignant, heart-rending story evoking the biblical expulsion from Paradise, relates in the grammar of the first person singular the fate of a man cast out—expelled—from the house in which he was living.[9] He is pushed out the door, falls down the steps and lands in the gutter. His hat is thrown out after him. We suppose him guilty of some offense; but as the story unfolds, it becomes apparent that his guilt and expulsion are without cause. "I had done them no harm," he says, bewildered by what befell him. The injustice cries out all the more loudly, the more we follow the man in his silent acquiescence, quickly adjusting to the humiliating conditions into which he has been thrown. We are tempted to wish that he would at least say, as a voice in the eighth of Beckett's *Texts for Nothing* says—on behalf, I think, of every human creature: "But whom can I have offended so grievously, to be punished in this inexplicable way?" (TN 113). However, at the very moment when his tale most captures our sympathy, he breaks the bonds, declaring it nothing but a story: "I don't know why I told this story. I could just as well have told another." For theodicy, however, there can be only the story it wants to tell: a mystifying story of guilt and a lifetime of punishments on earth before a final verdict decides one's everlasting fate. But the effect of the narrator's last words, his claim that he could have told a different story, turns what had seemed to be his fate into a mere contingency. And this obliquely casts a critical light on the fatalism in theodicy, indirectly subverting its power.

The guilt that theodicy imposes may be *nothing but* a story; nevertheless it is, as Beckett's stories imply, a story that has claimed real human lives for a "justice" beyond the bounds of reason. The anonymous voice that narrates *The Unnamable* tells us, appearing simultaneously to accept and to challenge this oppressive theological story of guilt: "Perhaps someday I'll know, say, what I'm guilty of" (UN 362).

In the story about Sapo that Malone relates, the rebellious youth should have been expelled from school, but was not. Why not? Malone is puzzled. "I have been unable to find out why Sapo was not expelled." But, after conceding that he "should have to leave this question open," he resolves to make sure that the boy is duly punished: "I shall make him live as though he had been punished according to his deserts." Conscious, however, of the arbitrariness of this "justice," he says, recognizing in the sky the corresponding darkness, "We shall not suddenly raise our eyes, far from help, far from shelter, to a sky black as night" (MD 184). What is carried out here on earth in God's name gets no confirmation from Heaven. Once again, it is a question of incomprehensible, arbitrary judgment and equally questionable punishment—just like what is wrought by a theodicy removed from daily life.

Guilt is the critical theme of the fifth of Beckett's *Texts for Nothing*. When this *Text* commences, Beckett seems to be evoking a scene of interrogation reminiscent of Kafka's *The Trial*. The scene is also, however, an elaborately exaggerated, ironic and mocking parody recalling Kant's phrase, "tribunal of reason," which announced his first *Critique* an interrogation of the legitimate claims of reason. The wording at the very beginning of the text, exceedingly enigmatic, certainly suggests a trial of some kind, taking place in a court of justice. This impression is immediately negated, however, for its representation is revealed as a mere projection of the narrator's mind, nothing but an imaginary event taking shape in a soliloquy. The narrator, withdrawn into an interior drama of introspection, has assumed all the character roles in a vertiginous proliferation of pronouns, although this in no way subverts the sharply critical edge (TN 95). However, the questions that the story raises regarding the terms of our morality, our justice, cannot be easily dismissed as mere fantasy. But at once, as in Kafka, the veracity or legitimacy of this experience is rendered problematic: "It's an image, in my helpless head, where all sleeps, all is dead, not yet born [. . .]" (TN 95). As he often does, Beckett sets up a story only to deconstruct it, implying that the same can be done with the theatrics in which theology casts us.

Writing in France, where the sovereign subjectivity that Descartes posited became the absolute point of reference for modern thought, Beckett never misses an opportunity to play mischievously with the assumptions of Cartesianism. But as Beckett's fifth *Text* continues, the narrator's introspection veers suddenly toward what is really at stake, namely, the metaphysical or theological question of an *ontological* guilt, the corrosive "original" indebtedness and guilt in being born, the guilt in existing—what the philosopher Levinas has called "usurpation"—that since ancient times has been made constitutive of our very essence, our sense of ourselves as human creatures:

> An instant and then they close again, to look inside the head, to try and see inside, to look [. . .] in the silence of a quite different justice, in the toils of that obscure assize where to be is to be guilty. (TN 95)

Inspecting his conscience for the slightest accusatory evidence of moral guilt in conformity to the prevailing cultural practice and finding nothing damning, the narrator rebels against his own obsession with the curse of this mythic guilt still haunting the modern soul; and he desperately searches for clues to the possibility of "a quite different justice." And, with subtle irony, he describes the scene of his moral examination in terms that recall Heidegger's thought, turning the profundity of the philosopher's ontological thesis regarding the human condition—a radical rewriting of the theological tradition, with its ancient story—into a buzzword, a catchphrase or jingle, parody of meaningful insight. Might this mischievous play with the story finally break the curse?

We learn that the entire "inquisition," conducted by "gentlemen of the long robe," has actually taken place only in the narrator's head, as he struggled to free himself from the harsh terms of divine justice and make sense out of its ceaseless vigilance, its terrible judgment, its still powerful, compelling hold on his conscience and sensibility. This justice, claiming always to speak inside him as "the voice of reason" (TN 96), keeps him imprisoned in a state of excruciating anguish, constantly compelled to examine with suspicion and condemnation the moral character of his motives, intentions, and deeds. He cannot even let himself enjoy the beauty of the earth and the sky without being tormented by guilt. But, as he records his broodings, consigning them to paper, he imagines that, if only he could laugh, the mythic spell might be vanquished, releasing him from its hold. Perhaps, he thinks, mischievously, blasphemously predicating of God totally contradictory attributes, "tomorrow will be different, perhaps I'll appear before the council, before the justice of him who is all love, unforgiving and justly so, but subject to strange indulgences " (TN 97). It is slowly taking away his life, he says to himself, contemplating the terrible "justice" of theodicy. If only he could treat the matter as if it were nothing but a game! But he cannot easily vanquish the phantoms—"all these voices"—that persist in haunting his mind, even though he knows that they are nothing but cultural projections, figments of the imagination (TN 98). Phantoms hurling accusations in his head: "sweet thing theology" (TN 98–99). He struggles to free himself; but in the end, the effort is exhausting, and, as he notes, his quill falls from his hand. After that fall is noted, the fifth of the *Texts for Nothing* comes to its end. The biblical Fall persists, resonating even in these little, seemingly insignificant falls. No period can mark here the end of theodicy at this time. But already the narrator has, after all, turned theodicy into a story made of words, words that, one might hope, other words could negate in a kind of proleptic mimesis of a world redeemed at least to the extent that it is released from the emotional damage caused by a theodicy formed around the assumption of guilt—a guilt made of nothing but words!

The narrating voice in the eighth of the *Texts*, "begging and imploring," expresses his hope in words, words like "day" and "night," "earth" and "sky":

> [. . .] if they could open, those little words, open and swallow me up, perhaps that is what has happened. If so let them open again and let me out, in the tumult of light that sealed my eyes [. . .]. (TN 112–113)

Can the simple life that such words evoke finally take hold and release him from the theological nightmare?

Theodicy reverses cause and effect; and it completes its triumph when it succeeds in the complete interiorization of guilt, making us into judges and executioners of ourselves. It is as if theodicy were setting up its court within our skulls. The narrating voice in *The Unnamable* records just how this possession operates:

> Let them put into my mouth at last the words that will save me, damn me, and no more talk about it, no more talk about anything. But this is my punishment, my crime is my punishment, that's what they judge me for. (UN 362–363)

His brooding continues:

> When all goes silent, and comes to an end, it will be because the words have been said, those it behoved to say, no need to know which, no means of knowing which, they'll be there somewhere, in the heap, in the torrent, not necessarily the last [. . .].

But the hoped-for release is instantly denied, as the old voices of theodicy interrupt, bringing him back into their system: the words that might rescue him "have to be ratified by the proper authority, that takes time, he's far from here, they bring him the verbatim report of the proceedings [. . .]." And the voice continues, while

> the messenger goes towards the master, while the master examines the report, and while the messenger comes back with the verdict, the words continue, the wrong words, until the order arrives, to stop everything or to continue everything [. . .]" (UN 363).

But somehow, the entire process remains inscrutable. A defense contesting the process is impossible.

Does not having acquired the language, the words of one's community, constitute, as such, though not an original guilt, at least some kind of indebtedness, a certain moral responsibility? Might the indebtedness to others that comes with the acquisition of language be involved in the mystical origination of guilt? The origin of the guilt imposed by theodicy remains beyond these questions. But we do know that, in the guilt that theodicy presupposes *a priori*, the past rules over the present.

*

The seriousness of Beckett's animadversions against theodicy is demonstrated by the fact that the theme of divine and profane justice figures in so many of his stories. He deeply cares about justice.

Calling attention to the inscrutability of divine justice and the vanity of efforts to understand its arbitrariness, Malone reports that Macmann, apparently an involuntary inmate, or prisoner, in a psychiatric hospital, the House of St. John of God, found singular pleasure in wandering around the garden that surrounded the hospital, and that, on one of his ventures there, overwhelmed by the beauty of a hyacinth he found, he uprooted it and carried it back to his room:

> No questions were ever asked in the House of St. John of God, but stern measures were simply taken, or not taken, according to the dictates of a peculiar logic. For, when you come to think of it, in virtue of what possible principle of justice can a flower in the hand fasten on the bearer the crime of having gathered it? Or was the mere fact of holding it for all to see in itself a felony [. . .]? And if so, would it not have been preferable to make this known, [. . .] so that the sense of guilt instead of merely following on the guilty act, might precede and accompany it as well? (MD 269)

Simply finding pleasure in the beauty of a flower must become a source of guilt and shame.

In modern times, keeping up with the times, theodicy has employed enlightenment, putting it to work for it in disciplinary practices of the self, the interiorization of theocratic terror. "Orders, prayers, threats, praise, reproach, reasons" (UN 330). And of course the secret confession—of "an old shame that kept me from living, the shame of my living that kept me from living [. . .]" (TN 134). How escape this terrible judgment? Beckett's narrator tells us, writing about Malone, that,

> not knowing how to go about it, in order to think and feel correctly, he would suddenly begin to smile for no reason, as now, as then, for already it is long since that afternoon [. . .] when the rain caught him far from shelter, to smile and give thanks for the teeming rain and the promise it contained of stars a little later, to light his way and enable him to get his bearings, should he wish to do so. (MD 233)

The rain's promise of stars is an intimation of the promise of happiness, a promise that appears in the beauty of the profane world as a profane illumination: a promise already partially redeemed in the lyricism, the very words, of Beckett's story, touched by the sense of *another* justice, free at last of theological guilt, free at last of its suffering. For the real guilt, the only guilt, issues from the suffering that we, the human species, have caused in nature and wrought for all of creaturely life—but most of all, it issues from what we have done to other human beings.

In his essay on *Endgame*, Cavell argues that "suffering has to stop being used, has to stop meaning anything, and become simply a fact of life."[10] But there *is* existential meaning in suffering: that must not be categorically denied. There is consequential exaggeration in Cavell's outrage. He is certainly right, though, to argue that suffering must never be "used." For Beckett's characters, there can be no doubt: theodicy is an abuse of the fact of suffering. Turning theological meanings into "facts of life," but without denying their existential meaning, is exactly what Beckett's stories are intended to accomplish. In the secret of guilt is the truth of its fiction: where it is supposed to be, there is absolutely nothing.

CHAPTER THREE

Political Theology:
Old Dictations, Old Knots

In these times, everything is political.

SØREN KIERKEGAARD, *Either/Or*[1]

*The sublation of religion, itself the illusory happiness of the
people, is the demand for their real happiness. [. . .] Thus
the critique of heaven is transformed into a critique of
earth, the critique of religion into the critique of law, and
the critique of theology into the critique of politics.*

KARL MARX, *Early Writings*[2]

One might reasonably wonder, I suppose, how a chapter on political theology could bear on the interpretation of Beckett's plays and stories. By way of an answer to that question, I would refer to Benjamin's account of his own engagement with theology: "My thinking," he said, "is related to theology as blotting pad is related to ink. It is saturated with it. Were one to go by the blotter, however, nothing of what is written would remain."[3] The same could be said, I believe, of Beckett's relation to theology and its theodicy: his works are saturated with their operations, even when nothing explicit appears. Thus one might understand Beckett's engagement with theology as a matter of grammar in Wittgenstein's sense: "Grammar," he suggests, "tells us what kind of object anything is. (Theology as grammar.)"[4]

Gathering and weaving together, in a reflection of far-reaching, revolutionary implications, three major philosophical works—Kant's *Religion within the Bounds of Reason Alone*, Hegel's *Faith and Knowledge*, and Bergson's *The Two Sources of Morality and Religion*, Derrida undertakes to rethink, for the sake of a just democracy-to-come, the fundamental role of faith, not only in religion but also even in the claims of knowledge proper to the natural sciences.

In the course of these subtle and intensely intricate reflections, Derrida defines what he means by "the messianic," or rather, by "messianicity without messianism,"—what I suggest we might also think of here as "radical utopian hope or faith without doctrine and dogma," arguing that it "would be *the opening to the future or to the coming of the other as the advent of justice*, but without horizon of expectation and without prophetic prefiguration." It is a question, namely, of a hope or faith invested in a future of democratic justice that is imagined *without* positing and imposing any more specific, determinate political form.[5] Further explaining this definition, he says:

> The coming of the other can only emerge as a singular event when no anticipation sees it coming, when the other and death—and radical evil— can come as a surprise at any moment. Possibilities that both open and can always interrupt history, or at least the ordinary course of history. [...] The messianic exposes itself to absolute surprise and, even if it always takes the form of peace or of justice, it ought, exposing itself so abstractly, be prepared (waiting without awaiting itself) for the best as for the worst, the one never coming without opening the possibility of the other. At issue there is a "general structure of experience." [...] *An invincible desire for justice is linked to this expectation.* [...]

"This abstract messianism," he continues,

> belongs from the very beginning to the experience of faith, of believing, of a credit that is irreducible to knowledge and of a trust that "founds" all relation to the other in testimony. This justice, which I distinguish from right, alone allows the hope, beyond all "messianisms," of a universalizable culture [and politics] of singularities, a culture [and politics] in which the abstract possibility of the impossible translation could nevertheless be announced. *This justice inscribes itself in advance in the promise, in the act of faith or in the appeal to faith that inhabits every act of language and every address to the other.*[6]

As object of faith and hope, "messianicity without messianism," or "utopia without doctrine and dogma," is thus *not* an *alternative* to displace a determinate set of principles. "Democracy-to-come" is not the name of an alternative to some determinate program or possibility, but that in the name of which a deconstruction of determinate forms of democracy, and, too, other political forms, might be carried out. Likewise, as the objects of faith and hope, "messianicity" and "utopia" are to be understood as strictly critical, deconstructive notions.[7]

*

I now want to introduce a brief discussion of Hegel's phenomenology of spirit, because his narrative of mutual recognition, breaking away from the archaic justice that prevails in the "state of nature," will be crucial to our reading, in Part Three, Chapter 6 of *How It Is*. In his early *Lectures on the Philosophy of Religion*, Hegel, saying about himself, "I am fire and water," tells of being caught in an aporetic struggle within himself between two equally necessary engagements or obligations: one holds him in the conditions of the finite, the other draws him away towards the freedom of the infinite.[8] In his later *Phenomenology of Spirit*, this conflict is characterized in world-historical terms, a reflection on the state of world, or at least the Occident, in his time. There was a time when, in the story he wants to tell, historical progress called for, as he put it,

> a frenzied effort to tear men away from their preoccupation with the sensuous, from their ordinary, private affairs, and to direct their gaze to the stars; as if they had forgotten all about the divine, and were ready, like worms, to content themselves with dirt and water.[9]

(I am reminded here of Beckett's *The Unnamable*, a story in the course of which the narrator invokes a certain lowly character named Worm.) But, in time, over time, dirt and dust—elemental substances that are also allegorical—lost their deathlike hold as a higher sense of Spirit was awakened and human beings turned with devotion towards "a heaven adorned with a vast wealth of thoughts and imagery." Hegel's story continues:

> The meaning of all that is, hung on the thread of light by which it was linked to that heaven. Instead of dwelling in this world's presence, men looked beyond it, following this thread to an other-worldly presence.

The excesses of this cast of mind needed, eventually, to be restrained. Consequently,

> the eye of the Spirit had to be forcibly turned and held fast to the things of this world; and it has taken a long time before the lucidity which only heavenly things used to have could penetrate the dullness and confusion in which the sense of worldly things was enveloped, and so make attentiveness to the here and now as such, attentiveness to what has been called "experience", an interesting and valid enterprise.

But "now", he thinks,

> we seem to need just the opposite: sense is so fast rooted in earthly things that it requires just as much force to raise it. The Spirit shows itself as

so impoverished that, like a wanderer in the desert craving for a mere mouthful of water, it seems to crave for its refreshment only the bare feeling of the divine in general.[10]

His thought concludes, acknowledging our time as a time of loss, a time of mourning and melancholy. Understanding this loss, however, is a decisive progressive step. A related thought is given expression in his *Philosophy of Right*: "It is only when actuality is mature that the ideal first appears over against the real."[11] But it is precisely at this moment, which should be a moment of triumph, that Spirit finds itself vulnerable, instead, to a strange incapacitation, the "ataraxia" of an "unhappy consciousness," seemingly unable to go on; for in finally becoming conscious of the ideal, it is compelled to realize how far it must journey to reach that objective and how ill prepared it is for the trials that await it. That is the moment when "philosophy paints its grey in grey"—the shading and indistinctness, the mistiness, that, as in *Lessness* and *Ill Seen Ill Said*, Beckett's story-images so often manifestly favor.

The *Phenomenology* diagnoses the mood of this historical moment, a moment in which we are still stuck, with astonishing perceptiveness:

> Faith has lost the content which filled its element, and collapses into a state in which it moves listlessly to and fro within itself.[12]

As Cervantes shows in the figure of Don Quixote, it is because of an investment in idealism as a sublime Romantic vision, an unearthly dream, that consciousness eventually falls prey to an irrefutable disenchantment and skepticism, and from there—at least for Hegel—into despair and melancholy, since skepticism works like an acid, corroding the hope, the faith, that lives in the very heart of idealism. The unhappy consciousness of modernity has lost faith in its guiding principles, values, and objects of belief; consequently, in the end, it has lost faith even in itself. But there are no completely satisfying alternatives to substitute for what has been lost—seemingly forever. As consciousness realizes that the "universal" it has been seeking is not the concept of the reconciled totality, it feels compelled to believe that what it has taken to be living reality is only, in truth, "the grave of its life." For it now seems to consciousness that consciousness is nothing but a struggle doomed in advance to failure.[13] In Hegel's story, unhappy consciousness is a consciousness that knows it is fragmented, agonizingly split into two, and caught in self-contradictions that deny the very possibility of a fulfilled journey through the ages of the world; but despite its knowledge, despite its self-consciousness, it is incapable of acting successfully.[14] Unhappy consciousness, stuck in pure, infinite feeling, unable to grasp the meaning of its situation, becomes an "infinite longing and languishing."[15] Although intensely aware that it cannot secure absolute truth by stoical detachment, that it cannot escape disenchantment and skepticism, and finally, that, challenged by the logic of reflexivity in skepticism, it cannot even defend its move to skepticism without falling into self-contradiction, unhappy consciousness nevertheless is not willing, or not able, to renounce its idealism, its dream, its commitment to the absolute. Renouncing neither its subjective truth nor its longing for the actualization, the truth, of the absolute, unhappy consciousness struggles to live with an almost unbearable aporia, swinging endlessly back and forth between the extremes of transcendence and immanence, hopefulness and despondency. The freedom from nature's powers that spirit sought in rising to the heights of stoicism now begins to feel more like eternal exile—its exclusion from the sensible beauty of a nature that it depends on for its very breath of life. Instead of an experience of triumph, having dispelled the powers of nature, this freedom becomes an experience of spiritual loss and disintegration.

It is thus not at all surprising that, in the "Conclusion" to *Faith and Knowledge*, Hegel is compelled to assert that,

> the highest totality can and must achieve its resurrection solely from this harsh consciousness of loss, encompassing everything, and ascending in all its earnestness and out of its deepest ground to the most serene freedom of its shape.[16]

But we, of course, are living in a post-Holocaust world—a world, moreover, that is still witnessing genocides. Beckett, therefore, finds it extremely difficult to believe in this task of "resurrection." As the *Dialectic of Enlightenment* argued, Hegel's "science of observing reason" cannot justify itself until it has actually transformed the world.

In my reading, however, Beckett recasts this "science," turning it into narratives: narratives that awaken a sense of promise in hope and skepticism, remembrance and mourning. And if indeed, as Hegel claims, the language that most accurately mirrors the condition of modernity is the "language of a disrupted consciousness," then in the grammar of Beckett's prose we find recognition of this condition, expressed in disjointed and paratactic sentences that suffer this disruptive pressure, thereby revealing just what is at stake in this condition.[17]

In his "Introduction" to the English translation of *Faith and Knowledge*, H. S. Harris discusses "infinite grief" as an intuition of the negative infinite:

> The infinite that is within the finite, and that reveals itself *negatively* in the perpetual perishing of the finite, reveals itself *positively* in the resurrection and perpetuation of the finite as a pattern of "inwardized," or "remembered," conceptual significance. [...] But nothing can be resurrected in the spirit, no finite particular can be "taken up" into the speculative infinite, until it has passed away into a remembering consciousness which values it, and hence mourns for it and grieves over it.[18]

To whatever extent there can be an aesthetic redemption of this "infinite grief," representing the possibility of reconciliation between the finite actuality of our suffering and the infinite ideality of our longing, it is correspondingly, for Beckett, the indeclinable calling of literature to bring Spirit to a moment of self-recognition, representing this possibility—and the liberating, utopian possibility of reconciliation—in the most compelling constructions of language.[19] And, as Hegel would have it, even the sentence constructions in Beckett's writings, painfully taking into themselves not only the disjointedness, the suffering, but also the work of memory and mourning, replicate the phenomenology of the Spirit's rhythms and moods, turns and returns, as it journeys towards self-recognition in otherness. For Beckett, however, both the course of this journey and the ending could not be more problematic. In reflecting on the story he tells in his *Phenomenology*, Hegel says: "By the little which now satisfies Spirit, we can measure the extent of its loss."[20] Beckett shows us our world suffering in its loss of the transcendent, the horizon of metaphysical meaning. But, instead of capitulating to desires for immediate substitutions, he *sustains* our sense of loss, our sense of something missing. In this way, he enables us to get some insight into what we are really missing and to "measure the extent of our loss." That might seem uncompromisingly, perversely negative, might even seem nihilistic; however, it could not in fact be more decisive in preparing the conditions for a world capable of recreating humanity without theology and its final justice.

*

Many of Beckett's stories seem, as we noted, to call for readings that cast them in a theological light.[21] Some readers might want to decline such readings; but it would be difficult to deny that *How It Is*, at least in its third part, where the question of justice is explicitly at stake, demands acknowledgment of its theological illumination. It is a story that draws on our cultural memory of religious and theological experience. And when we read this work, and indeed others Beckett wrote, we encounter as an operative fiction what Eric Santner terms "the psychotheology of everyday life": the persistent afterlife of the justice that once ruled in a world framed by political theology. The modern world does not ban or abolish its theological past; instead, as our world leaves behind a world-view that is primarily theological and founds a secular political order, it "redefines and rebinds politics and theology in an attempt to control their deepest antagonistic tendencies," hoping, if not to reconcile religious and secular impulses, at least to minimize their conflict.[22] In Beckett's stories, the ghosts of political theology continue to murmur; but they are never indulged and appeased. There are many allusive murmurings that, bearing implications for political theology, reverberate enigmatically in *How It Is*.

*

"Political theology" names the domain where questions about the religious and the political cross. Essentially, "political theology" concerns the historical influence of religion—and that means also its theology, theodicy, and eschatology—on political life. Since the very beginning of history, religion has played an overwhelmingly powerful role in political life, forming and informing everything from its institutions and myths of legitimation to its calendar of holidays. Monotheism and monarchy emerged together in mutual support.

Thus, as Schmitt argued in his 1922 work, *Political Theology*, careful study of the major political concepts and political institutions of the modern world would reveal that they are secularizations of theological origin, transposing or translating theological concepts, doctrines, and institutions into the context of secular political life.

In the world of the distant past, where the political was under the spell of religion, justice would be determined by reference to theological doctrines; and the judgments those doctrines authorized were to be executed by, or in accordance with, the appropriate religious institutions. For political theology, justice was theodicy: God's justice, its final verdict, final sentence, falling on mortal creatures at the end of their earth-bound time.

However, since the maturity, in the Western world, of that form of consciousness we call "late modernity," we have been living without any widely shared religious world-view. Today, indeed, the religious interpretation of life, death, and justice is no longer felt to be compelling—and yet, for many contemporaries, none of the radically secular alternatives that have emerged to fill the void is sufficiently satisfying. In the twentieth century, many thinkers have recognized this crisis of the spirit, engaging it in a form of critical thought. Some have tried to work out a world-view that would make it possible to continue thinking the political in the light of a religious dimension. And many modern writers of literature, recalling Dante, Milton, and Blake, have also responded to the crisis, creating fictional worlds where the political and the religious intersect, if only in the form of metaphor, fable, or allegory.[23]

It is into this historical moment, a time of emptiness and destitution, when the madness of theodicy is finished but a justice founded in humanity has not yet been realized, that Beckett has cast all his forlorn characters. But even though the terrible reign of theodicy has been broken, the political continues to be played out, as we know, in the disquieting light of religious symbols and theological tropes. And this is true in regard to the stories that Beckett tells. Not one of his stories unfolds without some references and allusions, or traces and echoes, evoking a theological dimension. And it is not possible to understand the treatment of justice in Beckett's stories without engaging in various ways the discourse of political theology, tracking down all the ways in which the theological illuminates or intervenes in the narrative.

But *why* are there such references and allusions, traces and echoes? As Graham Hammill notes in a summary of Hans Blumenberg's argument with Carl Schmitt, a summary that, I suggest, explains Beckett's frequent recourse to the "grammar" of theology: Blumenberg "begins to understand political theology as *a shaping fiction*, one whose strength comes not from a genealogy of the state [as in Schmitt's theoretical narrative], but instead from the persuasive force of theological metaphors that populate the early modern and modern landscape." Thus, as Hammill says, Blumenberg maintains that theological metaphors

> persist in the modern age not because they are structurally necessary, which is Schmitt's argument, but because, like all fictions, theological metaphors serve strategic ends. As fictions, theological metaphors have satisfied the need for cogent accounts of the world; and, at the same time, as tactical forms of mediation, they have sheltered against a literal-minded view of politics that [. . .] has polarized conflict into crisis.

For Blumenberg, "all modern politics is based in a fundamental way on rhetoric as a metaphorical practice."[24] In his account, the modern age is challenged by an "archive of theological metaphors" that it has inherited. Understanding this, Beckett exploits the stories carried by those metaphors and other rhetorical practices, drawing them out in a critical, dialectically reflective way.

Blumenberg's theoretical analysis, with its emphasis on language—rhetoric and metaphor—provides, I think, an illuminating explanation for Beckett's seemingly paradoxical recourse to religious and theological materials: not only despite the death of God, but precisely because of it. Only through these materials could he address the existential nihilism of his time, witnessing and expressing the longing, the mourning, and the despair. It is not only because in subtle ways the political, which Beckett's sustained concern for justice necessarily involves, is still, even today, drawing its legitimation, and even what we might call its theatricality, from the religious and the theological, above all in our inheritance of Christianity, but also because, whilst unrelenting and uncompromising in drawing us into the experience of human existence in a world without God, Beckett nevertheless wanted to connect his stories to the literary works of the tradition he inherited; and because, moreover, he has *depended* on the theological and religious materials—biblical stories, parables, liturgy, theological texts and doctrines, key words, symbols, metaphors and images—in order to see and express, through rhetorical devices of determinate negation, despite knowing all those materials to be nothing but props, the little encouragement he could muster, by grace of language, for the promise of happiness.

*

There are some enigmatic but intriguingly suggestive allusions in *How It Is*, the work that will be our subject in Part Three of this present book, for which I would like to venture an interpretation that, if not far-fetched and fanciful, would unquestionably draw us into the realm of political theology. The matter for thought concerns: [1] the curious reference to God's "old mill threshing the void," which nothing in the context illuminates (H 106); and [2] the metaphor of the sacks, sacks full of provisions—tins of sardines and various utensils—that, from the beginning to the end of Beckett's story, the denizens of the swamp-world, forming a procession, a "cortège" that challenges the Enlightenment assumption of a march of inevitable progress, must drag behind them on their long, slow, arduous journey—a journey with no destination.

The sacks, needed for survival, are, in their own way, as enigmatic as the old mill. At the very end of the first part of *How It Is*, in the course of describing the procession of "mortals" moving through the swamp dragging their sacks of provisions, many of which, including our narrator's, have burst open, the narrator suddenly speaks of "a celestial tin miraculous sardines sent down by God at the news of my mishap" (H 48). Early in the third part, the narrator again briefly turns all his attention on the sacks, speaking of their importance and of how he and the other mortals exchange or pass on their sacks. And he wants us to understand that, in these exchanges or inheritances, it is always a question of "a simple sack pure and simple a small coal sack" (H 111–112): there is, we are to believe, nothing at all very special about these sacks—and nothing special about their contents. But, recalling his earlier words about the tin of sardines, we must digest that assertion with a grain of salt. Not long after, the narrator's words provoke us to ponder a surprising question to which, until this moment, we had perhaps not given any thought: *Who* is the one, simply called "him," "in charge of the sacks"? (H 124) There is a strong intimation, here, that the one "in charge" is, might be, or should be, a "providential" God. When the sacks are again discussed, the narrator is talking about the fact that somehow he and the other mortals are being cared for, or at least looked after, by the one "in charge of the sacks." The narrator then speaks of "the sacks possible and food [. . .]/ the sack as we have seen there being occasions when the sack as we have seen is more than a mere larder for us yes moments when if needs be it may appear more than a mere larder to us [. . .]" (H 135). More than a mere larder? How so? What further meaning might there be? Soon thereafter, without having satisfied our curiosity, he calls attention to a "sudden light on the sacks at what moment renewed," seeming to suggest something supernatural or metaphysical, although after only a few words he cancels that mysterious claim, saying, "it's possible too there's a poor light." For all we know, that light does not augur something to come, but instead is nothing but the remaining trace of a sign of hope that is fading away, destined to vanish altogether. After that deflationary conjecture, he invokes someone "to whom at times not extravagant to impute that voice quaqua the voice of us all [. . .]" (H 138). The conclusion we come to is that the unnamed provider, the unnamed being in charge, is either God or Beckett, the god-like author who has dictated the narrator's words and, in one sense or the other, provided the characters in the story with their sacks and provisions: in any case, it is the one "who listens to himself and who when he lends his ear to our murmur does no more than lend it to a story of his own devising ill-inspired ill-told and so ancient so forgotten at each telling that ours may seem faithful that we murmur to the mud to him," this being "to whom," he says, "we are further indebted for our unfailing rations which inable us to advance without pause or rest," and "who God knows who could blame him must sometimes wonder if to these perpetual revictuallings narrations and auditions he might not put an end without ceasing to maintain us in some kind of being without end and some kind of justice without flaw who could blame him [. . .]" (H 139). Beckett wants us, it seems, to regard these sacks as if somehow providential. But who is the provider? God? How about mere circumstance?

In Beckett's story, then, one of his many "incredible stories," we encounter two truly enigmatic objects: God's "old mill threshing the void" and some rather mysterious or miraculous sacks. What might we make of them? What story might give them meaning? The meaning I want to propose—one, no doubt, among other possibilities, for Beckett has made sure that certain features, certain facts, are disguised, rendered only in displacement—ties them together in relation to a story with historical significance for political theology. Here, now, briefly recapitulated, is the story.

As the frontispiece for the English translation of Jacob Taubes's 1987 lectures, published in his book, *The Political Theology of Paul*, there is a photograph of one of the nave capitals belonging to the Romanesque church at Vézelay in Burgundy, France. What this photograph shows is a twelfth-century carving of the "Mystic Mill," a scene in a story important for Christian theology.[25] In typological iconography, we see Moses, or a prophet, representing the Old Testament, pouring grain from a sack into the funnel of a mill, whilst the apostle Paul, representing the New Testament, is working hard to catch all the refined flour in a sack. Reproducing in his lecture a commentary on the Mystic Mill written by the abbot of Saint-Denis around the time that the carving was made, Taubes told his seminar this story:

> One of these [roundels], urging us onward from the material to the immaterial, represents the Apostle Paul turning a mill, and the Prophets carrying sacks to the mill. The verses of this subject are these:
>
>> By working the mill, you, Paul, take the flour out of the bran.
>> You make known the innermost meaning of the Law of Moses.
>> From so many grains is made the true bread without bran,
>> Our and angels' perpetual food.[26]

Now, according to Kathleen Biddick, the poem "epitomizes the mediaeval Christian typological relation: Paul fulfills Moses, and the grain that will be baked into the sacred wafer of the Eucharist fulfills the Mosaic Law (from command to comestible)."[27] In other words, the sculpture is symbolically representing Christianity as the fulfillment and completion of messianic Judaism. This is theology with a political mission expressed in religious art.

Now, I do not want to claim that Beckett had this story in mind; nor do I even want to claim that he would have had something to say about the theological-political conflict that the sculpture is symbolically depicting. But I cannot resist the temptation to wonder about the mill and the sacks in Beckett's story, enveloped as they are in the miraculous and mysterious. Did he see this well-known carving? It would certainly not be unreasonable to suppose that, at some time during his long sojourn in France, he visited the church in Vézelay. And if that is so, he might well have learned about the story of the Mystic Mill, recapitulating it in his own way, hermeneutically disguising, displacing, and encrypting it in a new tale of his own devising. He was, after all, an ardent collector of stories. If, however, the connection I am suggesting is nothing more than a figment of my imagination, then the old mill remains an enigma, released for still other interpretive ventures; and the sacks, with their sardines and utensils, remain, miraculously, still providential. Good stories can be made out of these simple, everyday materials. There may be no connection between the two—or maybe only a connection emptied of meaning, as empty as the old mill, its wheels turning but grinding nothing, and as empty as the sacks that have burst open, losing all their provisions. But if there *is* a connection, it would, I think, be one more indication of Beckett's conviction that the struggle for justice in our time, the struggle for the fair distribution of the necessities for survival— sardines, bread from the mill, and utensils, is, at least in part, a political struggle for the happiness of Heaven on earth that has to be seen in the historical light of Judeo-Christian theology.

In Beckett's evocation of the old mill, though, the mill produces nothing. Instead of flour refined for the making of bread, this mill produces a void. Is this his comment on the politics in the New Testament claim to sublate and consummate the religion of the Old Testament? Or is it a subtle indictment of the politics of religious institutions, more concerned about winning theological debates than about providing bread for the hungry? We can only guess.

The reference to the mill might also recall another story. In Milton's *Samson Agonistes*, the greatest of modern poetic theodicies, Samson, "Eyeless in Gaza at the Mill with slaves," is being used, like the others, as a beast of burden, forced to turn the millstone with his bare hands. In his *Critique of Judgment*, Kant, familiar with Milton's poetic drama, borrowed the image of a hand mill in order to represent, as a symbol or metaphor, the despotic state ruled by "an individual absolute will" and also, at the same time, the moral heteronomy of a "blind and servile" will yielding to this state.[28] By extension, Beckett's image might be taken to suggest the despotism inherent in the ecclesiastical doctrines and institutions, imposing a theodicy that renders one "blind and servile" and offering nothing but empty consolations, rewards that amount to nothing.

The allegorical significance of the sacks is equally obscure, equally difficult to decipher. Dragged through the mud, they are subject to the injustices of chance, some bursting, others spared. They are also briefly touched—as if to be blessed—by a strange light. And at least one sack—the sack belonging to the unnamed narrator—is miraculously provisioned. But the way in which Beckett has given the sacks this mysteriousness is so transparently weak and unconvincing that it becomes impossible to take these dramas seriously. It is as if Beckett wanted to expose theological doctrines to a comedy of self-destruction by presenting in the most expressionless, deadpan manner the numinous phenomena, entertained with the appearance of utmost seriousness. In the solution of Beckett's irony, a mischievous skepticism, these theological doctrines quickly dissolve, leaving behind a tiny residue of melancholy longing, carried in hope for a world of "profane" happiness— and a justice that is wrought without supernatural appeal.

In thinking about epistemologies of emotion in eighteenth-century literature, Adela Pinch asks a provocative question: "Might the vertigo of skeptical demystification be as [. . .] gratifying as incredible stories?"[29] My question follows: Might one suspect that Beckett ultimately found as much entertaining material to work with in subjecting to the most radical skepticism the mysteries of political theology that hide behind our inherited forms of faith as the writers of earlier centuries found for the writing of their fictional tales?

CHAPTER FOUR

Ending the Endings:
The Endgame of Theodicy

*It is the heaviest stone that melancholy can throw at a
man, to tell him he is at the end of his nature;
or that there is no further state to come [. . .].*
SIR THOMAS BROWNE, *Urn Burial*[1]

*Where do we find ourselves? In a series of which we
do not know the extremes, and believe that it has none.*
RALPH WALDO EMERSON, "Experience"[2]

In *Texts for Nothing*, Beckett's anonymous voice declares that "it's the end gives meaning to words."[3] That might be true of language; but he will certainly fight against theodicies and their eschatologies. When, in *Molloy*, Beckett's character writes, "What I'd like now is to speak of the things that are left, say my goodbyes, finish dying,"[4] eschatology, the metaphysical endgame, a theology of ends and endings, of ultimate purposes and meanings, is called into question. He is not only saying farewell to his deceased mother; he is also saying "goodbye" to the endgame of eschatology. The stakes are *high*—indeed gambling the sky.

*

Have we finally cancelled the "flawed predictability" of God's extreme theatrical act?[5] Writing on the art of Francis Bacon, Gilles Deleuze opines that, "modern painting begins when human beings no longer experience themselves in terms of an essence [a determinate end], but instead as an accident."[6] I suggest that the same might be said of "modern" literature—Beckett's stories and plays, for instance, bringing this new shape of consciousness—and its world of contingency and catastrophe—to literary expression. It is not merely a question of showing life without metaphysics, without transcendence; for after Kleist and Kafka, literature will show life in its most extreme vulnerability, exposed to events without sufficient cause or reason.

*

In *The Call to Radical Theology*, Altizer notes that,

> What Blake could envision as the New Jerusalem, and Hegel could know as the advent of Absolute Spirit, [. . .] is the consequence of the end of history, an ending realized only through the death of God, which each could know as the most catastrophic ending in our history and precisely therefore as that ending able to call forth another beginning.[7]

Obsessed with beginnings and endings, ways and ends, ends natural and supernatural, matters that might all be nothing but "chimeras," Molloy tells the story of his search for his mother, ending up, apparently, in her bedroom, contemplating his own dying and "a world at an end, in spite of appearances, its end brought it forth, ending it began [. . .]."[8] The references to teleological and eschatological matters are so frequent that one might even suggest that that is what the subtext of the story is all about. Beckett's characters, especially those in his later works, inhabit a "closed immanence." Not merely finite, but closed, as if with "dead ends," even if they are venturing on a journey of some kind. However, precisely because of that very closure, denying any metaphysical end, the suffering in their lives is not only endless, misery without end, but it must be endured without ends of purpose and meaning. Thus, many of the characters are already living as if shrouded, stalked by death and obsessed with "last things." Even their corporeal movements and gestures are diminished, either minimal or somehow arrested, endlessly bereft of direction. Despite this, however, they cannot entirely get free of the eschatology that hangs over them, preparing them for final judgment.

The truth-claims of eschatology are promptly presented for questioning in both *Molloy* and *Malone Dies*. In both stories, the ending is declared already present in the beginning. The stories thus begin with sentences of death, references to their endings: eschatology, announcing the final judgment on a life that will soon come to its end. Contemplating "last things," Molloy's reflections turn sharply against this theology of ends and endings:

> For what possible end to these wastes where true light never was, nor any upright thing, nor any true foundation, but only these leaning things, forever lapsing and crumbling away, beneath a sky without memory of morning or hope of night. These things, what things, come from where, made of what? And it says that here nothing stirs, has never stirred, will

never stir [. . .]. Yes, a world at an end, in spite of appearances, its end brought it forth, ending it began, is it clear enough? (MO 35–36)

What he sees is the end already at work in the fatal beginning. It is frightening; but, despite seeing through the madness in eschatology, he cannot escape its hold. Victim of its madness, all he can do is imagine relief in the foretelling of the ending.

In a story without an existential journey, without settled destination and destiny, teleology is in trouble. And without teleology, the judgments and justice of theodicy are in trouble. Beckett's itinerary as a storyteller takes him from narratives of journeys to narratives with little or no movement: narratives that represent a world without the ends of teleology, the judgment of eschatology, and the justice of theodicy.

*

In *A Taste for the Secret*, Derrida discusses how he wants to think the connection between the promise of justice and eschatology:

> [. . .] justice—or justice as it promises to be, beyond what it actually is— always has an eschatological dimension. I link up this value of eschatology with a certain value of messianism, in an attempt to free both dimensions from the *religious* and *philosophical* contents and manifestations usually attached to them: philosophical, for eschatology, the thought of the extreme: the *eschaton*; or religious, the messianism of the religions "of the book."[9]

But if the customary meanings are to be avoided, why does he still want to claim, in his words, "that justice is eschatological and messianic?" He says, in a reply as lucid as it is brief:

> Perhaps because the appeal of the future [. . .], which overflows any sort of ontological determination, and which overflows everything that is and is present, the entire field of being and beings, and the entire field of history—is committed to a promise or an appeal that goes beyond being and history.[10]

Consequently, what he wants to understand with the word "justice" cannot be the same as, cannot be reduced to, the positivity of "right" or "law." Justice, he says, is,

> a relation to the unconditional that, once all the conditional givens have been taken into account, bears witness to that which will not allow itself to be enclosed within a context.

"It is clear," he explains, "that this relation—of the unconditional to justice— is a matter of life and death. Justice is not [reducible to] right [*droit*]; it is that which attempts, instead, to produce a new right."[11] Unlike theodicy, therefore, justice is an end that has no ending. There is no justice on earth. Not yet! And never without world-bound conditions. But that does not mean it is to be found somewhere else—in Heaven's verdict, say, or in our afterlife.

*

According to the biblical story, the world in which we find ourselves is, as Molloy says, playing on the double sense of "end," "a world at an end, in spite of appearances, its end brought it forth, ending it began" (MO 36). But neither the assumption of an originating purpose and ultimate meaning, nor the assumption of the apocalyptic termination of our world, can be rendered intelligible by empirical procedures. However, as a storyteller, Beckett wants to echo or reflect in the keenest, most moving prose, a deeply felt human need, letting us experience, in the concentrated intensity of literature and theater, its want of fulfillment. This is not a manifestation of Nietzsche's passive nihilism, but instead an expressive moment on the way to our self-recognition. That insightfulness is what great art can induce.

Beckett's writing repeatedly subverts whatever support grammar might have been thought to provide for such a claim, shaping a prose that relentlessly defies the dictum this *Text* enunciates. At a certain moment in his soliloquy, the writer in the sixth of Beckett's *Texts for Nothing*, invoking the temporal tenses, adverts to his "viewless form described as ended, or to come, or still in progress, depending on the words [. . .]" (TN 104). The obvious implication here is that teleology, and the divine justice it imposes, might be nothing more than a linguistic fabrication, a linguistically created possibility, consequence of what Wittgenstein characterized as "the bewitchment of our intelligence" by the grammatical contingencies of our language.[12] Turning this critique into an attack, the principal voice in *The Unnamable* says: "Set aside once and for all, at the same time as the analogy with orthodox damnation, all ideas of beginning and end" (UN 383). Should we—could we, even if we wanted to—renounce and abolish all such ideas? Or only those that lead us into the temptations of theology? What would our world be like without any orientations to beginnings and endings, origins and finalities? What about our sense of mortality? As when Montaigne, like a Beckett delegate, confides: "I have formed the habit of having death continually present, not merely in my imagination, but in my mouth."[13] That sense of mortality is not an end, or ending, controlled by the doctrines of theodicy.

*

In *Theory of the Novel*, Lukács suggests that "the writer's irony is a negative mysticism in times without a god."[14] With just that kind of ironic humor, the narrator in *Enough* (1965), a short story from Beckett's "middle years," says: "What do I know of man's destiny? I could tell you more about radishes."[15] Beckett's stories challenge predestination, challenge religious teleology and their judgments of life at the end, creating, as Alain Badiou notes, narratives and dialogues that reflexively expose their structure to the possibility of interruption by *chance* events: perhaps events offering "a different justice" and "a chance of happiness."[16] At every opportunity, Beckett attempts to break the spell of teleology, and therefore too of theodicy. And yet, in the tenth of his *Texts for Nothing*, a nameless voice acknowledges the continuing power in eschatology to compel a certain faith:

> That old past ever new, ever ended, ever ending, with all its hidden treasures of promise for tomorrow, and of consolation for today.[17]

But the promise of treasures is deferred, possibly only for the next life; and the consolation for today is nothing more than that empty promise. As Stanley Cavell says, writing about *Endgame*: "What it envisions is the cursed world of the Old Testament; and what is to be ended is that world, followed by the new message, glad tidings brought by a new dove of redemption, when we are ready to receive it."[18]

*

The promise of happiness—in a justice befitting our humanity—is a possibility only *after* the endgame of theodicy is played to its end. The curse of theological teleologies must be undone, its spell broken. Beckett will represent that in four ways: [1] *narratively*, in stories of journeys without ends, stories of journeys that take the unwitting character in a circle, or stories without a journey, without any progress towards an end; [2] *mimetically*, in retarded or arrested bodily movement; [3] *rhetorically*, in invocations of God's wrath and might, such as figure in curses, reduced to the banality of a literalism; and [4] *grammatically*, in interrupted, broken, and paratactic forms of expression, or in word-constructions without determinable sentence endings.[19] As Wittgenstein once remarked, theology is a grammar.

The existential or ontological condition of this world is indeed reflected in the very grammar in which Beckett's later stories are told: short, broken, paratactic sentences, isolated sentences often seeming to lead nowhere, or nowhere certain, expressed without any explanatory or justificatory connections, and sentence-like constructions without punctuation. What the increasing disintegration of Beckett's syntax symbolically represents is the interruption or suspension of the power of the end in the beginning. Every pause and silence in dialogue, every instance of parataxis, every breakdown and interruption in the continuity of the prose, potentially opens the situation to the possibility of chance events, metaphorically ending the rule of teleology and halting the cruel verdicts of theodicy.

Beckett's later, paratactic style is reminiscent of Hölderlin's use, in his translations of Sophocles, of the "counterrhythmic interruption," impeding and retarding the forward movement of the plot. This affinity with Hölderlin is what suggests an interpretation that reads in Beckett's style a symbolic gesture, blocking the stories from any straightforward, unexamined teleological or eschatological progression. But without such progression, without ends and endings, there is nothing left for theodicy to get hold of. Nevertheless, I think it undeniable that the promise of justice continues to be a philosophically important matter for Beckett.

*

The "punctum" in this regard is to be found in the construction of stories that lead us into what Benjamin described as "dialectics at a standstill." In *Aesthetic Theory*, Adorno called attention to this narratological strategy in his reading of the ending of *Waiting for Godot*:

> VLADIMIR: Well? Shall we go?
> ESTRAGON: Yes, let's go.
>   [*They do not move.*]

According to Adorno, this immobility or paralysis is Beckett's way of metaphorically representing the impotence of both the providential teleologies offered by religion and the political ideologies of progress that are dear to the enlightened, liberal bourgeoisie and the advocates of socialism.[20] "Without exception," he says, in Beckett's works, "the fulfilled moment reverses into a perpetual repetition that converges with desolation." In the most concrete, physical way, yet also allegorically, Beckett is showing the characters' not being moved any more by false promises, false teleologies and theodicies, false stories of progress: a rigorously determinate negative dialectics. At the same time, however, the fact that, according to Beckett's instructions, Vladimir and Estragon are not supposed to move tells us that they might still be under the spell of the false, still hoping for a messianic event, still waiting for the coming of Godot. The significance of their motionlessness is ultimately left radically ambiguous and uncertain. But the dialectical ambiguities surrounding movement, gesture, and journey in Beckett's stories do not diminish their power to make us reflect critically on the stories that sustain religion, although it might be argued that the journey narratives cannot entirely avoid encouraging a lingering sense that there must be rational meaning and truth, however obscure, in the teleology, eschatology, and theodicy of the religious stories. Until, in his late works, Beckett can leave that narrative structure completely and irrevocably, the claims of the theological, taking effect as destiny, theodicy, and eschatology, will persist in haunting the lives of his characters.

Perhaps, as even Nietzsche was willing to acknowledge, the old stories that religion provided once served humanity well; our ancestors needed the consolations of theodicy, needed faith in a supervenient, otherworldly salvation and redemption. But, as he also argued, those same stories are no longer needed; and they have become tyrannically oppressive and inimical to life. Salvation now lies in renouncing the old stories—the "endgame" of theology. In Beckett's *Endgame,* we see just how exhausted, how weak, those old stories have become. Cavell offers an interpretation of that work for the stage, stating what reflections the work provokes:

> The greatest endgame is Eschatology, the idea that the last things of earth will have an order and justification, a sense. That is what we hoped for, against hope; that was what salvation would look like. Now we are to know that salvation lies in *reversing* the story, in ending the story of the end, dismantling Eschatology, ending this world of order in order to reverse the curse of the world laid on it in its Judeo-Christian end. Only a life without hope, meaning, justification, waiting, solution [. . .] is free from the curse of God.[21]

Beckett's writing shows he increasingly understood the "grammar" that theology depends on and that it appropriates for the justice of its own designs.

*

In the tenth *Text,* a voice says: "you've got to go on without any of that junk, that's all dead with words, with excess of words, they can say nothing else, [. . .] but they won't say it eternally, they'll find some other nonsense, no matter what, and I'll be able to go on [. . .]" (TN 125). Can we go on—go on living—only if we cling to the old stories? Or can we go on only if we abandon them?

To those who need and want it, religion has always offered consolation. But for many, especially today, what religion requires in return for that consolation is suffocating, is life-denying. Ironically, it is the essential *otherworldliness* of religion, the very thing that has made religion powerfully appealing, even deeply needed, that is, for Beckett's characters, precisely what makes it also useless, empty-handed, oppressive. Many today are unable to endure its oppressiveness and otherworldliness; yet many others, we know, still feel that they cannot live without the transcendence, the meaningfulness that religion provides. And yet everyone, even the most stubborn skeptic, can feel something of the loss, the emptiness of a world without the story of God. A voice in the fourth of Beckett's *Texts* nicely sums up the argument:

> There has to be one, it seems [a story, namely], once there is speech, no need of a story, a story is not compulsory, just a life, that's the mistake I made, one of the mistakes, to have wanted a story for myself, whereas life alone is enough. (TN 93)

As long as there is life, there is speech; and speech makes stories. There will always be stories, and a need for stories—only, we might hope, not the theodicies that impose their mysterious curses, their finalities of fate. Those are stories we do not need. But there are many other stories inherited from religion that enrich life, giving it meaningfulness, when illuminated by those stories, from beginning to end.

As noted earlier, Beckett's narrator in *Texts for Nothing* declares that, "it's the end that gives meaning to words" (TN, 111). These loaded words, reminiscent of Eliot's verse in "East Coker" (1940), make a claim that bears on meaning both as language and as eschatology. The beginnings of his tales are always struggles against repetition: not only the power of the past to determine the new beginning, but also the power of the beginning to determine the fate of the ending. Correspondingly, the endings of his tales are always struggles against closure, closure of meaning: not only the power of the present to determine the future ending, but also the power of the ending to determine the meaning of the beginning.[22] Beckett's post-war stories show he understood how, in writing plays and prose fiction, his struggles to handle the narration of their beginnings and endings could become a source of inspiration, and an analogue, for his representation of the ways that our mortal creaturely life has struggled to survive—amid protest—in a world-order shaped and framed by the teleologies, theodicies, and eschatologies which the Judeo-Christian stories have imposed. In both their narrative content and their deviant grammatical form, his stories dramatically embody and enact the double-edged, often traumatic meaning of those theological inventions.

Just as Beckett sought to disrupt the tyranny of the logic of identity ordaining the ends and endings in the construction of the stories he wanted to tell, so he sought to disrupt the tyranny of that same logic in the narratives of Judeo-Christian theology. Mischievously using that logic, his stories will indeed show those old narratives "ordained to end" (TN 104). "And thank God for that!"

PART TWO

The Utopian Idea: Remembering the Future in the Past

CHAPTER ONE

Paradise: Nowhere—But Here!

When life is wretched toil, might a man look up and say:
even in these conditions I still want to exist?

FRIEDRICH HÖLDERLIN, "In lovely blueness . . ."[1]

I want to say about Beckett's stories and plays what Adorno argues in his dissertation on Kierkegaard: "eternity shines through"—but only "as the content of transience."[2] Gunnar Hindrichs is thus right in observing that "Adorno holds on to the Idea of salvation, as it were, but only *after* the angels, and the Messiah, have plunged down to earth and into their death."[3] On similar grounds, Jay Bernstein argues, in regard to Beckett, that, "If there is a Utopian moment in Beckett [i.e., a time of reconciliation], and I will agree that there is, it is not named or namable, for you cannot get there from here."[4] Although my own readings concur with these interpretations, my claim in this chapter is that, in Beckett, as in Adorno's reading of Beckett, there are moments when the Idea of an earthly paradise—the promise of happiness—shines through.[5]

The gods have departed; but the Idea of paradise still beckons—or perhaps, because we find ourselves in a god-forsaken condition, it beckons more than ever. And Beckett records the evidence, even when, thoroughly ambiguous and contestable, appearing briefly and in the negative, it is represented only by the art of fiction: "this voice its promises and solaces all imagination" (H 79). Is the happiness in justice possible for us? And the justice of that happiness? Why go on? And how? Beckett's persistent questions.

*

Beckett's allusions to paradise, the utopian Idea, are mostly expressed in very concrete images. In *Malone Dies*, the narrative treats us to the invocation of a certain "foretaste of paradise," but promptly declares it a mockery (MD 266). What are we to make of the traces and ciphers, metaphors and allegories evoking the promise of happiness that Beckett has woven into his stories? Might we understand them as word-images that attempt to redeem the hope for a kinder world—that world of happiness toward the creation of which all good-hearted people are ceaselessly striving? Understatement: "The world of the happy is different from that of the unhappy."[6]

Hölderlin's question is also Beckett's. When asking his question, the poet looks up into the sky. Occasionally, Beckett's characters will also look up towards the sky: a sky sometimes of the night, filled with the shimmering lights of the stars, sometimes a sky of the day, made radiant by the splendour of the sun—but at other times what appears is a sky clouded and gray, either promising or threatening the coming of rain. Does the sky announce any promise? Many of Beckett's skies are a lovely blue; but there are also some pitch-black skies, such as Blanchot, a careful reader of Beckett, recalls in *The Writing of Disaster*: skies that Beckett will describe—but not without inserting the vibrations of a "better" that leaves meaning suspended in the dark—as "black night or better blackness pure and simple" (IS 85).[7] These blackened skies would seem to bespeak a certain nihilism, voiding any hint of the sublime: "Blackness in its might at last. Where no more to be seen. [. . .] Absence supreme good" (ibid.) This would seem to assert that there is nothing to the beyond, although Beckett will immediately add, suggesting that there might still be the possibility of something promising: "and yet." Our metaphysical hopes persist, despite the fact that, as Beckett sees our world, promising "events" of encouragement have come to naught. We can no longer see in the sky its sublimity: neither the Christian nor the Kantian. In fact, city lights now totally block the light of the stars—stars which, by the time their light reaches us, might already be dead.

Despite the iconoclasm and the profound skepticism that Beckett's characters express or imply, sometimes in mockery or buffoonery, sometimes in biting contempt, with regard to religious rituals and doctrines; despite the scenery of nihilism—the desolate wastelands, the ruins, the empty places filled with loneliness—all of which is not so much an attack on religion as it is an unblinking look into the souls that inhabit our modernity; and despite sharply critical references and allusions to theodicy and the dispensations of divine justice it has authorized, the divine is an almost constant and pervasive presence in Beckett's stories and plays: an allegorical presence, even if only in the physiognomic distortions and other peculiarities of the prose. The world in which Beckett's characters dwell is a world that, whilst abandoned by God, remains coloured by that presence, still occasionally illuminated by world-disclosive epiphanies sustaining the felt significance of the divine operations. Because we still feel a need to keep in some kind of contact with the non-identical, an ideality that does not exist in our world, those momentary epiphanies encourage and confirm our aspirations for humanity. Indeed, virtually every appearance of beauty in Beckett's stories seems to speak to our utopian dreams; but this beauty is invariably ephemeral, and somehow ruined, its passing moment leaving the world once again dark, destitute and bereft, a charnel house of the spirit. Paradise appears in Beckett's stories—but only as so many metaphors substituting for the still missing profane translation of the utopian Idea, the promise of happiness his words are struggling to bear.

But at least there are occasional evocations of light and its transfigurations, promising words breaking into the darkness, words drawing our attention to the allegorical signs of hope: flashes, gleams, and rays of light, as in the tenth of the *Texts for Nothing*; images, as in *Enough*, of gentle green hills, a meadow abundant with flowers, and the shade and shelter of the forests; invocations of wondrous gardens, as in *Molloy*; references, as in *Malone Dies*, to stars lighting up the night sky; and, as in *Lessness*, evocations of an "open sky" and a "passing cloud," harbinger of rains for a parched earth. Beckett puts flowers in some of his stories. Typically, of course, they are a metaphorical indication of carefree happiness, hence of a world of freedom and justice, everything right, just as it should be; but invariably, he finds a way to make that association problematic. However, the nihilism is not yet absolute—Beckett's writing, even in the late works, still retains traces or hints of the promise, although whether these signs are promising indications of what is to come or ominous indications, instead, of what will eventually be denied, remains to be seen:

> And were there one day to be here, where there are no days, [. . .] a gleam of light, still all would be silent and empty and dark, as now, as soon now, when all will be ended, all said [. . .]. (TN 140)

The mood is subjunctive, densely intricate, expressing longing, the abandonment of hope and finally, perhaps, some measure of serenity. We cannot be certain, even if there is a gleam or ray of light, that it is a confirmation of the promise, an intimation of what is coming. For all we know, it might instead be nothing but the still glimmering vestige, the remaining trace, of a possibility no longer available. The flowers in that meadow, which Beckett, in *Enough*, conjures into being, are trampled underfoot. And in *The Calmative*, another story of calamity, as the title is telling us, there once were stars lighting the wretched man's way; but the character tells us that he raised his eyes to the sky without any hope, because, in his words, "the light I stepped in put out the stars, assuming they were there, which I doubted, remembering the clouds."[8]

In such luminous manifestations, there are some significant affinities with lyric poetry. Adorno notes, in this regard: "In industrial society, the lyric idea of a self-restoring immediacy becomes—where it does not impotently evoke a romantic past—more and more something that flashes out abruptly, something in which what is possible overcomes its own impossibility."[9] All the utopian Idea can do now, in our time, is appear in a flash, a gleam, a glimmer; conditions do not permit it to linger, to endure, to accomplish its promise.

*

Back home, after a year's futile journey in search of Molloy, Moran, in Part Two of the novel *Molloy*, records happily settling again into the routines of everyday life. "They were," he confides, reminiscing about the days immediately following his return, "the longest, loveliest days of all the year. I lived in the garden" (MO 169). He likes plants, he tells us, even seeing in them, possibly because of their organized beauty, or their sheer persistence, a "proof of the existence of God" (MO 94). There is one other invocation of a garden in the novel *Molloy*. In Part One, Molloy describes "a night of listening, a night given to the faint soughing and sighing stirring at night in little pleasure gardens, the shy sabbath of leaves and petals and the air that eddies there as it does not in other places [. . .]" (MO 44). There is another reference to a sabbath, once again suggesting, possibly, the promise of happiness, if not an earthly garden of paradise, as when Moran, about to set out on his quest for Molloy, tells us that "The sun's beams shone through the rift in the curtains and made visible the sabbath of the motes" (MO 94). He "rejoiced" in this sunlight. But the revelation this promising sunshine makes could be misleading: as the allusion to Matthew 7:3 implies, it might be just an illusion for the apparition of which a mote, a defect in the eyes— or, by metaphorical extension, a spiritual failing—is responsible. Soon, though, Moran concedes he was wrong in his forecast: "the weather was fine no longer, the sky was clouding over, soon it would rain." "But," he adds, "For the moment the sun was still shining. It was on this that I went, with inconceivable levity, having nothing else to go on" (ibid.). What encouragement does it take to "go on"? Why should the sun still shining not be enough for the moment?

Recalling Kant's words in concluding his *Critique of Practical Reason*,[10] Moran tells of a certain wonderful moment of happiness during his long and arduous journey: "I gave thanks for evening that brings out the lights, the stars in the sky and on earth the brave little lights of men" (MO 153). It is not God that inspires him to go on; it is the beauty of the stars in the sky and the welcoming lights in the homes where we mortals dwell that gives him the courage to go on. Later, however, approaching Ballyba, a distorted, garbled recapitulation of the ancient city, beloved for its paradisiacal gardens, he watches the spectacle of the urban lights briefly dispelling the darkness of the night and, perhaps reminded, in his proximity, of all the moral failings of humanity, he now curses the "foul little flickering lights of terrified men" (MO 156). But at least the stars are still twinkling in the sky—provided that the lights of the city do not render them—and a dimension infinitely beyond our powers of measurement, which their presence might remind us of—hopelessly invisible, as nowadays happens.

In the ninth *Text for Nothing*, seeking words of hope—a "way out"— for a world enduring unspeakable misery, a way out borne perhaps by his words, the narrating voice says:

If I could say there's a way out there, there's a way out somewhere, the rest would come, the other words, sooner or later, and the power to get there, and the way to get there, and pass out, and see the beauties of the skies and see the stars again. (TN 121)

The same images again, promising happiness, promising a way out. Have the words that bear the promise of happiness been found? They are all controlled by a conditional grammar, the grammar of hopeless longing. But is there not something redeeming in these words, connecting the promise of happiness and the beauty of nature? Kant saw in the beauty of nature a symbol of morality. Experiencing the beauty of nature is not sufficient as grounding for morality; nor can it suffice to create the world of peace and justice that the promise of happiness signifies. But if the power of our damaged words could be redeemed, so that they would have once again the power to reveal and redeem what they invoke in an act of creation and renewal, perhaps it would not be absurd to hope that, in both senses of "rest," "the rest would come."

*

Gazing out of the window after a heavy rain, Jacques Moran notices that the rain has stopped. And he records for us that significant moment:

Not only had the rain stopped, but in the west scarves of fine red sheen were mounting in the sky. I felt them rather than saw them [. . .]. A great joy, it is hardly too much to say, surged over me at the sight of so much beauty, so much promise. (MO 111)

But that moment of beauty does not last. There is promise in such beauty and beauty, too, in the promise: the redeeming of the promise of happiness, a redeeming that thoughtfully engaged words, poetic words, even damaged and corrupted words, as still bearing that promise, might set in motion. But what is that promise worth, if it does not release our world from the injustices that, as Beckett's stories show us in so many different ways, cause endless human misery, lives in abject desperation? Beckett's words see the beauty; they can even imagine paradise in a garden; but they cannot forget all the suffering that weighs heavily upon them.

In *The Unnamable*, the principal voice, obsessed with the fate of a character he calls Worm, hears a voice, or maybe just sounds, and imagines him "lost in the smoke"; but he goes on, in his monologue, to assure us that "it is not real smoke, there is no fire, no matter, strange hell that has no heating, no denizens." And then, suddenly, he ventures this momentous conjecture:

perhaps it's paradise, perhaps it's the light of paradise, and the solitude, and this voice the voice of the blest interceding invisible, for the living, for the dead, all is possible. (UN 352–353)

Perhaps, we might say. But the only thing we can say we know is that all is possible in the realm of fiction. But is the promise of happiness—the paradise of justice, peace, and happiness to be created right here on earth—nothing but fiction? Is it possible *only* in fiction?[11] In imagining how Kleist might have mischievously read Kant, James Phillips is provoked to declare: "Humanity *aspires* to paradise out of folly, humanity is *in* paradise out of folly, and humanity is *indifferent* to paradise out of folly."[12]

In the course of his long, brooding monologue, Malone, apparently confined to his deathbed, adverts to things reduced to "sand, or dust, or ashes," evoking "the blessedness of absence": an alchemical metamorphosis, one that seems to end in disappointment, but perhaps, instead, it is actually consummated in a strange, new experience of happiness, released from the oppressive weight of old theological stories (MD 216). Soon after that melancholy remark Malone, apparently hallucinating, tells us about the wondrous beauty he sees momentarily revealed in his room. The lyrical beauty of Beckett's prose, and the images it creates, now take us into the depths of a pathos that somehow belies its heart-rending abjection:

> When I open staring wide my eyes I see at the confines of this restless gloom a gleaming and shimmering as of bones [. . .]. And I can even distinctly remember the paper-hangings or wall-paper still clinging in places to the walls and covered with a writhing mass of roses, violets, and other flowers in such profusion that it seemed to me I had never seen so many in the whole course of my life, nor of such beauty. But now they seem to be all gone, quite gone, and if there were no flowers on the ceiling, there was no doubt something else, cupids perhaps, gone too, without leaving a trace. (MD 217)[13]

But in fact, that beauty *has* left a trace: after all, its apparition, however ephemeral, is at least preserved in the traces of print that now tell of it. Perhaps such beauty, with the modest but real happiness it offered, *requires* that transience, appearing suddenly, and only for an instant, leaving nothing but shimmering traces of its passage. Allegorical messengers of redeeming love, angels of care, *do* occasionally pass through our world, reminding us of our forgotten humanity and the moral claim of the past, its injustices crying out for correction, belatedly accomplishing what was missed. The messengers encourage faith and hope; but they will vanish into nothingness if not recognized and welcomed when they happen to appear. These redeeming angels of paradise are creations of grammar: their work retrieving from the past its missed or unfulfilled potentialities is written in the future anterior.[14] We should not be surprised that Beckett's lyricism draws him into the melancholy grammar of the conditional and the subjunctive.

In the first of the *Texts for Nothing*, the narrating voice evokes a "glorious prospect," only to remark, in a Nabokovian type of pun suggesting an act performed by the writer, that that promising prospect, that sudden appearance of paradise, is "blotted out" by the mist.

*

Lessness, a late work (1969), carries Beckett's prose experiments with subtraction and reduction close to the most extreme limit, forming units of thought contained in brief phrases that seem like gasps hoping for breath, some bearing immediately understandable meaning, some without: twenty-four paragraphs, each one composed of seven sentences, the units rhythmically repeated and assembled in different ways, like musical motifs, but creating a vertiginous experience.[15] The text, "*Sans*," in its original French title, is without conventional punctuation, hence without the determinate, fairly stable meanings that punctuation is designed to assure, and without finality or closure. Different configurations of words are accordingly possible, rendering different constellations of meaning.

There is just one character, a human being with a gray face and a little gray body, described by the narrator as appearing in a gray light and in the midst of a desolate landscape of ash-gray ruins, endlessness not only in the topographic sense, but also, I think, in the theological sense: "All sides endlessness earth sky as one." This is not a promising infinity, but rather endlessness without meaning, without purpose—mechanical. There is "no stir not a breath," on this desert of "endless flatness." Without sounds, without movement, time cannot be reckoned: the creature is lost in timelessness. "He will curse God again," the narrator says, "as in the blessed days face to the open sky the passing deluge." Even in "the blessed days," he was not satisfied. He has been facing life dependent on illusions, dreams, figments of the imagination. The illusions defied reason, chased its "light" away. So a dawn will come, dispelling the illusions, the fantasies; and with the dusk, their powerful spell will finally be ended: "Figment dawn dispeller of figments and the other called dusk." The figments are at last to be recognized as such: "Never but imagined the blue in a wild imagining the blue celeste of poesy." The spellbinding power of the dreams, the illusions of the imagination, no longer work. Nevertheless, "He will live again." Indeed: "On him will rain again as in the blessed days of blue the passing cloud." For now, though, there is no cloud to bring to the desert the rain of good fortune, the reign of happiness, "as in the blessed days of blue." And so, after the "blessed days" of the past, whether real or imaginary, "unhappiness will reign again." But at least the man can no longer find refuge in his fantasies, his illusions. And he did have a "foretaste" of paradise. The "happy dream," assuring us that life is blessed with divine purposiveness, some authoritative guarantee of meaningfulness, is just a dream. But the last words in this story affirm the possibility of a new life of freedom, a new "paradise" of the promised happiness, when life is at last lived in "lessness"—without any mystical assignment of destiny, hence of guilt, and without the false enchantments and consolations of the old religions: "Figment dawn dispeller of figments [. . .]." Language, bearing the promise, here spells out our enlightenment in the dispelling of the archaic, mythic spells of our culture.

As I noted earlier, the subtraction of punctuation creates ambiguities and instabilities of meaning, opening this text to alternative readings. *Lessness* might seem, at first, to be a story of the utmost hopelessness, all ruination, ash and grayness. But that impression overlooks the allusions to rain and an open sky—and, most significantly, the invocations of the color blue, the blue skies, and the flower that is blue.

*

In Novalis's novel, *Heinrich von Ofterdingen*, the character tells us about his "dream of a blue flower."[16] And in not one but two of Beckett's stories, stories belonging to his early, pre-war period, a blue flower appears, each time ambiguously symbolizing, or suggesting, love and happiness, an experience of paradise on earth. In *Assumption* (1929), an early pre-war story, we read about a strange character who longed "to be released in one splendid drunken scream and fused with the cosmic discord."[17] The man is engaged in a cosmic "struggle for divinity," in the course of which he "hungered to be irretrievably engulfed in the light of eternity, one with the birdless cloudless colourless skies, in infinite fulfillment," achieving "the blue flower, Vega, GOD. . . ." And in *Sedendo et Quiescendo* (1932), a crazy story that reads like a parody of Joyce, Belacqua is reported to have "inscribed to his darling blue flower some of the finest Night of May hiccupsobs that ever left a fox's paw sneering and rotting in a snaptrap."[18]

Other stories simply invoke flowers—meadows of flowers: as when, in *Enough*, an old man and a child are said to plod on through a field of flowers. But the image of beauty, typically implying happiness, is quickly destroyed, for, as pointed out earlier, Beckett's narrator tells us that, as they cross these fields, they are trampling on the flowers, crushing them under their feet. Recalling Hölderlin's metaphors, "words like flowers," "the flower of the mouth," we might wonder, knowing Beckett's fraught experience with words: Are these flowers they trample on also words?[19]

Now, as regards the significance of Beckett's invocations of "blessed days of blue," the "blue celeste of poesy," and the blue that figures "in a wild imagining," I think we need to recall some lines from Hölderlin's late poem, "In lovely blue":

As long as kindness lasts,
Pure, within his heart, he may gladly measure himself
Against the divine. Is God unknown?
Is he manifest as the sky? This I tend
To believe. Such is man's measure.
Well deserving, yet poetically,
Man dwells on this earth. But the shadow
Of the starry night is no more pure, if I may say so,

Than man, said to be the image of God.
Is there measure on earth? There is
None.[20]

In *Lessness*, as in Hölderlin's poem, the blue unquestionably refers to the transfer of the heavenly, the divine, to a utopian, *earthly* paradise of love and happiness. However, Beckett's words in these texts do not positively and unequivocally affirm the promise of happiness, and they certainly do not confirm its triumph. They are merely acknowledgements of our finest, most fervent hopes and dreams, ways of recognizing and expressing the spirit's irrepressible longing for beauty, and for the blessed happiness that is symbolized by the blue of the sky and the blue of the flower of love. Beckett shows us a desolate world, seemingly abandoned by God, in which, *nevertheless*, vestiges of the old story remain, fragments of faith kept alive in longing and languishment, and in the memories imagination invents to give that longing an object.

The old story is finished; but the new cannot yet be told. The words for that fail to come; the event fails to happen. In the meantime, Beckett tells stories in words that bear witness to our plight, our longing, and our hopes. No matter how gray and grim his words, no matter how impoverished and weak they are, by virtue of their struggle, they are still keeping and vouchsafing the promise: they are at least redeeming the spirit of language. For the time being, we must find contentment, an imperfect happiness, in our freedom from the consoling illusions of the past and in the courage to go on without them.

CHAPTER TWO

Tales for Children: Retrieving the Enchantment

*To reduce the imagination to a state of slavery—
even though it would mean the elimination of what
is commonly called happiness—is to betray all sense
of absolute justice within oneself. Imagination alone
offers me some intimation of what can be.*

ANDRÉ BRETON, *First Manifesto of Surrealism* (1924)[1]

*Infancy is the perpetual Messiah which comes into the arms
of fallen men, and pleads with them to return to paradise.*

RALPH WALDO EMERSON, "Nature"[2]

In "The Gigantic Toy as Legend," Ernst Bloch argues that "The fairy tale is just as much the first enlightenment as it is, in its proximity to humankind, its proximity to happiness, the model for the last enlightenment."[3] In keeping with this insight, one that Benjamin likewise expressed, I shall claim in this chapter that a compelling interpretation of how Beckett's works bear the utopian promise of happiness cannot ignore his inheritance of the fairy tale.

In "Serena II," part of "Echo's Bones," a long poem Beckett wrote in 1933, there is a significant invocation of fairy tales. Addressed to young children, it reminds them to say their prayers at bedtime:

[. . .] the fairy tales of Meath ended,
So say your prayers now and go to bed
your prayers before the lamps start to

sing behind the larches
here at these knees of stones
then to bye-bye on the bones[4]

Before all else a storyteller, Beckett drew for inspiration on the fairy tale tradition, not only acknowledging it in various allusions, but even, in his early years as a writer (October 1936–March 1937), attempting to produce, in German, a proper fairy tale of his own: "The Tale of the Young Man and the Old Man,"[5] only a fragment, a story he never finished, modeled after the traditional tales for young children, like something written by the Grimm brothers, Jacob and Wilhelm, who gathered ethnographic material for their folk tales, one of which is a story they called "The Old Man and his Grandson."[6] Surprising though it may seem, Beckett was, in his early years as a writer of fiction, a voracious reader of fairy tales. He got encouragement from reading them for his own work of storytelling. Besides studying stories by the Grimms, Beckett studied stories by Hans Christian Andersen and by the Comtesse Marie d'Aulnoy, whose "L'oiseau bleu" figures in "What a Misfortune," a tale in *More Pricks than Kicks*. In *Dream of Fair to Middling Women* (1931–1932), which also borrows from d'Aulnoy, Beckett reflects, at a certain moment, on his various appropriations of the fairy tale genre: "Extraordinary," he says, "how everything ends like a fairy-tale, or can be made to; even the most unsanitary episodes."[7]

Traces of narrative features typical of the fairy tale genre can be found in many of Beckett's stories. Indeed, the narrator in *How It Is* will explicitly describe the story he is recounting as "this faery" (H 132) and "this old tale" (H 106); and he will remind us of "the little fables of above," the stories of his childhood, that he occasionally likes to interpolate into the story of his present life (H 128).

In *The Unnamable*, the narrator pauses in his storytelling to reflect on what he has been telling us, saying, "I see myself slipping, though not yet at the last extremity, towards the resorts of fable" (UN 302). And in the course of mourning the death of his entire family, he recalls relating his life history as a bedtime story to his sleepy children (UN 312).

The narrator in *The Calmative*, telling us that, to calm himself, he will tell us a story, says "I'll tell my story in the past [. . .], as though it were a myth, or an old fable [. . .]."[8] And soon thereafter, awaiting a great transformative event, he declares:

But it's to me this evening something has to happen, to my body as in myth and metamorphosis [. . .]. Yes, this evening it has to be in the story my father used to read to me, evening after evening, when I was small [. . .].

And he then proceeds to tell us a story, presumably his own, although occasionally it seems he is living in the bedtime story his father told, a story that at many turns seems like a ghost story, with strange people, odd coincidences, events too improbable, too fantastic to be believed, and abrupt changes of place such as happen only in our dreams and tales for children.

In the first part of *Molloy* (also published in 1947), Molloy, venturing on a journey to find his mother, found himself in the menacing darkness of a primeval forest where "there reigned a kind of blue gloom" (MO 77). Day after day, and night after night, he sought ways to get out of this forest; but as time passed, he became increasingly convinced, enigmatically referring to an "imperative" he had disregarded, that his sojourn within its power was a question of his state of moral confusion. Eventually, however, after days and nights of great exertion, he was able to make his way out of the forest. But as the story ends, Molloy confessed that he "longed to go back into the forest." The forest is certainly not enchanting; but its mysterious grip on him is reminiscent of the forests under wicked spells that figure in many of the tales for children.

In Beckett's "Tale of the Young Man and the Old Man," which, as I said, is reminiscent of "The Old Man and His Grandson," the fairy tale is "exposed," as John Pilling has pointed out, "to the conditions prevalent in the world within which the characters dwell, and this breaks the tale's 'spell.'"[9] In writing to his German friend, Axel Kaun, Beckett defined this narrative trick as his "nominalist irony." The tale was halted mid-sentence; it offers no future, no "good news." And, as Pilling argues convincingly, although Beckett ventures into fantasy, the story gets "worsted by the force of reality."[10] Ultimately, therefore, Beckett invents only "the spectral suggestion of a fairy tale." "So it goes in the world," he will say, never satisfied to tell stories that encourage, as fairy tales often do, our most ill-conceived fantasies of wish fulfillment. "So it goes in the world": these words, which Beckett found many occasions to repeat, are the very words with which the Grimms end their story about "How the Cat and the Mouse set up House."

So Beckett abandoned his "Tale of the Young Man and the Old Man," but he did not forget it. In *Worstward Ho* (1983), one of his last stories, his unnamed narrator tells about an old man and a child, picturing them, in an image of incomparable poignancy and beauty, holding hands and plodding on, as if headed into eternity:

> Hand in hand with equal plod they go. [. . .] The child hand raised to reach the holding hand. Hold the old holding hand.[. . .] Slowly with never a pause plod on and never recede.[. . .] Joined by held holding hands. Plod on as one.[11]

And, varying the motif, in *Enough* (1965) he wrote a story about an old man and an old woman. Narrated this time by the woman in her old age, the story is formed by her reminiscences: their time together, walking through flowering meadows and climbing the gentle hills. The ending of the story is strikingly similar to the ending he will later write for *Worstward Ho*:

"Now I'll wipe out everything but the flowers. No more rain. No more mounds. Nothing but the two of us dragging through the flowers."[12] In both stories, the depiction of tenderness exudes an atmosphere of sadness. They are obviously not bedtime stories for children; yet they manifestly draw their inspiration from the fairy tale genre.

What explains Beckett's attraction to this genre? Why did he make use of it as a paradigm for telling stories? The first answer that no doubt comes to mind pertains to the craft and art of writing fiction: the genre is simply a good narrative form to learn from. But as I want the two epigrams that I placed at the beginning of this discussion to suggest, there is a much deeper motivation. No genre condenses the struggle between good and evil, fantasy and reality, enchantment and disillusionment more compellingly than the fairy tale. Moreover, in their magical power to conjure and annihilate, Beckett's words show the power of words over the very being of beings. This power is the essence of fairy tales. Furthermore, in the language of no other genre is the promise of happiness in the spirit of enlightenment brought so immediately into contact with our felt sense of its meaning. Beckett intuitively understood how the fairy tale again and again taps into the unconscious world of infancy, breathing life into the earliest version of utopian or messianic dreams, whilst at the same time it conjures into presence the terrifying monsters whose evil powers oppose and thwart the realization of those dreams.

Beckett will never sacrifice the storyteller's responsibility to truth for the sake of fantasy. Nevertheless, he does not hesitate to draw on the enchantments of fairy tales whenever they might serve the promise of truth. And, in his endings, the childhood dream-memory that was awakened will be shattered by a return to reality that emphasizes the difference, the non-identity, for the sake of revealing and intensifying the long-lost longing for paradise. Reproducing the infant dream-memory, Beckett's words make its spirit into material for a mature adventure in the world of the present. And nothing can convey the transformative energy of the word better than the fairy tale. And Beckett's little story, *Imagination Dead Imagine*, draws on that very energy.

*

Before concluding these reflections on children's stories and bedtime prayers, I want us to consider Benjamin's claim in his 1934 commemorative essay on Kafka. In this essay, he reflects on the German nursery folk song, "The Little Hunchback." "This little man," he says, "is only at home in distorted life; he will disappear with the coming of the Messiah [. . . .]."[13] Beckett's characters resemble this hunchback. And I would like to believe that he wished for them all a real life of happiness, the justice they deserve. There is textual support for this conviction. But Beckett could never share Benjamin's utopian or messianic faith. The closest he could let himself come to such faith was to tell stories in which, as if in response to the longing and the mourning they stirred, traces and echoes of the promise of happiness would occasionally appear for a moment of exquisite lyrical beauty before fading and passing away.

Benjamin concludes his remarks on this bedtime story, which bids children to pray for the poor hunchback, arguing that, "even if Kafka did not pray—and this we do not know—he still possessed in the highest degree what Malebranche called 'the natural prayer of the soul': attentiveness. And in this attentiveness he included all living creatures, as saints include them in their prayers." In Beckett, too, we encounter this painstaking attentiveness. It is the rigorous consciousness of the storyteller, one who serves as witness—witness for the beauty of the utopian or messianic Idea.

Infancy lives, perhaps, in a perpetual messianicity, a messianicity without messianism; however, as Mallarmé would soberly remind us, in the enlightenment of maturity, the infant must relinquish its ecstasy.[14] Paradise lost? What remains of that surpassed experience? Beckett never forgets, never betrays the child's memory of happiness; but his "nominalist irony" deprives us of the dream in the very instant that he awakens it, so that, for the sake of its promise, the meaning of our longing may be intensely felt. For him, the infant's paradise is a belated construction. In truth, it never was.

CHAPTER THREE

Hope and Despair in a Time of Mourning

[I]n hope we have been saved, but hope that is seen is not hope; for who hopes for what he already sees? But if we hope for what we do not see, we must wait with perseverance [. . .].

ST. PAUL, *Epistle to the Romans*

What's past and what's to come is strew'd with husks/ and formless ruin of oblivion.

WILLIAM SHAKESPEARE, *Troilus and Cressida*

§1

Dead End?

In an interview that took place late in his life, Heidegger avowed his desperate hope: "Only another God," he said, "could save us."[1] Is Heidegger right? I think it fair to say, at least, that Beckett wants no more gods. But is he waiting, as Badiou seems to think, for some apocalyptic event? Perhaps nothing more eventful than the coming of words—the words he needs to tell his stories.

In his attempt to understand Kierkegaard, Adorno formulated an insight that would remain with him throughout his intellectual life: "No truer image of hope can be imagined than that of ciphers readable as traces, dissolving in history, disappearing in front of our overflowing eyes, indeed confirmed in lamentation. In these tears of despair, the ciphers appear as incandescent figures, dialectically, as compassion, comfort, and hope."[2]

Beckett's characters are entangled in the aporia of an implacable dialectic, trapped between vainly hoping and abandoning all hope, unable to hope wholeheartedly, but unable to give up altogether: "A pity hope is dead. No. How one hoped above, on and off. With what diversity" (TN 84). Is there then no hope? "Good gracious, no, heavens, what an idea! Just a faint one perhaps, but which will never serve" (UN 359). We desperately need hope: "We must have the heavens and God knows what besides, lights, luminaries, the three-monthly ray of hope and the gleam of consolation."[3] However, the instant that a little hope emerges, it is vanquished, because "at each slow ebb hope slowly dawns that it is dying."[4] Nevertheless, it seems: "Better hope deferred than none. Up to a point. Till the heart starts to sicken. Company too up to a point. Better a sick heart than none. Till it starts to break."[5]

Many years earlier, in August 1936, Beckett had written in his "Clare Street" notebook this thought:

> There are moments when the veil of hope is finally torn apart and the suddenly liberated eyes catch sight of *their* world, as it is, as it must be. Unfortunately, it does not last long, the revelation ["*Wahrnehmung,*" usually meaning perception] quickly passes, the eyes can bear such pitiless light only for a brief time, the membrane of hope forms again and one returns to the world of phenomena.[6]

Beckett here conceives of hope dialectically, rendering it in the figure of a membrane, a veil. Hope, or faith, belongs simultaneously to the destitute world in which we actually live, as hope for release, and to the visionary world, that for which we long. But at the same time that hope connects us to the visionary world of which we dream, it is also a veil or membrane that keeps us sealed within our destitution, our mourning and melancholy. Hope, as a longing for what is other, diverts and drains our energy, our capacity to change the actuality of our world. Dead end?

§2

Ashes

In *Prometheus Unbound*, Shelley gives the final words in the play to Demogorgon, who urges all whom his words have gathered "to hope till Hope creates from its own wreckage the thing it contemplates."[7] It is only in that uncanny dialectical way, in ciphers that provoke "tears of despair,"[8] that Beckett will permit his stories and works for the stage to encourage a sense of hope. There is in this twist of negativity a rigorous faith in telling the truth.

In *Endgame* (1957), Beckett's Hamm tells a story that, in some ways, expresses with aesthetic perfection a vision that I believe to have a certain affinity with Beckett's own vision of the world:

> I once knew a madman who thought the end of the world had come. [...] I had a great fondness for him. I used to go and see him, in the asylum. I'd take him by the hand and drag him to the window. Look! There! All that rising corn! And there! Look! The sails of the herring fleet! All that loveliness! [*Pause.*] He'd snatch away his hand and go back to his corner. Appalled. All he had seen was ash.[9]

This deeply moving scene is an evocation of loss and mourning: an evocation, above all, of the vision of one who understands the finitude, the transience and ephemerality, of all earth-bound things. It is a vision that sees them in a dying light. Perhaps like that of Anaximander, who saw divine justice at work in the passing away of all things. Or like what Heraclitus saw, writing that the fairest universe is nothing but a heap of dust. Or like the vision of Empedocles, who leaped into the furious fires of Aetna, surrendering his body to purifications that would reduce him to ash. It is not, however, as most commentaries assume, a story that confirms Beckett's nihilism, but in fact a story that tells us the very opposite. It is not, as many readers have been tempted to suppose, a story about someone who rejects this life, but someone who loves it too much. The intensity of the man's reaction implies, rather, a strong emotional investment in the beauty of this world. He has seen all the loveliness, but also, like Sir Thomas Browne, author of *Religio Medici*, he sees, or foresees, the imminence of an inevitable transience, the final judgment of fate, always present in the whole of nature, turning everything to ash. And precisely because of his attachment, the immensity of his caring, the sight of so much doomed loveliness, or the distress over the prospect of loss, is unbearable. Its reduction to ash is appalling. And it is all the more so, says Beckett, "though you may stoop with fingers of compassion/ to endorse the dust,"[10] since the fate of that beauty seems to symbolize—to spell—the fate of the promise of happiness.

Will anything that that "madman" cares about remain for him in this life? Is ash—Malone's words in question—a sign of blessedness (MD 216)? Can ash be redeemed? Is it a redeemable substance? Remembering the Holocaust, we cannot argue that this is a foolish question. W. G. Sebald, an admiring reader of Beckett, claims that ash is in fact a redeemed substance: "It is," he argues, "the very last product of combustion, with no more resistance to it. [...] It represents the borderline between being and nothingness. It is a redeemed substance, like dust."[11] Is there anything that might be said to lift this man's spirits? Is he mad? Or is he a visionary who simply knows and sees how all worldly things end?

In *Lessness* (1969), written many years after *Endgame*, the ash motif takes over, reducing everything; and it no longer appears to be merely the vision of a madman. In this tale, "the blessed days of blue" have ended, replaced by a world in ruins, everything now ash gray.[12]

§3

Beckett: Baroque and Romantic poet?

Surprising though it will no doubt seem, despite Beckett's familiarity with the German language and with the phenomenologies of Husserl and Heidegger, I want to propose, drawing on the interpretations of our contemporary world in Benjamin's and Adorno's writings, that, more than any other writer in the twentieth century, Beckett inherited either directly or obliquely from what he knew about those writings something of the literary spirit that figured in the German Baroque *Trauerspiel* and, later, in early German Romanticism. Claims of inheritance and influence, claims of wide extension, such as the one I am suggesting here, will always generate skepticism, controversy, and the naming of counter-examples. This is as it should be. So if the interpretation I am proposing deepens and enriches the reading of Beckett's stories and plays, then it will have served its purpose. The merit of my claim depends in part, of course, on how the literary arts in these two periods are to be understood. The speech by Hamm that we have just read is, in this regard, exemplary for discerning the connection to a certain expressive formation in the German Baroque.

What, above all, characterizes the German Baroque, at least according to Benjamin's interpretation, is a vision of nature as an endlessly repeated process of generation, corruption, and dissolution, everything fated to return, as in Beckett's *Fizzles*, to dust and ash, leaving a world relentlessly gray, a "ruinstrewn land," with no manifest prospect of salvation, no firm hope for redemption. In Beckett, this repetition of the German Baroque world, the world of the *Trauerspiel*, is still a world bereft, a world shrouded in melancholy and mourning.

What characterizes early German Romanticism is its unresolvable tension between hope and despair: an irrepressible longing for a morally, politically, and spiritually enlightened world, an earth-bound paradise, and, threatening its "high hopes," an equally strong commitment to the skeptical truth. This Romanticism is torn between its longing for the fulfillment of its dream and its commitment to a sobriety of reason, and a reflectively grounded skepticism, that inevitably induce disillusionment and melancholy. The dialectic of longing and disappointment, its skepticism wrought in a pathos with affinities to the spirit engaged in early German Romanticism, is, after all, at the very heart of *Worstward Ho*, Beckett's very late work, one of his last stories.

§4

Melancholy longing

A dream world glimmers in the background of the soul.
KIERKEGAARD, *Repetition*[13]

Dialectical melancholy does not mourn vanished happiness.
It knows that it is unreachable. But it knows also of the promise
that conjoins the unreachable, precisely in its origin, with the wish.

[. . .] For the true desire of melancholy is nourished on the
idea of an eternal happiness without sacrifice [. . .].
ADORNO, *Kierkegaard: Construction of the Aesthetic*[14]

If, as Kierkegaard writes, 'longing alone is not sufficient for salvation,'
still, the images of beauty devolve upon longing, through which the course
of deliverance, disappearing, must travel if it is ever to lead to landing
and awakening; longing is accordingly the dialectical substratum of a
'doctrine of reconciliation' that Kierkegaard's theology of sacrifice would
like to emancipate from longing. [. . .] But it is [only] by the strength of
the immanence of their content [i.e., the content of the images] that the
sublation of longing is [to be] achieved.
ADORNO, *Kierkegaard: Construction of the Aesthetic*[15]

Worstward Ho (1983), one of the very last stories that Beckett wrote, is all
about longing for something forever unapproachable, something belonging
to the future of a past long lost. In a prose of the most sublime elegiac
lyricism, a voice speaks of this longing, repeating and prolonging the
syllables and liquid sounds that expressively embody and authenticate the
melancholy mood:

> Longing the so-said mind long lost to longing. The so-missaid. So far
> so-missaid. Dint of long longing lost to longing. Long vain longing.
> And longing still. Faintly longing still. Faintly vainly longing still. For
> fainter still. For faintest. Faintly vainly longing for the least of longing.
> Unlessenable least of longing. Unstillable vain last of longing still.[16]

As if Adorno and Beckett were in knowing conversation with one another,
Adorno likewise wrote about an unstillable longing: "The unstillable longing
in the face of beauty," he said, understanding "beauty" to have a moral-
political dimension, and indeed to bear within it, however broken, the
promise of happiness, "is the longing for the fulfillment of what was
promised."[17] This longing is dialectically intricate: not only is it longing for

an unattainable happiness; it is also longing for an end to the suffering inherent in longing, hence longing for an end to longing: "Longing that all go. Dim go. Void go. Longing go. Vain longing that vain longing go."[18]

The narrator in *How It Is*, one of Beckett's countless surrogates, laments the loss of his childhood faith, his belief in the religious doctrines he was taught. But at the same time that he mourns this loss and cannot entirely cease longing for that faith, he also longs to be free of its torments.[19] Is all lost? Not entirely, as long as there is memory and longing, not for the perpetuation of the past, but for something of meaning which was kept in that past.

*

In Kafka's "Before the Law," written in 1915 and first published in 1925, a man from the country is waiting before the open gates of the Moral Law, longing to enter; but for reasons that remain inscrutable he does not ever attempt to pass by the first gatekeeper and go on through the first of the countless gates. He waits at the first gate, perhaps immobilized by his timidity, until, after many years, when about to die, he is told that nothing ever would have prevented him from entering the precincts of the Law. In Beckett's inheritance of that enigmatic story, and of Thomas Mann's 1924 novel, *The Magic Mountain*, which takes place in a sanatorium occupying a mountain summit, Malone tells a story about the fate of Macmann, the young man who, as patient resident in the House of St. John of God, a psychiatric institution where a "principle of justice" (MD 269) is very much in question, watches as the gates of the institution are opened to the outside world by one of the keepers, who then retreated in dread. Are these gates opening the way into Hell or into Heaven? If the gates were opened to receive someone of great importance, the Messiah, perhaps, it seems that no one has come. The waiting has been in vain.

As in the story about the opening of the gates at the psychiatric hospital, Beckett offers many allusions to the coming of a Messiah or the return of Christ. But the allusions are like ephemeral apparitions, nothing more than occasional, fragmentary traces of an enigmatic figure whose very existence is so questionable that, if it did appear, must have already passed by, or if it were to appear, its presence would be so thoroughly unnoticed or unrecognized at the time of its passage that it is as if it had never come, or were never to come. The allusions are as elusive as the various conceptions of messianicity that appear in theological discourse.

In the House of St. John of God, the psychiatric hospital where young Macmann has been sequestered, a man said to look like the Messiah suddenly shows up and proceeds to read out loud a document of duties and prerogatives to be signed. Malone, reporting this event, observes that this strange man is actually improvising, not following a script (MD 249). Somewhat later, according to Malone's narrative, a group of people including the Director of the hospital and a lady noted for her philanthropy are gathered in Macmann's room. There, suddenly, the Director turns to one of the staff, a malevolent man by the name of Lemuel, and asks, "Where is the beautiful young man with the Messiah beard?" Why are they waiting for him? For what are they longing? But if that young bearded man were actually to come—what then?[20]

*

My argument is that, corresponding to the intimate dialectic between hope and despair, symbolically registered by the figures of Heaven and Hell, light and darkness, day and night, garden and swamp, and in rhythms of unrest and tranquility, a dialectic in which Beckett's characters are invariably entangled, despairing and hoping at the same time, there is an equally intimate dialectic, rhythmically expressed, between, in one movement, longing, lamentation, and mourning for the old religion and its theodicy, lost now forever, and, in the counter-movement, a lucid rejection of its sacrifices and a struggling, hopeful resistance to its deceptive consolations. Suspended between the extremes of this dialectic, rejecting yet needing, pushing away yet holding on, his characters drift and wander, like the one who, in Beckett's story *The End*, has ended up making his home in a small rowboat, cast about by the waves, "bereft of purpose," "seeking incessantly" a story, a meaning, words that would acknowledge the actuality of his condition.[21] One can always hear, through Beckett's prose, even when it is most frivolous, absurdly funny, or sarcastic and ironic, the strains of "muted lamentation, panting and exhaling of impossible sorrow, [. . .] as of one buried before his time" (UN 387). His characters live in the destitution of a wasteland, surrounded by ruins, garbage, dust, and ashes, a wasteland that, paradoxically, is also, somehow, as an uncanny effect of the lyricism of the prose, a world that can occasionally reveal its startling earthly beauty, hints—but nothing more than that—of a possible redemptive transformation of the earth-bound world.

*

In this regard, Adorno's emphasis on the utopian role of recollection is worth noting. It can explain why *How It Is* begins with the narrator's memories of childhood and why Beckett took such an interest in tales written for children, the genre that always begins by spelling "once upon a time":

> The reality of the work of art testifies to the possibility of the possible. The object of art's longing, [namely] the reality of what is not, is metamorphosed in art as recollection. Ever since Plato's doctrine of anamnesis, the not-yet-existing has been dreamed of in recollection, which alone concretizes utopia without betraying its existence. Recollection remains bound up with semblance: for even in the past the dream was not reality.[22]

At stake is a recollection moved by a longing for what has never existed: a memory of something that is possible only through the gift of language: in question, then, is how, drawing on the spirit in memory, the words in a literary work of art might bear witness to the promise of happiness.

Adorno will remind us, however, warning that the genuinely new appears only in "the longing for the new, not in the new itself." In an observation of the greatest significance, already recited at length in the Prologue, he argues:

> What takes itself to be utopia remains the negation of what exists and is obedient to it. At the center of contemporary antinomies is that art must be and want to be utopia; and the more utopia is blocked by the real functional order, the more this is true; yet at the same time, art must not be utopia, in order not to betray it by providing semblance and consolation. If the utopia of art were fulfilled, it would be art's temporal end. [. . .] *Through the irreconcilable renunciation of the semblance of reconciliation, art holds fast to the promise of reconciliation in the midst of the unreconciled* [. . .].[23]

This is what lies behind the little story Hamm tells: in his sorrow, his mourning, the man who can see nothing but ash is holding fast to the promise, despite already seeing in catastrophe the beauty of the world. Not to see it as ash would be to avoid seeing the most deeply concealed truth and betray the redeeming possibility.

In *Watt,* Mr. Knott rejects longing, wanting to be free of its inherent anguish: "the longing for longing gone [. . .] the ways down, the ways up, and free, free at last, for an instant free at last, nothing at last." But ceasing to long for something radically better might leave him with nothing: "nothing at last."[24]

I maintain that what is taken to be Beckett's "nihilism" is precisely his uncompromising renunciation, by way of subtraction—what he later calls "lessness"—of *almost* every semblance of reconciliation: a renunciation, a dialectics of negation, that is not advocating nihilism, but precisely holding fast, in faithful longing, to the *promise* of reconciliation, the *promise* of happiness—and the astonishing triumph of the weakest possible meaning, despite the crisis—in the midst of an unredeemed world. Whilst resisting the temptation of any counterfeit reconciliation, Beckett's fictional voices hold fast to that promise through both narrative content (occasional and brief allegorical figures and constellations) and narrative style (occasional moments when the prose rises to dithyrambic heights or shifts into an elegiac lyricism). Thus, for example, in the first of *Texts for Nothing*, after the narrator proclaims the sighting of a "glorious prospect," he immediately contradicts the actuality of the promise, the implicit reconciliation, in that prospect, holding on to it thereafter only as an object of longing: "but for the mist that blotted out everything, valleys, loughs, plain and sea." (TN 75) There are also texts in which the transcendent, renounced but still longed-for, returns, appearing in figures of displacement, its absence kept in presence only by words of remembrance.

*

Beckett's stories easily convince us that we must relinquish the old theodicy, with its guilt, sacrifices, and consolations. But with what are we left? What do we still need? What story, if any, can replace what has been forever blotted out? Later on, reflecting, as before, on his presumed dying, Malone admits that, "it is hard to leave everything." But then he says, in words of heartbreaking poetic beauty:

> The horror-worn eyes linger abject on all they have beseeched so long, in a last prayer, the true prayer at last, the one that asks for nothing. And it is then a little breath of fulfillment revives the dead longings and a murmur is born in the silent world, reproaching you affectionately with having despaired too late. The last word in the way of viaticum. Let us try another way. (MD 270)

In this passage, Malone gives us a key to this release, if there is one: the prayer that asks for nothing. Once despair has brought us to that understanding, that ultimate renunciation, we might be released, as if miraculously, from the despair. That is the "other way," the "way out" of the horror, the suffering: "The last word in the way of viaticum." And it is the interpretation that Malone, one of Beckett's many fictional "delegates," is approaching.

The question that Malone raises for us is whether ceasing to long for and await an impossible future paradise, and ceasing also, therefore, to lament the withdrawing or abandonment of God and the loss of the old theology, so beginning instead to make the most of opportunities here on earth for little steps towards the utopian transfiguration of this world, might, after all, be the only meaningful way for us to go on.

I like, in this regard, what Emerson, a most unlikely travel companion for Beckett, had to say about ends and endings, with far-reaching implications for theodicy: "To finish the moment, to find the journey's end in every step of the road, that is wisdom."[25] I think that something like this is what Heidegger must have had in mind when, in the late 1930s, sounding uncannily like Beckett whilst meaning something entirely different, he renounced the temptations in theology, all the distractions and consolations that figure in the Christian temporality of ends, and declared: "We know no goals, we are simply a going."[26] However, for Beckett's characters, the abjuring of all goals, all claims to a teleology, does not bring complete release from an oppressive theological metaphysics. No more purposes, no more goals, no more ends—and yet, these characters cannot cease longing, mourning, and waiting.

Might we get out of the linear time of aims and ends, the endless repetition of failure, to reinvent and renew ourselves in the radical temporality of contingent emergence? I am reminded of a remark in Wittgenstein's *Philosophical Investigations*: "It is in language that an expectation and its fulfillment make contact."[27] If the peculiarly deranged grammar of Beckett's prose may be read as an indication of that other temporality, that receptivity to the contingent, there is cause for some hope borne in the very flesh of the language. The derangements, however, repeatedly threaten that very contact.

CHAPTER FOUR

Waiting: In the Meantime

Hope and waiting exist in a dialectical relation: waiting is inherent in the very logic, or structure, of hoping. But the waiting in hope is a waiting that threatens to fall into dialectical contradiction. As Kierkegaard understood, the seemingly rational act of waiting for what we hope to see happen may be the very thing that makes what is hoped for impossible, retarding or arresting its coming. As we wait for what we think would answer our hope, what might matter most of all is *how* in the meantime we are waiting, for that waiting can also sustain a revolutionary fervor, a resistance to what was and what is, ending the world as we have known it, writing an ending for all the theodicies, all the eschatologies, that have failed to bring justice and its happiness to our earth-bound societies.

*

"There is no future in this."[1] Everything hinges on what, in Beckett's *Play*, the little word "this" designates. I shall take it to refer to the linear, irreversible historical continuum. Within the series of events in that continuum, the past is irrevocably past, denied a haunting afterlife, and there is only, as "future," more of the same. And that is a future *without* a future, a future that promises nothing new: no redeeming eventuality. What the suffering and misery of Beckett's characters cry out for is a new beginning, something that would inaugurate a time free of theodicy and of the worldly conditions that have moved people to turn in desperation to a metaphysical dispensation of justice. What on earth are we waiting for?

At stake in the promise of happiness is the institution of justice: the *coming* of justice here on earth. Always coming, always still-to-come, because it cannot be accomplished in any *present* time without corrupting and betraying its absolute demands. So justice requires a future-oriented waiting strong in hope. But it also requires a waiting steeped in remembrance, because the past belongs to the victims of injustice, whose claim on their future redemption constitutes our ineluctable historical obligation in living the present. And it also demands *no more* waiting!

In living the present, we live towards the future. Is there—might there be—a "witness for the future"?[2] A "witness" to vouch for the possibility of a *different* future, that is. I think Beckett's surrogate characters are such witnesses, sustaining our experience of both plight and hope.

*

In April, 1931, traveling from Paris to Kassel, Beckett was compelled to wait overnight in the train station in Nuremberg. Of this time waiting, he says, in a letter, that he has "the gloomiest memories."[3] This experience must indeed have haunted his memory, for he makes of it an important allegorical construction. The nameless voice in the seventh of Beckett's *Texts for Nothing* tells of sitting in the third-class waiting room of the South-Eastern Railway terminus, waiting day and night for a train that does not come. After the last train departed, the station closed for the night. So he must wait, looking outside through the glass of a locked door—"through the glass black with the dust of ruin," he says, reminding us of the biblical words (TN 108–110). Like so many of Beckett's other characters, his created "delegates," and like Kafka's man from the country, this narrator's life is consumed in futile waiting. Whilst waiting, his attention is drawn to the large clock high up on the wall in the waiting room and, in the course of his brooding, he is suddenly overcome by a sense of the discrepancy between the timelessness of eternity and the time that passes so slowly in his waiting that it seems like a counterfeit eternity (TN 108–110). But soon his uncanny vision of eternity vanishes, returning him to a Baroque, melancholy sense of the world as having been already doomed to damnation, sentenced from its very beginning to ruination and annihilation, obliterating all traces of its past. He is waiting for a train that will never come.[4]

*

In *The Calmative* (1946), an ironic title, its sound already suggesting *calamity*, Beckett's narrator tells of a man in distress, homeless, on the street. Someone comes to him solicitous. He asks the stranger for the time: "The right time for the love of God!" So the stranger tells him "a time," but that does not calm him. The narrator, reflecting on this situation, says: "But what time could have done that? Oh, I know, I know, one will come that will. But in the meantime?"[5] There is here, as we are undoubtedly supposed to detect, an enigmatic allusion to the time of the coming of the Messiah—or say, with Derrida, an allusion to an event that would inaugurate the time of messianicity, that is, a radically revolutionary time of utopian progress, but without a Messiah and without the doctrines, dogmas, orthodoxies, and other trappings of theology, theodicy, and messianism. An exhilarating thought—but the narrator's question concerns terrible struggles "in the meantime."

For too long, it has seemed that, in the meantime, all we could do is wait. But if that is really *all* that we could do—if that is really all we are *capable* of doing, and we cannot cease our waiting, then, as Cavell points out, it follows logically that what we are waiting for cannot—and will not—come. It will forever only be coming, endlessly coming.[6] There can be no end to the waiting game. Unless we resolve, in Cavell's words, "not to fulfill, but to dismantle all promises for which we must await fulfillment."[7] Beckett seems implicitly to be challenging us to consider the promise of happiness *after* the death of God and the end of religion. Must we continue now to wait? Malone, presumably dying, comments that, "he who has waited long enough will wait forever. And there comes the hour when nothing more can happen and nobody can come and all is ended but the waiting that knows itself in vain" (MD 234). But that hour has not come yet. And in the meantime? . . .

*

Krapp's Last Tape (1954), a one-act play written in the post-war, "middle-period," is of special significance because it so unequivocally presents a life resolutely abjuring transcendence: a life closed to revelation, closed to the theological dimension. Krapp is seen on stage listening to tape recordings he made over the years, reporting on his life. But he cuts off the machine each time the tape offers, or seems about to offer, some kind of revelation, some significant insight illuminating the meaning of his life, and perhaps life in general.[8] If we take Krapp to represent a character surrogate for Beckett, we will experience in the intensity of the theater the *withholding* of the fulfillment of meaning, compelled to acknowledge what it feels like, and what it means, to be denied the revelation or illumination that we wanted, waited for, and imagined we would be granted, if only Krapp had not stopped the machine. But why are we assuming there would be anything worth knowing? We are making, in fact, a wild assumption. Why the trust, why the blind faith? Perhaps he is turning off the recording because he recalls the banality, the triviality, of what was to follow. Nothing but crap! But we have fallen for the promise. We are disappointed; we were expecting a revelation. Krapp has denied us what we were waiting for. Symbollically, the play has foiled the possibility of a theophany; it has interrupted theodicy before it had a chance to judge. It is a play that, in the most unequivocal, most decisive way challenges the claims of a redeeming revelation, symbolically refusing the event that would set the stage for the teleological journey through life and the judgment of theodicy blessing or damning the end of that journey. The last tape refuses eschatology, the doctrine of last things. Off it goes!

What might we learn, eavesdropping on Krapp's solitary life? Perhaps we will be moved to reflect that the "chance of happiness," such as what theodicy offers, is nothing but a cheat. The staging of *Krapp's Last Tape* confines Krapp in the immanence of a finite, earth-bound world. This is where life must go on.

Our problem, our defeat, lies in waiting, waiting interminably for that great revelation, that miraculous event of messianic or utopian transformation, suddenly erupting into our world from outside, manipulating everything to make it all just right. Perhaps not today, but on the day after tomorrow.[9]

CHAPTER FIVE

In the Event of a New Word

Perhaps one of the most intriguing, but also most complex and elusive of Beckett's stories is *Ill Seen Ill Said*, a tale of mourning in which, through his surrogate narrator, the writer must persistently struggle against the most adverse conditions in order to imagine—to see and witness with the mind's eyes—scenes that might let him retell the crucial Christian stories and somehow retrieve from them, or from the very words themselves, as if from omens and auguries, a renewing sense of hope for the redemption of the promise of happiness.[1]

In this story, one of Beckett's last, a nameless narrator attempts to imagine and describe, as if present as spectator, scenes of the Crucifixion and Resurrection that evoke, at once with the greatest concreteness and yet also, paradoxically, with the most extreme referential indeterminacy, these historically decisive events. But the eyes of the imagination are weak, "a weak messianic force," and the words that come available for the telling of the story are equally poor.[2] In the story's background, evoking the longing and searching gaze of all creaturely life, determined to attain salvation and redemption, is St. Paul's "Epistle to the Romans" (Chapter 8:18–25), echoed in Friedrich Schelling's *Philosophical Investigations into the Essence of Human Freedom* (1809) and later in Walter Benjamin's *Origin of the German Mourning Play* (1925):

> I consider that the sufferings of this present time are not worthy to be compared with the glory that is to be revealed to us. For the anxious longing of the creation waits eagerly for the revealing of the sons of God. For the creation was subjected to futility, not willingly, but because of Him who subjected it, in hope that the creation itself will be set free [. . .]. For we know that the whole creation groans and suffers the pains of childbirth together until now. And not only this, but also we ourselves, having the first fruits of the Spirit, even we ourselves groan within ourselves, waiting eagerly for our adoption as sons, the redemption of our body. For in hope we have been saved, but hope that is seen is not

hope; for who hopes for what he already sees? But if we hope for what we do not see, with perseverance we wait eagerly for it.

The scenes are eerily evoked, naming significant details—"nails," a "zone of stone," "these millions of little sepulchers," an "empty tomb," "the body that scandal," a "shroud," "lambs," "the twelve"—all with the greatest concreteness, but also with the strictest referential indeterminacy. *Ill Seen Ill Said* is a remarkable text. On the one hand, of all the works Beckett created, it bears the most unmistakable, most explicit allusions and references to the Christian religion; but on the other hand, their meaning and significance necessitate interpretation. What are we to make of them? All the allusions and references, all the invocations and evocations, seem to be like shards from a nearby explosion that flew into the flesh of the text, splinters breaking into its texture, offering nothing more than that. Undergoing a frustration analogous to that of the narrator as we try to assemble the fragmentary details we have been given into a coherent story, we can only conjecture that what the narrator is trying to picture—as if somehow not in the imagination but in remembrance of what he witnessed, but now with inner eyes, "having no need of light to see," are crucial events in the story of Christ's life, death, and resurrection.[3]

The crucial theological events in this story have from the very beginning been denied objective confirmation, subtracted from the realm of the visible and from straightforward signification. However, what is at stake in the narrator's storytelling exertions is ultimately not, I think, imagining and telling well, once again, or somehow better, the familiar, old Christian story, rendering it, this time, in all its mystery, its awesome incomprehensibility, but rather an attempt to express our longing and our undying faith—faith in the prophetic promise of happiness, faith in the eventuality of the messianic "event"—and to invent poetic words to evoke what by its very nature precludes not only description, but even the possibility of naming: perhaps what, no doubt with Heidegger's "Ereignis" in mind, Alain Badiou calls an event of "ontological alterity," some kind of apocalyptic "breach in the ash-grey of being."[4] Something that could perhaps eventuate in the making of an enlightened world here on earth.

Is there "a gleam of hope" for us? If so, why expect that redemptive hope—the utopian promise of happiness—to continue unaltered the West's religious traditions and their theodicy? Might it perhaps be necessary to *imagine* that "gleam of hope" as calling for a radical destruction of those traditions, depriving us of their illusions, their fantastic dreams—but also releasing us from their sacrifices, their tyrannical, life-denying pressures? Might not Beckett's retelling of the old story be a story, after all, about his struggle to get at new words and new ways to evoke and interpret the meaning of messianicity, taking that term to signify the utopian promise that language bears? Could we experience a radically new *event*, or even think about the eventuality of an event that would radically interrupt and alter the historical continuum of a barbaric civilization, without new words, or familiar words redeemed, used in strange, new ways?

Adorno's *Minima Moralia* concludes with a paragraph that, although often cited, bears so directly on Beckett's symbolic and allegorical evocations of redemption in his narrative constructions that it seems to warrant here extensive quotation. The first sentence reads thus:

> The only philosophy that can be responsibly practised in the face of despair is the attempt to contemplate all things as they would present themselves from the standpoint of redemption.

After reading Beckett, one might argue, substituting "literature" for "philosophy" and "authentic fictional representation" for "thought" and "knowledge," that he must have believed that the only literature, the only story-telling that could be responsibly practiced in the face of despair would be the attempt to represent all things *both* as they are *and* as they would present themselves from the standpoint of redemption. Adorno's thought-prism continues, drawing us toward the very world into which Beckett throws us:

> Knowledge has no light but that shed on the world by redemption: all else is reconstruction, mere technique. Perspectives must be fashioned that displace and estrange the world, reveal it to be, with its rifts and crevices, as indigent and distorted as it will appear one day in the messianic light. To gain such perspectives without velleity or violence, entirely from felt contact with its objects—this alone is the task of thought. It is the simplest of all things, because the situation calls imperatively for such knowledge, indeed because consummate negativity, once squarely faced, delineates the mirror-image of its opposite. But it is also the utterly impossible thing, because it presupposes a standpoint removed, even though by a hair's breadth, from the scope of existence, whereas we well know that any possible knowledge must not only be wrested from what is, if it shall hold good, but is also marked, for this very reason, by the same distortion and indigence which it seeks to escape. The more passionately thought denies its conditionality for the sake of the unconditional, the more unconsciously, and so calamitously, it is delivered up to the world. Even its own impossibility it must at last comprehend for the sake of the possible.

"But," he warns, "beside the demand thus placed on thought, the question of the reality or unreality of redemption itself hardly matters."[5] Reading Beckett's stories and witnessing his works for the stage, experiments in literature that never cease to acknowledge, in a negative dialectic, the fact of their conditionality, reminding us at the same time of the absurdity and contingency—the conditionality—of the world they are representing, it is not difficult to realize with what intensity of anguish Beckett felt the impossibility to which Adorno is here giving thought. His was a lifelong struggle to wrest from language the words we need in order to make sense out of our experience of the world we are living in. And in his constructions of narrative and dialogue, he somehow finds ways to introduce momentary events, small events, almost nothing, which bespeak the possible.

This is what happens in *Ill Seen Ill Said*. In this story, a narrator struggles to imagine and tell once again, but in a new way, the story of events surrounding the Resurrection. Even though the narrator thinks the story that Christian faith believes may be nothing but a fiction, he struggles to find a way to retell it, making it not only emotionally moving but deeply compelling. "Imagination at wit's end spreads its sad wings" (IS 56). Beckett's retelling is like the telling of a ghost story, a tale not only haunted by a corpse that has vanished, leaving only a problematic trace and a ghostly old woman in clothes "immaculately black," but haunted also by a ghostly message promising a utopia of happiness that even words ill said are believed to impart, although our languages, themselves still in need of poetic redeeming, continue to withhold words for what is promised. It is a story that, as the narrator is forced at a certain point to acknowledge, "is not possible any longer except as figment" (IS 65). Or at least it is "not endurable" any more except as fiction (IS 65). But is there any reality at all to the story he wants to retell? "Such confusion now between real and—how say its contrary? No matter. That old tandem. Such now the confusion between them once so twain. And such the farrago from eye to mind. For it to make what sad sense of it may. No matter now. Such equal liars both" (IS 72). But could it be retold in a way that would convincingly revive or resurrect something in its content, something extracted from the no longer compelling theology, which might speak to our needs today? The narrator is deeply troubled: "Already all confusion. Things and imaginings. [. . .] If only she could be pure figment. Unalloyed. This old dying woman. So dead. In the madhouse of the skull and nowhere else. [. . .] How simple then. If only all could be pure figment" (IS 58). There are moments when, deeply immersed in the exertions of the imagination, the narrator finds himself pained by the thought that the story he is telling, ill seen and ill said though it is, could be nothing but fiction, a weave of words. There is too much suffering, too much pain, even if the events are just a story. The suffering, the pain: they are all too real for him.

The narrator in Beckett's tale, imagining himself to be a kind of witness, reports his observations of an elderly woman, whom he watches with ceaseless vigilance. The woman is living in a cabin in a pasture or meadow where lambs may be seen mournfully grazing. She is overcome by grief, not only listless, almost unable to move "in the deepening gloom," but without the will to move. Wallace Stevens's words in "Sunday Morning" (1923) exquisitely evoke the scene that Beckett's imagination transposes: "She dreams a little, and she feels the dark/ Encroachment of that old catastrophe [. . .]." Somehow, nevertheless, she eventually finds the strength to move, drawing that strength from the very depths of her sorrow. What stirs her most of all, and gets her to move around the cabin, is the interlude of happiness she is granted watching from the window the appearance of the planet Venus in the morning skies, announcing the return of a glowing sun. Sometimes, the narrator says, there are long stretches of time during which the woman cannot be seen, or seen at first only "darkly," before becoming "more and more plainly" visible, crossing the threshold of the cabin as she ventures out and goes back inside. But there are times when, from the narrator's location, she remains invisible, and all that can be seen—"ill seen"—is "a pallet and a ghostly chair" (IS 54). One time, watching her closely, the narrator sees her "stop dead": "Now," he tells us, is "the moment or never. But something forbids. Just time enough to glimpse a fringe of black veil. The face must wait. Just time before the eye cast down. Where nothing to be seen in the grazing rays but snow. And how all about little by little her footprints are effaced" (IS 55). Later, however, she "appears"—if that is the right word, hence the wrong word—seen in a cemetery, a "zone of stones," with twelve mysterious others, whom the narrator calls "witnesses," and "long shadows" (55).

The narrator is deeply moved, moved to tears, both by what, through imagination, he is "seeing" (or recalling having "seen"), and by what, struggle though he will, he can neither "see" in that way nor relate in words: "Riveted to some detail of the desert the eye fills with tears. Imagination at wit's end spreads its sad wings" (IS 56). But suddenly, the narrator's eye is distracted, the "vigil" interrupted and confused by something appearing in the sky (IS 57). How much easier it would be, he confesses, if only this old woman could be "pure figment" (IS 58). He is tempted to think his obsession with this story, and with its events, is madness: "In the madness of the skull and nowhere else. [. . .] If only all could be pure figment. Neither be nor been nor by any shift to be" (IS 58). He will go on imagining, as if remembering, and will go on with the story, but—"Gently, gently. On. Careful."

And go on he does, relating what he can imagine "seeing," or recall "seeing," of her visit to the cemetery in the dead cold of winter: "Shroud of radiant haze," he notes, following her passage north. "Where to melt with paradise" (IS 64). Back in the cabin, the woman, now identified with the Virgin Mary that figures in the rosary prayer, is imagined, sitting down to eat supper. "She waits. For it to cool perhaps. But no. Merely frozen again just as about to begin. At least in a twin movement full of grace she slowly raises the bowl toward her lips while at the same time with equal slowness lowering her head to join it" (IS 69).

Soon thereafter, the narrator's thoughts turn to the body of Christ and the mystery of the empty tomb. Punning on the word "matter," he says: "On resumption the head is covered. No matter. No matter now. Such the confusion now between real and—how say its contrary?" (IS 72). But of course, it is precisely a matter of the mattering of matter: the mystery of resurrection, the mystery of the flesh that becomes spirit. What happened? Where is the body? Is there a "trapdoor" in the coffin? "So cunningly contrived that even to the lidded eye it scarcely shows" (IS 73)? The narrator's skepticism cannot resist picturing the scene as a magician's vaudeville act. Raising the lid of the coffin, he raises doubts, risking a rebuff, perhaps from a guilty conscience: "Careful. Raise it at once and risk another rebuff?" (IS 73).

The narrator's thoughts soon return to the woman. "The silence merges into music infinitely far and as unbroken as silence. Ceaseless celestial winds in unison. For all matters now. The stones gleam faintly afar and the cabin walls seen white at last" (IS 73, 74). What, now, are we to make of that faint gleam from afar? Is it not the indication of some redemptive intervention in the world, some sign of messianicity? Soon after imagining that gleam, the narrator tells us:

> She is vanishing. With the rest. The already ill seen bedimmed and ill seen again annulled. The mind betrays the treacherous eyes and the treacherous word their treacheries. (IS 78)

His mind—reason—refuses to believe the story. The words fail to be compelling. Indeed, the inadequacy of the words betrays what they are trying to say:

> Haze sole certitude. The same that reigns beyond the pastures. It gains them already. It will gain the zone of stones. [. . .] The eye will close in vain. To see but haze. Not even. [. . .] How can it ever be said? Quick how ever ill said before it [the haze] submerges all. Light. In one treacherous word. Dazzling haze. Light in its might at last. Where no more to be seen. To be said. Gently gently. (IS 78)

The light of reason and the light of redemption are struggling against one another to own the truth. Which light will be victorious? Suddenly, the narrator can no longer see the woman in her cabin. He struggles to bring back before his mind's eyes some of the props in the scene—the pallet, her chair. And he tries to imagine the scene from different angles:

> With what word convey its change? Careful. Less. Ah the sweet one word. Less. It is less. The same but less. [. . .] See now how words too. A few drops mishaphazard. Then strangury. To say the least. Less. It will end by being no more. By never having been. Divine prospect. True that the light. (IS 81)

Despite these doubts, he draws on cultural sources of "remembrance" and returns to picturing the tomb and the body, so that he can retell the old story, reviving with strong words its power to compel faith:

Alone the face remains. Of the rest beneath its covering no trace. During the inspection a sudden sound. Startling without consequence for the gaze the mind awake. How explain it? And without going so far how say it? Far behind the eye the quest begins. What time the event recedes. When suddenly to the rescue it comes again. Forthwith the uncommon common noun collapsion. Reinforced a little later if not enfeebled by the infrequent slumberous. A *slumberous collapsion*. Two. Then far from the still agonizing eye a gleam of hope. By the grace of these modest beginnings. With in second sight the shack in ruins. To scrute together with the inscrutable face. All curiosity spent. (IS 83. Italics added.)

This passage, which Badiou rightly singles out for special reflection, certainly merits further thought. The narrator calls attention to an extraordinary "event," although he leaves it unclear what this "event" is. Is it the miraculous resurrection? Or is it rather the surprise coming of a new word, the "uncommon common noun collapsion"? And is the "gleam of hope" the grace of resurrection, sign of redemption? Or is it the grace, the hope—the promise— in the coming of a new word? Or is it both? "Two," as the narrator says, leaving its designation and meaning for us to determine (IS 83).

I am reminded here of Paul Celan's poem, "Flower," in which the poet says: "We baled the darkness empty, we found/ the word that arose in summer: flower."[6] Beyond joy in finding that word, and finding the essence of summer in the invocation of that word, the poet, his faith in the redeeming power of words restored, exults in the hope of finding another miraculous word: "One more word like this, and the hammers/ will swing over open ground." One more word that even the blind can see, and the darkness, emptiness, and wall of stony silence will be shattered and opened. Such is the promise that words bear. The word that Beckett's narrator receives rescues and redeems the hopes that stirred him to retell the old, old story once again.

Despite feeling that his imagination, never more than a "weak messianic force," is spent (IS 83), Beckett's narrator continues his efforts, both to see the crucial religious scenes with a vivid imagination and also find, if he can, new, strong, compelling words to revive it: "Full glare now on the face present throughout the recent future" (IS 84, 85). But he encounters insurmountable difficulties. Trying to picture what took place one April afternoon at the "place of the skull," the scene of the Crucifixion, he fails, unable to see any decisive traces. "No trace of all the ado" (IS 84). Just some bent rods and a nail.

Returning to the corpse, he focuses on the eyes. "Unspeakable globe." Are the eyes closed? He sees "two black blanks." So "unbearable" that he must seek shelter in a little blasphemous humor: "Fit vent-holes of the soul that jakes" (85). But his imagination once again is blocked:

Absence supreme good and yet. Illumination then go again and on return no more trace. On earth's face. Of what was never. And if by mishap some left then go again. For good again. So on. Till no more trace. On earth's face. Instead of always the same place. Slaving away forever in the same place. At this and that trace. And what if the eye could not? No more tear itself away from the remains of the trace. Of what was never. Quick say it suddenly can and [. . .] say farewell. If only to the face. Of her tenacious trace. (IS 85, 86)

But it is not just material traces of the Crucifixion and Resurrection that the narrator is in search of, to give his images and narrative the concreteness and vividness that would make these events compelling. It is, ultimately, a question of faith in the utopian promise of earthly happiness, a message to be borne in redeeming words, that Beckett's narrator is hoping for. That is the "event" at stake, regardless of the historical veracity of the Christian story. Without that, it seems that nihilism threatens, for as Nietzsche argued, we have lost faith in ourselves. Thus, earlier in his story, the nameless narrator confides his dread of the void: "Void. Nothing else. Contemplate that. Not another word. Home at last" (IS 66). But one should notice, in the metrical rhythm and rhyme of the two sentences, "If only to the face. Of her tenacious trace," there is a lengthening and prolonging of the claim: at least there is a trace that persists. Can that trace negate the void? Or does the rhyming, the repetition, make a mockery of the matter, reducing the seemingly passionate words, the desperate need for a trace, if nothing more, to the shallowness of a hissing limerick? Telling this story is a test of Beckett's faith in the redeeming power of words, weak though they may be, themselves in need of redeeming.

One might be reminded here of Nietzsche, a philosopher Beckett read with appreciation, who observed, in his *Genealogy of Morals*, that "mankind would rather have the void for purpose than be void of purpose."[7] But after so many futile efforts to resurrect the inherited Christian story, succeeding in conjuring only something ill seen and ill said, Beckett's narrator seems, finally, to find some relief in breathing that very void, well beyond the last things of eschatology:

> Decision no sooner reached or rather long after than what is the wrong word? For the last time at last for to end yet again what the wrong word? [. . .] No but slowly dispelled a little very little like the last wisps of day when the curtain closes. [. . .] Farewell to farewell. Then in that perfect dark foreknell darling sound pip for end begun. First last moment. Grant only enough remain to devour all. [. . .] One moment more. One last. Grace to breathe that void. Know happiness. (IS 86)

Did God come? There really are no compelling traces. Only a story ill seen, ill said. Happiness begins here and now with release from the afflictions of a tyrannical religion. Even the void that permits no meaning, no purpose, is better than those afflictions—shame, guilt, flagellations and mortifications of the flesh, the punishments of Hell. *Adieu à dieu.* Free at last? If we listen instead of read, Beckett's "Know happiness" might easily become "No happiness." We are left in the reverberations of a meaning in suspense.

Free at last? Perhaps. Or perhaps almost. The struggle against religion might be over, but it is not certain that Beckett thinks we are completely released from a metaphysical longing. We need to recall *Worstward Ho*: "Longing that all go. Dim go. Void go. Longing go. Vain longing that vain longing go."[8] The longing for a world that redeems the promise of happiness does not die. And as long as it continues to move us, there is a need for storytellers to find words, new words, to keep the faith, the hope for utopian reconciliation, alive. "Nohow on." From his earliest stories through his last, Beckett always gives sympathetic, indeed poignant expression to that longing. But for Beckett, the longing for a new, transfigured world is inseparable from his longing for new words, words with the power to redeem what they invoke. And this is why Beckett struggles so relentlessly, so sacrificially, with words. His narrator in *The Unnamable* says:

> When all goes silent, and comes to an end, it will be because the words have been said, those it behoved to say, no need to know which, no means of knowing which, they'll be there somewhere [. . .]

And then he adds:

> Perhaps they are somewhere there, the words that count, in what has just been said, the words it behoved to say, they need not be more than a few.

But no sooner has he given voice to this tentative faith than he gives expression to doubts:

> Where do these words come from that pour out of my mouth, and what do they mean, no, saying nothing, for the words don't carry any more, if one can call that waiting. (UN 363)

But even when words fail the author's intent, they still, I would argue, tell a story—and still carry the promise.

In his commentary on the invented word "collapsion" that comes to Beckett in the telling of *Ill Seen Ill Said*, Badiou points out that the syllable-word "on," suggesting our English word meaning "continue," is repeated many times in this story, and that it figures, moreover, in many important variations throughout the text. Among the words I found are: "once," "moon," "zone," "only," "stones," "alone," "gone," "beyond," "horizon," "wrongly," "reason," "nothing," "no longer," and "so on." Despite his eagerness to find in Beckett an apocalyptic "event," a radically disruptive opening to alterity, something like what he takes Heidegger to mean by "Ereignis," Badiou neglects to note that Beckett's newly invented, uncommon, common noun, "collapsion," is an event in language which joins the ancient Greek philosophers' word for being, namely ὤν (Ionic ἐών), the present participle of εἰμί, with the English word "collapse," hinting, perhaps, at the possibility, still "slumbrous", of a catastrophic or apocalyptic *ontological* event, a blessing, perhaps, in disguise, if the eventual collapse of the present epoch in the history of being should make way for revolutionary new ontological and existential possibilities. In Beckett, "on" should bespeak his hope, his courage to go on, despite having only so many old, weak words for his storytelling. It is, perhaps, his most important word. *Being* is a question of going *on.* Hence, slumbrous in the word—*collapsion*—there lurks a question: Will I collapse or go on? And of course, going on can be either more of the same or it can be invention. Beckett's stories are increasingly composed of words that are fragmented, broken, detached, collapsed, destroying, or in any case eliminating, continuities. Going on ventures beginning each time anew, making an opening for "the event," giving it a chance. There is a brief moment of triumph, I think, when that new "uncommon common noun," awaking from its slumber, comes to mind, as the right word, "flower," came to Celan, encouraging the glorious promise that bestirs a "weak messianic force." Is the promise in Beckett's new word resurrected? Could we be going on to a new ontology, a new way of being?

In *Endgame*, Hamm, left alone on stage, begins, obliquely, to call into question the plot that underwrites teleology.[9] Talking to himself, with words echoing Eliot's "East Coker," he declares:

The end is in the beginning and yet you go on.
[*Pause.*]

And so he wonders:

Perhaps I could go on with my story, end it and begin another.
[*Pause.*]

The entire play is, in fact, a meditation on story plots: on their beginnings and endings. Quietly at stake is the Judeo-Christian story, with its teleology and eschatology. What meaning, what *fullness* of meaning, is kept and promised "in the name of God"? And how can we continue to have faith in that promise, when it is to be so long in coming?

"On!" I wonder whether Nietzsche gave him that word. In the First Essay of his work *On the Genealogy of Morals,* the philosopher challenges his interlocutors, and eventually us, to acknowledge the true genealogy of our ideals, our values:

Would anyone like to take a look into the secret of how ideals are made on earth? Who has the courage? Very well! Here is a point we can see through into this dark workshop. But wait a moment or two, Mr. Rush

and Curious: your eyes must first get used to this false iridescent light.—
All right! Now speak! What is going on down there? Say what you see,
man of the most perilous kind of inquisitiveness—now I am the one who
is listening.—

—"I see nothing, but I hear the more. There is a soft, wary, malignant
muttering and whispering coming from all corners and nooks. It seems to
me one is lying: a saccharine sweetness clings to every sound. Weakness
is being lied into something meritorious, no doubt of it—so it is just as
you said"—

—Go on!¹⁰

Three times the interlocutors are invited to "go on." And after listening to
their chatter about "the triumph of [divine] justice," "the victory of God, of
the just God, over the godless," "the Last Judgment," "the Kingdom of
God," and all the "phantasmagoria of anticipated future bliss," the bliss
promised when our life here on earth has ended, Nietzsche finally shouts
"Enough! Enough!" And in *Enough*, a brief prose fiction published in 1967,
Beckett, as we know, shouted this too.

But Beckett's "Go on," his "nohow on," is profoundly different from
the meaning of the phrase in Nietzsche's dialogue: it is not Nietzsche's
contemptuous way of provoking his interlocutors to relate their theological
nonsense, but an expression of the determination and courage of one who
goes on *after relinquishing* the promise of happiness contained in the old
theodicy. Beckett's characters go on hoping, longing, and waiting—but for
the eventuality of a very different reign of happiness. Happy days might
come, perhaps—but this time without God; *our* achievement, *our* words,
and *our* deeds. What an event! But before we celebrate our freedom from the
word of God, we must not forget that, even in this story written near the end
of his life, Beckett makes his story-teller struggle with the Christian version
of the promise of happiness—and struggle with the old words, to make
them keep faith with that revolutionary promise: words of remembrance,
words for the future rescued from their past. However, the promise that the
words bear in their very existence as such cannot be taken hostage by the
Christian version—or indeed by any religious version.

In *Ill Seen Ill Said*, the redeeming of the promise that language, however
impoverished, still seems to bear is an eventuality that commences at long
last with the embracing of freedom from theodicy. And at long last, one
of the last things that one of Beckett's last narrators, all of them masks of
himself, wants to say is that, however poor, however weak the words, storytelling will somehow go on, striving to redeem what hope for the world
there may be in the words that have come. And so Beckett tells stories in
which the hopeful indications that we still long for in old metaphors, old
symbols, old, worn-out words—the eventuality of events promising a new
earthly reign of happiness, events suddenly revealing the world, if only for
an instant, in the light of redemption, or *as if* in that light—break into the

narratively enclosed world: a tiny gleam of light, a simple movement full of
grace, a dazzling, somehow radiant haze. And the coming of a new word,
an uncommon common noun, "slumbrous collapsion," giving language a
new life: this too is a promising event. Would Beckett still want to say, as he
does in ending the twelfth of his earlier *Texts for Nothing*: "nothing ever but
lifeless words" (TN 135)?

*

For Benjamin, there is not a single moment that does not carry within it its
distinctive reference or allusion to a "revolutionary chance in the fight for
the oppressed past."[11] However, in Beckett, as in Adorno, the utopia of
happiness can be represented only dialectically, and its chance glimpsed
most compellingly only through privation and destitution, the "determinate
negation" of its opposite, which must be resisted relentlessly. In words
reminiscent of Groucho's unforgettable comic line, words I hear voiced in a
certain self-parody, Beckett confided his anguished struggle against betrayal
by the language he is compelled to use: "Nothing," he said defiantly, though
perhaps also with a sense of irony, "will ever be sufficiently *against* for me."[12]
And defiant also, in the end, is his faith in language, despite all the struggles
with language and all his doubts about being able to say what needs to be
said (UN 363).

But if his works for the stage show virtually nothing but bleakness, a
grim reality occasionally interrupted by comedy in dialogue and vaudeville
gestures, there are, in his short stories and novels, surprisingly many moments
abandoned to, or overcome by, auratic enchantment, when, even in works
that, like *Texts for Nothing*, curse an inheritance of "lifeless words," "dead
letters,"[13] the prose suddenly begins to sing and echo, as if momentarily lifted
to the heights of sublime lyricism by some gracious infusion of hope.

So is there, in Beckett's dialectically charged words, "a chance of
happiness?"[14] I mean, of course, the chance promised by the very existence
of language, borne by our words, even when seemingly bereft. Perhaps
a chance, if only we could finally free ourselves from the ghosts of the
"providential" theodicies that persist in haunting us and, free of their severe
judgment, return to the promise that, "in the words that remain" (UN 406),
those capable of being released from commodification and other forms of
corruption, language by its very nature keeps in waiting, for us to use with a
new sense of justice in our relations with one another—"if that happy time
ever comes" (UN 331).

In the ninth of his *Texts for Nothing*, evoking the beauty of the natural
world, a world denied the denizens of *How It Is*, Beckett's surrogate "voice"
expresses, as if with overwhelming conviction, a hope that also seems to
move the narrator mired in the purgatorial swamp:

> There's a way out there, there's a way out somewhere, the rest would
> come, the other words, sooner or later, and the power to get there, and

the way to get there, and pass out, and see the beauties of the skies, and see the stars again. (TN 121)

These are certainly not "lifeless words," "dead letters" (TN 135). But the final words of this work, concluding the thirteenth *Text*, whilst acknowledging "a gleam of light," suggest, at most, considering its grammatical mood, what I would call, borrowing a phrase from Derrida,[15] a "spectral messianicity":

> And were there one day to be here, where there are no days, which is no place, born of the impossible voice the unmakable being, and a gleam of light, still all would be silent and empty and dark, as now, as soon now, when all will be ended, all said, it says, it murmurs. (TN 140)

Not even the presence of this gleam of light can portend or confirm the redeeming, utopian event, the longed-for revolutionary moment. The redemption of the utopian idea of justice—universal happiness—is always imminent, an incessant opportunity; but if it were actually to take place, it would at once be challenged, disputed and refused in the name of the demand for the absolute that it claims to represent. The paradise of justice must be here, here and now; but it can be nowhere actually fulfilled. So, despite that light, despite the presence of that enlightening idea, a skeptical, melancholy voice murmurs: "still all would be silent and empty and dark," since the perfection of justice must remain unfulfilled—until the end of this historical time.

In *Play*, a late work, Beckett's character is moved to declare, giving the first pronoun endless dimensions of meaning: "It will come. Must come. There is no future in this."[16] But a new word did come in the telling of a very old story. What, then, lies in that event?

PART THREE

After Hegel, Beckett's *How It Is*: Approaching Justice with Infinite Slowness

CHAPTER ONE

Swamp: Justice in
the State of Nature

§1

As we noted in the Prologue, Adorno is convinced that, as he puts it: "The more profoundly society fails to deliver the reconciliation that the bourgeois spirit promised as the enlightenment of myth, the more irresistibly humor is pulled down into the netherworld, and laughter, once the image of humanness, becomes a regression to inhumanity."[1] It is into such a netherworld, where the image of humanness appears in an archaic state of justice, that Beckett's *How It Is* casts us. He does not glorify regression, does not sing of any longing for that state, as Gottfried Benn does in two lines from one of his poems: "Ah, if only we were our primordial ancestors./ A clump of slime in a warm bog."[2] In Beckett's tale, the object of longing is the world said to be "above"—or rather, a world-order still bound to earth, but morally higher than that.

However, before we can live in a morally higher world, a world closer to utopia, we must understand the condition that sets in motion our need, our longing. Adorno's interpretation of artworks bears on this point. Artworks, he says, are the "after-images of pre-historical shudders in an age of reification, bringing the terror of the primal world against a background of reified objects . . . "[3] *How It Is* submerges us in the violence of a primal world—at once a state of nature we have in some ways left behind and yet also the reflection of a world not very different from the one we actually still inhabit.

Fighting all our battles over again, Beckett's evocations of theodicy take the form of familiar topographies, metaphors, and symbols, registering in the spirit of parody all old conventions that literature has used: Heaven and Hell, the realm above and the realm below, day and night, the light and the dark, summer and winter, weekdays and Sundays. Molloy describes living in a world of torments; but, with words that use echoing letters and syllables to make an emphatic description, he tells us its horizon is "burning with sulphur and phosphorous" (MO 22). This "Inferno," this "Purgatory," *our* world, would not be complete without the old literary trope of a swamp. So, in the region into which Molloy ventures in search of mother and home, he comes to a city situated near "a kind of swamp" that needs "redeeming" (MO 70). That swamp appears once again, this time in *How It Is*. In this later story, the central text for my argument in this book, Beckett casts his characters into the Purgatory of a dark, muddy swamp, a brutal state of nature where, as we learn in the third part of the tale, the hope for a more enlightened justice is at stake. Losing faith in the redeeming of language, he has also cast them, in prose of tortured grammar, into a purgatory of language, as this passage in *Texts for Nothing* suggests: "Blot, words can be blotted and the mad thoughts they invent, the nostalgia for that slime where the Eternal breathed and his son wrote, long after, with divine idiotic finger, at the feet of the adultress . . ."[4] Might redeeming words still emerge from this primeval slime?

As scholars and critics have noted, Beckett's stories and works for the stage increasingly situate and frame his characters in a space that in some way or other compels the felt impression of a closed world: either a world bereft of any dimension of transcendence from which salvation might come, or a world in which the light of hope and promise is faint and struggling to persist. In this regard, the situations, the worlds, into which he casts his characters resemble those in which the Baroque writers placed their characters. In his dissertation on Kierkegaard, with whose writings Beckett was familiar, Adorno, taking note of the fact that Kierkegaard occasionally refers to himself as "the Baroque thinker," suggests that, like the literary Baroque, he represented in his literary ventures "the condition of closed immanence no less than the allegorical conjuration of lost ontological contents."[5] The same might be argued, I think, in regard to Beckett—but with a crucial difference. For, in Beckett's world, God is finally dead; and if there is any redemption, its sense can only be sought here in our sojourn on earth—in the immanence of a profane world.

Resuming his story about the life of young Sapo, Malone's narration, told in a prose of heart-wrenching lyricism, places the boy in an eschatologically determined dimension, where a terrible Gnostic struggle between the forces of light and dark is once again re-enacted (MO 196–197). However, by showing this dramatic struggle as taking place in our familiar, ordinary world, Beckett redeems its allegorical power for our time, making it literally visible again for the renewal of our perception. At the same time, though, in case we readers forget the artifice behind the story we are absorbed in, we are occasionally reminded of the fictional nature of these orientating tropes, as when, for example, Molloy reports, with dark irony, that, "in order to blacken a few more pages," he will tell about his time at the seaside (MO 63). And at a certain point in the soliloquy, the unnamable narrator in *The Unnamable* exclaims, using art not only to vanquish any remnants of aesthetic semblance, but to utterly demystify the reality of the all-too-human struggles we live through in quotidian life: "What rubbish all this stuff about light and dark" (UN 300).

*

Before elaborating the themes that surround the question of justice and accordingly bear on the interpretive argument I wish to make, I think it would be useful for us now to have a brief summary of the three parts of *How It Is*, reading some especially pertinent textual passages, in order both to give some substance to the story and to convey something of the uncanny, felt quality of Beckett's remarkable prose. In this novel, he is not merely describing, but creating an almost overwhelming visceral sensation and feeling of oppressive proximity and viscosity, of inhibited movement and broken speech, through a prose breathless and panting, gasping for breath, not only because of its relentlessly racing speed and pounding rhythms, but also because of its syntactical subjection to a suffocating existential reality. Submerged in a swamp of mud, a mud so thick that it is clogging the tongue, the nameless narrator of the novel struggles to speak, to tell his long story. From beginning to end, this story takes place in the mud, making the facts of the story themselves muddy and murky. If mud, the elemental substance in the biblical story of Creation, is an indication of life, of beginnings, it is also an indication of death and endings. And with so many spell-binding repetitions, so many citation-like fragments jumbled and repeated, each time differently contextualized and ambiguously indexed in the narrative temporal order, Beckett's readers are again and again brought to the very edge of dizziness, as if they themselves were about to slip and fall into the bottomless vortex of mud, helpless and hopeless, like the mortals in the story.[6]

In the absence of punctuation, Beckett leaves it to his readers to constellate meaningful unities of words. Frequently, the prose is hospitable to different configurations of words, hence different renderings of sense. Thus, in a way, his readers are made responsible for the stories that are constructed. And, implicitly, therefore, we the readers become participants in the stories we have constructed, complicit in their grammatical and narrative substance.

In *Twilight of the Idols*, Friedrich Nietzsche remarked: "I fear we are not getting rid of God because we still believe in grammar."[7] In *How It Is*, Beckett experiments with as much grammatical anarchy as is possible, without falling into the utter incomprehensibility of madness. That deconstruction of grammar is, I suggest, one of the ways he leaves traces of an attempt to move beyond the historical reach of providential justice and its endings.

§2

Now, to the story: "this life in the dark and mud its joys and sorrows journeys intimacies and abandons" (H 139). In Part I, said to be about the narrator's past, his childhood, his life before encountering Pim, the narrator, in the mud, tries to remember meaningful events from his earlier life. But the adversity of his present situation is distracting, and, as he struggles to organize his sack, with its tins of sardines and utensils for eating, all that he can recall, to sustain some hope, are "bits and scraps," mere "rags of life." Moreover, the exertions required by his situation are exhausting, causing interruptions, repetitions, and moments of incoherence. I quote three passage fragments to convey as concretely as possible an exact image of the narrator's situation and state of mind:

- I turn on my side which side the left it's preferable throw the right hand forward bend the right knee these joints are working the fingers sink the toes sink in the slime these are my holds too strong slime is too strong holds is too strong I say it as I hear it (H 19)

- semi-side left right leg right arm push pull flat on face curse God bless him beseech him no sound with feet and hands scrabble in the mud what do I hope a tin lost where I have never been a tin half-emptied thrown away ahead that's all I hope (H 47)

- the sack my life that I never let go here I let it go needing both hands as when I journey that hangs together ah these sudden blazes in the head as empty and dark as the heart can desire then suddenly like a handful of shavings aflame the spectacle then (H 35)

Even in this terrible darkness, even in this watery gloom, hope will persist, urging a fierce courage to go on. And perhaps memory, weak and fragmentary though it is, can provide the much-needed encouragement, as when, in Part I, the narrator escapes present misery by recalling, with the assistance of the imagination, images of childhood that awaken desires and longing for a paradise of happiness. But this would not be the childhood he has lost; rather, it would be a paradise that has never existed, a paradise of which childhood could be only a hint.

*

Beckett's narrator, sometimes one of his surrogate voices, sometimes not, and sometimes merging with the identity of the characters in his story, divides his story into *three temporal parts*, representing, in temporal succession, a childhood past remembered (Part I), a present told as it is happening (Part II), and a present that, reducing to absurdity attempts to set in motion a calculative, mechanical form of justice as a "rational" replacement for the archaic justice of nature, provokes us to imagine the possibility of a different, more enlightened institution of justice (Part III). The allegorical topography of the story is correspondingly divided into *three spatial dimensions or worlds*: the present takes place in the underworld, the realm of the swamp; the past took place in the world above, the sun-drenched world of the narrator's childhood; and the future above all belongs to the "celestial" realm of possibilities—a lovely blue.

It is worth noting here the curious fact that the narrator in *The Unnamable* describes Paradise as "like slime" (UN 358), possibly not intending, or not only intending, to describe the nature of the environment, as we might have thought, but indicating instead, or also, that he regards evocations and promises of "Paradise" as nothing but mean-spirited deceptions: "like slime" in that sense. Bearing that earlier text in mind, we might wonder, if Beckett conceives the "purgatory" of *How It Is* as a realm of slime, whether he believes that there is no difference between paradise and purgatory. In the sixth of the *Texts for Nothing*, the nameless narrating voice acknowledges "nostalgia for that slime where the eternal breathed and his son wrote, long after, with divine idiotic finger [. . .]" (TN 103). This of course suggests a very different conception of the mud-realm: the swamp is not, or not only, a purgatory, or a time to learn the meaning of justice, but also a realm of fertility and creativity.

The mud-realm, the primordial realm out of which the promise of life emerged, is the "purgatory" where the narrator in *How It Is*, and all the other mortal creatures like him, must work out the terms of their existential condition. This realm of mud, terrible though it is, seems also to be the primordial site of redemption, the metaphorical realm where people must go to work out the pathologies of everyday life, learning, or remembering, what it is—how it is—to be a worthy human being. Such a purgatory would be a necessary stage on the way to a finer justice and a higher stage of humanity: the redeeming of the justice that the existence of language as communication promises. This interpretation is suggested by Molloy, who, in the much earlier work of fiction, suggests *redeeming* a swamp, transforming it into a beautiful garden (MO, 44, 70).

The allegorical topography in *How It Is* represents a *moral universe* of three conditions: the past is the world of errant ways; the present is the swamp of guilt and purgatory learning, and the future is the possibility of redeemed life, a world in which—quoting four words that, quite surprisingly, appear in the text and that seem not to be meant ironically or cynically—the true "dignity" of "humanity" would be realized and "regained" or "restored" (H 26–27). The topography also represents, although in a different ordering, the dimensions of *a political universe*: the past was lived in the "state of nature," the present is lived in a struggle, still within the state of nature, for the justice of recognition and acknowledgement, and the future is imagined in the flashing of images that correspond to our longing for a utopia or paradise of justice—not in heaven, but here in *our* world of light, a rational order of justice built under the sun on the surface of the earth.

*

In Part II, the narrator leaves behind the remembering of things past, life in the "world above," the paradise of childhood close to his mother. Part II relates his life down below that world, lost in a swamp of darkness where the denizens of this realm, moving about in it without any reason to hope for release, seem to undergo a kind of hellish purgatory recalling Dante's images. The very first words of Part II conjure the scene, beginning without the customary capital letter:

> here then at last part two where I have still to say how it was as I hear it in me that was without quaqua on all sides bits and scraps how it was with Pim vast stretch of time murmur it in the mud to the mud when the panting stops how it was my life we're talking of my life in the dark in the mud with Pim part (H 51)

In Part II, we witness the narrator as he moves through the muddy swamp and with an uncanny slowness and indirection approaches an other, his victim or his tormentor, in scenes of exorbitant primal justice. The present is about his time entangled with Pim. We learn that, after struggling mightily, as if, perhaps, with longing and love, to approach Pim, his "other," another "mortal" likewise caught in the mud, the narrator, having finally reached Pim, suppresses his tender sentiments and undertakes to torment and torture him. Pim cries out to him, begging for an end to the torment; but the narrator, although hoping to hear "a human voice" and desperately anxious to hear his victim speak, resorts to "extorting" a voice, a speech (H 122, 142–143). But he finds that he can't make out the words. Perhaps there are no words, just the murmuring of sounds, a groan or a cry. Or perhaps the mud interferes with the intelligibility of the communication.

Reminiscent of Kafka's story "In the Penal Colony," the narrator attempts to communicate instructions by inscribing words in Pim's flesh. He is desperate to get Pim to acknowledge him, to speak, and to "love" him, as it were (H 71–75). Passively enduring the narrator's torments of the flesh, Pim at first cries out, but then, submitting to the narrator's efforts to extort speech from him, he suddenly begins to "sing" (H 55–64). Mocking Pim's "singing," the narrator intensifies the torture (H 62). But Pim is a mere link in a seemingly infinite chain of violence and suffering—a sequence without rational purpose and justification: "an infinite number of damned, moving blindly through the mud in a great chain of torment."[8]

Part III relates the narrator's experience "after Pim." In this part of the tale, the narrator encounters a mortal named Bem, or Bom, who will now, in turn, torment him, giving him a name and making him "talk of a life said to have been mine above in the light before I fell" (H 109). By the end of the tale, the narrator has been, is, or will have been, both victim and tormentor (H129).

Near the closing of the narrative we are told that, besides Pim, Bom and the narrator, there are actually, in this Hell-realm, thousands, maybe millions of couples, each couple paired as tormentor and victim, and that, after a considerable stretch of time, these couples break up, moving in a kind of endless procession or caravan to form new pairs with their roles reversed, repeating and perpetuating this brutal dialectic in a "state of nature" (H 111–127). But the swamp is not only a realm of archaic justice; it is also, I believe, a realm where our "species," having "suffered morally" and needing moral and spiritual enlightenment, must pass its allotted time, somehow learning the meaning of a more caring, more humane sense of justice (H 23, 26).

*

Above the mud-realm, as already noted, is a realm of light: a realm lived in the light and, at night, under the guidance of the stars (See H 43, 72).[9] Although frequently evoked, very little is actually said about his time in this realm, except that it seems to be, or to have been, a much happier time, a time that the narrator often relates in recollections of his childhood and early years of life, evoking images from his earlier "other life," a life "said to have been" his, a "golden age," which passed "above in the light" (H 8–9). Momentarily escaping into his past from the misery of his present conditions, Beckett's narrating voice tells us: "my life above what I did in my life above a little of everything tried everything [. . .]" (H 78). At one point, he says: "two more years to put in a little more then back to the surface ah," suggesting that his time in the swamp might be only temporary, depending, perhaps, on repentance for torturing and forgiveness from the victims (H 83). Although, for the narrator, the world of life in the light above seems to be, and to have been, a happier place than the swamp into which he has fallen, he recalls that, in his "life above," "all I wanted I got nothing left but go to heaven," suggesting, perhaps, that the satisfaction of material desires— the "production line of happiness"—might still leave one bereft of meaningful existence (H 78). Thus he declares, referring to this realm of light above: "had a life up above down here I'll see my things again a little blue in the mud a little white our things little scenes skies especially and paths [. . .] that will be good good moments the good moments I'll have had up there down here nothing left but to go to heaven" (H 76).

Even in the gloom and darkness of the swamp, the light from the world above occasionally penetrates, bringing, if only for an instant, a ray of hope: "my life again above in the light the sack stirs grows still again stirs again the light through the worn thread strains less white [. . .]" (H 88). The consolation of memories, however small, however brief, however faded by the passing of time, is somehow deeply sustaining. Speaking of Pim, the narrator says: "ABOVE the light goes on little scenes in the mud or memories of scenes past he finds the words for the sake of peace HERE" (H 98).

Near the beginning of his tale, still, it seems, not altogether accepting his present plight, lost in the swamp, the narrator tells us, contradicting the impression of muteness in the interactions taking place in the swamp, that "others who had always known me here in my last place they talk to me of themselves of me perhaps too in the end of fleeting joys and of sorrows of empires that are born and die as though nothing had happened" (H 12). Such is life above, the world above, built on the earth, subject there to the conditions—the fate—inherent in natural history.

*

Freud reports a story that bears on the ascription of light to the world above. It seems that a three-year-old boy whom he knew found himself in the interior of a very dark room. "Auntie," he cried, "Please speak to me. I'm frightened because it is so dark." The aunt replied, "What good would that do? You can't see me." The boy declared: "That doesn't matter; if anyone speaks, it gets light."[10] In Beckett's "world of light above," there is the light of speech; but in the world below, there is no speech: the swamp is silent, dark. And its justice is without enlightenment. However, the speech in the world above is mostly idle chatter emptied of meaning, a defense against the silence of death. Beckett is compelled to take us down into the realm of mud, where we might catch at least some seeds of meaning, the murmuring of syllables emerging from the experience of suffering. That is how it is.

*

Above the world of light ("above" in either the biblical, theological sense or the moral-political sense), is a realm that has been named, in the course of Western history, Heaven, Paradise, and Utopia. Clarifying the topography of his tale, the narrator relates that he received a dream "of a sky an earth an under-earth where I am" (H 37). There is even a moment when he suddenly and briefly imagines "ascending heaven at last no place like it in the end" (H 104). And in that moment, he conjures up "days of great gaiety thicker than on earth since the age of gold above in the light" (H 108). But, in the end—the narrative's final reckoning with truth—this realm above is denied reality. Its justice is nothing but the narrator's fantasy.

However, the narrating voice in Beckett's earlier *Texts for Nothing*, evoking a realm very much like the realm of mud in *How It Is*, had already stated:

> No, something better must be found, a better reason, for this to stop, another word, a better idea, to put in the negative, a new no, to cancel all the others, all the old noes that buried me down here, deep in this place which is not one, which is merely a moment for the time being eternal, which is called here (TN 130–131).

The narrator in the next of the *Texts for Nothing* expresses this hope in more detail, but in the allegorical language of theology, declaring that he is waiting "for as long as it takes to die again, wake again, long enough for things to change here, for something to change, to make possible a deeper birth, a deeper death, or resurrection in and out of this murmur of memory and dream" (TN 133).

The "justice" at stake here would require a justice of humanity emerging, metaphorically, from the primitive, creative mud of the state of nature. A justice promised in words, for words are how we share.

*

Where on earth can justice be found—or founded? If through suffering we could begin to learn mutual recognition, the acknowledgement of our shared humanity, our belonging to a community of mortal creatures, and could finally leave behind us the purgatory of the swamp, where divine justice, punishing the guilty, reigns uneasily with the barbaric justice of a state of nature, perhaps our words with one another might fulfill their promise in the light of a justice finer than any theodicy can imagine. However, lest we forget the tragic lessons of the past, we are reminded, with words that evoke Benjamin's interpretation of Klee's painting, *Angelus Novus*, that "progress properly so called ruins in prospect" (H 22). According to Benjamin, the painting shows the angel of history,

> looking as if he is about to move away from something he is fixedly contemplating. [...] His face is turned toward the past. Where we perceive a chain of events, he sees one single catastrophe which keeps piling wreckage upon wreckage [...]. The angel would like to stay, awaken the dead, and make whole what has been smashed. But a storm is blowing from Paradise [...]. This storm irresistibly propels him into the future to which his back is turned, while the pile of debris before him grows skyward. This storm is what we call progress.[11]

Beckett's grammar carries a certain complexity of thought. His rejection of teleologies and eschatologies extends to assumptions and predictions of progress: all the projections of the Enlightenment, and also the prospect that Marxism imagines it can foresee. However, he seems to be expressing skepticism not only about these assumptions and prognostications, but even about the very concept of progress as such. What has been left in ruins for the sake of "progress"? How might our supposedly enlightened notion of progress ruin the very prospect of the future? What might be tragically wrong with this entire way of thinking about our existential situation and its future prospects? What sunny, happy, *credible* prospect lies outside, and above, the swamp we are in?

CHAPTER TWO

The Struggle for Acknowledgement and Recognition

Everyone vaguely apprehends a good in which the soul may rest; and longing for it, each one struggles to come to it.

DANTE ALIGHIERI, *Purgatorio*[1]

§1

In Part One of this book, we considered Beckett's literary works in relation to Judeo-Christian teleology, theodicy, and eschatology, arguing that, for Beckett's surrogate characters, there is no grand teleological design determining the course of human existence, no redemption beyond the time of mortal life, no last judgment as imagined in eschatology, and, to borrow Malcolm Bowie's phrase in *Proust Among the Stars*, no "celestial exit from loss and waste."[2] In Part Two, we reflected on hope and despair in relation to Beckett's various articulations of the utopian Idea, venturing an earthly "paradise." Now, in Part Three, we shall be developing a reading of *How It Is* (1958–1961), in which, shifting from the question of divine justice to the question of justice in the institutions we create, our attention will be drawn to the struggle for freedom and justice here on earth—a struggle that Beckett understands, I suggest, as a struggle for the sense of our humanity. The story is divided into three parts, oriented, in the usual, linear time-order, towards the past, the present, and the future. It is in the third part that justice, the promise of happiness, arises.

*

Molloy tell us that, "What I liked in anthropology was its inexhaustible faculty of negation, its relentless definition of man, as though he were no better than God, in terms of what he is not." "But," he adds, alluding to Heidegger, "my ideas on this subject were always horribly confused, for my knowledge of men was scant and the meaning of being beyond me."[3] All of Beckett's works are invitations to reflect on our lives and question our most steadfast convictions. In keeping with the spirit that undoubtedly moved him to commit himself to the art of storytelling, I propose to give a reading of Beckett's middle-period epic story, *How It Is* (1961), in particular its third part, interpreting it as a dramatic allegory of the slow, halting historical journey of the human species from a violent state of nature toward a just and humane world, or, more specifically, as a representation of the struggle for a civil society organized around a concern for social justice, a concern for the welfare of all.

In "The Affirmative Character of Culture," originally published in 1937, Herbert Marcuse's description of the individual in a society structured by late capitalism and its political institutions illuminates the character of Beckett's narrator and the conditions within which he struggles:

> The individual has the character of an [apparently] independent, self-sufficient monad. His relation to the (human and non-human) world is either abstractly immediate (the individual constitutes the world immemorially in itself as knowing, feeling, and willing ego) or abstractly mediated (determined by the blind laws of the production of commodities and of the market). In neither case is the monadic isolation of the individual overcome. To do so would mean the establishment of real solidarity; and it would presuppose the replacement of individual society by a higher form of social existence.[4]

Whereas, in Part One, I argued that Beckett's work shows *divine* justice in its destructiveness and in its final capitulation to the enlightened forces of modernity, here in Part Three, I want to argue, contrary to what all too many critics have claimed, reading in his works nothing but a ruthless nihilism, that Beckett in fact shows us an impassioned concern for *terrestrial* justice, the conditions necessary not only for our survival, but for our living on, as earth-bound mortals, the only creaturely life charged with the promise that language bears.

Whilst drawing inspiration from the topography in Milton's *Paradise Lost* and, even more from Dante's *Divine Comedy*, to replay the hellish conditions of morally unredeemed creaturely life in the darkness of a realm of existence where the light of redemption—if there is such enlightenment—can just barely penetrate, *How It Is* also draws on evocative allusions to a Hobbesian "state of nature," to narrate in word-images a fictional, allegorical genealogy of the movement, an infinitely slow progress, precarious and halting, towards social justice, terrestrial justice. There is no other work in which Beckett bears witness so powerfully to this movement. I want accordingly to suggest that what Beckett's compelling images are plotting to rehearse is Hegel's dialectical account of the struggle for mutual recognition—recognition of "that other who is me" and "that me who is the other," the necessary condition for the possibility of justice and its freedom—that takes place, in the "state of nature," between the lord or master and his bondsman or slave (TN 113). According to this reading, Beckett's epic is a work of phenomenology—phenomenology more or less in Hegel's sense—that gives concrete, embodied exemplification to that struggle as a movement not only towards freedom and the peace of justice, but really towards a new humanity, a humanity moved by love and sympathy, instead of fear, self-interest, and violence. As Christopher Holman summarizes Hegel's phenomenology in this regard, "what the will wants is to have its own power recognized; the fulfillment of human capacities proceeds through the development of ever more refined modes of recognition."[5] But this does not happen without a struggle over power—the dialectic of domination and submission.

*

In *The Claim of Reason*, Stanley Cavell makes an observation I want our reading of Beckett's story to bear in mind: "Being human is the power to grant being human. Something about flesh and blood elicits this grant from us, and something about flesh and blood repels it."[6] In no work before or after *How It Is* does Beckett explore the phenomenology of this ambivalence, this duplicity, and the dialectic it generates, more thoroughly.

If there can be, and should be, as Benjamin rightly demanded, a "history of the vanquished" that would be "dedicated to the remembrance of the nameless,"[7] all the nameless victims of ancient fears and hatreds, cruelty and injustice, then one of the more compelling ways to understand Beckett's stories, novels such as *How It Is* and *The Unnamable*, might be to read them as works recalling and, in a certain sense, representing, the voices and lives of those whose suffering, destitution, and living death are not recognized in the dominant representations of life in our present time.

In the Prologue, I suggested that we might most appropriately characterize Beckett's storytelling as a form of remembrance and testimony, as bearing witness to the human condition in the twentieth century. In his study on Hobbes, whose writings, like those of Hegel, are unquestionably in the background of Beckett's novel, Leo Strauss pointed out Hobbes's recognition of the role of collective memory in sustaining an understanding of the need for institutions of justice: "The bourgeois existence that no longer experiences these terrors [of the state of nature] will endure only as long as it remembers them."[8] In Beckett's plays and stories, the terrors and horrors of our time—the time within our living memory today—are represented for collective memory; they figure frequently as events that, although past, continue nevertheless to haunt and shape the present, leaving in their wake wastelands of physical, moral, and emotional devastation. In these wastelands, we confront the injustices of mortal existence, along with a smoldering longing for justice. And we are compelled, in effect, to imagine very different relations with others: the possibility of a more enlightened humanity, a kinder, gentler humanity, coming to its senses—coming to itself.

It cannot be merely by chance that, in the study of Beckett's last, carefully chosen residence, the writing desk was placed in front of the window, so that, as he sat there writing, his gaze, whenever he looked up, would fall on the prisoners in the yard of the Santé prison.[9] In *Beckett Writing Beckett*, H. Porter Abbott argued against a common interpretation that reads an unequivocal nihilism into Beckett's intentions and overlooks the social critique:

> Without question, Beckett wants us to feel the weight of political injustice, the outrage of tyranny, the stifling in humanity of engineered lives, the bitter residue of a system of self-interest. [. . .] From beginning to end, Beckett's art is one long protest. It is written out of horror in the face of human wretchedness and with yearning that this wretchedness be lessened.[10]

At a certain moment in *How It Is*, a question is raised about how many unfortunates there are, or were, surviving in the swampy purgatory where Beckett has set the story. We read the narrator's ruminations, making the question of justice the key to the interpretation of this text:

> So neither four nor a million/ nor ten million nor twenty million nor any finite number even or uneven however great because of our justice which wills that not one were we fifty million not a single one among us be wronged/ not one deprived of tormentor as number 1 would be not one deprived of victim as number 50000000 (H123)

Following this claim, this declaration of justice, Beckett gives it an ironic twist, as if to call attention to the perversion of justice—especially that perversion that often takes place in the very name of justice. Significant assertions follow: "We have our being in justice I have never heard anything to the contrary" (H 124). Of course, this tells us nothing about what "justice" is. However, the protagonist narrator, who remains nameless, broods over what "he," presumably the biblical God, whose judgment is supposed to have condemned him to live in the swamp, must have in mind for him: this God must wonder, "if finally he might not with profit revise us by means for example of a pronouncement to the effect that [. . .] in reality we are one and all from the unthinkable first to the no less unthinkable last glued together in a vast imbrication of flesh without breach or fissure" (H 140).

*

When the narrator tells us that "it's like my sack when I had it still this providential flesh I'll never let it go," his remark is recognizing, and indeed realizing, or enacting, a prophetic promise, a providential hope, already marking his body, already inscribed in his flesh (H 55). He may fall into the realm of mud, the realm of muddling reason, muddled justice, and he may lose his sack, with its tins of sardines and its utensils for eating; but as long as he lives on, he still has his body, bearing in its flesh, or as its flesh, the promise that it provides. But does this flesh, this embodiment, provide more than bare life? I would suggest that Beckett's recognition of our intercorporeality—this "vast imbrication of flesh"—implies that the flesh is "providential" in a morally profound sense.

In theological terms, the flesh is a palimpsest in which the word of God might be read. But, whereas Christian theodicy judges the flesh to be the source of sin and immorality, Beckett seems to believe that it is time to recognize that the flesh, for too long regarded as solely in opposition to the spirit, is "providential" in a new sense: it provides shelter for the spirit. The word of God inscribed in the flesh says, or means, not only the gift of life, with whatever suffering that incarnation requires of us, but also the acknowledgement of the moral claim of the other in the condition of a shared fate or destiny, for we are "glued together in a vast imbrication of flesh without breach or fissure" (H 140). As Emmanuel Levinas has argued, drawing on ancient biblical scriptures and Talmudic commentaries, the body is a text bearing a message from paradise.[11] And, as already noted, in Merleau-Ponty's late phenomenology, our bodies are composed of a "universal flesh" and emerge from a certain "intercorporeality." This experience, which he describes in "The Intertwining—The Chiasm," suggests that human bodies are "providential" in nature, since they carry and provide, if not the divine inscription and its promise of paradise, at least something of an elemental, preliminary, and provisional sense of the just and humane community, a community of singular individuals all determined, through the flesh, by an equally shared mortality.[12] Such is the promise that enlightens the flesh. But nothing of that promise is guaranteed.

*

In *How It Is*, as in many of Beckett's other stories, there are vertiginous vacillations in the pronouns, creating confusions and uncertainties; and there are games that Beckett plays with proper names, making identities elusive. Sometimes, as in this story, we cannot even really know for sure whether the narrator is alone or joined in this purgatory to the fate of countless others. But perhaps that ambiguity is not relevant, if, from a certain moral-political standpoint, the standpoint of justice, the many are, or must become, one: a community—but of singularities.

If all those in this swamp, this purgatory, are in some sense, some way, "linked bodily together" (H 140), joined in their lives through what is described earlier in the story as "this providential flesh" (H 55), it is difficult not to think that the operation of a certain conception of justice is at stake, as indeed it was for Merleau-Ponty, when he spelled out, in a hermeneutical phenomenology of the flesh, the "intercorporeality" that is constitutive of our embodied existence.[13] This "intercorporeality," engaging a certain "reversibility" and "reciprocity of positions," yours and mine, mine and the others', defeats the philosophical assumption that justice in social relations must somehow be grounded in, and derived from, an original solipsism and egoism—the theoretical position of the solitary individual.

The phenomenological ground for a theory of justice that Merleau-Ponty explicates completes the earlier grounding for justice that Hegel worked out in his phenomenological narrative regarding the struggle between lord and bondsman for recognition and acknowledgement. Hegel's narrative of this struggle in his *Phenomenology of Spirit* will thus be the touchstone for our reading of Beckett's *How It Is*. My hope is that this reading, concentrating on a theme that has not received sufficient attention, will illuminate Beckett's concern for justice in our ethical life, showing what is at stake in the substance of his narrative.

Before we delve further into the intricacies of Beckett's story, however, it might be useful to consider what, in "Love and Law: Hegel's Critique of Morality," Jay Bernstein says regarding Hegel's thinking in his early essay, "The Spirit of Christianity and its Fate" (1788–1789). Bernstein argues that this text, preceding the *Phenomenology of Spirit*, "provides the most direct and eloquent presentation of the logical structure and moral content of Hegel's ethical vision." According to Bernstein:

> This is a vision of ethical life itself, of how Hegel conceives of the meaning of ethics, what it is about and its internal dynamic logic, and of ethicality so understood as constitutive of our relation to ourselves, others, and the natural world. In working out the substance of ethical living, above all in opposition to Kant's morality of universal law, Hegel is simultaneously elaborating the structural contours of human experience. [. . .] Hegel's ethical vision is hence the vision of the demands and fatalities of ethical life becoming the pivot and underlying logic for the philosophical comprehension of human experience in general. [. . .] At the center of Hegel's ethical vision in the "Spirit" essay is the idea of a causality of fate, an ethical logic of action and reaction: to act against another person is to destroy my own life, to call down upon myself revenging fates; I cannot (ethically) harm another without (ethically) harming myself. In this way the flourishing and foundering of each is intimately bound up with the flourishing and foundering of all. Social space is always constituted ethically, as a space in which subjects are necessarily formed or deformed, freed or oppressed through the structures of interaction governing everyday life. It is this that is Hegel's great idea since it reveals how ethical life matters independent of any particular moral norms, laws, ideals, principles, or ends. Ethical life is not, in the first instance, about moral principles, but about the ways in which both particular actions and whole forms of action injure, wound, and deform recipient and actor

alike; it is about the secret bonds connecting our weal and woe to the lives of all those around us.[14]

It is precisely those "secret bonds" that Hegel demonstrated in his phenomenology of the struggle over recognition and acknowledgement and that Merleau-Ponty, steeped in Hegelian thought, sought to bring to light in his phenomenology of embodiment, recasting them in the last years of his life in terms of a phenomenological hermeneutics of the flesh.

This "chiasmic intercorporeality" that phenomenology brings to light unquestionably constitutes, at the most elemental and universal level of flesh, a sympathetic, pre-moral community among all human beings. This nature is a good beginning for moral development. However, the fully mature, enlightened consummation of that initial structure of sociability— what Bernstein has described as "the secret bonds connecting our weal and woe to the lives of all those around us"—is by no means assured. It is, in fact, inherently precarious, its future always contingent, a question of its constant and consistent encouragement or else, mostly due to adverse and inimical conditions in early life, its tragic displacement by antipathies and violence. Casting us, from the very beginning of our mortal lives, in networks of interdependence, this structure can eventuate in fear and hate, as when dependence on others makes one feel vulnerable, weak, and insecure. And this, in turn, can motivate forms of social life that, in some way or other, involve acts of rage and violence—or exploitative relations of domination and submission, as in the primitive and barbaric "justice" of the state of nature dramatized by Beckett in *How It Is*.

*

Thomas Altizer elaborates another dimension of Hegel's phenomenology that bears on the reading we shall be pursuing in this chapter and its three sequels. "The past generation," he says, "has witnessed a discovery of the deeply theological ground of modern philosophy, one initiated by Hegel's *Phenomenology of Spirit*, a work that not only revolutionized philosophy but for the first time created a philosophical realization of the death of God."[15] What Nietzsche interpreted as "nihilism" figures in Hegel's narrative in a dialectic that requires a moment of "self-negation" or "self-emptying": "This revolutionary theological thinking is also thereby the advent of a purely apocalyptic philosophical thinking, one reflecting the advent of the final Age of the Spirit, an advent inseparable from the absolute self-negation or self-emptying of Absolute Spirit."

According to Altizer, the death of God is reflected in the self-negation or self-emptying of Absolute Spirit. It is "the first conceptual apprehension and enactment of the Crucifixion." And "just as the Crucifixion is at the center of St. Paul's theology, so the death of God is at the center of Hegel's philosophy." This, he argues, "is the center making possible the first full philosophical enactment of an absolute immanence, an absolute immanence that is the total self-negation or self-emptying of an absolute transcendence [. . .]."[16] This immanence, bearing in this new emptiness a memory, a bodily felt sense, of what has been lost, sacrificed for the cause of freedom, is precisely, of course, the irrevocably finite—or closed—world into which Beckett's characters have been thrown, left to survive on their own.

In Hegel's narrative, this revolutionary moment, drawing to a close the time of transcendence, a moment that Altizer wants to call "apocalyptic," certainly inaugurates a new and universal freedom, essential condition for the possibility of justice. But, as Altizer notes, this freedom and justice are initially conceived—in the Enlightenment commitment to Reason—as cold and abstract, an abstract universality destroying all historical traditions and reducing the individual to "a bare integer of existence."[17] (In Part III of *How It Is*, Beckett draws attention to this reduction of the individual to an integer. More on this later.) The Hegelian narrative, however, does not rest when the moment of social revolution has achieved recognition of the *concept* of "universal freedom," because freedom and justice still remain at this stage empty abstractions. The struggle for freedom and justice has barely begun—and must continue.

Hegel's *Phenomenology* accordingly leads us through the dialectic of a brutal struggle for freedom and justice. Universal freedom and justice are possible concretely only when there actually is, in all relationships, *mutual* respect, *mutual* recognition, and *mutual* acknowledgement. This requires respect for the *humanity*, or *dignity*, of all human beings: all must be treated as ends in themselves, never as means to other interests and ends. In a compelling narrative, Hegel shows why, and how, the contradictions in the relationship that the lord or master demands make that relationship inherently self-contradictory and unstable; and his analysis, challenging the authority of the lord or master, shows the way toward the resolution of the struggle, ending it in the revolutionary emergence of a new social system.

However, in the final sections of the *Phenomenology*, we are to learn, it seems, that the evolution of Spirit is consummated in a freedom and justice that essentially presuppose the death of God. Only that death makes us truly responsible for our world; and only that death liberates us from the power of inscrutable judgment operative in theodicy. But, instead of giving us happiness, that freedom and justice, having finally been won by sacrificing God, leaves us in a vulnerable, desperate and vertiginous condition: without any firm grounding, any secure footing, without certainty, ignorant of the future, we must nevertheless act. We see that what Hegel calls "Unhappy Consciousness" is embodied in mournful immobility, knowing there is a need to act but unable to move. This is an immobility or paralysis that many of Beckett's characters enact. It is as if the death of God had somehow left them without motivation, without any capacity to posit ends and endings—left them to survive, indeed, without promise. And yet, despite their "unhappy consciousness," a painfully sharp and lucid sense of their abandonment and deprivation, and despite their longing for rescue, these characters never indicate a desire for immortality: on the contrary, some wish only to return to the stillness of dust, just like the words that Beckett assigns to paper; or, insofar as they long for redemption, what they want is to enjoy here and now, in mortal life, the happiness that language has promised in the story of redemption. But Beckett's characters cannot escape the fate of "unhappy consciousness," which is "capable of peace, reconciliation, and order," as one scholar has put it, "only at the cost of a ceaseless and restless reflection on division and disorder."[18]

§2

In commenting on Beckett's early short story, *The Expelled* (1946), S. E. Gontarski notes that the opening "focuses not on the trauma of rejection and forcible ejection but on the difficulty of counting the stairs down which the narrator has, presumably, been dispatched." And he argues that, strangely, "there is little resentment here at the injustice of having been ejected from some place like a home." Thus, from the absence of any complaining and from the flat, inexpressive tone, Gontarski draws a conclusion that is, I think, debatable: "The focus of injustice in Beckett is *almost never* local, civil, or social, but cosmic, the injustice of having been born, after which one finds one's consolations where one may—in counting, say."[19] Certainly, what always concerns Beckett, in this story as in all his others, is a cosmic dimension, witnessing the "human condition" in all its dimensions: our loss of traditions; our cultural disorientation; our metaphysical homelessness; our existential abandonment and loneliness, bereft of God's omnipresence and authority; our subjection to a paradigm of objectivity that denies us any authentic interiority; but also, finally, our ontological exposure to finitude, contingency, mortality, and nothingness. Beckett's characters may regret having been born, having been thrown into the injustices of existence; but they never regret mortality as such, seeking immortality instead. Most of all, Beckett's works exemplify Richard Rorty's conception of fiction, the greatest works of which, he says, "give us details about the kinds of suffering endured by people to whom we had previously not attended [. . .] and details about what sorts of cruelty we ourselves are capable of [. . .]."[20] And these are issues that, in our time, can be separated neither from a cultural history of theodicy, which is the metaphysical dimension of justice, nor from centuries of struggles for justice in its earth-bound forms.

If justice is ultimately a question of how people today engage one another, how people treat other people, then Beckett's plays and stories witness much about the injustices in today's world; and they express or induce a certain longing for an enlightened world released from cruelty, violence, and suffering. Wherever there is cruelty, or violence, or a homeless beggar on the streets, there is injustice. There are, in fact, surprisingly many allusions to justice and injustice scattered throughout Beckett's works, more than one might suppose: allusions that cannot be interpreted as (exclusively) signifying cosmological, ontological, or metaphysical dimensions of our creaturely life.

In any case, I hear the matter-of-fact tone in which the expelled boarder tells his story to register the shock and shudder of the injustice he has just suffered; the man is, quite simply, numb. What Beckett has given us is indeed an allegorical story about unkindness and injustice. Thus I want to suggest that it is precisely in the expressionlessness with which the expulsion is reported that the full horror of the injustice is expressed. And in its concrete immediacy, the expulsion is quite simply mean and cruel; it is not at all a cosmological or metaphysical injustice—although it can of course become the core of an expanded, allegorical interpretation, seeing in the event a cosmological or metaphysical meaning.

However one interprets *The Expelled*, I will argue that at least *How It Is* is one work that cannot be understood unless it is read in the light of the principle of *mutual recognition and acknowledgement* that is required for the eventuality of social and civil forms of justice: justice understood as a question of the very meaning of our humanity; justice, therefore, as the struggle against all forms of inhumanity.

I have called attention to Beckett's description, in *How It Is*, of the characters in the swamp of purgatory: creatures of "providential flesh" (H 55), they are "linked bodily together," "glued together" (H140). In this story of "life in the dark and mud its joys and sorrows journeys intimacies and abandons," a story told "as with a single voice perpetually broken now" (H 139), the characters will suffer their fate, their justice or injustice, together.

Now if, as Adorno has lucidly argued, "the true basis of morality is to be found in bodily feeling, [that is to say,] the moment of aversion to the inflicting of physical pain on what Brecht once called 'the torturable body,'"[21] then it seems to me that one must read *How It Is* as exposing and exploring that very basis—and the cruelties and injustices that time and again betray it.

Returning for a moment now to Gontarski's argument about justice, formed in his reading of *The Expelled*, I find myself coming to a different interpretation: justice as civility, as social-political economy, is in fact very much Beckett's concern. And nowhere is this more in evidence than in the third part of *How It Is*. But even in the much earlier story, *The Expelled*, Beckett is already engaging the question of human justice and injustice, using the power of a rhetorical minimalism to impart the story. Instead of making his character moan and groan, crying out in pain, and weeping profusely at his plight, Beckett gets a more unsettling, more chilling effect by using what in 1915 Paul Klee described as "cool Romanticism without pathos": Beckett simply tells us, in a flatness of style free of sentimentality and akin to the post-Expressionist style emerging in the mid-1920s known as "Neue Sachlichkeit," that the man expelled from his room in the boarding house was struggling to count the number of steps down which he thrown.[22] The cold objectivity in the report of that difficulty counting the steps is the bitterly ironic reproduction of that horror: the cold inhumanity, the singular injustice, or at least cruelty, in the gesture of expulsion. Are we not, perhaps, to imagine it as an allegorical retelling of God's angry deed? No reason or cause is given for such heartbreaking abandonment. In the course of recounting his expulsion, the man reflects, at a loss to explain it: "And yet I had done them no harm." Was there fairness, or justice, in that expulsion and estrangement? We cannot read his words without confronting the question of justice. And what is at stake here is not divine justice, not metaphysical justice, or not only that, but the humane sense of justice: how we treat one another in everyday life.

I am reminded here of the rigorous sobriety—the "discretion"—manifest in Claude Lanzmann's cinematographic techniques in his filming, some years ago, of *Shoah*, a work of remembrance and testimony: what makes his images so moving, so powerfully compelling, is precisely their "lessness," subtracting as much as possible all traces of subjectivity from the images of the camps: we do not witness acts of Nazi brutality, herding the doomed on and off the cattle cars; we do not see naked women and children on their way into the gas chambers; we do not see piles of naked corpses; instead, in long shots, we follow the train rails leading to the camp; in eerie images, impossible to see without a shudder, we see the stark emptiness, the ordinariness, the banality, of the site, as if nothing unspeakable could ever have happened there; and we hear the ghostly silence. It is the *absence* of corpses that is the more powerful indictment here.

The expelled lodger counts the steps! The overwhelming moral effect in Beckett's story is produced by a similar, morally sensitive aesthetic: at work is a deeply compassionate discretion, a restraint that, by a dialectical twist of irony, makes use of an exaggerated, uncompromising quantitative objectivity to "attest" the inhumanity of the scene. With all emotional warmth subtracted from the event, reducing the expelling of the lodger to a stark facticity, Beckett's words become a mocking *repetition* of the ill will, the cold-heartedness, that we sense must be behind the closed door.

*

How It Is was first published in French, bearing the title *Comment c'est*, which, to Francophone ears, can sound like a verb that refers to some kind of commencement.[23] In "Beginning Again," his perceptive commentary on *How It Is*, H. Porter Abbott, noting the two great historical models for Beckett's work, argues that,

> In the epic tradition, showing how it is has meant showing how things fit, how they work out. In the Bible and in epics coming out of the biblical tradition, this has meant in addition showing how the working-out

of things is just: justifying, as Milton described his task in *Paradise Lost*, "God's ways to man." It has meant showing how even pain and suffering have their place in the order of things, and how in the long run punishments fit crimes, as Dante sought to do with such exacting attention to detail in *The Divine Comedy*.[24]

But the time of these theodicies, using a conception of divine justice in which we of today can no longer happily believe in order to authorize and legitimate the institutions of justice erected here on earth, is irrevocably past. So Beckett's setting, although drawing on Dante and Milton, casts the existential struggle for justice in an elemental realm so primeval that it is virtually unrecognizable as a social order. Beckett's story also draws on the political writings of Hobbes, whose story about the origin of justice in the state begins with a representation of our mortal lives in the "state of nature," as well as on the writings of Hegel, whose story takes us from that state of nature into a political order of constitutionally grounded justice.

In *Dialectic of Enlightenment*, Max Horkheimer and Theodor Adorno claimed that, "In the most general sense of progressive thought, the Enlightenment has always aimed at liberating men from fear and establishing their sovereignty. Yet the fully enlightened earth radiates disaster triumphant." Their first statement is true; but their second one must be amended: if disaster is triumphant, that is because the world has not yet been fully enlightened. And that is what writers like Beckett show us.

Beckett consciously writes in and for an age that has experienced the withdrawing of the divine, a concealment of the metaphysical spirit, abandoning us, God's mortal creatures, to work out our history, our justice, our fate, in a godless world. However, because we are still coping with the afterlife of this momentous event, the topography in *How It Is*, as in virtually all of Beckett's stories and plays for the stage, is presented, even if only dimly, in the metaphorical light of a theological dimension—a dimension illuminated, as all philosophical thought according to Adorno must be, by the remembrance of the promise of social reconciliation, a redemption of our humanity borne by language in its irreducible alterity, hospitality indebted to the other.

In *Texts for Nothing*, one of Beckett's surrogate voices says, opening his words to endless possibilities, among which, however, we surely must include the eschatological: "It's the end [that] gives meaning to words" (TN 111). What end, and what ending, can give meaning to justice? In *How It Is*, what is at stake is much more than the institution, here on earth, of the human sense of justice; breaking into the text are fragmentary reminders of a time in which human history was interpreted in the light of the redemptive justice we projected into a far-off vertical height: Heaven. Is there anything left of that distant justice for us here on earth?

Whereas "universal history, making false claims to universality," has always been written by the victors, the more enlightened discourses of religion have given their voices to the oppressed and the destitute. Nevertheless, the struggle for freedom and justice compels a questioning of the compromises made in the name of the old theodicy—a questioning, that is, of the dispensations and consolations of divine justice, the subject that Hegel takes up for thought in his interpretation of Antigone's tragic choice. The struggle also compels a questioning of ends, endings, and the assumption of last things: a questioning, finally, of the persistent appeal of eschatology.[25] And, more urgently: How and when will we end the violence of the Hobbesian "state of nature," its injustices and cruelties continuing today wherever an economy of uncontrollable avarice and ruthless power prevails? Is there a promising ending for the struggle unto death that Beckett, like Dante, situates in the darkness of the swamp?

Like *The Divine Comedy*, *Paradise Lost*, and Hegel's *Phenomenology of Spirit*, Beckett's novel is not only a work of mourning wrought from suffering and its tragic wisdom; it is also, like them, a reflection on the meaning of universal social happiness, a possibility the promise of which depends on the realization of justice and its peace—here on earth, as it was projected, not long ago, in Heaven. Unlike those earlier works, however, *How It Is* broods on these matters without achieving any resolution, any happy ending, or peace of mind. Whilst words occasionally intervene, evoking spectral images of paradise or traces of a passing moment anticipating happiness, in the end they seem to leave the reader in something like what Hegel might have wanted to call the unhappy consciousness—except that the characters in Beckett's underworld remain perpetually stirred by a desperate desire to break out of the swamp of oppression in which they are hopelessly languishing.

In *The Inferno*, Dante conjures up the poet's experience, coming upon a swamp: "Thus we made our circle round that filthy bog,/ staying between the bank and the swamp, with our eyes turned on those who were swallowing mud."[26] The swamp of mud into which Beckett's story casts its characters is a world virtually bereft of any references to transcendence, and what references there are offer paltry consolation. Reminders of a divine order, the ancient source of redemption, persist, occasionally breaking into the narration, although language in its irreducible alterity, the voice in its frustrating resistance to the assignment of a determinate meaning, is already an indication of the prophetic, the promise made in a "prophetic present,"[27] the time of a gift that paradoxically cannot ever be made present.

The seemingly "otherworldly" interruptions in the narrative remind us, if any are needed, that the presence of evil cannot be resolved by the calculated equivalence of "an eye for an eye", the archaic justice of vengeance.[28] Beckett, however, keeps us inextricably mired in the existential struggle, showing us still capable of only the most elementary human gestures— still immeasurably far from a radically new commencement, utopian or messianic, for historical humanity. For that, after all, is, "in the meantime," how it was and how it is.[29] But Nietzsche's Zarathustra gestures towards a world where "a different justice" might someday rule: "that man be delivered from revenge, that is for me the bridge to the highest hope, and a rainbow after long storms."[30] Revenge is a purely destructive type of justice—nothing but an endless cycle of violence.

In an interview late in his life, Heidegger expressed his hope for the future; but, as in his earlier writings, published with the title *Contributions to Philosophy*, he could imagine a world released from nihilism only in terms of an apocalyptic, absolutely supervenient event, terms, therefore, that seem to deny human beings the capacity, or the will, to transform and redeem. "Only another god can save us," he declared, speaking, as he often would, in an exalted and oracular tone of voice.[31] What might Beckett have replied? Perhaps an ironic line that von Hofmannsthal gave to Zerbinetta, playing a "*commedia dell'arte*" character in Strauss's opera, *Ariadne auf Naxos*. She says what one can imagine that Beckett himself, with his subtle sense of the deepest, ultimately inconceivable affinity between comedy and tragedy, might, among other, equally enigmatic things, have said: "When a new god comes along, we are struck dumb!"[32] Would he not have wanted us at least to acknowledge, even if only to ourselves, that that, after all, is how it is?

We are told, however, that, in their "couplings journeys and abandons," the characters in the swamp feel a need for something like God, "an intelligence somewhere a love who all along the track at the right places according as we need them deposits our sacks," an "intelligence" "to whom given our number not unreasonable to attribute exceptional powers or else at his beck assistants innumerable," to whom they might appeal, murmuring their demands, their needs, "that minimum of intelligence without which it were an ear like ours and that strange care for us not to be found among us" (H 137–138) .

A nameless voice, an uncanny voice, not his own, that the protagonist-narrator says is murmuring "within" him, seems to respond to the need, offering, so he says:

> bits and scraps barely audible certainly distorted there it is at last the voice of him who before listening to us murmur what we are tells us what we are as best he can/ of him to whom we are further indebted for our unfailing rations which enable us to advance without pause or rest (H 139–140)

This prompts the protagonist-narrator to ruminate on the source of the authoritative voice, the voice of the nameless one who has provided what those condemned to the swamp of purgatory are in need of:

> of him who God knows who could blame him must sometimes wonder if to these perpetual revictuallings narrations and auditions he might not put an end without ceasing to maintain us in some kind of being without end and some kind of justice without flaw who could blame him and if finally he might not with profit revise us by means for example of a

pronouncement to the effect that this diversity is not our portion nor these refreshing transitions from solitary travelers to tormentors of our immediate fellows and from abandoned tormentors to their victims (H 139–140)

But we know that, for the justice we need, we cannot depend on God. We must institute that justice ourselves. We must "revise" ourselves. And we know that, in the real world, there can be no "justice without flaw." And yet, nevertheless, in Beckett's stories we will find echoes and traces, hints anticipatory of a finer justice, a justice more enlightened than the ancient justice of revenge that still rules and torments our passions.

Too many domestic relations, economic relations, and political relations continue to be structured in terms of dominance and submission; relations of this nature were not abolished, as Hegel believed, in the system of justice created by the state of law. Thus Beckett's protagonist-narrator wonders whether it is possible to leave behind the injustices inherent in relations not grounded in recognition and acknowledgement, relations the cruelty of which he signifies using the extreme image of tormentor and victim. We shall see, though, that there is reciprocity in that relationship, as the roles are in time reversed. But the violence in the relationships remains, compelling us to give thought to the meaning of justice.

§3

How It Is has been assigned to the very beginning of Beckett's so-called "middle period," coming soon after the trilogy. But like the stories in his earlier, "post-war period," it is still in fact the narration of a journey—or perhaps of countless journeys, destination uncertain. Some readers think of it, therefore, as a work of transition. According to Alain Badiou, after *Texts for Nothing* (1950), Beckett succumbs to his own "failures" and does not emerge from that cast of mind until *How It Is*.[33] In the later novel, Beckett has made significant changes in prose style and narrative form. It is indeed a strange and bewildering form of novel, consisting, not of grammatically well-formed sentences ordered into paragraphs according to a linear narrative temporality, but instead of sentence-fragments that have been assembled to form blocks of text with no punctuation marks at all and with no obvious principles of coherence, unity, and temporality in operation. It seems to be a monologue, an "enormous tale" supposedly told to us as it was heard, with the words given to our narrator: "scraps of an ancient voice in me not mine" (H 7). The story, "ill-said ill-heard ill-recaptured ill-murmured" (H 7), is expressed by a nameless narrator, a voice, presumably male, frequently seeming to quote the dictations, and even the murmurs, of another anonymous voice, perhaps the voice of Beckett, or perhaps that of some other superior author, as when, for example, the narrator calls attention to the constructedness and arbitrary manipulation of the narrative and tells us, possibly expressing his own thought but possibly giving voice to the intentions of the author who has invented him as well, "I'll quicken him you wait and see how and can efface myself behind my creature when the fit takes me" (H 52). Exhausted by his physical exertions and constantly panting and gasping for breath, forced at times to break off, the narrator struggles to tell his story of chance encounters in the darkness of a swamp.[34] This is how the story unfolds, indeed divided into three parts, spanning "vast tracts of time," but only ambiguously staying with the temporal structure of past, present, and future. In Part I, taking place in a time before the narrator's encounter with Pim, the narrator is on his belly crawling in the mud toward Pim and recalling his earlier life in an "age of gold," mostly the years of his childhood, lived in a world said to be above where he is now, a world bathed in a golden light, with blue skies and a green earth (H 7, 44, 108). In Part II, the narrator tells of his encounter and time with Pim in a sort of macabre *dance mécanique*: a strange relationship, predominantly one in which, with their limbs entwined, as Alvarez says, "like amorous primeval reptiles," the narrator concentrates on tormenting and torturing his partner, although there are also moments when he seems to feel a certain tenderness and affection and even crave love instead of brutality.[35] In Part III, the narrator moves away from Pim, seeking another mortal, someone who will treat him as he treated Pim.

As Badiou rightly observes, the narrative represents its characters, its subjects, in just four "figural positions."[36] The top position in each coupling is said to be that of the "tormentor," the "torturer," whilst the bottom position is declared to be that of the "victim":

[1] Wandering in the dark, crawling or swimming—and ceaselessly murmuring—whilst dragging a sack full of survival necessities described, no doubt with irony, in mocking jest, as including "a celestial tin miraculous sardines sent down by God" (H 48)

[2] Meeting someone in the "active" position and coming down on top of him, torturing or tormenting him

[3] Being motionless, abandoned by the one encountered

[4] Encountering another who comes down on top of one whilst one is motionless and "passive," submitting to a time of torture and torment.

Connecting the relations in this narrative construction—always a coupling that involves the torturer, or tormentor, and his victim—to Hegel's phenomenology of recognition, I think it clear that the positions should also be thought of in terms of the "lord" and the "bondsman," or the "master" and the "slave." In Beckett's story, there is, to be sure, reciprocity or reversibility in the violence of the encounters. But what kind of justice is this? It is ultimately repeating the archaic justice of revenge. As the couplings change, the torturer or tormentor becomes the one tormented or tortured. There is symmetry, but it is the symmetry of a justice still bound to violence. The violence of a lawless "state of nature" continues. In any case, Badiou wants to say that these generic figures are intended to represent "everything that can befall a member of humanity."[37] That is an extravagant and questionable interpretation.

§4

In a prose absolutely bereft of embellishment, its minimalism tolerating few adjectives and adverbs and an equally minimal use of explanatory clauses, Beckett leaves it to his readers to catch the rhythms that have replaced punctuation and hear what speaks even from the silence of the caesuras. This is a prose that compels readers to undergo a semblance of what his characters are experiencing. Seldom giving us time to pause, the prose leaves us panting, gasping for breath, as breathless as the narrator claims to be, struggling to move through the mud, murmuring, choking on the mud-laden words, and panting from the exertions. It is as if the mud were forcing us to struggle for survival, clinging to the very words that are drowning us. The repetitions of words, the rhythms, are, like diabolic chants, extremely hypnotic—but also, in consequence, radically disorienting. Finally, the prose sucks us into the oppressiveness of its dark, muddy swamp, insisting on describing in excruciating objective detail the bodily movements of the narrator and the mortals he encounters.[38] Thus, for example, the narrator tells us:

> moving right my right foot encounters only the familiar mud with the result that while the knee bends to its full extent at the same time it rises my foot we're talking of my foot and rubs down one can see the movement all along Pim's straight stiff legs [. . .]/ my head same movement it encounters his it's as I thought but I may be mistaken with the result it draws back again and launches right the expected shock ensues that clinches it I'm the taller/ I resume my pose cleave to him closer he ends at my ankle two or three inches shorter than me (H, Part II, 57–58)

There is cruelty in this interaction—but also a certain estranged eroticism. Something Adorno says in "Lyric Poetry and Society" sheds light on this eroticism: "the chimerical yearning of language for the impossible becomes an expression of the subject's insatiable erotic longing, which finds relief from the self in the other."[39] In the swamp where a "state of nature" prevails, the yearning of language, bearing the promised happiness of justice, struggles in metaphor to connect bodies.

§5

Now, as we know, according to the Old Testament, God made Adam from mud or clay, bestowing upon that elemental material the life of breath and the gift of the word. In his poem "Germanien", Hölderlin writes of the "golden word" as a "flower of the mouth."[40] Beckett, without necessarily abrogating this thought, turns the poet's phrase into "the mud in the mouth" (H, Part I, 27). For him, this mud, representing the ancient mud of the Old Testament, is still the primordial creative substance, that from which all life on this planet emerged and to which, in death, all life must return, submitting to an inexorable mortality. Thus, it seems that, for Beckett, recognition of this fact, and reflection on its humbling meaning, its pathos and its hope, are essential moments in our understanding of ourselves as human beings, creatures who are mortal, being wrought of earth, "humus":

> the mouth opens the tongue comes out lolls in the mud that lasts a good moment they are good moments perhaps the best difficult to choose the face in the mud the mouth open the mud in the mouth thirst abating humanity regained (ibid.)

Beckett's nameless surrogate narrator tells us:

> the tongue gets clogged with mud that can happen too only remedy then pull it out and suck it swallow the mud or spit it out it's one or the other and question is it nourishing and vistas last a moment with that/ I fill my mouth with it [. . .] and question if swallowed would it nourish and opening up of vistas they are good moments/ rosy in the mud the tongue lolls out again [. . .] (H, Part I, 28).

Recalling God's creative act, giving life to Adam, Beckett's narrator, assuming the same creative powers, says: "we're talking of Pim never be but for me anything but a dumb limp lump flat for ever in the mud but I'll quicken him you wait and see and how I can efface myself behind my creature when the fit takes me" (H, Part II, 52). The storyteller creates with words, nothing but words.

Everything in this story, including the narrator's monologue, takes place in the primeval mud, elemental source of all earthly life.[41] Why and how the narrator, and the other mortal creatures there with him, if there are any, originate or end up in that swamp, "warmth of primeval mud impenetrable dark" (H, Part I, 11), is never explained. Near the beginning of the story, the narrator says: "others knowing nothing of my beginnings save what they could glean by hearsay or in public records nothing of my beginnings in life" (H, Part I, 12). Little by little, though, we learn about the narrator's earlier life, if not about his beginnings, as every now and then moments of this much happier life, an almost enchanted, idyllic life in the realm "above," a life secure in the loving care of his mother, are brought back in flashes of memory. But the golden light of that world, the world above the swamp, is always quickly extinguished. Fallen into the realm of the mud, moving with difficult and painful exertion, carrying an old coal sack cluttered with tins, utensils, and foodstuffs, the narrator records, in the "bits and scraps" of memory he can recall, the journey he undertook to move towards "another"—in fact, as he phrases it, in a seemingly endless cycle, "from mortal to mortal" (H, Part II, 62). Struggling to approach and finally encounter one of the others, someone called Pim, who, like him, is swimming, or rather, restlessly and aimlessly moving about, submerged in the mud, the narrator at once becomes his relentlessly cruel tormentor (H, Part III, 131). In Part III, the narrator records his journey *away* from Pim the victim and *towards* Bom, the one who will, for a time, become his own cruel tormentor. And he suggests or implies that there is in fact an infinite "procession," a "cortège," of unfortunates like him, all of them submerged in the mud and journeying through its confusion.

Narrator, Pim and Bom: three morally muddled creatures mired in the mud of a Hobbesian state of nature and somehow muddling through. In their estrangement and loneliness, they each desperately seek out another like themselves; they seem to long for some creaturely relationship, some warmth and affection, perhaps even love. But the violence towards which they gravitate with one another leaves them in a condition more like death than life.

Why, when they finally succeed in getting together, do the relationships turn to violence, a conflict of wills, a brutal dialectic of domination and submission? Beckett's tale offers no answer; but this dialectic is like the negative image of the dialectic that moves toward mutual recognition, the mutual acknowledgement of a shared humanity, a shared suffering and mortality, a journey that could be on the way to a world order of enlightened justice.

§6

Raising questions about our present conception of justice, questions about its humanity, Beckett retells Hegel's narrative about the emergence of our modern sense of humanity from an archaic form of justice. The narrator hears ghostly voices, voices murmuring in the mud, voices dictating, speech badly distorted, swamped, by the terrible medium through which it must pass. Quoting, or say parroting these "dictations," Beckett is satirizing the authority of the "author" behind the theological narrative: fate, prophecy, and God's power. Among the unfortunate denizens in this realm, there is, despite these voices, virtually no communication by speech: instead, they interact, in their coupling, one of them acting, the other reacting, one dominating, the other submitting, one "speechless," the other briefly "reafflicted with speech" (H 140), in an endless cycle or procession, perpetuating the virtually mute state of nature. Recalling the Commandant's way of serving the demands of justice in Kafka's "Penal Colony," Beckett's narrator reports the inscribing of something painful on Pim's back. This reader cannot be certain, but it seems possible that the narrator desperately wants Pim, his victim, to speak, to talk with him, and that his assault is an effort to compel Pim to respond. The victim does respond, though: he cries out in pain—he "sings" (H 64–65, 69–71). And whatever minimal speech does take place in this situation is speech "extorted" by torture. It is not "free speech" (H 92, 130, 143). Despite the manifest brutality, however, the narrator declares, "I am not a monster" (H 64). But if he is not a monster, then his brutality must be all-too-human. The peculiar "justice" that reigns in Beckett's realm of mud is actually nothing but violence in disguise, even if the roles are eventually reversed.

Despite the elemental intertwining, the "imbrication of flesh" that joins the couples, there is only, or almost only, instead of a sense of shared destiny, a common wealth and common task, only a compulsion to repeat, endlessly, the ancient ritual of absolute power, determining what "justice" is in a simulacrum of the state of nature. For Merleau-Ponty, our "intercorporeality" constitutes an initial community of sympathies, the first moment in the formation of an enlightened institution of justice, a justice of reversibility and reciprocity, prototype for what he will describe as "an ideal community of embodied subjects,"[42] whereas for the denizens of Beckett's realm of mud, the elemental intertwining of flesh, of limbs, is little more than an agonizing struggle with no apparent purpose.

There is, in Beckett's earlier work, *The Unnamable*, a passage that anticipates the story in *How It Is*, succinctly dramatizing the nature of this struggle, the archaic justice of "an eye for an eye," and catching, at the same time, the psychological ambiguities that frequently characterize relationships involving sadism and masochism: "[. . .] he'll come and lie on top of me, lie besides me, my dear tormentor, his turn to suffer what he made me suffer, mine to be at peace" (UN 374). Undertaking "imaginary journeys," the narrator in *How It Is* speaks of "imaginary brothers in me" (H 114). Cain and Abel? And he characterizes the "journeys and abandonings" as times in which all the mortals caught in the mud are "forsaking" one another, each one determined "to go toward his other," but only in order to torment a different "brother" or be, in turn, tormented. They do not go toward one another in order to talk, learn, grow, offer help, share, or love.

As Robert Pogue Harrison points out in his review of recent translations of *The Divine Comedy*:

The basic "plot" has to do with the pilgrim's efforts to complete a long, self-interrogating, and transformative journey at the end of which his inner being—which, like human history, suffers from the perversion of self-love—becomes harmonized with the love that moves the universe. Salvation means nothing more, and nothing less, than such harmonization.[43]

In *How It Is*, no such harmonization takes place. Painfully missing, in Beckett's swamp-realm, is the *capacity* for love—which, as Hegel's phenomenology of spirit suggests, is crucial for mutual recognition and thus, too, for a society structured to make possible the justice that happiness demands. Nevertheless, there is some hope for a passage beyond violence. For, conflicting with the need to dominate, and with the violence it requires, intense outbursts occasionally interrupt the narrator's story-telling and indicate sentiments approximating love or the need for love. And there are even some moments of tenderness as well, as when, in the narrator's words:

> In the dark the mud my head against his my side glued to his right arm round his shoulders his cries have ceased we lie thus a good moment they are good moments/ how long thus without motion or sound of any kind were it but of breath vast a vast stretch of time under my arm now and then a deeper breath heaves him slowly up leaves him at last and sets him slowly down (H 54–55)

And there are, awakened in this intertwining of bodies, dreams, fantasies, of a time of shared happiness:

> One day we'll set off again together and I saw us the curtain parted an instant something wrong there and I saw us darkly all this before the little tune oh long before helping each other on dropping with one accord and lying biding in each others arms the time to set off again (H 57)

In a moment of self-knowledge, grasping the muddiness of his sentiments, the narrator tells us: "my right arm presses him against me love fear of being abandoned a little of each no knowing not said" (H 66). In fact, the narrator, confessing a need for affection, a need for love, seems desperate to know whether, despite the tormenting, Pim might actually love him in return:

> [. . .] no knowing life above life here God in heaven yes or no if he loved me a little if Pim loved me a little yes or no if I love him a little in the dark the mud in spite of all a little affection find someone at last someone find you at last live together glued together love each other a little love a little without being loved be loved a little without loving [. . .] (H 74)

He becomes violently enraged and verbally abusive, in fact, when Pim, suffering from the torture, remains unresponsive to his gestures of affection (H 75–96). But of course love, like truth and justice, is not something that can be extorted. In the swamp of mud, the state of nature, rationality is muddled; and without rational dialogue, relations become confused and distorted. Justice requires dialogue, mutual recognition and acknowledgement: "mon semblable, mon frère," as the poet Baudelaire expressed it. That is what, in a muddled way, the narrator's "love" is all about. As we shall learn in Part III of *How It Is,* behind the violence is a deep, passionate longing for justice, social relations no longer determined by power and force: love embodied in a sense of shared humanity, the kind of love that, sharing the good and the bad in a common fate, is kept open by the promise in words exchanged.

CHAPTER THREE

Cruelty and Kindness: Humanity in Question

In a letter to Thomas MacGreevy, that I briefly discussed in the Prologue, Beckett writes: "I am reading Schopenhauer. [. . .] An intellectual justification of unhappiness—the greatest that has ever been attempted. [Unhappiness] reminds us of what are the most necessary of all things: tolerance, patience, forbearance and charity, which each of us needs and which each of us therefore owes."[1] Beckett writes, I claim, in aspiration to an idea of the human. Despite efforts to resist a grim view of the world, and an equally grim conviction regarding the means to express this view, a consciousness almost bleak enough to tempt ending his tormented life, despite efforts to limit his emotional vulnerability, Beckett cannot escape caring deeply about the fate of humanity, and in fact, suffering the agonies of all creaturely life, as his repeated evocations not only of human cruelty and misery, but also of slaughterhouse brutality tell us. In a mode of writing that shows its expressive impoverishment, weakness, and struggle, telling stories about characters living in a time of spiritual emptiness, a time of destitution, Beckett occasionally permits himself to share that sympathetic caring with his characters and readers, giving way—but only with the most heartbreaking restraint—to expressions of sentiment sublime in their very plainness and austerity, letting us hear "the little murmur of unconsenting man, to murmur what it is their humanity stifles" (UN 319). But, despite the bleak images of creaturely life on this earth—images suggesting nihilism—that his words so frequently materialize, one finds, in his stories, occasional moments evocative of warmth, tenderness, and kindness. We must not overlook these surprising passages, invariably expressed in a prose of restrained lyricism, in which Beckett affirms his faith in the promise of humanity. His stories remind us to attend to the suffering of others. This is not nihilism. The reading I am offering here supports Gerhard Richter's claim: "The screaming that Beckett claims as the structure of his writing [. . .] reverberates both in the imperative that writing intervene in unnecessary human suffering and in the acknowledgement of writing's impotence to transform the world in which this suffering occurs."[2]

Beckett's characters are not created out of nothing. They are the creations of feelings and sentiments that must be given expression. In *Open City*, Teju Cole gives voice to a sense of life that I believe could not have been foreign to Beckett as he created all his characters—all his "delegates," as he was wont to call them: "[S]ometimes it is hard to shake the feeling that [. . .] there really is an epidemic of sorrow sweeping our world, the full brunt of which is being borne, for now, by only a luckless few."[3]

We must not ignore, or interpret otherwise, the expressions of anguish over the human condition that he puts in the mouths of his characters—his "delegates": "I know my eyes are open, because of the tears that pour from them incessantly." I take these eyes to express, in their abjection, something of our almost "dead longings" for a way to the redeeming of the utopian promise: "The horror-worn eyes linger abject on all they have beseeched so long, in a last prayer, the true prayer at last, the one that asks for nothing."[4] Asks for nothing—but still is hoping. And still is pouring his tears into words, giving them new life:

> But I am silent, it sometimes happens, no, never, not one second. I weep too without interruption. It's an unbroken flow of words and tears. With no pause for reflection. But I speak softer, every year a little softer. [. . .] Slower too, every year a little slower. [. . .] If so the pauses would be longer, between the words, the sentences, the syllables, the tears, I confuse them, words and tears, my words are my tears, my eyes my mouth.[5]

Beckett transforms his tears because he cannot relinquish his faith, despite a nagging skepticism, in the redeeming power of words.

*

What I claim is at stake for Beckett is the prospect of a morally transformed world, a more just, more humane world. The "promise of happiness" is borne by language in its very existence as medium of communication; but it also appears allegorically in Beckett's stories: negatively in meanness and cruelty, affirmatively in affection, empathy, and kindness.

The suffering of many of Beckett's characters is ontological: they suffer simply from being, from existence, regretting they were ever born, a condition they did not choose; and they suffer from the knowledge of their mortality, not because they fear death or because they are not assured of an immortal afterlife, but because they do not want to depart from their life in this world. But many in his stories suffer from the actions of others. It is about this, now, that I want to write. Nothing refutes more unequivocally, more decisively the reading that interprets Beckett as a nihilist, denying that there is anything at all of meaning and value in the world, that there is anything worth fighting and dying for, than what Beckett shows us about cruelty and kindness.

Why are many of Beckett's characters victims? If not the victims of circumstance, survivors of catastrophes, disasters, and calamities, many are victims of indifference, meanness, and cruelty. Many are deprived: deprived of mobility, deprived of home, deprived of purpose, and deprived, most tragically, of human warmth, sympathy, and kindness. They are people like us—except that, whether as victim or as agent, they have suffered the loss of what connects them to a sense of humanity.

In the course of his inner monologue, Molloy wonders: "From where did I get this access of vigour? From my weakness perhaps."[6] In one way or another, Beckett's characters are disabled, powerless to move, impotentialized, profoundly weak—weak in the distinctive sense that figures in Paul's Corinthians (1 Cor 7: 27–28). Bearing witness to the suffering of the weak, Paul wrote: "God chose what is weak in the world to shame the strong. God chose what is low and despised in the world, even things which are not, to bring to nothing the things that are." Might Beckett have chosen to tell stories about weak and disabled characters in order to shame the strong and remind us of the kindness, sympathy, and justice we owe to others? Might he have chosen to show us the world of the low and the despised in order to provoke us to question our acceptance of such a world—the world as it is?

With a sympathy that avoids sentimentality and a moral lucidity that avoids moralism, Beckett tells stories that call attention to acts of wanton cruelty and the suffering those acts cause. Pointing out that, when Beckett was a young man, he took part in the Irish struggles for independence, Richard Toscan argues that he always felt "tremendous compassion for humankind. Man's inhumanity to man upsets him gravely." In keeping with these sentiments and convictions, Beckett consistently refused to tolerate the arbitrary justice in divine caprice: there can be, he thought, no rational ground for so much hatred and brutality, so much inhumanity. On a related theme, Toscan tells of an interview with Jack MacGowran, who reported that Beckett often said to his friend, "People must think I had a very unhappy childhood, but I hadn't really. [. . .] But I was always more aware of the unhappiness around me than of happiness."[7] So much unredeemed misery (TN 118).

*

Beckett's affections and sympathies, and, correspondingly, his distress and outrage over acts of cruelty extend, in fact, beyond the human—to the animals we abuse and kill. In one of Beckett's earliest short stories, *Dante and the Lobster* (1932), he shows great sympathy even for the lobsters that are sacrificed for our feasts, dropped alive into pots of boiling water. The second act of *Waiting for Godot* (1952) begins with Vladimir singing a song about a dog:

A dog came in the kitchen
And stole a crust of bread.

Then cook up with a ladle
And beat him till he was dead.
Then all the dogs came running
And dug the dog a tomb—

He pauses and broods, deeply moved by this wonton cruelty, this injustice, before continuing the song and repeating the verse. When Estragon enters, Vladimir, who broke off singing the song, is moving "feverishly" about the stage, trying to shake off his sadness. We are not surprised when, as Estragon nears, he expresses a desire, perhaps rather a need, to embrace him (WG 37–38). In all three novels in his trilogy, *Molloy* (1947), *Malone Dies* (1951), and *The Unnamable* (1953), the thousands of animals we cruelly slaughter every day of the work-week are also remembered with unreserved sympathy. Indeed, in these novels, vividly concrete images of the slaughter taking place where animals are slaughtered erupt into the narrative again and again, each time catching us off guard and compelling our attention. It is impossible not to read these disruptive evocations, which by their repetition insist on our thought, as intensely passionate protests against a society that requires indefensible cruelty.

*

Unprovoked acts of meanness and cruelty appear in many of Beckett's works. They cannot be ignored. Watt, for instance, is the object of several such acts. On his way to Mr. Knott's house, where he will assume the duties of a servant, Watt is ejected from the tram. He is also knocked over by a railway porter, and has a stone thrown at him by Lady McCann. The narrator in *The Expelled* is summarily rejected and thrown out the door of his boarding house. He falls down the steps and is left to lie helpless on the sidewalk. In *Malone Dies*, Beckett takes us into the House of St. John of God, a psychiatric hospital where Lemuel, one of the "keepers," is shown taking sadistic pleasure in brutally beating up and tormenting the helpless patients in his care.

Waiting for Godot (1952) shows us some of the most memorable and most thought-provoking instances of both cruelty and kindness. We cannot take in the drama that unfolds without being compelled to answer its moral questions. Pozzo, who is blind, badly mistreats his "guide" Lucky, whom he drives and beats with a whip, constantly insulting, humiliating, and scolding him. Estragon, too, mistreats him, kicking him and hurling abuse at him—but in revenge for how, in an earlier episode, Lucky had mistreated him. Cruelty so often goes on and on in endless cycles, its origin lost in the ambiguities of the conflict. The archaic justice of revenge still rules.

In the second act of the drama, Lucky, staggering under the weight of the baggage he is carrying, falls down, causing Pozzo to fall down too. Vladimir and Estragon—"Didi" and "Gogo"—see Pozzo crawling on the ground and begging for help getting up. Didi's spontaneous urge is to give the needed assistance. But instead, he and Gogo debate whether or not to go and help.

Gogo, recalling the chicken bone that he gave yesterday to Pozzo, says: "We should ask him for the bone first. Then if he refuses we'll leave him there" (WG 50). Didi replies, asking "You mean we have him at our mercy?" The conversation continues:

ESTRAGON: Yes.
VLADIMIR: And that we should subordinate our good offices to
   certain conditions?

Didi thinks that would be an "intelligent" course of action and pursues the thought of helping "in anticipation of some tangible return" (WG 51). And, since Gogo is still not moving, still not moved by sympathy, he vehemently urges action, but mixes up the altruism of an immediate, spontaneous responsiveness and the utilitarian calculations of negotiated self-interest in a jumble and tangle of arguments that shift without so much as an interval of breath from an assertion invoking the highest moral ground to an assertion of the lowest and meanest motivation:

Let us not waste our time in idle discourse! (*Pause. Vehemently.*) Let us do something, while we have the chance! It is not every day that we are needed. Not indeed that we personally are needed. Others would meet the case equally well, if not better. To all mankind they were addressed, those cries for help still ringing in our ears! But at this place, at this moment of time, all mankind is us, whether we like it or not. Let us make the most of it, before it is too late! Let us represent worthily for once the foul brood to which a cruel fate has consigned us! What do you say? (*Estragon says nothing.*)

"It is true," he continues, fully aware that he is reducing to absurdity a morally demanding situation that in any case should require no deliberations at all,

that when with folded arms we weigh the pros and cons we are no less a credit to our species. The tiger bounds to the help of his congeners without the least reflexion, or else he slinks away into the depths of the thicket. But that is not the question. What are we doing here, *that* is the question. (WG 51–52)

"And," he adds, "we are blessed in this, that we happen to know the answer. Yes, in this immense confusion one thing alone is clear. We are waiting for Godot to come." What is sadly, tragically funny about Didi's claim is that, whilst they are waiting for God, or for the Messiah, whose presence would symbolize, or represent, a morally transformed humanity and world, they have delayed helping Pozzo, missing the call to enact, immediately and spontaneously, a good-hearted, benevolent deed: exactly the kind of act that would have embodied the virtue of that morally transformed humanity for which, presumably, they are longing. Their debating and waiting is what, ironically, is delaying the "arrival," metaphor for the realization of the potential claimed by the word "humanity."

To be human is to respond to others with kindness and, if need be, with charity and forgiveness; it is to assume some responsibility for the welfare of others. But, by the end of Vladimir's ruminations, that sense of responsibility, that sense that others have a moral claim on our humanity, has vanished. Didi and Gogo are waiting for the impossible messianic event, an event that cannot happen without their transformed hearts. It does not cross their minds that transformation is in *their* hands. Nothing is delaying the time of redemption, the time of justice and its share of happiness—nothing at all, that is, except their ruminating and waiting.

Vladimir eventually goes to give Pozzo a hand, telling him, in a mockery of messianism, "We've arrived." When Pozzo asks, "Who are you?" Didi answers by saying something that, precisely because it is obvious, should provoke us to thought: "We are men" (WG 53). Are they? Can their comportment be reconciled with our conception of humanity? After trying several times to pull Pozzo to his feet, Didi stumbles and falls himself. The three pitiful characters exchange more words, and eventually, with Estragon's encouragement, Vladimir strikes Pozzo, who cries out in pain and crawls away. That is Estragon's revenge for Pozzo's assault on him. Despite his anger, however, when he hears Pozzo's cries for help, Estragon says, "He's all humanity" (WG 54). That says infinitely more than he seems capable of understanding. Nevertheless, after Vladimir gets up, the two friends finally lift Pozzo onto his feet.

Pozzo and Lucky are paired as master and slave: Hegel's dialectic, staging a phenomenology of the struggle for mutual recognition. Pozzo keeps Lucky on a rope. But Vladimir and Estragon, though occasionally quarrelsome, are bound to one another in friendship. Sometimes, although awkwardly, and not without one or the other showing a little reluctance, they even embrace (WG 37–39). Despite the quarrels, they obviously take care of one another, as when, for instance, Didi, seeing Gogo asleep and imagining him in need of warmth, takes off his overcoat and wraps it around Estragon's shoulders. And when Gogo wakes up, startled and anxious, Vladimir hastens to comfort him. Beckett's stage directions say that he *"runs to him, puts his arms around him"* (WG 46).

Kindness and affection also figure, even if only implicitly or by indirection, in some of Beckett's later stories. In *Molloy*, Jacques Moran shows hospitality and kindness in his encounter with a stranger, a "foreigner," offering the hungry man a tin of sardines—more nourishment than he had hoped for (MO 140–141). In *Enough* (1965), the narrator, an old woman now, reminisces about her life with a man now deceased, possibly a guardian, with whom, from the age of six, she lived. She recalls their frequent walks together, hiking hand in hand across meadows in flower, through forests, and up the steepest hills in the region, sometimes hiking for many days at a time, even in the rain. Her tale concludes with her recognition of the emotional dimensions of their relationship.[8] Although gestures of tenderness and affection are not explicitly expressed, it is manifest that their relationship was indeed a close, warm, and intimate one, a sharing of kindness, and that she remembers their time together with fondness and nostalgia. The reminiscences are bittersweet.

In *Worstward Ho* (1983), there is a somewhat similar image of affection. Here, in a prose of heart-rending beauty, Beckett asks us to imagine, along with him, an old man and a child:

> Hand in hand with equal plod they go. In free hands—no. Free empty hands. Backs turned both bowed with equal plod they go. The child hand raised to reach the holding hand. Hold the old holding hand. Hold and be held. Plod on and never recede. Slowly with never a pause plod on and never recede. Backs turned. Both bowed. Joined by held holding hands. Plod on as one. One shade. Another shade.[9]

The elegiac poignancy of this image is almost unbearable, precisely because it so rigorously avoids all sentimentality, reducing the affection, the tenderness, to the simplicity of a gesture. The closing words of that strophe, that textual unit, representing them as two shades, intensify the emotional impact, rendering them as images fading away. But the images of tenderness, of affection, remain, lingering in our longing—a longing all the more overwhelming because of the indeterminacies that Beckett imposes. As the story unfolds, though, we find ourselves accompanying them to an old graveyard, a place of shades.

In *Endgame* (1957), Nagg and Hamm are storytellers. But Beckett gives Hamm an especially meaningful story to invent and tell.[10] It takes place on the eve of Christmas and is about a man, pale and thin, who came crawling towards him on his belly, raised his face to him, "black with mingled dirt and tears," and implored him to give him something—some bread, say—for his starving son, his "little boy," to eat. Hamm, however, was unmoved and angrily rebuffs the father's entreaties: "Use your head, can't you, use your head, you're on earth, there's no cure for that!" After a pause, he says to him, violently: "But what in God's name do you imagine? That the earth will awake in spring? That the rivers and seas will run with fish again? That there's manna in heaven for imbeciles like you?" Once his irritation passes, though, Hamm relents and offers to take the man into his service. The man then asks if he would consent to take in the child as well—"if he were still alive." At this point, Hamm is not sure how to continue the story and breaks off, waiting for further inspiration to come. "Nothing you can do about it, just wait for it to come. (*Pause.*) No forcing, no forcing, it's fatal." But it becomes apparent that, despite the interruptions and distractions, Hamm is still brooding on the story. He tries to treat it with levity, but his heart is heavy. He was getting in the mood to continue the story; but finds himself overcome by sorrow. "He takes out a handkerchief, unfolds it, and holds it spread out before him." "We're getting on," he says, struggling to avoid the claim on his emotions:

> You weep, and weep, for nothing, so as not to laugh, and little by
>   little . . . you begin to grieve.
> (*He folds the handkerchief, puts it back in his pocket, raises his head.*)
> All those I might have helped.
> (*Pause.*)
> Helped!
> (*Pause.*)
> Saved.
> (*Pause.*)
> Saved!
> (*Pause.*)

And then, seeming to change the subject and refer to an earlier discussion with Clov about all the rats in the kitchen, although he could be talking about all the people needing help in the world, he says, "The place was crawling with them!" And then he attempts to continue telling the story, at first repeating his reply to the supplicant, but, after a pause, he seems to be talking to himself. It is not made clear, however, why he is angry, and whether his anger is directed against this man, who is making a moral claim on his compassion and charity, or whether it is directed against himself. Is he angry because he is too soft-hearted or because he is too cold-hearted? Is he angry because he feels helpless, unable to help all those in need? Does he think that the man has been making demands he feels no obligation to meet? Is he angry, perhaps, because the demands make him feel guilty? When he repeats his earlier words, it now seems possible that, instead of being addressed to the supplicant, he might be addressing himself. But he ridicules one of the fundamental principles of morality:

> Use your head, can't you, use your head, you're on earth, there's no
>   cure for that!
> (*Pause.*)
> Get out of here and love one another! Lick your neighbor as yourself!
> (*Pause. Calmer.*)
> When it wasn't bread they wanted it was crumpets.

He pauses at this point and abruptly changes the subject. Various distractions arise here, but Hamm is haunted by this story and its resolution never ceases to summon him. What is the fate of the boy? Does it not depend entirely on Hamm?

If he exists he'll die there or he'll come here. And if he doesn't
(*Pause.*)
It's the end, Clov, we've come to the end. I don't need you any more.

If the storytelling is finished, no listener is needed.

But Beckett's own story, the story that constitutes his play, his own endgame, has not ended with those words. Hamm has one more, one final monologue. After responding to Clov, his obsession returns. It bears the signs of a conscience burdened by a guilt that refuses to be repressed:

If he could have his child with him. . . .
(*Pause.*)
It was the moment I was waiting for.
(*Pause.*)
You don't want to abandon him? You want him to bloom while you
    are withering? Be there to solace your last million last moments?
(*Pause.*)

His next words are, like so many others, ambiguous:

He doesn't realize, all he knows is hunger, and cold, and death to crown it all. But you! You ought to know what the earth is like, nowadays. Oh I put him before his responsibilities!

Whatever we imagine as answers to the riddles in Hamm's words, we cannot be uncertain about Hamm's intentions. He will be done with that story. He will "speak no more about it." But it will not be easy for *us* to dismiss or forget the moral challenge, the moral claim that Hamm's story, fragmented, incomplete and enigmatic though it is, sets before us. What does kindness—benevolence, if you will—require of us? In witnessing that dialogue, we cannot evade its summons to our own moral conscience. How would *we* respond to similar supplications? Making us witnesses to acts of kindness and acts of indifference and cruelty, Beckett's stories are provocations for us to examine our acknowledging, or failing to acknowledge, the moral claims of others. What does our most deeply felt sense of humanity require of us? What does the suffering of others require of us? Without the cultivation of our capacity for kindness, sympathy, charity, and forgiveness, how could there possibly be a justice befitting our presumption of humanity?

In *Waiting for Godot*, Vladimir asks himself: "Was I sleeping while others suffered? Am I sleeping now?"[11]

CHAPTER FOUR

The Human Voice:
Of Promises and Solaces

In this brief chapter, we shall reflect on two intriguing phrases that appear in *How It Is*: "this voice its promises and solaces all imagination" (H 79) and "hang on to humankind" (H 94). I shall argue that what Adorno says about the subject's voice in lyric poetry may also be said here about the voice that can be heard murmuring through the words that Beckett gives his profoundly lonely narrator in *How It Is*: "Only one who hears the voice of humankind in the poem's solitude can understand what the poem is saying."[1]

One of the most striking and consequential features of Beckett's story, *How It Is*, is the absence of words exchanged among the presumed characters. We hear some moans and cries, but only the words, the murmurings and mutterings, of the story's narrator. In the darkness of the swamp, the narrator at times cries out, but he receives no response; and even in his real or imaginary encounters with others, no words are exchanged. But the possibility of justice in the promise of happiness depends on words. Our humanity, as Beckett will remind us, is "made of words" (H 45). And it abides in the *keeping* of words, the words that remember and must redeem our institutions of justice for the promise of happiness, taking us out of the state of nature. It is words that make an enlightened justice, hence communities of peace, more than a possibility.

*

How It Is, like the stories in the earlier trilogy, is haunted by voices, many different ones. And it is told or narrated in, and by, at least two seemingly distinct voices, although there are perhaps more. There is one especially strange voice which, compelling but anonymous, seems, quite frequently, to be dictating what the narrator is telling us. In a frequent refrain, seemingly more and more derisive each time it is announced, the narrator, in a sort of ventriloquism, declares, "I say it as I hear it."[2] What voice is the narrator hearing? Whose voice is it? Early in the telling of the story, the narrator states that he hears "an ancient voice," a voice that is "in him" but "not his" (H 7). Is this the voice of God? Is it the "voice of Reason"?[3] Or is it the voice of moral conscience? There is no definitive answer. It is surely important, though, that we are told about times when it is only through hearing other *human* voices that the unfortunates consigned to the mud-realm might be able to "hang on to humankind" (H 94). So it seems to me that we must somehow read what the narrating voice says about the voice according to that understanding. As when, for example, that voice says: "if he heard a voice if only that if he had ever heard a voice voices if only I had asked him that I couldn't I hadn't heard it yet the voice the voices" (H 74).

Very often, when the narrator invokes a voice he hears—an "ancient voice," said to be "the voice of us all," "all those here before me and to come," that invocation is followed by the phrase "quaqua of us all," or by some variant of that phrase (H 107–108): "I hear of an ancient voice quaqua on all sides the voice of us all [. . .]" Is this nothing but "a gibberish garbled six-fold" (H 134)? The second "qua" seems to be making a mockery of essentialism, reducing the philosopher's solemn idealisms to idle chatter—or mere gibberish. Significantly, however, all but one of these strange invocations are in the third part of the work: the part specifically related to justice and to a future. Hence, another way of reading the "quaqua" would take the repetition of the Latin to be a rhetorical form of emphasis, suggesting that what really matters in the voice—its deepest sense—is its humanity: its being the "voice of us all." If we take "quaqua" together with the other words that are most frequently placed near it, namely, as "the voice of us all" or "the voice on all sides," then we can hear it emphatically reverberate throughout the mud-realm, where it would be audible, perhaps, to all who long to hear it, as the voice that gives expression to our still weak sense of a shared humanity. The "voice of us all" would be the voice that speaks in the name of justice—or for its sake. We shall return to this emphatic characterization of the voice in the final chapter.

But questions remain: Is this voice-of-us-all Rousseau's enlightened voice, representing the "*volonté générale*"—or is it the dangerous voice of the mob, the "*volonté de tous*"? Two very different representations of ethical life, and of justice in particular, are here at stake. In its concern for justice, *How It Is* raises provocative questions about the truly human voice, the voice *qua* human. Beckett is listening intently for that strangest of all voices. It is a voice that, by virtue of its character as a singular plural, singular in its pluralism, irreducible in its alterity, is recalling us all to our humanity: "this voice its promises and solaces all imagination" (H 79). Beckett's surrogate leaves us to go on, questioning this voice, this voice that becomes many, a voice that, bearing the promise of happiness, belongs to the alterity of a "prophetic present"[4] that can never be made present, and that therefore cannot belong to the future of our historical continuum, but only to a future event that has interrupted and broken that historical template.

How are we to go on, however, if this voice, the voice that promises, in its otherness, to redeem a wayward mankind, were recognized to be nothing but a delusion, a consolation created by the poetic imagination? Beckett is not afraid to make fun of the philosopher's formal use of the Latin "*qua*," as in its essentialisms. But attributing promises and consolations to the imagination does not imply that they are illusions; for, after all, there can be no creative relation to the future without the work of imagination. Ultimately, Beckett's answer to that question is the same as Adorno's. In *Negative Dialectics*, the philosopher says, unequivocally: "To lend [an ear and] a voice to suffering is a condition of all truth."[5] We must go on, courageously defending our ideals and dreams, not discouraged by having had to renounce conceptual essentialism as the way to rescue the *promise* in the voice of humanity. That renunciation, though, is not a loss but a gain, for we now can understand how a certain form of violence, a certain neglect of singularities, of differences, was always secretly operative in that essentialism—even when, in the course of the last three centuries, its inclusive universality has served the cause of social progress. Beckett is listening to all the voices of suffering and giving them all a voice, trying to make them audible—and audible, within their singularity, a voice that speaks for—and also to—all of humanity. In that sense, it is with an "ancient" voice he is speaking.

*

What, now, shall we think about the "solaces"? Sometimes, the encouragement of hope comes, not by way of an image preserved through memory, but by way of a nameless voice, an uncanny voice, said to be "inside" the narrator, but not his. In "bits and scraps barely audible certainly distorted," the narrator hears a voice he seems to be attributing symbolically, metaphorically, to the "God" that speaks of "some kind of justice without flaw," radically different from the "justice" of violence in the state of nature, where speech, if there is any, is "extorted" by torture:

> there it is at last the voice of him who before listening to us murmur what we are tells us what we are as best he can/ of him to whom we are further indebted for our unfailing rations which enable us to advance without pause or rest/ of him who God knows who could blame him must sometimes wonder if to these perpetual revictuallings narrations and auditions he might not put an end without ceasing to maintain us in some kind of being without end and some kind of justice without flaw who could blame him/ and if finally he might not with profit revise us by means for example of a pronouncement to the effect that this diversity is not our portion nor these refreshing transitions from solitary travelers to tormentors of our immediate fellows and from abandoned tormentors to their victims (H 139–140)

The gripping story that Beckett has made out of words should remind us that, however impoverished our lives, we are still blessed with the fertile ooze of language. "God" is nothing but the metaphor for that blessing. Language is still giving itself to us, still "providential," a medium of creation, of beginnings, even when the story it must tell is of endings—including the ending of the myth of its own origins. Near the end of his story, the narrator, overwhelmed, marvels at the gift he has received:

> when the panting stops ten words fifteen words a murmur to the mud/ and later much later these aeons my God when it [the panting] stops again ten more fifteen more in me a murmur (H 136)

Words—a few—continue to come: enough words, enough consolation, to make a promising end for the story, and evoking at the same time the prospect of other stories, "other worlds" (H 143). As long as there are words, words coming, hope endures. And what the narrator touches with those words he emphatically reclaims for a sense of humanity at once promising and provocative, "all imagination":

> then from mouth to mud brief kiss brush of lips faint kiss (ibid.)

Words can sometimes be redeeming—like kisses.

CHAPTER FIVE

Redeeming Words

For the one who is yearning/ The hint was enough, and hints are/ From long ago, the language of the gods.

FRIEDRICH HÖLDERLIN, "Rousseau"[1]

In *Truth and Method*, Hans-Georg Gadamer remarks that, "the light which causes everything to emerge in such a way that it is evident and comprehensible in itself is the light of the word."[2] Words can be deceptive, hostile and hateful; but they can also bring light, revealing, uncovering, reminding—and, with that light, much that is good. As I recall, Kafka says, somewhere: "Through words come remnants of light." Freud tells a story about a child that poignantly confirms this uncanny event.[3] And Adorno will maintain that, "even artworks that incorruptibly refuse celebration and consolation do not wipe out the radiance."[4] The reading of *How It Is* proposed in this chapter, and indeed throughout this volume, supports this claim.

In Beckett's story, there is a seemingly miraculous moment of illumination, hardly to be expected, of course, but immediately subject to skepticism: "[. . .] sudden light on the sacks at what moment renewed [. . .] it's possible too there's a poor light"[5] In this chapter, we shall give thought to Beckett's rhetoric of "illuminations"—some of the metaphors and allegorical figures, such as the light that suddenly falls on the sacks, through which, in that tale, a few hints and intimations of the promise of happiness appear, despite the abysmal darkness of the swamp. Even if meant to be teasing, jocular, and ironic, the invocation of that miraculous light sustains, against all nihilism, the possibility of its presence in the world. What the words in this work are ultimately illuminating is the presence of the promise of happiness in the state of nature, where mortals are struggling with one another in an infinitely slow movement toward a higher justice. Insofar as this promise is in the keeping of language, the redeeming of this promise is the same as the redeeming of words—of their power to redeem.

*

Yielding to despair is of course a temptation; but the narrating character in *How It Is* resists completely abandoning hope, despite the extreme deprivation, finding moments of consolation in recalling his life as it was in the world said to be above, the world of a happy childhood. Recalling the past, the words of Beckett's narrator become lyrical, mournful, yet filled with longing and hope:

> I look to me about sixteen and to crown all glorious weather egg-blue sky and scamper of little clouds [. . .]/ we are if I may believe the colors that deck of emerald grass if I may believe them we are old dreams of flowers and seasons (H 29)

The frequent naming of the blue in his reminiscences here (as in his later story, *Lessness*) calls to mind the blue sky that appears in Hölderlin's very late poetic fragment, "In lovely blue"—and this passage recalls, too, the "blue flower," symbol in early German Romanticism of a longing for the Absolute, that life of the spirit sought so ardently in *Heinrich von Ofterdingen*, Novalis's story of a journey not only toward self-knowledge, but toward an understanding of the world that might make possible the redemption of that world—its achievement of universal enlightenment.[6] Beckett makes the narrator's dream-moment, returning to his childhood in the world above, both bitter and sweet; it is a flashback, happening in a flash. He sees a magical world of blue skies, white clouds, radiant sunshine, emerald grass, and blue flowers. Although it does not last, there is an after-image of the lost beauty and joy, a heart-warming glow in the keeping of memory that lingers on for a while:

> blue and white of sky a moment still April morning in the mud it's over it's done I've had the image the scene is empty a few animals still then goes out no more blue I stay there [. . .]/ it's going let it go I realize I'm still smiling there's no sense in that now been none for a long time now/ my tongue comes out again lolls in the mud I stay there no more thirst the tongue goes in the mouth closes [. . .] it's over it's done I've had the images/ that must have lasted a good moment (H 31)

In these rare and precious moments, the narrator feels as if he were floating up, returning to the world above, the world he thinks of as home (H 70): "life above [. . .] our little scenes blue by day always fine a few fleece clouds the stars by night heavenly bodies never dark" (H 93). In the world above, one is of course nearer to a sense of things infinite and eternal. These daydreams are invariably tinged with a lyrical sense of paradise. But when reality breaks into the vision of the dream, the voyage skyward is over:

Sea beneath the moon harbor-mouth after the sun the moon always light day and night [. . .] all those I see are me all ages the current carries me out the awaited ebb I'm looking for an isle home at last [. . .] a little turn at evening to the sea-shore seawards then back drop sleep wake in the silence eyes that dare open stay open live old dream [. . .] (H 86)

He soon yields to skepticism: "what isle what moon you say the thing you see the thoughts that sometimes go with it it disappears" (H 86). The isle, symbolic promise of paradise, vanishes into the darkness. But even in the confusion, it seems that after-images continue to haunt the chambers of memory. Drawn to the life he once enjoyed in the world above, the narrator's restless thoughts struggle to defy reality and soar upward, even rising above earth-bound life, deep into the blue sky, realm of infinite possibility, where a different justice, a different paradise, may be imagined for our earth-bound world.

Throughout *How It Is*, as when the narrating character tries to recall the faith in the biblical Christian stories he once felt as a child so long ago, the themes of salvation and redemption—a new interpretation though still signified by the old familiar names—are brought into our consciousness, evoked many times and in many different ways:

that belief said to have been mine the feeling since then vast stretch of time that I'd find it again the blue cloak the pigeon the miracles he understood/ that childhood said to have been mine the difficulty of believing in it [. . .] the belief the blue the miracles all lost never was/ the blue there was then the white dust impressions of more recent date pleasant unpleasant (H 70)

As the narrator watches the procession of men, "an endless cortège of sacks" moving slowly through the mud, he must leave his daydreams and childhood memories to confront his present harsh reality. He is hungry. But despite a skepticism verging on the cynical, he is so worried about surviving that he cannot resist wondering whether he might possibly receive "a celestial tin miraculous of sardines sent down by God at the news of my mishap" (H 48). Whether sent by God or not, he does seem to have some sardines in his sack. In any case, he reports seeing "[. . .] sudden light on the sacks," although he cannot resist questioning that hint, that sign: "at what moment renewed [. . .] it's possible too there's a poor light" (H 138).

Not long after, he is seized by a dreadful question: "is it possible the old business of grace in this sewer why want us all alike some vanish others never" (H 61). Theodicy can no longer justify itself. Its gracious dispensations of justice are arbitrary and unjust; they make no rational sense. But although the time of theodicy is past, the old words still bear the Idea that might inspire a transformation of the institutions of justice here on earth, redeeming its promise, the potential that Kant and Hegel, like Hobbes, glimpsed in the monstrous justice, inevitably tragic, that had been inherited from the archaic world. And it is, I suggest, solely for the sake of that inspiration, that potential, with its circumstantial illuminations, that Beckett preserves and draws upon the rich allegorical figures of Christianity. The "old business" of grace must be translated into a concern for justice on earth—a truly human justice, favoring no one: Why should a God decree that some vanish, others never?

*

In an intricate, richly allegorical image alluding to Christ's last Passover supper and Dante's *Inferno*, the narrator reflects on his determination to survive the journey through the darkness of the swamp, a state of nature where justice is still mired in violence:

> When the last meal the last journey what have I done where been that kind mute screams abandon hope gleam of hope frantic departure [. . .]/ abandoned here effect of hope that hangs together still the eternal straight line effect of the pious wish not to die before my time in the dark the mud [. . .] (H 46)

The narrator's thinking, reflected in the writing, is sometimes muddy and muddled; but at other times, as here, it reaches the most intense lucidity and resolve, the words touched by that gleam whose promise they carry into expression.

Despite the darkness and gloom of the mud-realm, it seems that there are, occasionally, hopeful signs, "rags of life in the light," interventions coming from the realm above:

> it dies and I see a crocus in a pot in an area in a basement a saffron the sun creeps up the wall a hand keeps it in the sun this yellow flower [. . .]/ the light goes on in the mud the prayer the head on the table the crocus the old man in tears the tears behind the hands skies all sorts different sorts on land and sea blue of a sudden gold and green of the earth of a sudden in the mud (H 21)

So many words evoking the promise of happiness: the sun, the crocus, the blue of sea and sky, a yellow flower, the saffron, the green and gold of the earth. To be sure, these things all belong to his past. They are things remembered. Nevertheless, the names that invoke them bring them back into the present: the crocus is blossomimg again, the sun is again creeping up a wall, the earth is once again gold and green. However briefly, they were rescued by words, words saving them for yet another day. This beautiful image, and the glorious light of hope it casts, is said to last hours; but, inevitably, it eventually fades away, leaving him, and all the other unfortunates in this realm of mud, once again in the dark. But, whilst it lasted, was it not an intimation of happiness? If only he could "catch a glimpse," as he phrases it, of "the good moments I'll have had up there down here nothing left but to go to heaven" (H 76). The memories are full of promise: they bespeak future possibilities. But, as he acknowledged earlier, "fewer gleams no gleams what does that mean that I was once where there were gleams."[7] What kind of consolation can memories of the past possibly give (H 22)? Having abandoned the hope that theodicy offers to the devout, the faithful, the narrator stoically bears his profound loss of faith, even refusing the illusions that would make the nothingness of death less frightening. It is not immortality he wants, not the consolations of the hereafter, not condolences for having been born, but happiness in a mortal's measure of life. The only redemption of time passed on earth that is worth the wanting is to be found in the beauty of a crocus, the patterns of sunlight on a wall, the deep blue of the sky, a faint ray of light—and the moments of kindness, affection, respect and love that bring people together.

*

Torn between moments of hope and moments of despair, the unfortunates in nature's mud-realm suffer the conditions of a terrible form of justice. The narrating voice speaks of the "effect of our justice":

> though in what this diminished by a general free for all one does not see/ involving for one and all the same obligation precisely that of fleeing without fear while pursuing without hope/ and if it is still possible at this late hour to conceive of other worlds/ as just as ours but less exquisitely organized/ one perhaps there is one perhaps somewhere merciful enough to shelter such frolics where no one ever abandons anyone and no one ever waits for anyone and never two bodies touch/ and if it may seem strange that without food to sustain us we can drag ourselves thus by the mere grace of our united net sufferings from west to east towards an inexistent peace we are invited kindly to consider/ that for the likes of us and no matter how we are recounted there is more nourishment in a cry nay a sigh torn from one whose only good is silence or in speech extorted from one at last delivered from its use than sardines can ever offer (H 142–143)

Another world? A world ordered by the mercy of a different justice? A world in which a just peace might finally prevail? Are we contemplating the world said to be of "life above"—that is, life as *we* know it here on earth? Or are we instead conjuring up an image of an impossible paradise? Let us read again, but now in a larger context, the narrator's agonized invocation of a "paradise" whilst recollecting his childhood years:

> [. . .] I have suffered must have suffered morally hoped more than once despaired to match your heart bleeds you lose your heart drop by drop

weep even an odd tear inward no sound no more images no more journeys
no more hunger or thirst the heart is going you'll soon be there I hear it
there are moments they are good moments/ paradise before the hoping
from sleep I come to sleep return between the two there is all the doing
suffering failing bungling achieving until the mud yawns again (H 23)

In these words, making suffering and hope *share* in the fate of ethical life,
one can hear the voice of a weary and despairing, but still undefeated
revolutionary spirit.

But the memories of the past haunt the present, and the narrator's
tale echoes Dante's words. Those memories work against hope. At the
gate to the Inferno (III, 1–9), we read the solemn and terrifying words:
"*Lasciate ogne speranza, voi ch'entrate*". In English translation, those
words, even more chilling in the "*terza rima*" of their original Italian, still
reverberate with frightening power: "Abandon all hope, you who enter
here."[8] According to Boccaccio, the poet "always wore an expression of
melancholy and contemplation." In the story Beckett gives his narrator, we,
his readers, are bidden, as in a passage we quoted earlier, to contemplate
both hope and despair:

the last meal the last journey what have I done where been that kind
mute screams abandon hope gleam of hope [. . .] a dog/ abandoned here
effect of hope . . . (H 46)

In Goya's late painting, *El Perro Semihundido* (1818–1823), there is an
abandoned dog, Baroque symbol of mourning and melancholy, about to
drown in a vast flood or sea of darkness. Only its head is still visible above
the water, as the frightened animal looks up towards the sky, waiting for a
divine intervention that, if its probability may be judged by the ominously
dark color of that sky, will never be coming to the rescue. Interpretations of
this enigmatic work abound; but in terms of the interpretation that I wish to
propose, the dog, almost drowning, represents Goya's bitter disillusionment
and sorrow as he witnessed the horrors of war in Spain and saw the hopes
and dreams of the Enlightenment, the ideals borne by the French Revolution,
ruthlessly negated by the Terror that followed. Like the dog in his painting,
his hopes were drowning—but in human blood and a sea of tears.

Is happiness—a chance of happiness—nevertheless still possible? The
narrator resolves at least to continue pondering the question, even if happiness
itself eludes him: "I'm going end of the journey/ to speak of happiness one
hesitates those awful syllables" (H 25). So he does, occasionally, touch on
the question. And sometimes, despite the elusive allusiveness even of the
word, conjuring up life in the world above is sufficient for a measure of
solace, evoking something like happiness, something approaching what
seems like it might commonly be called happiness, although peace of mind,
as Christ's apostles remind us, is not what life is about. In any case, what

we are wont to think of as "happiness" is nothing but an illusion, shadowed by its contrary (H 43). What, then, is happiness? What is it necessary to know? (H 51) If we take seriously the "imbrication of flesh," we must ask ourselves: Can any individual be happy when even one other among us is without nourishment and shelter? How might justice become the hospitality of a utopian, messianic time?

*

Even in the misery of the underworld mud-realm, there is at least a small chance for the promise of universal happiness to begin its transformative work. Despite so much against it, images reminding of paradise, and the redeeming light of another moral order, are made to appear in Beckett's story: "just enough to be thankful for" (H 104). For one who is yearning, the hint is enough. Not for nothing have his words conjured up blue skies and a crocus in the sun, redeeming the significance of their presence even in the forbidding darkness of the swamp.

CHAPTER SIX

Where in the World is Justice?

*Just as our eyes avoided looking at the heavens
above them, fastened upon earthly things, so
justice holds them here on the earth below.*

DANTE, *Purgatorio*[1]

§1

In *Dialectic of Enlightenment*, Horkheimer and Adorno look with eyes as coldly clear as Dante's at the course of history:

> Each advance of civilization has renewed not only mastery but also the prospect of its alleviation. However, while real history is woven from real suffering, which certainly does not diminish in proportion to the means of abolishing it, the fulfillment of that prospect depends on the concept. For, not only does the concept distance human beings from nature, but [. . .] it enables the distance that perpetuates injustice to be measured.[2]

Hegel too contemplated that history and desperately sought within it some rational explanation for the horrors he could not deny: "But as we contemplate history as this slaughter-bench, upon which the happiness of nations, the wisdom of states, and the virtues of individuals were sacrificed, the question necessarily comes to mind: What was the ultimate goal for which these monstrous sacrifices were made?"[3] Hegel's image of history is as relevant today as it was in his years, but his attempt at an answer gets no support from the dialectical narrative that, in the wake of the Holocaust, Horkheimer and Adorno propose.

Reflecting on the application of that narrative, Susan Buck-Morss argues in her recent book that, "to arrive at the Universal, one must immerse oneself in the Particular. [Thus], the truly productive 'universal' experience of reading Hegel is [. . .] through the liberation that one's own imagination can achieve by encountering dialectical thinking in its most concrete exemplification."[4] This is what she attempts in *Hegel, Haiti, and Universal History*. It is also, I suggest, what, in his own way, hence as a story-teller, a writer of fictional stories, Beckett attempts to accomplish in *How It Is*, immersing us in the phenomenology of the master-slave relation, revealed in all the brutality of its concrete particularity. We may wish to deny it, but the story is a mirror.

Now, as Buck-Morss notes,

> By the eighteenth century, slavery had become the root metaphor of Western political philosophy, connoting everything that was evil about power relations. Freedom, its conceptual antithesis, was considered by Enlightenment thinkers to be the highest and universal political value. Yet this political metaphor began to take root at precisely the time that the economic practice of slavery—the systematic, highly sophisticated capitalist enslavement of non-Europeans as a labor force in the colonies— was increasing quantitatively and intensifying qualitatively to the point that by the mid-eighteenth century it came to underwrite the entire economic system of the West, paradoxically facilitating the global spread of the very Enlightenment ideals that were in such fundamental contradiction to it.[5]

But how far are we, even today, from the injustices of the past? In *How It Is*, Beckett cunningly draws us into a realm that it is not easy to dismiss as pure fantasy—or as a story about an archaic condition of humanity, a state of nature we left behind centuries ago. The images his words create are compelling.

§2

In the later years of his life in Paris, Beckett reserved for himself, quite detached from the rest of the apartment that he shared with his spouse, a small, plainly furnished study in which he sat, writing his stories. His desk was placed in front of a window—the only window in the small, dark room. Looking out that window, what he saw, surrounded by high walls, was the desolate courtyard of a prison. . . . It is as if Beckett wanted a constant reminder to reflect on questions of justice and injustice, circumstance and fate; wanted that penitentiary perspective on the existential, ontological, and metaphysical dimensions of mortal life. But what a prospect for the freedom of the imagination! A prison courtyard might kill the imagination— or it might spur it to rebellion. Sometimes we react to imposed limits by rebelling, taking them as a challenge to be exceeded. Imposed limitation— negativity—may do what comfortable accommodations cannot do! Too much comfort, too much accommodation, can tempt the spirit into complacency, softness in thought. The threat to spirit might be just what it needs! The prison outlook could certainly be depressing. But it could also be a powerful provocation—to freedom of spirit, freedom as imagination. A provocation, perhaps, to the imagining of another story—a very different story—about injustice and the way to justice.

"In all art that is still possible," says Adorno, "social critique must be raised to the level of form, to the point that it wipes out all manifest [i.e., unmediated] social content."[6] As we shall see, Beckett's *How It Is*, the principal story with which this chapter is concerned, engages "social critique," as do in fact many of his stories, in a mediated, but oblique and enigmatic way. In *How It Is*, Beckett introduces problems of sociality, whether with real others or with the imagined presence of others; and ultimately, as I shall argue, the narrative turns on questions regarding justice and fairness, a theme that recalls *The Expelled*, a much earlier narrative. In this later work, retelling Hegel's story, we shall find ourselves moving with infinite slowness toward the time of justice.

*

In his essay on "Fate," Emerson reflects on the human condition with words that, when I read them, evoke Beckett's narrative imagery in *How It Is*, retelling: "Man," he says, as if interpreting the meaning hidden in the barbaric life this story records, "is not order of nature, sack and sack, belly and members, link in a chain, nor any ignominious baggage, but a stupendous antagonism, a dragging together of the poles of the Universe." Emerson then goes on to say that mankind "betrays his relation to what is below him,— thick-skulled, small-brained, fishy, quadruminous,—quadruped ill-disguised, hardly escaped into biped, and has paid for the new powers by loss of some of the old ones."[7] The meaning of this sentence is elegantly forked, for the betrayal is twofold. Are we not still, in fact, too thick-skulled, small-brained, fishy, and ill-disguised? And what if "some of the old ones," representing our primordial, biological connectedness to nature, have been betrayed by rejection rather than by sublation—the progressive development and maturation of our *sympathetic* "powers," nature's innate sociability, impulses suppressed and lost in the egoity compelled to emerge in the Hobbesian "state of nature"? Emerson's words contain an indictment for the sake of a humanity whose originary possibility has still not been grasped in its newer powers. Mutual victimization—or mutual redemption? For which, in his tale, will Beckett's words declare?

There is no authentic art that does not appeal to the redeeming potential of a humanity that does not yet exist. Beckett's stories bring us close to the calamities and sufferings of life; but in that proximity, they summon us to take the measure of injustice. What is the justice of the Judeo-Christian God, judged by the suffering of humanity?—and what is human justice, measured by the impossible, the utopian or messianic promise of happiness? In one way or another, Beckett's characters are, all of them, embodiments of these questions, their lives and words cast into the grammatical structures of a temporality of justice that stretches, in memory and mourning, between hope and despair, loss and promise.

In the story of his journey in search of his mother, Molloy tells us that he kept moving restlessly from town to town, never finding the hospitality and peace of mind he sought. "But," he says, with the suggestion of an allusion to Kafka's story about the "man from the country": "in the country there is another justice, other judges, at first" (MO 60).[8] Another justice? Is that what he has been seeking? In any case, he stopped in a town as night fell, reflecting that there was little likelihood he would be attacked by any creaturely life, whether humans or wild animals, that he might chance to encounter. "Morning is the time to hide" from predators, he says: "They wake up, hale and hearty, their tongues hanging out for order, beauty and justice, baying for their due" (MO 61). What justice is at stake here?

In *How It Is*, Beckett takes us into a realm where, although the "vertical" justice of theodicy is virtually inoperative, the "horizontal" justice of humanity, precondition for the utopian possibility of universal happiness, has not yet been realized. This incompleteness and indeterminacy is emphatically registered in the syntax of Beckett's prose.

The justice we need, the justice on which universal happiness depends, is a profane justice for the world we live in, a justice without which there can be no beauty and no truth untouched by human suffering, no beauty or truth free of the guilt we must bear for turning away from those who, in their destitution, ask only for justice now—not in the heaven of an afterlife, but right here, in this very world. This is the happiness for which, often in silence, his characters patiently plead. All there is.

§3

Near the end of *How It Is*, Beckett's narrator speaks of "the faint sign for us of a change some day nay even of an end in all honour and justice" (H 135). He also invokes "refreshing alternations of history, prophecy, and latest news" (H 129).

At the same time that he was conceiving the dialectic of lordship and bondage, Hegel wrote in a note:

> Reading the newspaper in early morning is a kind of realistic morning prayer. One orients one's attitude against the world and toward God [in one case], or toward that which the world is [in the other]. The former gives the same security as the latter, in that one knows where one stands.[9]

As we are nearing the end of *How It Is*, the narrator, speaking of his life, his journey, evokes a temporality not experienced in linear terms as past, present, and future, but instead in what might be thought to be the more hopeful terms of "refreshing alternations of history prophecy and latest news" (H 129). But, as the story draws to a close, the narrator is alone, still feeling trapped in the mud and an oppressive darkness. Now there is, as Adorno says of Kierkegaard's situation, "only an isolated subjectivity, surrounded by a dark otherness." [10] All the others, whom we were encouraged to believe present with the narrator, there in that swamp, that state of nature, have been erased by the author's decree, their independent existence no longer recognized. Unable, in the mud of the swamp, to orient toward God and somehow banished from the familiar world of light above, the protagonist is thrown into the most extreme estrangement and dread: "I shall die," he screams, adding the word "good" (H 147). A strange ending to this tale! Is this a moment when "the theatricalization of the self becomes the sole proof of its freedom and its existence"? [11] It is indeed as if everything except the nameless narrator has suddenly vanished into absolute darkness: the swamp, the faint light from above, Pim, Pam, Bem, Bom, Krim, Kram and all the other mortals supposedly part of the caravan, dragging their sacks on a journey without end. All apparently gone! Is the narrating speaker objecting to the story-teller's intention to end the tale—making him die, as it were, into, and as, the silence of its ending? He calls out—perhaps hoping his pleas will reach God, perhaps just hoping that the others suffering in the mud, if in fact there are any, might come toward him and, simply by the warmth of their presence, their nearness, console or reassure him. But if there is a God, this God is unmoved by his plight: unmoved and unresponsive. And no other mortals, if there are any in this swamp, respond to his cries, his screams. He begins to feel that even death might be better than going on in his present isolation and estrangement. In the realm of brutal power relations where it seems he has been cast, our narrator can count on neither "historical prophecy nor the latest news."

Speaking of dying and death, a frequent and important theme in Beckett, we might think of the narrator's resistance to dying in the context of the history of philosophical thought. Ever since Aristotle (*Politics* 1253a9), the human has been understood *metaphysically* as "the animal that 'possesses' language." That defining interpretation displaced and suppressed a much older defining interpretation, emphasizing the human as finite and mortal. The bearing of this older understanding for Beckett's story is that, whereas the realm of the swamp is the state of nature, essentially a condition of animal existence, the narrator's screaming, declaring his dread of dying, is an assertion of his belonging among the mortals—human beings capable of dying, unlike the other animals, which merely perish and cease to live. And this means that, whereas in the swamp, what prevails is a justice reduced to mere bodily existence, "bare life," what the narrator in his expression of mortality is longing for is a more humane justice that belongs to a properly human world. To be a mortal able to die is to be released from the state of nature and from the injustice that rules in that realm as "justice"—or it is, at the least, to be yearning for that release.

In this regard, it is pertinent to note that the word "realm," which I have used to describe the swamp in which Beckett's story takes place, derives from words bespeaking the regulations and regimentation of governing regimes; and these, in turn, derive from the ancient Greek words ὀρέγω, which means "stretch out" and "extend," and ὄρεξις, meaning "longing or yearning after." Beckett represents the narrator, and perhaps also the others whom he names, as inhabiting a realm or medium in which they are ceaselessly reaching out towards an other to couple with in longing and yearning—not only for others, if there are any, but also for a different justice.

The textual passage upon which I have been commenting comes at the very end of *How It Is*. It marks the end of the story of a journey engaging the dramatic interactions in which, by my reading, a new justice is at stake. Are the screams only, or mainly, lamenting ontological mortality? Whatever else these screams could be, might they be metaphorical ciphers, registering the sacrifice, the martyrdom of the particular to the universal: the sacrifice of nature, including its own, that the self must make in order to overcome, for the sake of a different, more enlightened justice, the brutal nature that rules in the state of nature? "Objective is the fractured landscape; subjective, the only light in which it glows."[12] Might the "dying" in question be the metaphorical "dying"—or, in Hegel's terms, the sublation—of the solitary, self-centered, pre-ethical ego? Freedom and justice, actualizing the promise of happiness, require a series of mediations in the course of which each of the individuals in the community progressively embodies the ability and the willingness to take into consideration the perspective of the other. At stake, then, would be the overcoming of "*first nature*," the passing away, or rather the surpassing, of the human being in the "state of nature," as when the narrator as pre-ethical ego comes to full self-realization and forms its "*second nature*" in terms of a genuine *intersubjectivity*—which is to say, it enters the life of a discursive community grounded in the light of *reciprocal recognition and acknowledgement*, the essential substance of justice and ethical life.[13] Beckett makes us conscious of our desperate need for this absent light, precisely by showing the subjective in its undergoing and enduring a time of immeasurable distress.

And might the screams, the shattering of conceptual meaning, be also the cipher of a mythic terror? If so, they would be not only a lament for the dying of his hope for the realization of justice, not merely an expression of the most extreme disillusionment, recognizing that the journey is not going forward to end in a glorious justice. They would also convey something of the terror in perpetual violence. In the end, the narrator, forsaken, must struggle on alone. Progress is still taking the form, here in this swamp-world, of a struggle for domination. The journey is still caught up in a cycle of violence: freedom enacted as domination remains in mere nature. As Hullot-Kentor points out: "Progress as domination is inextricable from domination as regression—not, however, regression in the sense of a movie running backward, but as the return to what was never solved in the first place: the struggle for self-preservation."[14] So justice is still requiring sacrifice, still subject to its fateful logic. Before ending his tale, the narrator invokes a martyr's cross. The screams would accordingly be a register of the dread this mythic condition, a freedom without justice, a false, counterfeit freedom, imposes—and a recognition of the burden that those among us committed to the struggle for justice must learn to bear. What should not die, must not die, is hope—and the recording of memories, as in this story by Beckett, handing down the long history of struggles and sacrifices, a story written for the sake of a more humane justice.

*

Earlier (Part Two, Chapter 3), we gave thought to the question whether ash and dust are redeemed substances. A more urgent question, though, is whether the sufferings of the dead, the victims of injustice, cruelty and violent hatreds, might ever be redeemed. Can we ever "bring justice" to those victims? Can we retrieve and redeem such a past? For Benjamin, it seems, such redemption is possible only *sub specie aeternitatis*, because all efforts to redeem *within* historical time would be inherently corrupt, inherently "utilitarian," not serving the dead but only the interests of others, we the living and those to come. This is not intended as an argument for nihilism; but the eschatological concept of eternity on which the argument depends is extremely problematic, especially in a secular age. First of all, by discouraging action here and now, it perpetuates the suffering and continues to pile up the corpses. Can any redemption that is other-worldly, outside history, beyond time, really be redeeming?

When Benjamin asserts that the suffering of the victims of violent injustice can be redeemed only in "eternity," what meaning is he assuming for these enigmatic concepts? It seems to me that he is in effect configuring an impasse; because as Adorno has insisted, after all is said and done, the dead are really still dead, dead for all eternity, the victims are really victims, victims for all eternity, and what they suffered cannot be undone by any actions we might undertake within our world as we know it. Thus, on the one hand, it is true that any redemptive actions within historical time, even just calendar events of remembering, would necessarily be, *in some sense*, "utilitarian" in character, doing another injustice to the victims of injustice, since our actions could serve only the interests of people present and future. But, on the other hand, locating "redemption" in the "eternity" of the Judeo-Christian tradition is also of no benefit to those whom malevolence and injustice caused to suffer and die, because, unless "eternity" means life-after-death, a notion that is—regardless of its persistence—logically incoherent, the translation of suffering into the realm of "eternity," at least on one other interpretation of that notion, would eternally delay, postpone, and defer the desired redemption, perpetuating the injustice, the crime, the suffering.

Even Beckett's bleakest works, bearing witness in remembrance to past and still present forms of injustice and suffering, serve at least to redeem the *future* of that suffering: most of all, the hope and longing that formed within it. And that redeeming of consequence could take place only *within* historical time—but a historical time the present course of which would be halted, interrupted, broken into by the actions of a moral consciousness. All we can do by way of redemption, redeeming the responsibility for justice, is to acknowledge our indebtedness and keep the dead, the victims of injustice, in our historical remembrance, giving them a forever protected place for the last word in our historical records, an "eternal" after-life within the community that embraces both the living and the dead. This is a "far cry" indeed from the utilitarianism of Bentham and Mill. And it is, as Adorno sought to make Benjamin concede, the most that can be morally required of us as human beings cast adrift into a world the fundamental nature of which we can neither dominate nor transcend. Is it not this remembrance that, in *How It Is*—and also in *The Lost Ones*—Beckett is salvaging?[15]

*

In *Hegel, Haiti and Universal Justice*, Susan Buck-Morss allows herself to speculate, noting Hegel's silence regarding the slave's struggle for freedom in Haiti, despite his writing—during that very revolution, with full knowledge of the struggle—philosophical arguments for freedom and justice as the rational meaning of the history of spirit:

> What if every time that the consciousness of individuals surpassed the confines of present constellations of power in perceiving the concrete meaning of freedom, *this* were valued as a moment, however, transitory, of the realization of absolute spirit? What other silences would need to be broken? What undisciplined stories would be told?[16]

The last words of Beckett's story confront us with numerous possible but undecidable resolutions (H 146–147). However, whenever that ending threatens to pull us, the readers of the tale, into a swamp of despondency, we need to be reminded of some words we encountered earlier in the story, telling of one

> who listens to himself and who when he lends his ear to our murmur does no more than lend it to a story of his own devising ill-inspired ill-told and so ancient so forgotten at each telling that ours may seem faithful that we murmur in the mud to him/ and this life in the dark and mud its joys and sorrows journeys intimacies and abandons [. . .] (H 139)

How It Is, Beckett's extremely "undisciplined" story, invites an allegorical reading that would connect the struggle for freedom to the institution of justice, situating the primeval history of that struggle—or, I suppose, the origin of its not impossible future—in a moral swamp, a state of nature in which individual consciousness has none of its rational powers, not even its ability to express in words its experience of this brutal, alienated condition. The alienation has cut so deeply into subjectivity that consciousness has not yet found—or else lost—its ability to know and understand itself. Moreover, compelled to acknowledge the voice of the Other at the origin of its interiority, consciousness now confronts the fact that its own voice, its very identity, has been irrevocably pluralized. As Catherine Chalier has noted in her book on ethical life in the writings of Kant, Hegel, and Levinas:

> The crisis of the subject [...] is causing man to lose all certainty about his being. The cogito no longer constitutes the certain and the unquestionable "Archimedean point" that Descartes hoped would serve as a basis on which to reconstruct the order of truths. The I, denounced as an illusion, can no longer posit itself and leaves confusion about the self in its wake. It can no longer find its identity "within" and must be content to play a role in a private, social, historical drama whose author and stakes no one really knows. The I—forgetful of the infinite, which, according to Descartes, dwells within the subject and confers permanence on its self-certainty, and incapable of finding the law that governs its thoughts and acts in the innermost depths of its finitude—reaches the point where it expects the sense of its being to come from a social or historical exteriority, where it hopes to be recognized by others, and at the same time demands that recognition with a violence commensurate with its own precariousness. But the riddle of the subject's new identity seems to have become pointless, given the chasm opened up by the rise of the human sciences, which would eliminate the very idea of the subject, as if that idea were nothing but a fiction or a humanist or spiritualist nostalgia.

Thus, she wonders: "Must the subject succumb to these attacks?" That question calls forth the rest of her argument, in which we see reflected something of the very world in which Beckett has cast his characters:

> The moral and political consequences [...] ought to command our utmost attention. [...] The moral subject is now looking for itself in a world deserted by the hope for sense. Often, it seems that to speak of sense is purely and simply to confess one's incapacity to take on the burden of nihilism, which has paralyzed every value. But the moral subject is also looking for itself in a world still marked on a daily basis by human resistance to humiliation, oppression, injustice, and death.[17]

After registering his convictions, in a number of different works, regarding how Spinoza's sublime cosmology, Descartes' indulgent egoism, and Kant's severe morality of conscience have shaped and informed the world we live in, Beckett takes us, in *How It Is,* on an arduous and demanding journey, venturing into a realm of biopolitics where, after Hegel, we become witnesses to a dialectic the historical violence of which has not yet been adequately resolved. Not even today. And in the persistence of this violence, the very

meaning of our humanity—indeed the end of our humanity—is at stake. We
must think it in its duplicity, to the end.

*

In the course of his journey through the swamp, and through the purgatory
of language, the narrator tells us that, "with someone to keep me company
I would have been a different man, more universal" (H 67). This is a
significant claim; but if it is to be compelling, we need to resolve, first, what
we are to make of Pim, whom he wants us to believe he encounters and
subjects to violent and dehumanizing torments, and second, what we are to
make of all the evocations that imply the existence of countless other mortals
moving through the muddy swamp-realm. If he, or his "sense of humanity,"
has not become "more universal," who is to be blamed? And why would the
company of others have enabled him to become "more universal"?

As we know, Hegel's *Phenomenology of Spirit* answered that question,
dramatizing in the violence of a relationship of domination and submission
the dialectical emergence of a more universal sense of humanity—and a
corresponding sense of justice—in the form of mutual recognition and
acknowledgement. However, this mutuality is not possible unless each
of the subjects comes into the moral lucidity of self-recognition and self-
understanding.[18] In Beckett's story, as in Hegel's, there is a journey toward
that moral lucidity. But, whereas in Hegel's, the stage of redeeming self-
knowledge is reached, in Beckett's it is dissolved in a delirious fantasy.

§4

However many plausible interpretations of Beckett's epic novel there may
be, I want to claim that his story lends itself, as becomes especially evident
in the third and final part, to a reading that interprets it as a dramatization
of Hegel's dialectic of lord and bondsman—or, in Beckett's terms, tormentor
and victim. As such, it is a powerful, compelling story, throwing us into the
phenomenology of this dialectic and never letting us really escape from the
macabre dance of its violence, its archaic institution of justice, although of
course we can always escape it by a sleight of hand in the aesthetic semblance
of fiction. Voices, words come to the narrator, and he conjures images of
"another age," suggesting that "progress," a word dear to philosophers
committed to the project of enlightenment, is nothing but an illusion:
"progress properly so called ruins in prospect [. . .] ah if you had seen it four
hundred years ago what upheavals" (H 22).

What is at stake in this epic tale is nothing less than the humanity of
justice, or the humanity in justice: going on from the brutality, the barbarism
of the Hegelian dialectic, overcoming the "justice" that prevails in the state of
nature, the "dark ages," to realize a justice worthy of our "higher" spiritual

nature as mortal human beings. The message that words bear, the promise, namely, of happiness, thus concerns happiness understood as the justice of a humanity coming to itself. The syntax of this passage, denied punctuation, creates stubborn uncertainties in meaning; but the words, reminiscent of Benjamin's interpretation of Paul Klee's *Angelus Novus*, seem to suggest, even whilst they continue to bear their promise, that, looking backwards at the past, its "progress" appears as nothing but a prospect in ruins.[19]

*

Again and again, the narrator's tale refers or alludes to a matter of justice, "our justice": sometimes it is the violent justice of the swamp, sometimes the justice that exists in the realm of light above, and sometimes, the divine justice that no longer rules the still incompletely enlightened world above the realm of the swamp (H 114). To be sure, there is, in the swamp, sameness or reversibility of roles in the biopolitics of the various physical encounters, but not anything we would want to call "justice." What rules in this swamp is "naked self-preservation": what Benjamin called "*bloßes Leben*," human life reduced to mere animal survival, its minimum conditions of possibility. The justice and injustice in this strange process are explained in great detail:

> The spectacle on the one hand of a single one among us towards whom no one ever goes and on the other of a single other who never goes towards anyone it would be an injustice and that is above in the light/ in other words in simple words I quote on either I am alone and no further problem or else we are innumerable and no further problem either/ save that of conceiving but no doubt it can be done a procession in a straight line with neither head nor tail in the dark the mud with all its various infinitudes that such a conception involves/ nothing to be done in any case we have our being in justice I have never heard anything to the contrary (H 124)

Somewhat later the narrator reports "the faint sign for us of a change some day nay even of an end in all honour and justice" (H 134–135). A "faint sign" of a "change"! A change that presumably commences with the questioning of the prevailing system of "justice." At stake is a justice not to be expected as a gift from heaven, but as an institution to be accomplished by mortals in an enlightened world of light—the world said to be "above."

Evoking a stanza in Dante's *Purgatorio* in which the poet tells us that, "from the left, a procession of souls appeared to me, moving their feet so slowly that they seemed not to be towards us,"[20] the movement that Beckett describes is said to take place "in a procession without end or beginning languidly wending from left to right straight line eastward strange in the dark the mud sandwiched between victim and tormentor" (H 127). "Progress" is thus rendered only in the most physical, most literal terms; no "higher," more ideal, more distinctly ethical conception is recognized here. In this connection, the narrator remarks:

impossible that at every journey we should have had to scale a mountain of sacks and should still have and should for ever have each one of us at every journey in order to reach his victim to scale a mountain of sacks our progress as we have seen while admittedly laborious yet the terrain the terrain try and understand no accidents no asperities our justice (H 136)

He laments the asperities of the situation, the "injustice" in being compelled to move on—to "progress"—with extreme exertion; but the violence and injustice inherent in relations of domination and submission not only continue without complaint; they are essentially denied, on the grounds that the roles are, in the course of time, reversed. The "justice" in this oddly muddled realm is consequently figured in the symmetry and reciprocity of violence: "all alike our justice, one life everywhere" (H 134).

Spelling out the implications for hope, but creating more confusion than clarity, the narrating voice says:

only the victims journeyed/ the tormentors as though struck numb with stupor instead of giving chase right leg right arm push pull ten yards fifteen yards lying where abandoned penalty perhaps of their recent exertions but effect also of our justice/ though in what this diminished by a general free for all one does not see/ involving for one and all the same obligation precisely that of fleeing without fear while pursuing without hope/ and if it is still possible at this late hour to conceive of other worlds/ as just as ours but less exquisitely organized/ one perhaps there is one perhaps somewhere merciful enough to shelter such frolics where no one ever abandons anyone and no one ever waits for anyone and never two bodies touch/ and if it may seem strange that without food to sustain us we can drag ourselves thus by the mere grace of our united net of sufferings from west to east towards an inexistent peace we are invited kindly to consider/ that for the likes of us and no matter how we are recounted there is more nourishment in a cry nay a sigh torn from one whose only good is silence or in speech extorted from one at last delivered from its use than sardines can ever offer (H 142–143)

Another world? A world ordered by the mercy of a different justice? A world in which a just peace might finally prevail? Are we contemplating the world said to be of "life above"—that is, life as we live it here on the earth? And are we then to imagine earth-bound life as it might be in some possible future? In the course of reflecting on questions of justice, the narrative voice slips vertiginously from the serious to the ironic, from the understandable to the incomprehensible, and from the rational to the nonsensical in a speech full of contradictions that confirms Adorno's claim: in a damaged world, thought that is true cannot itself escape damage, but its truth consequently consists in honestly exhibiting the damage. Nevertheless, by the end of this muddled peroration, we might feel that an inkling of the desired justice, or at least a sense of the desire for justice, has begun to emerge.

§5

What prevails in the swamp is, for the most part, an inhuman justice, coldly objective, and strictly mathematized; a rigid, merciless "justice" of calculation:

> At the instant I reach Pim another reaches Bem we are regulated thus our justice wills it thus fifty thousand couples again at the same instant the same everywhere with the same space between them it's mathematical it's our justice in this muck where all is identical (H 112)

In the pages that follow (113–128), the narrator takes us through a maze of mathematical calculations regarding the successive couplings of tormentors and victims, their coming together and forsaking one another, as each moves after a while toward the next one with whom to couple, reversing the roles of torturer and victim. The narrator undertakes to register all the different possible mathematical permutations, assuming that there are perhaps millions consigned to the realm of mud, endlessly cycled into and out of the brutal dialectic, even calculating the speed of the procession and the duration of each coupling.[21] Giving the appearance of great seriousness, he takes pains to estimate and calculate just how many mortals there are in this situation, "because of our justice which wills that not one were we fifty million not a single one among us be wronged" (H 123). In the next block of prose, however, the irony in this explanation is fully revealed: it turns out that the seemingly admirable "justice" here is really just a question of ensuring that no one be deprived of a tormentor nor deprived of a victim! There is even a calculus of sacks, because their numbers threaten to impede the "progress" of the alternations: the caravan, it seems, could be "arrested for ever and frozen in injustice" (H 136–137). The "injustice" here, though, consists in the fact that the reversibility of roles is arrested, so that the victim never gets a chance to dominate and torture.

There is, therefore, as much madness in calling this arrest an "injustice" as there is in thinking of "justice" as something measurable, something calculable. Reading these speculative pages of numbers, page after page, one must take them to be a parody, a compelling *reductio ad absurdum* of the notion of justice as a matter of calculating the symmetries and equalities. For, these symmetries and equalities are nothing but measures of violence. Whereas the *law* requires calculations—the commensurability, for instance, of crime and punishment, true *justice* remains incalculable. (Such justice is *aporetic*, however, because it cannot be effective without the enforcement of the law, even though the law cannot be properly questioned without an appeal to the moral authority of a justice irreducible to law.) We need to remember that, for centuries, philosophical thought represented reason itself as *ratio*. Hobbes, for example, thought all reasoning, all uses of reason, to be a matter, ultimately, of addition and subtraction:

> By RATIOCINATION, I mean *Computation*. Now, to compute, is either to collect the sum of many things that are added together, or to know what remains when one thing is taken out of another. [. . .] So that all ratiocination is comprehended in these two operations of the mind, addition and subtraction.[22]

As Buck-Morss has pointed out, Hobbes endorsed domestic slavery in England, praising it as a rational solution to the problem of social discipline among the so-called "masterless men"—vagabonds, paupers, criminals, and sexual degenerates.[23] But given his definition of rationality, a distorted sense of justice is perhaps not out of order.

Beckett's lengthy accounts of numbers, seemingly endless calculations, dramatize in a devastatingly critical way the true nature of the exchange economy in late capitalism, which reduces individuals to exchangeable factors. The calculated tracking of the mortals moving through the swamp is, moreover, a grotesque parody of instrumental rationality, a critique of the reduction of reason as a faculty of critical judgment to reason as nothing more than a utilitarian method of calculation, a calculation of means and ways that neglects critical reflection on the ends. The most extreme instance of this reductionism was the Nazis' use of rationality in their technologies of genocide.

Beckett's assignment of numbers to the people fallen into this hellish realm also calls to mind the Nazis' tattooing of death camp prisoners, reducing them to numbered "items," "superfluous" and "eliminable."

Making a mockery not only of the utilitarian definition of happiness, but also of the swamp's "regulated" system of "justice," the narrator's voice turns into a text that takes us as readers through many pages of arithmetical calculations regarding the pairing of tormentor and victim (H 112, 125). But, as Levinas argues in *Otherwise than Being*, "Justice is not a legality regulating human masses, from which a technique of social equilibrium is drawn, harmonizing antagonistic forces."[24] Such is the "regulated" but perverted "justice" that prevails in the realm of mud. So, "here where justice reigns" (H 134),

> Nothing to be done in any case we have our being in justice I have never heard anything to the contrary (H 124)

No voice of conscience speaks out in protestation. The practice goes on without question:

The spectacle on the one hand of a single one among us towards whom no one ever goes and on the other of a single other who never goes towards anyone it would be an injustice (H 124)

In other words, even the "unsocial sociability"[25] of the state of nature, suffering in its dialectic of violence, might be preferable to absolute estrangement from others. But a calculus of justice, justice *as* calculus, is radically dehumanizing: the greatest conceivable injustice. And, according to the narrator, or the one he frequently "quotes," it is precisely that dehumanizing estrangement which still prevails, even after centuries of "progress," in the realm "above"—the realm said to be "above in the light" (H 124).

Beckett's absurd procession of men and calculations represents a strong protest against the ancient conception of justice as revenge, as getting even— justice reduced to the reckoning of retribution. An eye for an eye. This is the "justice" of a state of nature, a cruel purgatory, forgetting that justice must be helpful, redeeming instead of punishing.

We read in the narrator's notes: "the procession which seemed as if it must be eternal our justice the advantage of stopping it without prejudice to a single one among us" (H 141). Stopping it would mean "one half of us tormentors in perpetuity victims in perpetuity the other." And this, of course, makes impossible *their* justice, which counterfeits the principle of reversibility and reciprocity that is at the heart of a radically different conception of justice:

So neither four nor a million nor ten million nor twenty million nor any finite number even or uneven however great because of our justice which wills that not one were we fifty million not a single one among us be wronged/ not one deprived of tormentor (H 123)

What begins in this textual excerpt with a comment that seems at first to argue against historians who squabble over calculating the exact number of Holocaust victims whilst neglecting more important responsibilities, such as discovering the records of still concealed atrocities, explaining the pogroms, and accounting for the appeal of fascism, soon turns into an inspiring assertion of justice, insisting that, no matter how many lives are involved, "not a single one" among them should be harmed. But that stirring notion of justice, uncompromising in its authority, sounding like a revolutionary battle cry, is quickly and abruptly negated by the five words at the end that interpret it.

And yet, this stirring notion is supported by other episodes in the story. When some of the sacks that the men are dragging have burst, the narrator, whose sack remains intact, perhaps because of its "better quality jute," says: "there's no justice or else one of those things that pass understanding" (H 61). Of course, I suppose that one could always take this comment to be accepting the perpetuation of the "equality" demanded by an archaic and brutal form of justice. Nevertheless, it is, I think, significant that, even in this realm where everything is muddled, there is a longing for peace, for a "life above in the light a little blue little scenes for the thirst for the sake of peace" (H 127): consolatory images drawn with difficulty from memory and imagination. And there are splinters of hope for a life "in justice and the safeguard of our essential activities" (H 142). In the occasional evocations of justice, no matter how distorted and perverted they are, the ideal that is longed for is still kept in mind. "There's no justice," as a comment on the misfortune that only some of the sacks have burst, sounds like a defense of justice as equality, as solidarity, as caring for others. It sounds like an acknowledgement of the idea that there is no justice when, for no compelling reason, some must suffer devastating losses whilst others are spared. And paradoxically, the mockery expressed in the negation of an enlightened sense of justice only intensifies the desirability of the utopian ideal, experienced through the sharpness of its very absence. Indeed, the narrator urges us to listen carefully for "the faint sign" of another justice: "a change some day nay even of an end in all honour and justice" (H 135): a justice not to be expected as a gift from heaven, but as an institution to be accomplished by mortals in the world of light that will rise above the swamp.

§6

To learn a little more about life in the swamp, let us accompany the narrator in his comments and reflections on the character of its justice. First of all, he tells us that, although there is much suffering in this swamp caused by acts of violence, there is a certain "justice" in this realm, because everyone without exception is subject to this violence: "it's someone each in his turn as our justice wills and never any end it wills that too all dead or none" (H 132). And everyone is ultimately confronted with the very same obstacles and adversities (H 137). The narrator also confides that, despite the wretched conditions, there is comfort in the nearness of others similarly struggling to survive: "what comfort in adversity others what comfort" (H 48). He then goes on to invoke "the interests of all":

> Those dragging on in front those dragging on behind whose lot has been whose lot will be what your lot is endless cortège of sacks burst in the interests of all/ or a celestial tin miraculous sardines sent down by God at the news of my mishap (H 48)

The significance of this reference to "the interests of all" cannot be underestimated, even though the meaning of the phrase remains obscure. As already noted, the narrator's thoughts about justice are set in motion by the sight of some burst sacks: some have burst, some have been spared; and this inequality stirs him to ruminate on the question of justice and injustice. As far as he can determine, though, there is nothing that makes the inequality understandable. So he is left briefly to wonder about the operation of chance or grace, and, even more importantly, about the democratic ideal of justice as equality: "is it possible the old business of grace in this sewer why want us all alike some vanish others never" (H 61). What does justice for all mean? What does "all alike" mean? What does equality before the law of justice require?

Suggesting that the "justice" that prevails in the purgatory of the swamp is, however, topsy-turvy, with the lowest form of justice (the justice that arises in the state of nature, the purgatory swamp-world below) displacing the highest (the enlightened justice of the world above), the narrator has occasion to say that,

> We leave our sacks to those who do not need them we take their sacks from those who soon will need them we leave without a sack we find one on our way we can continue on our way (H 111)

Why does Beckett go out of his way to include this obviously unacceptable comportment? The only explanation that comes to mind is that, in this perverse parody of Marxist doctrine, he wants in this extreme way to provoke an intense process of reflection and self-examination, compelling us to question our own beliefs and convictions regarding the right and the just in ethical life.

§7

Inseparable from the question of our justice is the question regarding our humanity. Describing his situation, the narrator speaks of his "face in the mud the mouth open the mud in the mouth thirst abating humanity regained" (H 27). Somewhat later, he tells us "I'll fall asleep within humanity again just barely" (H 44–45). And still later, he describes himself as "hanging on to humankind" (H 94). He fears losing his humanity, losing his sense of what his humanity demands of him, and he attempts to redeem, or at least hold on to, that sense—whatever might "restore me to my dignity" (H 26), in part by bringing it into words, words to be shared. But words from others—if there are any—are "extorted," not freely forthcoming. There are also numerous invocations of the human species,[26] as when, for example, he recalls "before Pim the golden age the good moments the losses of the species" and says, "I was young I clung on to the species we're talking of the species the human" (H 47). He thus shows that he realizes that the preserving or redeeming of his humanity is impossible apart from the fate of all the others in the swamp. He recognizes in Pim "a fellow creature" (H 54), speaks of "our life in common" (H 55), "clinging almost to each other" (H 55), and reminds himself that, "even beasts observe one another" (H 55). Imagining the future, he says: "one day we'll set off again together and I saw us the curtains parted an instant [...] and I saw us darkly all this before the little tune oh long before helping each other on" (H 57).

§8

In Beckett's tale, our attention is claimed by an anonymous voice, the narrator's voice, that sometimes says, or implies, that it is the only voice, but at other times says, or implies, that there are, in this swamp, many voices, many mortals like himself. Moreover, whereas sometimes these other voices are said to be "outside," at other times they are said to be "inside"—that is, nothing but murmurs and rumblings inside the narrator's skull. What is the singular voice that the narrator claims to hear? Is it the voice of conscience, "an ancient voice in me not mine" (H 7)? Is it the voice of reason, "this voice its promises and solaces all imagination" (H 79)? And what does it have to tell us about justice: the archaic justice in the state of nature, what the narrator calls "our justice," or another, different justice, such as the narrator in the fifth of Beckett's *Texts for Nothing* (TN 95) has invoked? We must, the narrator says, lend our ear to hear the voices, hear their murmuring, and hear, if there are any, their words (H 139).[27]

The story also seems haunted, however, by a voice that might be divine. Beckett does not underestimate how difficult it is for us to leave behind our infantile dependency on the justice of a God said to be "caring," despite the history of cruelties and atrocities not only carried out in his name, but with his acquiescence or approval—or else carried out, at least, without his power to stop them. However much the narrator wants to escape the tyrannical justice of the divine voice, he cannot, it seems, entirely silence it:

> It's the voice of him to whom we are further indebted for our unfailing rations which inable us to advance without pause or rest/ [the voice] of him who God knows who could blame him must sometimes wonder if to these perpetual revictuallings narrations and auditions he might not put an end without ceasing to maintain us in some kind of being without end and some kind of justice without flaw (H 139)

But more significant, for our purposes, than the question of the possible voice of God are the murmurs and voices that, as I want to argue, represent in some way Beckett's concern, in this story, for the cause of an enlightened justice. This concern appears in the enigmatic "quaqua" that accompanies his character's repeated invocations of a voice. That emphatically doubled Latinism, upon which we briefly reflected earlier, might be taken to express the voice's struggle, its redoubled exertions to become, or be true to, what it is called upon to be:

[1] "this voice quaqua of us all never was only one voice my voice never any other" (H 87)

[2] "[I hear] an ancient voice quaqua on all sides the voice of us all as many as we are as many as we'll end if we ever end by having been" (H 108)

[3] "to hear and note one of our murmurs is to hear and note them all" (H 138)

[4] "this anonymous voice self-styled quaqua the voice of us all that was without on all sides then in us when the panting stops bits and scraps barely audible certainly distorted there it is at last the voice of him who before listening to us murmur what we are tells us what we are as best he can" (H 139)

My claim, proposed earlier (Part Three, Chapter 4), is that this "voice of us all" is the voice that bespeaks, and speaks for, our humanity. It is "my" voice, "my own" voice; and yet, it is also *not* "my own" at all, but a voice I inherit, an ancient voice, a universal voice *within mine* that belongs to us all. And this means it bears the promise of a justice radically different, not only from the justice that reigns in the state of nature and from the archaic justice of revenge, but even from the justice that rules in our own, "more enlightened" day. The "voice of us all" is invoked in a lyrical mode of speech about which we might say what Adorno says in writing about the late poetry of Stefan George: it "becomes the voice of human beings between whom the barriers have fallen."[28]

But we must not ignore what Beckett surely wants us also to hear in the repetition of this "quaqua," hearing what our ears are telling us. The double "qua," doubled and redoubled, ends up sounding like the quacking of a duck, or maybe the quack-quacking of a flock of ducks. Beckett is certainly turning the philosophically very august and imposing Latin term, positing an ontological essentiality, into sheer quackery. Then is the "voice of us all," the recognition of a common humanity, nothing, in the end, but idle prattle?[29] Is essentialism in the utopian or messianic defense of humanity unavoidable? And if there is a certain injustice coiled within essentialism, can we ever hope to escape reenacting its scenes of injustice? I suggest that what Beckett wants is to *release* the "voice of us all" *from* the quackery of philosophical essentialism, so that it may finally speak without violence.

Beckett's appeal to this Kantian voice might not, however, be very comforting. There is a much earlier appearance of the "quaqua." Significantly, it figures in a scene of brutal injustice. In the first act of *Waiting for Godot*, we watch Pozzo subjecting Lucky, his rope-bound slave, to appalling and degrading abuse.[30] And as he pulls on the rope around Lucky's neck and cracks his whip, Pozzo yells at Lucky, commanding him to think: "Think, pig!" After a brief silence, Lucky begins a very long "tirade," a rambling, incoherent monologue that can only be regarded as a burlesque parody, turning philosophical thinking into the quackery of a pompous academician. But Lucky, ostentatiously presuming to engage in a profound meditation on the existence of God and various other important matters, twice resorts to a "quaquaquaqua," altogether missing the opportunity to compel Pozzo—and Vladimir and Estragon too—to give thought to the cruelty and injustice of enslavement. His in particular. The speech is funny, but the situation is not. What, though, can mere words accomplish? What good are the eloquent, finely wrought discourses of the philosophers, scholarly treatises composed in configurations of words as abstruse and incomprehensible as Lucky's? In the laughter that avoids thinking, injustice is released from judgment.

§9

So, are we "arrested for ever and frozen in injustice" (H 137)? The thirteenth, and final, text in Beckett's late work, *Texts for Nothing*, apparently written three years before *How It Is*, concludes without leaving much hope, despite God's word, despite the presence of his voice and light:

> And were there one day to be here, where there are no days, which is no place, born of the impossible voice the unmakable being, and a gleam of light, still all would be silent and empty and dark, as now, as soon now, when all will be ended, all said, it says, it murmurs. (TN 140)

Are going on, "refreshing alternations of history" (H 129), and beginning history over again—a radically new "commencement"—impossible? Perhaps not, as long as any telling words, any prophetic words from the past (H 129), remain within our cultural memory, and there are still in our midst any storytellers, any poets compassionately fearless, to receive those words and bring them to life. That could be one of the ways we might understand "it says, it murmurs." The lyricism, the beauty with which Beckett's dark thought is expressed defies the hopelessness even whilst sustaining a sense of loss. There is hope wherever language still retains some of its power to reveal, to originate—the power that Arendt named with the word "natality."

But there is much that we should have to learn. In beginning his "Theological-Political Fragment," Benjamin, using the figure of the Messiah as metaphor for the commencement of a new age of justice, the realization of the promise of happiness, argues that the possibility of real justice on earth—the messianic or utopian Idea—requires the ending of history as we have known it.[31] The time of justice cannot be the *goal* of history, because that would place it *within* the continuation of history; whereas it must instead be the interruption and end of history as we have known it. Levinas says something quite similar: "Justice does not result from the normal play of injustice. It comes from the outside, 'through the door', above the fray; it appears as a principle external to history."[32] There is much, for Beckett too, that we should have to learn! We would need to free ourselves from incapacitating myths, the old theodicies, learning to live without "the nostalgia for that slime where the eternal breathed and his son wrote, long after, with divine idiotic finger [. . .]" (TN 103). We would have to relinquish theological hope, and the endless waiting it imposes, in order to realize the possibility of hope ambiguously "gleaming among the imaginary ashes," "the faint hope of a faint being after all, human in kind, tears in its eyes before they've had time to open [. . .]" (TN 138). And yet, without keeping in mind the prophetic power of the word, how might we nevertheless find the courage to end the tragedy of history as we have known it, approaching one another in the spirit of the truly human justice that its storytellers darkly announced?[33]

Remembrance too we must learn. But what is this remembrance? Maurice Blanchot offers an interpretation that I should like to embrace: in difference from ordinary memory, remembrance is, paradoxically, a kind of forgetfulness, a poetry that preserves "what men, peoples, and gods do not yet have by way of their own memory, but in the keeping of which they abide even as it is entrusted to their keeping."[34] I want here to recall an argument which Adorno made, that carries forward Blanchot's thought regarding what we do not yet have in remembrance, whilst also illuminating Beckett's struggle, in a time when we have not yet realized the condition of our humanness, to say what cannot be said without betraying the unsayable:

> That it is spoken, that distance is thus won from the trapped immediacy of suffering, transforms suffering just as screaming diminishes unbearable pain. Expression that has been objectivated as language endures; what has once been said never fades away completely, neither the evil nor the good, neither the slogan of "The Final Solution" nor the hope of reconciliation. What accedes to language enters the movement of a humanness that does not yet exist; it is compelled towards language and alive only by virtue of its helplessness.[35]

The language in *How It Is* registers with implacable power both this compelling movement and its helplessness.

Almost drowning in the mud and struggling against it, panting, for the breath needed to speak is being squeezed out of him, the narrator is still able to recall a few scraps from the ancient prophecy; but his voice, in heart-rending cries, dies out unheard, unanswered. There is no one in the heights of

Heaven to answer the cries, the prayers, the questions. And there is no end, no purpose, no ultimate metaphysical meaning or design: or in any event, nothing confirmed, nothing signified. That is how it is. But a deeply moving story, recalling us to ourselves, has nevertheless been imparted. However, as Franz Rosenzweig states in his *Star of Redemption*: "[T]he word is mere inception until it finds reception in an ear and response in a mouth."[36]

I think it of the utmost significance that the figures in *How It Is* do not communicate, do not relate to one another by way of the word. In the swamp, the mouth is filled with mud. It cannot speak; it cannot kiss. The voice is a monologue, without reception, without response. The voice dies out; leaving no echoes, no vibrations, it is obliterated even before it ceases.

In *Aesthetic Theory*, Adorno affirms a minimal measure of hope for "what accedes to language." In Beckett's story, we can find expressions of suffering and helplessness that begin to move towards "a humanness that does not yet exist"; but there is almost no encouragement.

In §671 of his *Phenomenology of Spirit*, Hegel declares: "The reconciling *Yea* [*Das versöhnende Ja*], in which the two I's let go their antithetical *existence* [*Dasein*] is the *existence* of the 'I' which has expanded into a duality."[37] As *How It Is* draws us towards its ending, there is a dialectical struggle, increasingly interrupting the flow of words, between "yes" and "no." The "yes," Hegel says, in the final words that conclude his "Morality" section, "is God manifested in the midst of those who know themselves in the form of pure knowledge." The muddy, confusing conflict into which Beckett's narrator, the very antithesis of the "beautiful soul," is cast, and into which, therefore, we too, as readers, are dragged, implicitly challenges this claim (H 144–147). Without referring to the *Phenomenology*, Beckett struggles with, and finally gives up on, Hegel's story regarding the procession of Spirit in human history. Language has not yet fulfilled its role in the unfolding of Spirit as long as injustice persists in the world. Instead of inspiration, there is breathless panting, and gasping for breath. No real communication.

In the last four pages, a vertiginous, delirious, bewildering prose, perhaps simply attempting to banish all pretense in the fiction, Beckett seems at moments to be speaking directly to us, confiding his struggles and conflicts as a writer of the tale we have been reading, whilst at other moments, he seems to be making his nameless narrator painfully acknowledge that everything he has told us is nothing but a fiction screaming in his skull. Here the "yes" and the "no" struggle for the truth:

> If all that all that yes if all that is not how shall I say no answer if all that is not false yes/
> All these calculations yes explanations yes the whole story from beginning to end yes completely false yes/
> That wasn't how it was no not at all no how then no answer how was it then no answer [. . .]

There was something yes but nothing of all that no all balls from start
to finish yes this voice quaqua yes all balls yes only one voice here yes
mine yes when the panting stops yes/ [. . .]

Hard to believe too yes that I have a voice yes in me yes when the panting
stops yes not at other times no and that I murmur yes I yes in the dark
yes in the mud yes for nothing yes [. . .]/

But all this business of voices yes quaqua yes of other worlds yes of
someone in another world yes whose kind of dream I am yes said to be
yes that he dreams all the time yes tells all the time yes his only dream
yes his only story yes/ [. . .]

And this business of a procession no answer this business of a procession
yes never any procession no nor any journey no never [. . .] never
anyone no only me no answer only me yes so that was true yes it was
true about me yes [. . .]

Only me in any case yes alone yes in the mud yes the dark yes that holds
yes the mud and the dark hold yes nothing to regret there no with my
sack no I beg your pardon no no sack either no not even a sack with
me no/ [. . .]

The shifts in the one who is speaking and the one who is being addressed are
dizzying. Sometimes, it seems that Beckett is speaking to us, sometimes
speaking to his character, sometimes speaking to himself; sometimes the
character—his narrator in the story—seems to be addressing us, sometimes
appealing to Beckett, his inventor, and sometimes just thinking out loud. But
what is striking in these concluding pages of the story is the compelling
sense that the difference between truth and semblance cannot be maintained,
that communication has broken down, and that, without a responsive other,
the meaningfulness of language itself is threatened.

Language, Hegel says, manifests the existence of Spirit: "Language is self-
consciousness existing *for others* [. . .]" (*Phenomenology of Spirit*, §652).
But as the final four pages of Beckett's drama show, this communicative
function has in our time been severely disrupted. In fact, the disruption is
not only in relation to other worldly subjectivities; it is also an absolute
severance of communication with a transcendent, metaphysical being—
namely, with God. Commenting on Hegel's text regarding the reconciling
"Yes," Rebecca Comay observes:

The speech act describes nothing, asserts nothing, and points to nothing
beyond its own enunciation: [at most] it offers a kind of ontological
proof of the inaugural extension of the speaking subject. [. . .] This
reflexivity accounts for the otherwise disappointing emptiness—I dare
say 'flatness'—of Spirit's last monosyllable. The "reconciling *yes*"
functions as an empty performative: it is a communication without a
message, without any content to communicate other than the fact that
there is, or could be, communication, that the machine is once again

working; [...] a minimal gesture of recognition, whose only function is to prolong or reestablish contact, to check the channel or test the microphone, the audible breath drawn by the speaker as he opens his mouth to say something [...].[38]

Moreover, "like every counterphobic measure, the test needs to be endlessly repeated; the more it succeeds the more it opens itself to failure; it keeps on generating the very indeterminacy it wants to settle [...]."[39]

In Hegel's recourse to this little word, she argues, the forgiveness and reconciliation it seems to offer "is reduced to a zero degree of meaning and expressivity: spectral, citational, referentially opaque. Speech hovering on the verge of empty reverberation."[40] Beckett's "yes" is contested by the "no," but it does seem to be longing for some kind of reconciliation, struggling—but without success—to find, or achieve, some kind of meaningful engagement with the world. "Yes" is not Beckett's last word. The novel stops, without the punctuation of a period, oscillating between defiance and resigned acceptance of a dispirited reality—what Hegel, writing that grammatical mark at the very end of his history of absolute Spirit, called its "Calvary," "*die Schädelstätte des absoluten Geistes*" (§808). More than that—if even that—Beckett's narrator will not know. For Hegel, in the course of his narrative it has become certain that this moment will be decisively sublated, making way for a glorious realization. A compromising—and compromised—"yes" wins out, retroactively erasing so much that called into question the possibility of just such an affirmation. So it is to *dispute* Hegel's seemingly naïve faith that the spirit of language—hence its justice, we might say, as existing for the sake of others—has already been fully realized, that Adorno remarks that, "What accedes to language enters the movement of a humanness that does not yet exist."[41] It is precisely towards the expression of that movement in language that Beckett is struggling. Struggling against the language he has inherited, which otherwise operates to keep us in the captivity of what-is. That is his journey and the journeys, or movements, of his characters. Is there a "way out"? Conveying an answer in a dialectical image, in words that allude to the redeeming of the promise of happiness, Beckett's narrative voice ends the ninth of his *Texts for Nothing* evoking, even if only conditionally, the beauty in the movement of freedom:

> I have no doubts, I'd get there somehow, to the way out, sooner or later, if I could say, There's a way out there, there's a way out somewhere, the rest would come, the other words, sooner or later, and the power to get there, and the way to get there, and pass out, and see the beauties of the skies, and see the stars again. (TN 121)

This Kantian image of the stars, allegorical figure for the possibility of the world's redemption, is implicitly present throughout *How It Is*, serving as an allegorical recollection of the promised moral justice.

*

Stories are necessary cultural treasures, because, despite their fictional character, they are sources of cultural remembrance: remembrance as destruction, remembrance as inception, commencement of the new. In his essay on the question of memory in Proust, Beckett wrote of "that double-headed monster of damnation and salvation—Time—with its necessary corollary, Memory."[42]

Might the last word be given to justice? In the eighth text in *Texts for Nothing*, a voice asserts that, "it's the end that gives meaning to words" (TN 111). As this strange work concludes, it invokes an "impossible voice," perhaps that of "the unmakable being"—what in Jena Romanticism would have been called the Unconditioned, hence the Absolute—and, along with that voice, "a gleam of light."[43] But in a grammatical construction of bewildering temporality, the sentence seems to declare, in spite of this hopeful presence, that "all would be silent and empty and dark, as now, as soon now, when all will be ended," except that, "when all will be ended, all said," something, something nameless, might still remain to say and to murmur: as we read in the text, "it says, it murmurs" (TN 140). Last words. We do not know what is being said, what is being murmured. But perhaps it is just enough to sustain our faith in the possibility of redemption—the utopian or messianic promise of happiness—that there is still an audible murmur, still, from somewhere, a communicative interruption—saying, trying to make meaning. The murmur in *Texts for Nothing* is, however, silenced by the author's placement of a punctuation mark: after the word "murmur" there is a peremptory period. By contrast, the very last words in the epic—"how it is"—are followed by no punctuation mark, no period signifying the ending of the storytelling. So now the struggle for justice—for something beyond the calculus of justice, something beyond the justice of revenge, something even more demanding of human nature—must somehow go on. Even if without the words we desperately need ancient stories ill-told.

In *The Origins of Totalitarianism*, a work of incomparable critical analysis, Hannah Arendt argued that,

> Beginning, before it becomes a historical event, is the supreme capacity of man; politically, it is identical with man's freedom. *Initium ut esset homo creatus est*—"that a beginning be made man was created," said Augustine (*City of God* 12, 20). This beginning is guaranteed by each new birth; it is indeed every human being.[44]

We must commence wherever we can, if necessary, again and again, for that is how it is: *comment c'est. Commencez!* Begin! Like Beckett's narrator, slowly moving through the swamp, we must begin approaching a humane justice—even if, as his tale suggests, that demands an infinite slowness.

The realm into which Beckett's story throws us reminds me of some lines in a poem by Gottfried Benn, one of the most important German expressionist poets: "Oh, that we were our primordial ancestors./ A clump of slime in a warm bog."[45] Willing evolutionary regression is, it seems, his only remaining hope in a world that threatens to exterminate the humanity in our nature. Must we not try to go on, to go ahead of ourselves? In my reading, Beckett is closer in spirit to the post-Holocaust poet Celan, who, despite grave doubts, expresses in *Breathturn* his *longing* for some saving words, words of release. It is as if the words that have come to him, although weak and wrong, are nevertheless grasping for other words, patiently working their way toward the ones that might serve. The imagery in Beckett's tale is remarkably similar to the imagery in this poem by Celan; and there is also an affinity, or proximity, in the thought:

Oozing, then
weedy stillness on the banks.
Just one more sluice. At the
wart tower,
cleansed in the brackish waters,
you emerge.
In front of you, among
giant drifting spore-vessels,
a brightness cuts though as if words
were grasping.[46]

Might words be coming, words that, like a sickle, would cut through the swamp-weeds in which we are entangled, bringing the brightness of hope? The poet imagines the possibility of our breaking out of the swamp of despair and making a new, more humane world—a world, we might perhaps believe, in the light of an earthly redemption.

Is there really, in Beckett's tale, a movement toward justice? The characters in Beckett's swamp, whether representing one man or many, *seem* to be drifting toward justice—toward their humanity—in a movement of infinite, or nearly infinite slowness. But like Benjamin, Beckett would remind us that nothing *for us* has been promised. The very last words in Benjamin's essay on "Goethe's Elective Affinities" (written during the years 1919–1922 and published in 1925) say: "Only for the sake of the hopeless ones have we been given hope."[47] Near the end of the story of Malone's struggle against the death that awaits him, Malone, or perhaps the narrator of his story, expresses in deeply moving words the ontological understanding of creaturely life at which, in the midst of the horror, he has arrived. The true prayer is a prayer for the other. And then, in fact, there is a "breathturn":

The horror-worn eyes linger abject on all they have beseeched so long, in a last prayer, the true prayer at last, the one that asks for nothing. And it is then a little breath of fulfillment revives the dead longings and a murmur is born in the silent world, reproaching you affectionately with having despaired too late. (MD 270)

As if enveloped in fog or smoke, some of the images in *How It Is*, Beckett's post-Holocaust tale, seem vaguely to evoke the enclosed biopolitical world of the death camps and, in uncanny ways, to connect with another one of Celan's poetic works, a verse written in remembrance of the victims of the Holocaust:

The colliding temples,
naked, in the rending of masks:

before the world
the unbidden hope thrown out
the dragging rope.

In the oceanic wound-edges lands
the breathing number.[48]

In the darkness of the swamp, where justice obeys only the power of violence, the laws of nature, and where, in a movement of infinite slowness, the justice to displace it can seem to be nothing but the fiction of a dream, enigmatic and spectral, as elusive in concept as in reality, something possible, if ever, only in the realm of light said to be "above," Beckett throws out to the unfortunate mortals cast down there, to the men assigned a number and forced to go on dragging their sacks of provisions, exhausted, panting and out of breath, the rope of an unbidden hope. This is the hope that has abandoned all hope, a longing or prayer that waits patiently for nothing, but still lives for what might be possible even in the belatedness of words—in "the words that remain," "this dust of words."[49]

NOTES

Prologue

1   Dante Alighieri, *Purgatorio*, bilingual edition, W. S. Merwin, trans. (New York: Alfred A. Knopf, 2000), III, ll. 40–42 (pp. 24–25): Translation altered.

2   Søren Kierkegaard, *Either/Or,* trans. Walter Lowrie, with revisions by Howard A. Johnson (Princeton: Princeton University Press, 1971), vol. II, 19.

3   Martin Heidegger, "Nietzsches Wort, 'Gott ist tot'," *Holzwege* (Frankfurt am Main: Vittorio Klostermann, 1950), 200. My translation.

4   Heidegger, "The Nature of Language," in *On the Way to Language*, trans. Peter D. Hertz (New York: Harper & Row, 1971), 90. Translation revised. "*Zuspruch*" may be translated as "promise" in the sense of "potential" and "opportunity."

5   Jacques Derrida, "A Certain Impossible Possibility of Saying the Event," trans. Gila Walker, *Critical Inquiry* (Chicago: University of Chicago Press, 2007), vol. 33, no. 2, 458. On the promise, also see his *Avances* (Paris: Les Éditions de Minuit, 1995). On language, see his *Monolingualisme de l'autre* (Paris: Galilée, 1996); *Negotiations: Interventions and Interviews, 1971–2001*, ed. and trans. Elizabeth Rottenberg (Stanford: Stanford University Press, 2002); and "Language Is Never Owned," Interview with Evelyne Grossman, June 29, 2000, in Thomas Dutoit and Outi Pasanen, ed., *Sovereignties in Question: The Poetics of Paul Celan* (New York: Fordham University Press, 2005). And on religion, see *Le Tombeau du Dieu Artisan: Sur Platon* (Paris: Les Éditions de Minuit, 1995) and "Faith and Knowledge: The Two Sources of 'Religion' at the Limits of Reason Alone," trans. Samuel Weber, in Gil Anidjar, ed., *Acts of Religion* (New York: Routledge, 2002).

6   Theodor W. Adorno, *Notes to Literature*, trans. Shierry Weber Nicholsen (New York: Columbia University Press, 1992), vol. II, 90. Italics added. Explaining, in his "Paralipomena," how this utopian idea of "happiness" differs from the self-centered hedonism cynically promoted and exploited by our political economy, Adorno says: "Because all happiness found in the status quo is an ersatz and false, art must break its promise in order to stay true to it. But the consciousness of people, especially that of the masses who in an antagonistic society are separated by cultural privilege from consciousness of such a dialectic, holds fast to the promise of happiness; rightfully so, but in its immediate, material form. This provides an opening for the culture industry, which plans for and exploits the need for happiness." See *Aesthetic Theory*, trans. Robert Hullot-Kentor (Minneapolis: Minnesota University Press, 1997), 311.

7 Theodor Adorno, *Aesthetic Theory*, trans. Robert Hullot-Kentor (Minneapolis: University of Minnesota Press, 1997), 52.

8 Theodor W. Adorno, "Is Art Lighthearted?", *Notes to Literature*, trans. Shierry Weber Nicholsen (New York: Columbia University Press, 1992), vol. II, 251.

9 Theodor W. Adorno, *Minima Moralia: Reflections from Damaged Life*, trans. E. F. N. Jephcott (London: Verso Editions, 1974), 247.

10 Beckett, *How It Is* (New York: Grove Press, 1964), 17. Hereafter cited by H.

11 Beckett, *The Unnamable*, in *Three Novels: Molloy, Malone Dies, The Unnamable*, 319.

12 Benjamin, "Theologico-Political Fragment," *Reflections: Essays, Aphorisms, Autobiographical Writings*, ed. Peter Demetz (New York: Schocken, 1986), 312.

13 Benjamin, "Theses on the Philosophy of History," in *Illuminations*, trans. Harry Zohn (New York: Schocken, 1969), 253–254.

14 Marie-Aude Baronian and Mireille Rosello, interview with Jacques Rancière, trans. Gregory Elliot, in *Art & Research*, vol. 2, no. 1 (summer 2008), 1–20.

15 See Beckett's anatomy of laughter in *Watt*, part I (Paris: The Olympia Press, 1953; New York: Grove Press, 1953), 48: "The bitter laugh laughs at that which is not good, it is the ethical laugh. The hollow laugh laughs at that which is not true, it is the intellectual laugh. [. . .] But the mirthless laugh is the dianoetic laugh [. . .] the laugh of laughs, the *risus puris*, the laugh laughing at the laugh [. . .] at that which is unhappy."

16 See Adorno, "Trying to Understand *Endgame*," *Notes to Literature*, trans. Shierry Weber Nicholsen (New York: Columbia University Press, 1991), vol. I, 257.

17 Gilles Deleuze, *Francis Bacon: The Logic of Sensation*, trans. Daniel W. Smith (Minneapolis: University of Minnesota Press, 2003), 53. There are numerous affinities between Bacon and Beckett.

18 Friedrich Nietzsche, *The Will to Power*, trans. Walter Kaufmann (New York: Random House Vintage Books, 1967), 56.

19 Beckett, *Endgame* (New York: Grove Press, 1958), 18–19.

20 Stanley Cavell, *Must We Mean What We Say?* (New York: Charles Scribner's Sons, 1969), 121.

21 Adorno, "Commitment," *Notes to Literature*, vol. II, 90. See *Aesthetics: Lectures on Fine Arts*, 300. As Hegel says: even when art *fails* to embody the Idea, the form in which art appears is always "adequate" to its content, because its "defectiveness of form" nevertheless expresses the truth of that particular historical moment.

22 The first volume is *Redeeming Words and the Promise of Happiness: A Critical Theory Approach to Wallace Stevens and Vladimir Nabokov* (New York: Lexington Books, Rowman & Littlefield, 2012). The second volume is *Redeeming Words: Language and the Promise of Happiness in the Stories of Döblin and Sebald* (Albany: State University of New York Press, 2013).

23 See Leo Bersani and Ulysse Dutoit, *Arts of Impoverishment: Beckett, Rothko, Renais* (Cambridge: Harvard University Press, 1993).

24 Beckett, *Worstward Ho*, in *Nohow On*, ed. S. E. Gontarski (New York: Grove Press, 1996), 89.

25 Adorno, *Negative Dialectics*, trans. E. B. Ashton (New York: Continuum Publishing Company, 1973), 191. Translation altered.

26 Adorno, *Minima Moralia: Reflections from Damaged Life*, 182. Translation altered.

27 Heidegger, "Building Dwelling Thinking", in Albert Hofstadter, trans. and ed., *Poetry, Language, Thought* (New York: Harper & Row, 1971), 363.

28 Adorno, "Resignation," in *Critical Models: Interventions and Catchwords*, trans. Henry W. Pickford (New York: Columbia University Press, 1998), 293. In conversation with Max Horkheimer, with whom, during the war years 1939–1944, he wrote *Dialectic of Enlightenment*, Adorno commented that, "What gives knowledge the stamp of authenticity is the reflection of possibility. This is what my fundamental philosophical experience is [. . .]." And he continued, saying, "I believe that there is a certain sort of concrete insight [*Erkenntnis*] with a force that, even in its particularity, contains the possibility of the whole. The fragmentary concrete. [. . .] My comment [about the fragmentary concrete] has been criticized as naïve. But is this criticism not already an admission that one no longer believes in happiness?" Horkheimer replied: "I have not given up the claim of happiness, but I do not believe in happiness. Whoever believes in happiness is in the worst sense naïve." To that Adorno reaffirmed his dialectical thinking: "We must be," he said, "at once more naïve and much less naïve." See Horkheimer, *Gesammelte Schriften, Dialektik der Aufklärung und Schriften 1940–1950* (Frankfurt am Main: S. Fischer Verlag, 1987), vol. V, 506–508. My translation.

29 At the end of *Watt*, we find these words: "no symbols where none intended." The amusing catch is that there is no way for readers to know Beckett's intentions. Nevertheless, his works are full of metaphors, symbols, and allegorical constructions. See *Watt* (New York: Grove Press, 1953), 254.

30 Marcel Proust, *In Search of Lost Time*, trans. Andreas Mayor and Terence Kilmartin, revised by D. J. Enright (New York: Random House, 2003), 261. Regarding John Milton, whose poetry, especially *Paradise Lost*, Kant read with great care, thought and enthusiasm, see Sanford Budick, *Kant and Milton* (Cambridge: Harvard University Press, 2010), 304.

31 Beckett, *Watt*, 247.

32 Beckett, *The Letters of Samuel Beckett 1929–1940*, ed. Martha Dow Fehsenfeld and Lois More Overbeck (Cambridge: Cambridge University Press, 2009), vol. I, 33.

33 Arthur Schopenhauer, *Essays and Aphorisms*, ed. and trans. R. J. Hollingdale (London: Penguin, 1970), 42 and 50.

34 A. Alvarez, *Beckett* (London: Fontana Press, 1973, 1992), 31. See also Gilles Deleuze on Beckett's word-images, in "The Exhausted," trans. Anthony Uhlmann, *Sub-Stance*, vol. 78 (1995), 3–28.

35 Georges Bataille, *The Absence of Myth: Writings on Surrealism*, trans. Michael Richardson (New York: Verso, 1994), 66.

36 Adorno, *Minima Moralia: Reflections from Damaged Life*, §143, 223–224.

37 Ludwig Wittgenstein, "Lecture on Ethics," in *Philosophical Occasions: 1912–1951* (Indianapolis and Cambridge: Hackett Publishing Co., 1983), 43–44. In *Emerson's Transcendental Etudes* (Stanford: Stanford University Press, 2003), Stanley Cavell opines that in Wittgenstein's sentiments regarding Shakespeare, what disturbs him might be the sense conveyed in the playwright's language that there is a "continuous threat of chaos clinging to his creation, an anxiety produced as the sense that it is something miraculous that words can mean at all, that there are words" (237). I am not sure about this, but I think it undeniable that such a sense attaches to Beckett's use of language.

38 Regarding "arche-writing," see Derrida, *Of Grammatology* (Baltimore: Johns Hopkins University Press, 1976).

39 Derrida, "How to Avoid Speaking," in Sanford Budick and Wolfgang Iser, ed., *Languages of the Unsayable* (New York: Columbia University Press, 1989), 14.

40 Derrida, "How to Avoid Speaking," 11.

41 Maurice Blanchot, "Language and the Right to Death," in *The Work of Fire*, trans. Lydia Davis (Stanford: Stanford University Press, 1995), 300–301.

42 See Hannah Arendt, *Eichmann in Jerusalem* (New York: Penguin revised and enlarged edition, 1992), 49: "The longer one listened to him [Adolph Eichmann], the more obvious it became that his inability to speak was closely connected with an inability to think, namely, to think from the standpoint of someone else."

43 See Lorna Martens, *The Promise of Memory: Childhood Recollection and Its Objects in Literary Modernism* (Cambridge: Harvard University Press, 2011).

44 Friedrich Hölderlin, "Celebration of Peace," trans. Michael Hamburger, in Eric L. Santner, ed., *Hyperion and Selected Poems* (New York: Continuum, 1990), 235.

45 G. W. F. Hegel, *Aesthetics: Lectures on Fine Art*. 2 vols. Trans. T. M. Knox (Oxford: Clarendon Press, 1975), vol. I, 128.

46 Hegel, *Aesthetics*, vol. I, 128.

47 See my essay, "Civilized Cruelty: Nietzsche on the Disciplinary Practices of Western Culture," *New Nietzsche Studies*, vol. 5, nos. 1/2 (spring/summer 2002), 72–94.

48 Adorno, "In Memory of Eichendorff," *Notes to Literature*, vol. I, 73.

49 On Walter Benjamin's representation of historical potentialities, aborted revolutionary projects, and missed opportunities, see Samuel Weber, *Benjamin's "-abilities"* (Cambridge: Harvard University Press, 2009).

50 See Rebecca Comay, *Mourning Sickness: Hegel and the French Revolution* (Stanford: Stanford University Press, 2011), 34.

51 Walter Benjamin, *Gesammelte Schriften* (Frankfurt am Main: Suhrkamp Verlag, 1978), vol. I, part 3, 1238–1239. My translation.

52 Maurice Merleau-Ponty, "Le philosophe et son ombre," in *Signes* (Paris: Gallimard, 1960), 210. My translation.

53 See below, endnote 91.

54 See Shane Weller, *A Taste for the Negative: Beckett and Nihilism* (London: Legenda, 2005).

55 In my understanding of utopianism, it is not necessarily at odds with meliorism. I concur with Richard Rorty's argument in *Achieving Our Country: Leftist Thought in Twentieth-Century America* (Cambridge: Harvard University Press, 1998).

56 See Stanley Cavell, *In Quest of the Ordinary: Lines of Skepticism and Romanticism* (Chicago: University of Chicago Press, 1988), 135.

57 W. G. Sebald, "Echos aus der Vergangenheit," in *"Auf ungeheuer dünnem Eis": Gespräche 1971 bis 2001* (Frankfurt am Main: Fischer Verlag, 2011), 72. My translation.

58 W. G. Sebald, "Echos aus der Vergangenheit," 149–152: whereas, Sebald argues, we have always believed that it is great figures and great events that have moved history, in reality it is "on the tiny, invisible, unfathomable details that hope rests—if indeed it can count on anything."

59 Derrida, "A Certain Impossible Possibility of Saying the Event," trans. Gila Walker, *Critical Inquiry* (Chicago: University of Chicago Press, 2007), vol. 33, no. 2,458. And see Asja Szafraniec, *Beckett, Derrida, and the Event of Literature* (Stanford: Stanford University Press, 2007).

60 Derrida, *Mémoires: For Paul De Man*, trans. Eduardo Cadava, Jonathan Culler, Cecile Lindsay, and Peggy Kamuf (New York: Columbia University Press, 1989), 150.

61 Derrida, *Negotiations: Interventions and Interviews, 1971-2001*, ed. and trans. Elizabeth Rottenberg (Stanford: Stanford University Press, 2002), 362.

62 Derrida, "Faith and Knowledge: The Two Sources of 'Religion' at the Limits of Reason Alone," trans. Samuel Weber, in *Acts of Religion* (New York: Routledge, 2002), §30, 67.

63 Derrida, "Faith and Knowledge," §38, 83.

64 Derrida, "Faith and Knowledge," §21, 56.

65 Derrida, "Faith and Knowledge," §21, 56.

66 Michael Naas, *Miracle and Machine: Jacques Derrida and the Two Sources of Religion, Science and the Media* (New York: Fordham University Press, 2012), 161. Also see Leonard Lawlor, "What Happened? What Is Going to Happen? An Essay on the Experience of the Event," in Amy Swiften and Joshua Nichols, ed., *The Ends of History: Questioning the Stakes of Historical Reason* (London and New York: Routledge, 2013), 179–195.

67 Derrida, "Faith and Knowledge," op. cit., §21, 56.

68 Derrida, "Faith and Knowledge," §22, 56.

69 See *Islam and the West: Conversations with Jacques Derrida*, trans. Teresa L. Fagan (Chicago: University of Chicago Press, 2008). Derrida argues, giving Benjamin's highly abstract formulations the concrete definition they need: "What distinguishes the idea of democracy from all other ideas of political regimes [. . .] is that democracy is the only political system [. . .] that accepts its own historicity, that is, its own future, which accepts its self-criticism, which accepts its perfectability. [. . .] To exist in a democracy is to agree to challenge,

to be challenge, to challenge the *status quo* in the name of a democracy to come. Democracy is always to come, it is a promise, and it is in the name of that promise that one can always criticize, question that which is proposed as de facto democracy" (42–43).

70 *Islam and the West.*

71 Michael Naas, op. cit., 164.

72 John Caputo, "Hospitality and the Trouble with God," in Richard Kearney and Kascha Semonovich, ed., *Phenomenologies of the Stranger: Between Hostility and Hospitality* (New York: Fordham University Press, 2011), 90 and 92. Benjamin's "event" is appropriated not only by Derrida, but by Giorgio Agamben and Alain Badiou.

73 Gershom Scholem, *Diaries 1913–1919*, trans. and ed. Anthony D. Skinner (Cambridge: Harvard University Press, 2007), 144.

74 Adorno, *Negative Dialectics*, 381.

75 See my essay, "*The Lost Ones*: A Tale for Holocaust Remembrance," forthcoming in the journal *Philosophy & Literature*.

76 However, Beckett's nihilistic longing is "Gnostic," according to Jacob Taubes's definition: the new, as yet still unknown apocalyptic God is "an annihilating God who crushes the world." This "nonexistent" God puts in question "the validity and finality of what exists," responding to a "nihilistic, revolutionary longing." See Jacob Taubes, *Occidental Eschatology*, trans. David Ratmoko (Stanford: Stanford University Press, 2009), 10.

77 David Hume, *Essays Moral, Political, and Literary*, ed. Eugene Miller (Indianapolis: Liberty Classics, 1985), 153.

78 Benjamin, "Theologico-Political Fragment," *Reflections: Essays, Aphorisms, Autobiographical Writings*, 312.

79 Adorno, "Die Idee der Naturgeschichte," *Philosophische Frühschriften, Gesammelte Schriften* (Frankfurt am Main: Suhrkamp, 1973), vol. I, 365. My translation.

80 Hegel, "Introduction," *The Philosophy of History*, trans. Leo Rauch (Indianapolis: Hackett Publishing Co., 1988), 29.

81 See Leo Bersani, *The Culture of Redemption* (Cambridge: Harvard University Press, 1990).

82 This is the formulation in Martin Hägglund, *Dying for Time: Proust, Woolf, Nabokov* (Cambridge: Harvard University Press, 2012), 52.

83 See Vladimir Nabokov, *Pale Fire* (New York: G. P. Putnam's Sons, 1962; Lancer edition, 1963), 37.

84 Nabokov, *Ada, or Ardor: A Family Chronicle* (New York: Random House, Vintage International, 1990), 521.

85 Nabokov, *Ada, or Ardor: A Family Chronicle* (New York: Penguin, 1971), 458.

86 Giorgio Agamben, "The Idea of Language," in *Potentialities: Collected Essays in Philosophy*, trans. Daniel Heller-Roazen (Stanford: Stanford University Press, 1999), 45.

87 Beckett, *Disjecta: Miscellaneous Writings and a Dramatic Fragment*, ed. Ruby Cohn (London: John Calder, 1983), 52. And see Matthew Feldman, "But What was the Pursuit of Meaning in this Indifference to Meaning?: Beckett, Husserl, Sartre and Meaning Creation," in Ulrike Maude and Matthew Feldman, ed., *Beckett and Phenomenology* (New York: Continuum, 2009), 13–38.

88 Maurice Merleau-Ponty, *The Visible and the Invisible*, trans. Alphonso Lingis (Evanston: Northwestern University Press, 1968), 125.

89 Beckett, *Proust and Three Dialogues with Georges Duthuit* (London: John Calder, 1987), 103.

90 Adorno, *Aesthetic Theory*, 117: "Authentic art knows the expression of the expressionless, a crying from which the tears are missing." Paradoxically, it is in some of Beckett's late prose fiction, where he is experimenting with "lessness," a style virtually expressionless, that one encounters a prose of almost overwhelming emotional power: "a crying from which the tears are missing." And see Duncan M. Chesney, *Silence Nowhen: Late Modernism, Minimalism, and Silence in the Work of Samuel Beckett* (New York: Peter Lang, 2013).

91 Adorno, "Late Style in Beethoven," in *Essays on Music*, ed. Michael Lappert, trans. Susan H. Gillespie (Berkeley: University of California Press, 2002), 566. The more reified and commodified individual life and language become, the more difficult it is to form a meaniful narrative. Beckett's prose "minimalism" or "lessness" is radically different from the aesthetics of minimalism in the "sculptural" works of the 1960s. Whereas the artworks of minimalism capitulate to the conditions of an exhausted, hollow, empty rationalization, embracing it in order to reveal the stark beauty of its logic, its grammar, Beckett's "lessness" is much more ambiguous: whilst defying the rules for discursive sense-making in order not only to free prose language from the rationalizing forces of reification and commodification at work in contemporary culture, but also to manifest the damage to language that those forces have wrought, preserving and transmitting its language in its destitute state, Beckett's "lessness" wrests from that damage, that suffering, that deadness, a prose language that sustains a literature which is, despite everything, compellingly meaningful, redeeming thereby, or at least rescuing from total oblivion, fragments of its ever-broken promise.

92 Johann G. Hamann, "Aesthetica in Nuce," trans. Joyce P. Crick, in J. Bernstein, ed., *Classic and Romantic German Aesthetics*, Cambridge: Cambridge University Press, 2003, 1–23. "But if we raise up the whole deserving righteousness of a scribe upon the dead body of a letter, what sayeth the spirit to that? [. . .] Shall we be but a groom of the chamber to the dead letter, or perhaps a mere esquire to the deadening letter? God forbid! [. . .] But how are we to raise the defunct language of nature from the dead?"

93 Ralph Waldo Emerson, "Nature," in *Essays and Lectures*, ed. Joel Porte (New York: The Library of America, 1983), 46: "Infancy is the perpetual Messiah, which comes into the arms of fallen men, and pleads with them to return to paradise."

94 See Martin Seel, *Aesthetics of Appearing*, trans. John Farrell (Stanford: Stanford University Press, 2005), 127–134 for a discussion of the aesthetic operation of prose in literature.

95 Alain Badiou, *Conditions*, trans. Steven Corcoran (New York: Continuum, 2008), 266.

96 Badiou, *Conditions*, 267. And see Leonard Lawlor, "What Happened? What Is Going to Happen? An Essay on the Experience of the Event," in Amy Swiften and Joshua Nichols, ed., *The Ends of History: Questioning the Stakes of Historical Reason*, 179–195.

97 And see Asja Szafraniec, *Beckett, Derrida, and the Event of Literature* (Stanford University Press, 2007).

98 Adorno, *Aesthetic Theory*, 82. Translation modified, italics added.

99 See Jay Bernstein, *Against Voluptuous Bodies: Late Modernism and the Meaning of Painting* (Stanford: Stanford University Press, 2006), 46. I quote, as bearing very much on my project, what Bernstein says about a painting by Chaim Soutine: "It must seem an insult to commitments to justice and a travesty of the feelings that support such commitments (compassion for the sufferings of others, or righteous anger at those who calculate the worth of human lives as if it were a simple matter of profit and loss) that the intelligibility and validity of those commitments and feelings could be thought to hang on or be found in just "this" painting or "this" urgent brush stroke of red. The disproportion between these two, the unjust ruination of human lives on the one hand and the velleities of some cultural artifacts on the other, is so immense that to consider the latter as a, or the, voice of the former, perhaps even the condition in which the latter has a voice, appears outrageous, even blasphemous. And because the disproportion at issue here is actual, hence the sense of insult and travesty actual (and so apparently always possibly justified), the need to make sense of the intimate connection between concern for the worth of human lives that are systematically denied worth, the validity of a passion for justice and happiness, and the refinements of high cultural artifacts is constant." Beckett is painfully conscious of this problem.

100 Bernstein, *Against Voluptuous Bodies*, 13.

101 Stanley Cavell raises this question, without offering any definitive answer, in *The Claim of Reason: Wittgenstein, Skepticism, Morality, and Tragedy* (New York: Oxford University Press, 1979), 416. And see Gerald Bruns, *On Ceasing to Be Human* (Stanford: Stanford University Press, 2011), 31–46.

102 "Civilized cruelty" is meant, of course, to catch a terrible irony, a contradiction in our culture. See David Michael Levin, "Civilized Cruelty: Nietzsche on the Disciplinary Practices of Western Culture," in *New Nietzsche Studies*, vol. 5, numbers 1–2 (summer 2002), 72–94.

103 Most of the Beckett works with which we will be concerned are English translations; but they are translations that Beckett himself worked on, drawing from the original French. Unfortunately, I cannot in this study undertake to compare the English and French translations, fascinating and valuable though this would be. For more on the question of Beckett's translations, see Sinéad Mooney, "Beckett in French and English," in S. E. Gontarski (ed.), *A Companion to Samuel Beckett* (Malden, MA: Wiley-Blackwell, 2010), 196–208.

104 Beckett, *Dream of Fair to Middling Women*, ed. Eoin O'Brian and Edith Fournier (New York: Arcade Publishing Co., 1992), 28. Belacqua, Florentine lute maker, was required to sit, in Dante's *Purgatorio*, leaning forward with his head bent down between his knees: the characteristic depressive position. His immobility became, for Beckett, the source of an important allegorical demonstration. On Beckett's modernist reflexivity in the construction of narrative, see Mark Nixon, "Between Art-World and Life-World: Beckett's Dream of Fair to Middling Women," in Ulrika Maude and Matthew Feldman (ed.), *Beckett and Phenomenology*, 97–100.

105 See Stéphane Mallarmé, "Crisis in Poetry," in Mary Ann Caws, ed. and trans., *Selected Poetry and Prose* (New York: New Directions, 1982), 76: "I say: a flower! And outside the oblivion to which my voice relegates any shape, insofar as it is something other than the calyx, there arises musically, as the very idea and delicate, the one absent from every bouquet [*l'absente de tous bouquets*]." Speaking of *the absent*, the poet celebrates the power of language, but also notes its fateful connection to death.

106 See Friedrich Hölderlin's phrase "the flower of the mouth," in "Germanien," his metaphor in the elegy "Der Gang aufs Land," where the word blossoms as do "the sky's blooms," and his simile in "*Brot und Wein*," where the poet speaks of "words, like flowers." See Hölderlin, *Hymns and Fragments*, trans. Richard Sieburth (Princeton: Princeton University Press, 1984) and *Hyperion and Selected Poems*, ed. Eric L. Santner (New York: Continuum, 1990).

107 Beckett, *Worstward Ho*, in *Nohow On* (New York: Grove Press, 1980), 89. Hereafter, this tale will be cited by WH. In *How It Was: A Memoir of Samuel Beckett* (London: Faber, 2001), 95, Anne Atik quotes from a December 1977 conversation with him: "All writing is a sin against speechlessness. Trying to find a form for that silence. Only a few, Yeats, Goethe, those who lived for a long time, could go on to do it, but they had recourse to known forms and fictions. So one finds oneself [today] going back to *vielles compétences* [know-how, as opposed to the creative act]—how to escape that. One can never get over the fact, never rid oneself of the old dream of giving form to speechlessness."

108 Northrop Frye, "Verse and Prose," in Alex Preminger, ed., *Princeton Encyclopedia of Poetry and Poetics* (Princeton: Princeton University Press, 1974), 886.

109 Discussing in a letter (March 1954) why there could not be a musical interpretation of *Waiting for Godot*, Beckett tells Edouard Coester that, "what is at issue is a speaking whose function is not so much that of having a meaning as of putting up a struggle, poor I hope, against silence, and leading back to it." See Samuel Beckett, *The Letters of Samuel Beckett: 1941–1956*, ed. George Craig, Martha Dow Fehsenfeld, Dan Gunn, and Lois More Overbeck (Cambridge: Cambridge University Press, 2011), vol. II, 474–476.

110 Maurice Merleau-Ponty, *The Visible and the Invisible*, trans. Alphonso Lingis (Evanston: Northwestern University Press, 1968), 125.

111 In a 1941 letter to Max Horkheimer, Theodor Adorno, refers to the difficulties he was encountering in finding a way to think the *theologoumena*: "I have a weak, infinitely weak, feeling that it is still possible to think the secret [. . .]."

The difficulty: it lies in silence. See Rolf Wiggershaus, *Die Frankfurter Schule: Geschichte, theoretische Entwicklung, politische Bedeutung* (Munich: Karl Hanser, 1986), 503.

112 Jacques Derrida, *Monolingualisme de l'autre* (Paris: Galilée, 1996), 125–126. My translation. Derrida might here be responding to Heidegger's assertion that we are human "only because we are granted the promise of language." See Martin Heidegger, "The Nature of Language," in *On the Way to Language*, trans. Peter D. Hertz (New York: Harper & Row, 1971), 90.

113 Beckett, *The End*, in S. E. Gontarski (ed.), *Samuel Beckett: Complete Short Prose 1929–1989* (New York: Grove Press, 1995), 99. One should notice the rhymes ("cold" and "told," "likeness" and "life"), the repetition ("story," "story"), and the rhythm or melodic line ("the courage to end or the strength to go on"). These features, characteristic of the oral tradition of storytelling, recuperate that tradition, redeeming it for the expression of present experience. They are also moments of reconciliation, hence of redemption, making the two senses of "sense" work together without privileging the cognitive.

114 Beckett, *Enough*, in *Samuel Beckett: Complete Short Prose 1929–1989* (New York: Grove Press, 1995), 186.

115 Georg Lukács, *The Theory of the Novel*, trans. Anna Bostock (Cambridge: The MIT Press, 1971), 56.

116 Lukács, *The Theory of the Novel*, 88.

117 Lukács, *The Theory of the Novel*. And see Jay M. Bernstein, *The Philosophy of the Novel: Lukács, Marxism, and the Dialectic of Form* (Minneapolis: The University of Minnesota Press, 1984).

118 For a really fine-grained discussion—the best I know about—of specific examples of what Beckett calls his "syntax of weakness," see Christopher Ricks's 1990 Clarendon Lectures, in *Beckett's Dying Words* (Oxford: Oxford University Press, 1993).

119 Benjamin, "The Storyteller," in *Illuminations*, trans. Harry Zohn (New York: Schocken, 1969), 84. And see, e.g. Roger Cohen's story, "Experience as it once was," *The New York Times*, 10 October, 2013. Empirical support for Benjamin's claim can be found in a story by Richard Hamilton, *BBC News Magazine*, April 12, 2014: "The Storyteller in Marrakech," www.bbc.com/news/magazine-26988777. But see Anu Anand, "Storytelling Returns to Delhi's Streets: The Lost Art of Urdu Storytelling", BBC Online, April 2, 2011.

120 Benjamin, "The Storyteller," *Illuminations*, 87.

121 In his 1827–1828 *Lectures on the Philosophy of Spirit*, trans. and intro. Robert R. Williams (New York: Oxford University Press, 2007), 233, G. W. F. Hegel supported Herder's emphasis on language, challenging Kant's indifference to the role of language in philosophical discourse. And see Jere O'Neill Surber, "Hegel's Linguistic Thought in the Philosophy of Subjective Spirit: Between Kant and the 'Metacritics'," in *Essays on Hegel's Philosophy of Subjective Spirit*, ed. David S. Stern (Albany: State University of New York Press, 2013), 181–200. Today, neither philosophers nor poets and writers of

fiction can disregard the questioning language and its powers of signification and representation.

122 Nietzsche, "On Truth and Lies in a Nonmoral Sense," in Daniel Breazeale, ed., *Philosophy and Truth: Selections from Nietzsche's Notebooks of the Early 1870s* (New Jersey and London: Humanities Press International, 1979), 84.

123 Nietzsche, *Beyond Good and Evil: Prelude to a Philosophy of the Future*, trans. Walter Kaufmann (New York: Random House Vintage Books, 1966), part I, §16, 23.

124 Nietzsche, *Beyond Good and Evil*, §21, 29.

125 See Linda Ben-Zvi, "Samuel Beckett, Fritz Mauthner, and the Limits of Language," *PMLA*, vol. 95 (March 1980), 183–200. Also see William Franke, "Franz Rosenzweig and the Emergence of a Postsecular Philosophy of the Unsayable," in *International Journal for the Philosophy of Religion*, vol. 58 (2005), 161–180.

126 Husserl's contributions included reflections in the 1930s on a crisis in the natural sciences in which he proposed a phenomenologically grounded rational reconstruction of their procedures for the formation of the concepts they need: a reconstruction that would exhibit the fundamental concepts of the sciences in precise, intuitively transparent language. See his *Crisis of European Sciences and Transcendental Phenomenology*, trans. David Carr (Evanston: Northwestern University Press, 1970).

127 Hugo von Hofmansthal, "The Lord Chandos Letter," trans. Joel Rotenberg. *New York Review of Books*, 2005, 121.

128 Ibid., 122.

129 Ibid.

130 Ibid.

131 In "Laoköon oder Über die Grenzen der Sprache," *Rapporte* (Frankfurt am Main: Suhrkamp, 1965), vol. I, 187, Peter Weiss wrote a comment on the Hofmannsthal "Letter" that bears on Beckett's experience of writing. Whilst acknowledging the "decay" of language, the possibility that "behind every word the danger of a fall into silence always threatens," his essay concludes with the encouraging thought that failure in terms of the old conventions might be liberating rather than defeating.

132 I am borrowing the phrase in quotation marks from André Bleikasten's commentary on William Faulkner's great novel, *The Sound and the Fury*. See Bleikasten's book, *The Most Splendid Failure* (Bloomington: Indiana University Press, 1976), 87.

133 Stefan George, *Das Neue Reich, Sämtliche Werke*, 18 vols (Stuttgart: Klett-Cotta, 1982), vol. IX, 133–34. My translation.

134 See Martin Heidegger, *On the Way to Language* (New York: Harper & Row, 1971).

135 Martin Jay, "Is Experience Still in Crisis?" in Tom Huhn, ed., *The Cambridge Companion to Adorno* (Cambridge: Cambridge University Press, 2004), 140.

136 Ralph Waldo Emerson, "Nature," *Essays and Lectures*, ed. Joel Porte (New York: Library of America, 1983), 22.

137	Rainer Maria Rilke, *Sämtliche Werke in zwölf Bänden*, ed. Rilke-Archiv, Ruth Sieber-Rilke and Ernst Zinn (Frankfurt am Main: Insel Verlag Werkausgabe, 1976), vol. I, 194–195. My translation.

138	Wallace Stevens, "Esthétique du Mal," in Frank Kermode and Joan Richardson, ed., *Collected Poetry and Prose* (New York: The Library of America, 1997), 282. Stevens is alluding to Hölderlin's poem, "Bread and Wine."

139	T. S. Eliot, "East Coker," *Collected Poems 1909–1962* (New York: Harcourt, Brace & World, 1963), 188–189.

140	Concerning this "transcendental reduction," see my book, *Redeeming Words and the Promise of Happiness: A Critical Theory Approach to Wallace Stevens and Vladimir Nabokov* (New York: Lexington Books, Rowman & Littlefield, 2012).

141	In painting, Manet unquestionably showed the way. His *Déjeuner sur l'herbe*, a "reconstruction" of Marcantonio Raimondi's engraving, *Judgment of Paris* (1510–1520), designed by Raphael, compels one to oscillate between the mimetic illusion, the semblance of dimensional reality, and seeing the image in its flatness—as just an image painted on a canvas surface. For discussions of reflexive modernism in painting, see Clement Greenberg, *Art and Culture: Critical Essays* (Boston: Beacon Press, 1961) and Michael Fried, *Art and Objecthood* (Chicago: University of Chicago Press, 1998).

142	See my recent book, *Redeeming Words and the Promise of Happiness: A Critical Theory Approach to Wallace Stevens and Vladimir Nabokov.*

143	Beckett, *Disjecta: Miscellaneous Writings and Dramatic Fragments*, ed. Ruby Cohen (New York: Grove Press, 1984), 171–172. Also see Beckett's letter to Axel Kaun, in Martha D. Fehsenfeld and Lois M. Overbeck, ed., *The Letters of Samuel Beckett* 1929–1940 (Cambridge: Cambridge University Press, 2009), vol. I, 513–520. A. Alvarez argues, in *Beckett* (London: Fontana Press, 1992), 67, that Beckett's expressions of extreme despair regarding language should be understood as "aesthetic nihilism." I repudiate that interpretation, unless "aesthetic" carries all the weight.

144	Beckett, *Disjecta*, 173.

145	Cavell, "Ending the Waiting Game: A Reading of Beckett's *Endgame*," *Must We Mean What We Say?*, 120.

146	See Cavell's examples, op. cit., 124–125. *First, literalism*: Hamm says to Clov, "I'll give you nothing to eat." Clov replies: "Then we'll die." Hamm then says: "I'll give you just enough to keep you from dying. You'll be hungry all the time." And to that Clov says, simply drawing the logical conclusion: "Then we won't die." Dying is at stake, but the logic is impeccable; and precisely therein lies the humor. *Secondly, the defeat of normal meaning*: Hamm to Clov, seeming with his words to make a confession: "I've made you suffer too much." Pause. "Haven't I?" Clov answers him: "It's not that." Hamm, shocked, then asks: "I haven't made you suffer too much?" Clov replies with an ambiguous "Yes!" Hamm, showing he is relieved, says "Ah you gave me a fright!" And after a pause, he says, coldly: "Forgive me," seeming to be asking for forgiveness. He pauses, waiting no doubt for Clov to respond to that.

But when Clov remains silent, Hamm, louder now, says, "I said, Forgive me," turning his plea into a command. Again, we are witnesses to a breakdown in communication, showing isolation and estrangement.

147 Adorno, "On Lyric Poetry and Society," *Notes to Literature*, vol. I, 52–53.

148 Jean-François Lyotard, "The Psychoanalytic Approach," in *Main Trends in Aesthetics and the Sciences of Art*, ed. Mikel Dufrenne (New York: Holmes & Meier, 1979), 143.

149 Beckett, *Worstward Ho*, in *Nohow On*, 93. Hereafter WH. Beckett's title is a parody playing with the title of *Westward Ho!*, an 1855 British historical novel about Francis Drake in the Caribbean.

150 See Gontarski and Ackerly, "The Knowing Non-Exister," in S. E. Gontarki, *A Companion to Samuel Beckett* (Malden, MA: Wiley-Blackwell, 2010), 392. The contemporary self, liberated from its Cartesianism, is still on trial in Beckett's first-person narrator stories. But "equally on trial is the language through which identity is shaped and asserted, the sentence sentenced, so to speak."

151 Maurice Blanchot, *Faux Pas* (Paris: Gallimard, 1943), 3.

152 Ann Atik, *How It Was: A Memoir of Samuel Beckett* (London: Faber, 2001), 95.

153 Beckett, *From an Abandoned Work*, in *The Complete Short Prose 1929–1989*, 162.

154 See John Calder, "Philosophy and Language," in John Calder, *The Philosophy of Samuel Beckett* (London: John Calder, 2001), 85–105.

155 See Cavell, "Ending the Waiting Game: A Reading of Beckett's *Endgame*," in *Must We Mean What We Say?*

156 Sartre, "The Paintings of Giacometti," *Situations*, trans. Benita Eisler (Greenwich: Fawcett, 1969), 128–129.

157 Stéphane Mallarmé, "Quant au livre," *Oeuvres complètes*, ed. Henri Mondor and G. Jean-Aubry (Paris: Bibliothèque de la Pléiade, Gallimard, 1945), 186.

158 See Vladimir Nabokov, *Ada, or Ardor: A Family Chronicle* (New York: Vintage International, 1990), 267 and see Georg W. F. Hegel, *Hegel's Science of Logic*, trans. A. V. Miller (New York: Humanities Press, 1969), 32 and *The Encyclopaedia Logic, with Supplements*, trans. T. F. Geraets, W. A. Suchting, and H. S. Harris (Indianapolis: Hackett Publishing Co., 1991), 154. On the two traditionally opposed senses of "*Sinn*," or (in English) "sense," see Hegel, *Aesthetics: Lectures on Fine Arts*, trans. T. M. Knox (Oxford: Clarendon Press, 1975), vol. I, 128–129. And see the discussion of the dialectical or speculative proposition in my book, *Redeeming Words and the Promise of Happiness: A Critical Theory Approach to Wallace Stevens and Vladimir Nabokov*, 165–168.

159 Edmond Jabès, "The Key," in *Midrash and Literature*, ed. Geoffrey Hartman and Sanford Budick (New Haven: Yale University Press, 1986), 352.

160 Thomas Altizer, *The Call to Radical Theology*, ed. Lissa McCullough (Albany: State University of New York Press, 2012), 139. Also see Martin Hägglund,

Radical Atheism: Derrida and the Time of Life (Stanford: Stanford University Press, 2008).

161 Ibid., 64.

162 Ibid., 52.

163 Ibid., 56–57.

164 Ibid., 58.

165 Ibid., 62.

166 Ibid., 61.

167 See my essay, "*The Lost Ones*: A Tale for Holocaust Remembrance," forthcoming in the journal *Philosophy & Literature*.

168 Ibid.

169 Ibid.

170 Ibid.

171 Derrida, "This Strange Institution Called Literature," in Derrida, *Arts of Literature*, trans. and ed. Derek Altridge (New York and London: Routledge, 1992), 66.

172 Alain Badiou, *Conditions*, 263.

173 Badiou, *Conditions*, 258.

174 Sandra Wynands, *Iconic Spaces: The Dark Theology of Samuel Beckett's Drama* (Notre Dame: University of Notre Dame Press, 2007), 46.

175 Nietzsche, *The Will to Power*, 4. Hereafter WP.

176 See David Michael Levin, "Civilized Cruelty: Nietzsche on the Disciplinary Practices of Western Culture," in *New Nietzsche Studies*, vol. 5, nos. 1–2 (summer 2002), 72–94.

177 See Ludovic Janvier, *Beckett par lui-même* (Paris: Seuil, 1979).

178 Beckett, *Murphy* (London: Routledge & Sons, 1938), 246. And see Shane Weller, "Phenomenologies of the Nothing: Democritus, Heidegger, Beckett," in Ulrike Maude and Matthew Feldman, ed., *Beckett and Phenomenology*, 39–55.

179 Beckett, *Watt*, 76.

180 See Lawrence E. Harvey, "Watt," in E. Gontarski (ed.), *On Beckett: Essays and Criticism* (New York: Grove Press, 1986), 91–116.

181 Beckett, *Waiting for Godot* (New York: Grove Press, 1956), 58.

182 Friedrich Schiller, *On the Aesthetic Education of Man in a Series of Letters*, trans. Reginald Snell (New York: Frederick Unger Publishing Co., 1965), 106. Italics added.

183 Schiller, *On the Aesthetic Education*, 57.

184 Ibid., 63.

185 After the Second World War, Beckett had something of a "revelation" regarding his approach to writing fiction. He realized that, whereas "Joyce had gone as far as one could in the direction of knowing more, [being] in control of one's material," his "own way" had to be "in impoverishment, in lack of knowledge and in taking away, in subtracting rather than adding."

See James Knowlson, *Damned to Fame: The Life of Samuel Beckett* (London: Bloomsbury, 1996), 352.

186 Benjamin, "Imagination," *Selected Writings 1913–1926* (Cambridge: Harvard University Press, 1996), vol. I, 280–282.

187 Beckett, *Company*, in *Nohow On* (New York: Grove Press, 1986), 39. "Company" was first published in 1980.

188 Beckett, *Imagination Dead Imagine*, in Richard W. Seaver, ed., *I can't go on, I'll go on: A Samuel Beckett Reader* (New York: Grove Press, 1976), 550.

189 Beckett, *Enough*, in S. E. Gontarski (ed.), *Samuel Beckett: The Complete Short Prose 1929–1989*, 192. Is Beckett here challenging Mallarmé's "annihilation" of the flower? See Stéphene Mallarmé, "Crisis in Poetry," in Mary Ann Caws, ed. and trans., *Selected Poetry and Prose* (New York: New Directions, 1982), 76: "I say: a flower! And outside the oblivion to which my voice relegates any shape, insofar as it is something other than the calyx, there arises musically, as the very idea and delicate, the one absent from every bouquet [*l'absente de tous bouquets*]." Is he commenting also on Hölderlin's poetic invocations of flowers—"words like flowers," "the flower of the mouth"?

190 Edmund Husserl, *Ideas: General Introduction to Pure Phenomenology*, trans. W. R. Boyce-Gibson (New York: Collier-Macmillan, 1963), 139.

191 Ibid., 97.

192 Ibid., 132.

193 Ibid., 136–137.

194 Ibid., 157.

195 Jay Bernstein, "Philosophy's Refuge: Adorno in Beckett," in David Wood, ed., *Philosopher's Poets* (New York: Routledge, 1990), 177–191.

196 See the 1937 letter to Axel Kaun, in Beckett, *Disjecta: Miscellaneous Writings and a Dramatic Fragment*, ed. Ruby Cohn (London: John Calder, 1983), 52. And see Matthew Feldman, "But What was the Pursuit of Meaning in this Indifference to Meaning? Beckett, Husserl, Sartre and Meaning Creation," in Ulrike Maude and Matthew Feldman, ed., *Beckett and Phenomenology*, 13–38.

197 Beckett, *Fizzles* (New York: Grove Press, 1976), 37. Also in S. E. Gontarski, ed., *The Complete Short Prose 1929–1989*, 236.

198 Beckett, *Fizzles*, in *The Complete Short Prose 1929–1989*, 232. This phrase appears at the beginning of the fifth "Fizzle."

199 On the proper name and identity, see Derrida, *A Taste for the Secret*, trans. Giacomo Donis (Cambridge: Polity Press, 2001; Malden: Blackwell Publishers, 2001), 67–69 and *On the Name*, trans. David Wood, John P. Leavey, Jr., and Ian McLeod (Stanford: Stanford University Press, 1995).

200 See Gerald Bruns, *On Ceasing to be Human* (Stanford: Stanford University Press, 2011), 79–97.

201 Heidegger, "Letter on Humanism," trans. Frank A. Capuzzi, in William McNeill, ed., *Pathmarks* (Cambridge: Cambridge University Press, 1998), 243.

202 Beckett, *Endgame*, 32–33.

203 Badiou, *Conditions*, 269.

204 Ibid., 269.

205 The conception of time and history in Beckett is a topic deserving a work of its own, especially insofar as it is a question of a time of redemption, which would require another temporality somehow breaking into the irreversible linear flow of time. Agamben follows Heidegger's radical attempt to think the renewal of history in terms of "event," but he thinks it in the context of Benjamin's appropriation of Pauline Hebraicism, reconfigured in Benjamin's aphoristic notes "On the Concept of History." Badiou likewise follows Heidegger's movement of thought, proposing that we read Beckett's experiments with language in these terms. But he leaves in the dark the implications of these experiments for the course of time and history engaged by Beckett's stories. On the Hebraic conception of time and history, open to a redemptive event-possibility, see Marlène Zarader, *The Unthought: Heidegger and the Hebraic Heritage*, trans. Bettina Bergo (Stanford: Stanford University Press, 2006).

206 Adorno, *Aesthetic Theory*, 154. See also op. cit., 244, 249, and 271.

207 See Stanley Cavell, "Ending the Waiting Game: A Reading of Beckett's *Endgame*," *Must We Mean What We Say?*, 115–162.

208 Beckett, *Three Dialogues*, 145.

209 Badiou, *Conditions*, 46ff.

210 Badiou, *Conditions*, 255. Also see his "Etre, existence, pensée," in *Petit Manuel d'inesthétique* (Paris: Seuil, 1998), 137–187.

211 I am told that more has been written on Beckett than on Shakespeare. Writing anything to add to this florilegium is, therefore, daring a grave risk. I will accordingly provide only an abbreviated bibliography, indicating some of the works I have used. Also, I wish to note that, for reasons of economy, I will not be discussing the original French versions of Beckett's works, important though they are. In almost every instance, however, Beckett himself was involved in the preparation of the English translation.

212 Beckett's *Molloy* (1947), *Malone Dies* (1951) and *The Unnamable* (1959) were all written initially in French and subsequently translated into English by Beckett himself. In *Strong Opinions*, Vladimir Nabokov observed, in this regard: "I've read him in both French and English. Beckett's French is a schoolmaster's French, a preserved French, but in his English you feel the moisture of verbal association and of the spreading live roots of his prose." Nabokov, *Strong Opinions* (New York: Vintage International, 1990), 172. Beckett himself said that, since his knowledge of the French language was limited, it would be easier for him to achieve a bare, stripped-down English prose, a minimalist prose without embellishment, by writing first in French and then translating what he wrote into English: see Michael Robinson, *The Long Sonata of the Dead* (New York: Grove Press, 1969), 133. Paul Auster has opined that, "However stripped his style in French may be, there is always a little extra added to the English renderings, some slight twist of diction or nuance, some unexpected word falling at just the right moment, that reminds

us that English is nevertheless Beckett's home." Paul Auster, "From Cakes to Stones: A Note on Beckett's French," in *The Art of Hunger and Other Essays* (London: Menard Press, 1982), 54.

213 Dante, *Purgatorio*, op. cit., VIII, l. 139 (80–81): "se corso di guidizio non s'arresta." My translation.

214 Paul Celan, "Breathturn," in Michael Hamburger, trans., *Poems of Paul Celan* (New York: Persea Books, 1972), 252–253. My translation.

215 Regarding the divine turned to dust, see G. W. F. Hegel, *Hegels theologische Frühschriften*, ed. H. Nohl (Tübingen: J. C. B. Mohr, 1907), 300; *Early Theological Writings*, trans. T. M. Knox (Chicago: The University of Chicago Press, 1948), 252. But, for others—W. G. Sebald, to name just one—dust, like ash, is a redeemable substance, perhaps already redeemed. As Lynne Sharon Schwartz notes in *The Emergence of Memory: Conversations with W. G. Sebald* (New York: Seven Stories Press, 2007), dust, like ash, is a substance finally at rest, a substance released from longing. "Man" (Hebrew *adam*) is derived from earth, or dust (Hebrew *adama*) as *adam* is derived from *adama*, and "*humus*," the English word "human," is related to "*humus*," the Latin word for earth or soil.

216 Benjamin, "The Task of the Translator," *Illuminations* (New York; Schocken Publishing, 1969), 82.

217 Giorgio Agamben, *Remnants of Auschwitz: The Witness and the Archive*, trans. Daniel Heller-Roazen (New York: Zone Books, 1999), 34.

218 Georges Bataille, "Molloy's Silence," in S. E. Gontarski, ed., *On Beckett*, 131.

219 John Calder, *The Philosophy of Samuel Beckett* (London: Calder; New Jersey: Riverrun Press, 2001), 1.

220 Derrida, "Demeure: Fiction and Testimony," in *The Instant of My Death/ Demeure: Fiction and Testimony*, trans. Elizabeth Rottenberg (Stanford: Stanford University Press, 2000), 29.

221 See Beckett's *The Unnamable*, 297, where the narrating voice speaks of serving as witness to the sufferings of all the Murphys, Molloys, and Malones. And see also, in that same novel, 311–318, the narrator's desperate, agonizing efforts, upon returning home from his journey, to find out exactly what happened to his family, all dead, having died, according to Mahood, in the course of the most horrible imaginable suffering. But there are different versions of the event. These strange, unsettling pages, suggesting a nightmarish atrocity, the scene, perhaps, of some brutal crime, reveal the narrator's obsession with the question of what makes a witness credible and what constitutes genuinely authoritative testimony. On witnessing, see Derrida, *A Taste for the Secret*, trans. Giacomo Donis (Cambridge: Polity Press, 2001; Malden: Blackwell Publishers, 2001), 72–74. This is one of several texts where he discusses the witnessing of the witness.

222 Beckett, *Watt*, 202–203.

223 See Paul Celan, "Ash-glory," in *Speech-grill and Selected Poems*, trans. Joachim Neugroschel (New York: Dutton, 1971), 240. And see "Nihilism in Samuel

Beckett's *The Lost Ones*: A Tale for Holocaust Remembrance," forthcoming in the journal *Philosophy & Literature*. I read Beckett's story as an attempt to imagine what happened inside the Nazi's gas chambers—as if, paradoxically, he is both inside and outside.

224 Regarding the role of the witness in Beckett, see J. E. Dearlove, "The Voice and Its Words," in S. E. Gontarski, ed., *On Beckett*, 150–168. See also David Houston Jones, ed., *Samuel Beckett and Testimony* (London and New York: Palgrave Macmillan, 2011); Daniel Katz, "What Remains of Beckett: Evasion and History," in *Beckett and Phenomenology*, 144–157; and John Banville, "Words from the Witness," in *The Irish Times Weekend Review* (September 25, 2004), 10, quoted by Jackie Blackman, "Beckett's Theatre: 'After Auschwitz'," 83 in Sean Kennedy and Katherine Weiss, ed., *Beckett: Memory, History and Archive* (New York: Palgrave Macmillan, 2009), 71–87.

225 Regarding the redeeming "event" and promise in the context of Christian theology, see Derrida, *Avances* (Paris: Les Éditions de Minuit, 1995), 41–42.

226 Years later, Paul's "as if not" is explicitly invoked in *The Unnamable*; but here the narrating voice, longing for death, expresses the wish—a wish that seems like a prayer calling upon God's mercy—that he "might be left in peace at last" and "given quittance, and the right to rest, and silence, if that is in his gift." He next adds: "It's a lot to expect of one creature, it's a lot to ask, that he should first behave as if he were not, then as if he were, before being admitted to that peace where he neither is nor is not, and where the language dies that permits of such expressions" (UN 328).

227 Benjamin, *The Origin of the German Tragic Drama*, trans. John Osborne (London: New Left Books, 1998), 81. That translation of the German title is mistaken, because the whole point of Benjamin's study is to show the difference between tragedy, for which the ancient Greek dramas are the paradigm, and the German Baroque "*Trauerspiel*," or "mourning play."

228 Benjamin, *The Origin of the German Tragic Drama*, 129.

229 Benjamin, *The Origin of the German Tragic Drama*, 166.

230 Benjamin, "On Language as Such and on the Language of Man," *Reflections: Essays, Aphorisms, Autobiographical Writings*, 328–329.

231 Emmanuel Levinas, *Totality and Infinity: An Essay on Exteriority*, trans. Alphonso Lingis (Pittsburgh: Duquesne University Press, 1969), 213.

232 Jürgen Habermas has committed a lifetime of work showing that the theory of justice and the theory of language must be thought in terms of their connection. And, in "The Child's Relations with Others" and other writings, Maurice Merleau-Ponty has elaborated the phenomenological stages in the child's sense of justice, showing the correlation between those stages and the stages in the child's acquisition of language.

233 Benjamin, "Theologico-Political Fragment," *Reflections: Essays, Aphorisms, Autobiographical Writings*, 312.

234 Hölderlin, *The Death of Empedocles: A Mourning-Play*, trans. David Farrell Krell (Albany: State University of New York Press, 2008), Act I, scene 7, lines 860–862, 67. I have slightly altered Krell's fine translation.

235 "I give you my word" appears not once but twice in Beckett's *Texts for Nothing*. See Beckett, *Texts for Nothing*, in *Stories and Texts for Nothing*, trans. Samuel Beckett (New York: Grove Press, 1967), *Text* III, 86 and *Text* VI, 105. It also appears in *Molloy*, 49. This surely confirms its importance for Beckett—precisely, indeed, as an expression of promise.

236 Max Horkheimer, "The Rationalism Debate in Contemporary Philosophy", in *Between Philosophy and Social Science: Selected Early Writings*, ed. and trans. G. Frederick Hunter, Matthew S. Kramer, and John Torpey (Cambridge: The MIT Press, 1983), 262. Translation altered, italics added.

237 Beckett, *Endgame* (New York: Grove Press, 1958).

238 Paul Celan, *Gesammelte Schriften*, ed. Beda Allemann and Stefan Reichert (Frankfurt am Main: Suhrkamp Verlag, 1983), vol. I, 159. My translation.

239 Derrida, "Language Is Never Owned," Interview with Evelyne Grossman, June 29, 2000, in *Sovereignties in Question: The Poetics of Paul Celan*, ed. Thomas Dutoit and Outi Pasanen (New York: Fordham University Press, 2005), 106–107. And see Celan, *Gesammelte Werke* (Frankfurt am Main: Suhrkamp, 1983), vol. III, 186.

240 Benjamin, "On Language as Such and on the Language of Man," *Reflections: Essays, Aphorisms, Autobiographical Writings*, 331. And see Jean-Luc Nancy, *La partage des voix* (Paris: Éditions de Galilée, 1982).

241 But see *Molloy*, 156, where Moran writes of the "foul little flickering lights of terrified men." But there could be truth in both descriptions of the lighting mortals have achieved. We are terrified, and that makes the flickering illumination of the earth, the incomplete enlightenment we have achieved, all the more heroic.

242 Ralph Waldo Emerson, "Nature," *Essays and Lectures*, ed. Joel Porte (New York: Library of America, 1983), 22.

243 On the oath, the pledge, the promise in giving one's word, see Derrida, *A Taste for the Secret*, 72–74.

244 Beckett, *Texts for Nothing*, in *Stories and Texts for Nothing*, trans. Samuel Beckett (New York: Grove Press, 1967), text VIII, 111. In *The Unnamable*, the narrator says "I know my eyes are open because of the tears that pour from them incessantly" (UN 298). In *The Opening of Vision* (London and New York: Routledge, 1988), published before Derrida's own reflections on the fact that the eyes not only see but also weep, I noted the connection and argued that weeping, the involuntary, hence strongest expression of sympathy, is the *root* of vision, the moral source of sight and insight. In *Aesthetic Theory*, 117, Adorno, drawing on Benjamin's thoughts on "the expressionless," remarks: "Authentic art knows the expression of the expressionless: a weeping from which the tears are missing."

245 "I give you my word": See supra, endnotes 235 and 243. This utterance also appears in *Molloy*, 49.

246 See Christopher Ricks' Clarendon Lectures, *Beckett's Dying Words* (New York: Oxford University Press, 1993).

247 Adorno, *Kierkegaard: Construction of the Aesthetic*, trans. Robert Hullot Kentor (Minneapolis: University of Minnesota Press, 1989), 122.

248 See Giorgio Agamben, *The Sacrament of Language: An Archaeology of the Oath*, trans. Adam Kotsko (Stanford: Stanford University Press, 2011).

249 One must recognize the problematic character of the witness's testimony, the oath, the pledge, the promise, the giving of one's word (whether or not in the context of fiction), and the relation between literature and truth. See Derrida, "Faith and Knowledge," in *Acts of Religion*, ed. Gil Anidjar (New York: Routledge, 2002) and Michael Naas, *Miracle and Machine: Jacques Derrida and the Two Sources of Religion, Science, and the Media* (New York: Fordham University Press, 2012).

Part One

Chapter One

1 Theodor Adorno, *Negative Dialectics*, trans. E. B. Ashton (New York: Continuum Publishing Co., 1973), 5. Also see Jean-Luc Nancy, *Hegel: L'inquétude du négatif* (Paris: Hachette, 1977).

2 Herbert Marcuse, "The Concept of Essence," in *Negations: Essays in Critical Theory*, trans. Jeremy J. Shapiro (Boston: Beacon Press, 1968), 73.

3 Adorno, *Aesthetic Theory*, trans. Robert Hullot-Kentor (Minneapolis: University of Minnesota Press, 1997), 199.

4 Samuel Beckett, *The Letters of Samuel Beckett: 1941–1956*, ed. George Craig, Dan Dunn, Martha Dow Fehsenfeld, and Lois More Overbeck (Cambridge: Cambridge University Press, 2011), vol. II, 97. In this August 1948 letter, I hear Groucho Marx's famous words in the 1932 film, *Horse Feathers*, which I have quoted as my book's epigram. Might those words have been echoing in Beckett's head? In any case, I suggest that they share a certain cast of mind: not only skeptical but dialectical, able to see the comedy in life's tragedy. "No matter what it is or who commenced it, I'm against it." Whereupon, Groucho creates as much disorder as he can.

5 Theodor W. Adorno, "On Lyric Poetry and Society," in *Notes to Literature*, trans. Shierry Weber Nicholsen (New York: Columbia University Press, 1991), vol. I, 45. And see Jay M. Bernstein, *The Philosophy of the Novel: Lukács, Marxism, and the Dialectic of Form* (Minneapolis: The University of Minnesota Press, 1984).

6 Stanley Cavell, *Emerson's Transcendental Etudes* (Stanford: Stanford University Press, 2003), 173.

7 Adorno, "On Lyric Poetry and Society," op. cit., vol. I, 43.

8 Adorno, *Negative Dialectics*, 380–381. Italics added. Nietzsche's distinction is to be found in *The Will to Power*, trans. Walter Kaufmann (New York: Vintage, 1968), §22, 17.

9 Adorno, *Aesthetic Theory*, 367.

10 Adorno, *Aesthetic Theory*, 362–363.

11 "A chance of happiness": see Beckett's play, *Krapp's Last Tape*, in *A Samuel Beckett Reader* (New York: Grove Press, 1976), 499. There are an extraordinary number of evocations of happiness in Beckett's works. The quest for happiness represents one of Beckett's most important questions: it is like a thread, woven into many texts.

12 Jay Bernstein, "Melancholy as Form: Towards an Archaeology of Modernism," in John J. Joughin and Simon Malpas, ed., *The New Aestheticism* (Manchester: Manchester University Press, 2003), 167–191.

13 Meanwhile, in his *Philosophical Investigations*, ed. G. E. M. Anscombe (New York: Macmillan, 1953), Ludwig Wittgenstein took up, as an epistemological problem ill conceived, the question of going on, arguing against the Cartesian paradigm, according to which a claim to understanding does not hinge on the presence of some logically private mental state or process, but on demonstrating "mastery of a technique," the ability to go on. Immersed in the intellectual life of Paris, Beckett, bringing to bear his own philosophical education, mercilessly subjected the sovereign subjectivity in Cartesianism to ridicule. His novels and plays reduce the logic of its dualisms, its "antagonisms," to comical absurdities—but as a real, lived experience, the estrangement in solipsism is dreadful and tragic.

14 Friedrich Hölderlin, "Becoming in Dissolution," *Essays and Letters on Theory*, trans. and ed. Thomas Pfau (Albany: State University of New York, 1988), 96–100.

15 Søren Kierkegaard, *Stages on Life's Way*, trans. Walter Lowrie (Princeton: Princeton University Press, 1940), 201.

16 Paul Celan, *Fadensonnen*, *Gesammelte Werke* (Frankfurt am Main, Suhrkamp Verlag, 1968), vol. II, 177. My translation.

17 Jacques Derrida, "How to Avoid Speaking," in Sanford Budick and Wolfgang Iser, ed., *Languages of the Unsayable* (New York: Columbia University Press, 1989), 14.

18 Derrida, "How to Avoid Speaking," op. cit., 11.

19 Robert Hullot-Kentor, *Things Beyond Resemblance: Collected Essays on Theodor W. Adorno* (New York: Columbia University Press, 2006), 230.

Chapter Two

1 Walter Benjamin, *The Origin of German Tragic Drama*, trans. John Osborne (London: NLB, 1977), 129. The English title is misleading because the *punctum* of Benjamin's study is precisely the *difference* between tragedy and *Trauerspiel*.

2 Beckett, *The Unnamable*, in *Three Novels: Molloy, Malone Dies, The Unnamable*, 360.

3 Beckett, *Endgame* (New York: Grove Press, 1958), 80–81.

4 Thomas Altizer, *The Call to Radical Theology*, ed. Lissa McCollough (Albany: SUNY Press, 2012), 114. The chapter on guilt runs from 107–119.

5 Altizer, *The Call to Radical Theology*, 116–117.

6 Beckett, *Malone Dies*, 235–236.

7 Adorno, *Kierkegaard: Construction of the Aesthetic*, trans. Robert Hullot Kentor (Minneapolis: University of Minnesota Press, 1989), 120.

8 See, e.g., Walter Benjamin, "Zum Problem der Physiognomik und Vorhersagung," *Gesammelte Schriften* (Frankfurt am Main: Suhrkamp Verlag, 1985), vol. VI, Fr. 64, 91. Also see "The Meaning of Time in the Moral World," *Selected Writings 1913–1919* (Cambridge: Harvard University Press, 1996), vol. I, 286–287, "World and Time," *Selected Writings 1913–1919*, vol. I, 226–228, and "On Language as Such and on Human Language," *Reflections: Essays, Aphorisms, Autobiographical Writings*, trans. Peter Demetz (New York: Schocken, 1986), 327–328.

9 Beckett, *Expelled*, in S. E. Gontarski, ed., *Samuel Beckett: The Complete Short Prose 1929–1989* (New York: Grove Press, 1995), 46–60.

10 Stanley Cavell, "Ending the Waiting Game: A Reading of Beckett's *Endgame*," op. cit., 151.

Chapter Three

1 Søren Kierkegaard, *Either/Or*, trans. David F. Swenson and Lillian M. Swenson (Garden City, NY: Doubleday, 1959), vol. II, 234.

2 Karl Marx, *Der historische Materialismus: Die Frühschriften*, ed. Siegfried Landshut (Leipzig, 1932), vol. I, 264ff.

3 Walter Benjamin, "Theory of Knowledge, Theory of Progress," N7a,7, *Arcades Project*, trans. Howard Eiland and Kevin McLaughlin (Cambridge: The Belnap Press of Harvard University Press, 1999), 471.

4 Ludwig Wittgenstein, *Philosophical Investigations*, bilingual edition, trans. G. E. M. Anscombe (London: Macmillan, 1953), §373, 116.

5 See Michael Naas, *Miracle and Machine: Jacques Derrida and the Two Sources of Religion, Science, and the Media* (New York: Fordham University Press, 2012).

6 Jacques Derrida, "Faith and Knowledge," trans. and ed. Gil Anidjar, *Acts of Religion* (New York and London: Routledge, 2002), 56. Italics added. And see Immanuel Kant, *Religion Within the Bounds of Reason Alone*, trans. Theodore M. Greene and Hoyt H. Hudson (New York: Harper & Row, 1960); G. W. F. Hegel, *Faith and Knowledge*, trans. Walter Cerf and H. S. Harris (Albany: State University of New York, 1977); and Henri Bergson, *The Two Sources of Morality and Religion*, trans. R. Ashley Audra and Cloudesley Brereton, with assistance of W. Horsfall Carter (Notre Dame: University of Notre Dame Press, 1986).

7 See Michael Naas, "The Promise of Other Voices," *Research in Phenomenology*, vol. 43, no. 1 (2013), 122.

8 G. W. F. Hegel, *Vorlesungen über die Philosophie der Religion*, *Sämtliche Werke*, H. Glockner, vol. XV, 80. My translation.

9 Hegel, *Phenomenology of Spirit*, trans. J. N. Findlay (Oxford: Clarendon Press, 1977), 5.

10 Hegel, *Phenomenology of Spirit*, 5.

11 Hegel, *Philosophy of Right*, trans. T. M. Knox (Oxford: Oxford University Press, 1967), 12–13.

12 Hegel, *Phenomenology of Spirit*, 349.

13 Ibid., 132.

14 Ibid., 126ff.

15 Ibid., 131.

16 Hegel, *Faith and Knowledge*, trans. Walter Cerf and H. S. Harris (Albany: SUNY Press, 1977), 191.

17 Hegel, *Phenomenology of Spirit*, 316.

18 H. S. Harris, "Introduction" to Hegel's *Faith and Knowledge*, 40–41.

19 See Hegel, *Faith and Knowledge*, 149, 157–158, 182, and 190.

20 Hegel, *Phenomenology of Spirit*, 5.

21 See Mary Bryden, *Samuel Beckett and the Idea of God* (New York and London: Palgrave Macmillan, 1998) and Simon Critchley, *The Faith of the Faithless: Experiments in Political Theology* (London and New York: Verso, New Left Books, 2012).

22 See Graham Hammill and Julia Reinhard Lupton, "Introduction," *Political Theology and Early Modernity* (Chicago: The University of Chicago Press, 2012), 1–4.

23 Regarding Milton, whose *Paradise Lost* Kant read with great appreciation, see Sanford Budick, *Kant and Milton* (Cambridge: Harvard University Press, 2010).

24 Budick, *Kant and Milton*, 86.

25 For a photograph of the twelfth-century basilica capital, with its representation of the story of the "Mystic Mill," and for the analysis and interpretation of the story that the carving represents, see Kathleen Biddick, "Dead Neighbour Archives: Jews, Muslims, and the Enemy's Two Bodies," in *Political Theology & Early Modernity*, 130.

26 Biddick, "Dead Neighbour Archives," 131.

27 Ibid.

28 On the hand mill, see Immanuel Kant, *Critique of Judgment*, trans. Werner S. Pluhar (Indianapolis: Hackett Publishing Company, 1987), §59, 227. On the despotic will and heteronomic will, see Kant, *Critique of Practical Reason*, trans. Lewis White Beck (New York: The Liberal Arts Press, 1956), Book II, ch. 2, §2, 122.

29 Adela Pinch, *Strange Fits of Passion: Epistemologies of Emotion, Hume to Austen* (Stanford: Stanford University Press, 1996), 20. "Incredible stories": as in the eighteenth- and nineteenth-century Gothic novels of mystery and horror.

Chapter Four

1 Sir Thomas Browne, *Urn Burial* (New York: New Directions Pearl, 2010), 77, 85.

2 Ralph Waldo Emerson, "Experience," in Joel Porte, ed., *Essays and Lectures* (New York; The Library of America, 1983), 471.

3 Beckett, *Texts for Nothing* (New York: Grove Press, 1967), 111.

4 Samuel Beckett, *Molloy*, in *Three Novels: Molloy, Malone Dies, The Unnamable* (New York: Grove Press, n.d.), 3.

5 Adorno, *Aesthetic Theory*, trans. Robert Hullot-Kentor (Minneapolis: University of Minnesota Press, 1997), 290.

6 Gilles Deleuze, *Francis Bacon: The Logic of Sensation*, trans. Daniel W. Smith (Minneapolis: University of Minnesota Press, 2003), 101.

7 Thomas Altizer, *The Call to Radical Theology*, ed. Lissa McCollough (Albany: SUNY Press, 2012), 147.

8 See some of Beckett's numerous allusions to teleological and eschatological matters in *Molloy*, 4, 6, 10, 35–36, and 108–109. And see the allusions in *Texts for Nothing*, 82–83.

9 Jacques Derrida, *A Taste for the Secret*, trans. Giacomo Donis (Cambridge: Polity Press, 2001; Malden, MA: Blackwell Publishers, 2001), 20.

10 Derrida, *A Taste for the Secret*, 20.

11 Derrida, *A Taste for the Secret*, 17.

12 Ludwig Wittgenstein, *Philosophical Investigations*, §109, 47.

13 Michel de Montaigne, "That to philosophize is to learn to die," *The Complete Essays*, trans. Donald M. Frame (Stanford: Stanford University Press, 1965), 62. Beckett's characters borrow many traits from Montaigne.

14 Georg Lukács, *Theory of the Novel*, trans. Anna Bostock (Cambridge: The MIT Press, 1971), 90.

15 Beckett, "Enough," in *Samuel Beckett: The Complete Short Prose 1929–1989* (New York: Grove Press, 1995), 192.

16 See Alain Badiou, *Conditions*, trans. Steven Corcoran (New York: Continuum International Publishing, 2008), 266. The phrase "a chance of happiness" comes from *Krapp's Last Tape*, in *I Can't Go On, I'll Go On: A Samuel Beckett Reader* (New York: Grove Press, 1976), 499.

17 Beckett, *Texts for Nothing* (New York: Grove Press, 1967), 123.

18 Stanley Cavell, "Ending the Waiting Game: A Reading of Beckett's *Endgame*," *Must We Mean What We Say?* (New York: Charles Scribner's Sons, 1969), 143.

19 See S. E. Gontarski, "Introduction" to *Samuel Beckett, Nohow On* (New York: Grove Press, 1996), vii–viii.

20 Adorno, *Aesthetic Theory*, 30–31 in the English translation.

21 Cavell, *Must We Mean What We Say?*, 149. Italics added. Also see 33 and 53 on curses turned literal.

22 On revolutionary beginnings and endings, see Paul A. Kottman, "Novus Ordo Saeclorum: Hannah Arendt on Revolutionary Spirit," in *Political Theology & Early Modernity*, ed. Graham Hammill and Julia Reinhard Lupton (Chicago: University of Chicago Press, 2012), 143–158. Recapitulating Hannah Arendt's argument in *On Revolution*, Kottman says that, "perhaps the clearest sign of the rift between past and future [or say beginning and ending] is the separation

of the experience of revolution from the experience of happiness, as though the latter were no longer intrinsic to the former. If revolutionary spirit has lost its sense of [. . .] the promise of earthly happiness—and, for us, it clearly has— then it remains not only divided from itself but also doomed to failure, 'loaded down with misery.'" Thus, he continues, "if this division *is* our inheritance of revolutionary spirit [. . .], then it is not the historical march of some positive content ('freedom,' or 'happiness') but rather a different 'strange and sad story that remains to be told and remembered.' [. . .] Which is to say that the earthly happiness intrinsic to freedom is not separable from its renewed worldly pursuit as politics—from the experience and inheritance of crushed dreams, lost hopes, and thwarted chances for a sharable happiness into which newcomers are born." Op. cit., 154–155.

Part Two

Chapter One

1 Friedrich Hölderlin, "In lovely blueness . . .," in Richard Sieburth, trans. and ed., *Hymns and Fragments* (Princeton: Princeton University Press,1984), 249. Altered translation.

2 Adorno, *Kierkegaard: Construction of the Aesthetic*, trans. Robert Hullot Kentor (Minneapolis: University of Minnesota Press, 1989), 132.

3 Gunnar Hindrichs, "Scheitern als Rettung: Ästhetische Erfahrung nach Adorno," *Deutsche Vierteljahrschrift für Literaturwissenschaft in Geistesgeschichte*, vol. 74, no. 1 (March 2000), 146–175. My translation. And see Anselm Kiefer's "Merkaba" (Gagosian Gallery), showing an aeroplane, the Messiah's Chariot, lying in a meadow where it crashed and shattered.

4 Jay Bernstein, "Philosophy's Refuge: Adorno in Beckett," in David C. Wood, ed., *Philosophers' Poets* (New York: Routledge, 1990), 185. But might there be a "backdoor" way into Paradise? See the suggestion of Herr C, in Heinrich von Kleist's "On the Puppet Theater," in *An Abyss Deep Enough: Letters of Heinrich von Kleist, with a Selection of Essays and Anecdotes*, trans. Philip B. Miller (New York: E. P. Dutton, 1982), 216. Beckett would perhaps enjoy playing with that suggestion.

5 We must, of course, constantly remind ourselves to penetrate the ideological mystifications surrounding the prevailing experience of happiness. In *What Is Called Thinking*, Heidegger observes that "[T]he devastation of the earth can easily go hand in hand with a guaranteed supreme living standard for man, and just as easily with the organized establishment of a uniform state of happiness for all men" See Martin Heidegger, *What Is Called Thinking?*, trans. J. Glenn Gray (New York: Harper & Row, 1968), 30.

6 Ludwig Wittgenstein, *Tractatus Logico-Philosophicus*, trans. David Pears and B. F. McGuiness (London: Routledge, 1995), §6.43.

7 See Maurice Blanchot, *L'Écriture du désastre* (Paris: Gallimard, 1980), 117.

8 Beckett, *The Calmative*, in S. E. Gontarski, ed., *Samuel Beckett: The Complete Short Prose 1929–1989*, 76–77.

9 Adorno, "On Lyric Poetry and Society, in *Notes to Literature*, trans. Shierry Weber Nicholsen (New York: Columbia University Press, 1991), vol. I, 50.

10 See Immanuel Kant, *Critique of Practical Reason*, trans. Lewis White Beck (New York: The Liberal Arts Press, 1956), 166: "Two things fill the mind with ever new and increasing admiration and awe, the oftener and more steadily we reflect on them: the starry heavens above me and the moral law within me."

11 See Adorno on semblance, *Negative Dialectics*, 399–400.

12 James Phillips, *The Equivocation of Reason: Kleist Reading Kant* (Stanford: Stanford University Press, 2007), 98.

13 See W. G. Sebald's allegorical image of "flowers running around the ceiling" in *Austerlitz*, trans. Anthea Bell (New York: Random House, 2001), 99. In Beckett as in Sebald, flowers, roses, are figures of redemption. And see Sebald's allusion and homage to Beckett's image of cupids suddenly appearing in fissures, or cracks in the ceiling but abruptly disappearing, leaving no trace, in *Vertigo*, trans. Michael Hulse (New York: New Directions, 1999), 145–146. In "Central Park," Walter Benjamin says: "Redemption [*Die Rettung*] depends on the tiny fissure [*Sprung*] in the continuous catastrophe [that is history]." See Benjamin, "Central Park," *Selected Writings 1938–1940*, vol. IV, 185. Sebald reminds us of this claim in telling a fictional story that draws its inspiration from Beckett, turning Beckett's cupids into angels of justice, messengers of hope in the possibility of redemption. Such "fissures," inviting a leap of hope—or a leap, say, of faith—appear, allegorically, in Sebald's story about Dr. K. in his hotel room, half asleep in bed, exposed to the phantoms his subconscious mind will acknowledge when the censorious egological defenses are down.

14 Let me provide a concrete example in literature of redemption in the *future anterior* grammar. As I have noted, Beckett was a significant influence on W. G. Sebald. They shared similar world-views. In Sebald's *Austerlitz*, the narrator reports Jacques Austerlitz telling him of his distress over living in a world that lets its present time be severed from the past and hence from the dead, the victims, in particular, of the Holocaust. Hoping for some redemptive justice for the dead, Austerlitz says: "A clock has always struck me as something ridiculous, a thoroughly mendacious object, perhaps because I have always resisted the power of time out of some internal compulsion which I myself have never understood, keeping myself apart from so-called current events in the hope [. . .] that time will not pass away, has not passed away, that I can turn back and go behind it, and there I shall find [. . .] that all moments of time have co-existed simultaneously, in which case none of what history tells us would be true, past events have not yet occurred but are waiting to do so at the moment when we think of them, although that opens up the bleak prospect of ever-lasting misery and never-ending anguish" (*Austerlitz* 101). The sentence moves swiftly through a succession of brief assertions boldly denying the conventional order of historical time, gradually slowing down in longer clauses, before coming to its dialectical counterpoint, a twist ending in a moment of disenchantment, a moment of truth shattering the futile hope invested in a quixotic metaphysical fantasy of transcendence. But Austerlitz

hints at the radical, redemptive restructuring of historical temporality that is proposed in Benjamin's manifesto "On the Concept of History." Benjamin expresses his faith that there is a past in which opportunities for revolutionary action emerged, only somehow to be missed: a past, therefore, that has never yet been present; a past that is still awaiting its time to take place, its right moment, its "*kairos*," to use St. Paul's term. This requires an "awakening" of our collective consciousness. *In this awakening, another dimension of time might appear, intersecting and interrupting the linear, irreversible series of discrete, punctate historical moments. This future anterior is the dimension that brings the possibility of redemption.* Benjamin's conception, grammatically formulated in terms of a future anterior, is a radical reconfiguration of historical temporality and historical memory: although we cannot undo the harm that people suffered, cannot redeem the dead, victims of injustice, we can, when we give ourselves over to historical remembrance, at least make sure that the suffering and misery these victims endured will never be forgotten and will accordingly serve as a powerful force to encourage us in changing the present, so that such wrongs will never take place in the future. In this way, a haunting past that never was present returns, becomes present, and fulfills its moral claims in shaping its future. But in Sebald's narrative, all that this consciousness can see is "the bleak prospect of ever-lasting misery and never-ending anguish." Beckett's characters would no doubt form the same conclusion. See W. G. Sebald, *Austerlitz*, trans. Anthea Bell (New York: Random House, 2001).

15 Beckett, "Lessness," in Richard Seaver, ed., *I Can't Go On, I'll Go On: A Samuel Beckett Reader* (New York: Grove Press, 1954), 557–561.

16 Novalis (Friedrich von Hardenberg), *Heinrich von Ofterdingen*, trans. Palmer Hilty (Prospect Heights: Waveland Press, 1990; New York: Continuum Publishing Co., 1992), 20–22.

17 Beckett, "Assumption," in S. E. Gontarski, ed., *Samuel Beckett: The Complete Short Prose 1929–1989*, 3–7.

18 Beckett, "Sedendo et Quiescendo," in *The Complete Short Prose 1929–1989*, 13.

19 See Friedrich Hölderlin's phrase "the flower of the mouth," in "Germanien;" the elegy "Der Gang aufs Land," where the word blossoms as do "the sky's blooms;" and "Bread and Wine," ("Brot und Wein") where the poet speaks of "words, like flowers." See the poet's *Sämtliche Werke*, ed. Paul Stapf (Berlin and Darmstadt: Der Tempel-Verlag, 1960), 271, 276, and 320. And see Heidegger's discussion of these poetic word-images in Hölderlin, in *On the Way to Language*, trans. Peter Hertz and Joan Stambaugh (New York: Harper & Row, 1971), 99.

20 Friedrich Hölderlin, "In lovely blue. . .," in Richard Sieburth, ed. and trans., *Friedrich Hölderlin: Hymns and Fragments* (Princeton: Princeton University Press, 1984), 248–253.

Chapter Two

1 André Breton, *Manifestoes of Surrealism*, trans. Richard Seaver and Helen R. Lane (Ann Arbor: University of Michigan, 1969), 31.

2 Ralph Waldo Emerson, "Nature," in *Essays and Lectures*, ed. Joel Porte (New York: The Library of America, 1983), 146.

3 Ernst Bloch, "Das Riesenspielzeug als Sage," *Erbschaft dieser Zeit*, in *Gesamtausgabe*, vol. 4 (Frankfurt am Main: Suhrkamp, 1977), 184.

4 Beckett, *Echo's Bones and Other Precipitates* (Paris: Europa, 1935), 155. The poem contains allusions to "Jack and the Beanstalk" and other children's fairy tales.

5 Thanks to John Pilling and John Wieczorek, in Pilling's "The Uses of Enchantment Beckett and the Fairy Tale," published in *Samuel Beckett Today/Aujourd'hui: Des éléments aux traces. Elements and Traces* (Amsterdam and Atlanta: Rodopi, 2009), vol. 21, no. 1, 75–85. There is an English translation of Beckett's story, a torso, abandoned abruptly. It begins with the words "Once upon a time there was an agreeable enough young man, with no social contacts and no vocation, as little within as without, who could find no belief in even the most beautiful and hallowed things."

   Archives of the Beckett International Foundation, University of Reading, MS 5002.

6 See Chris Ackerley, "Fairy-Tales and Flagellations: Samuel Beckett's "Sanies II," *Fulcrum*, no. 6 (2007); Lawrence E. Harvey, *Samuel Beckett: Poet and Critic* (Princeton: Princeton University Press, 1970); Lois G. Gordon, *The World of Samuel Beckett: 1906–1946* (New Haven: Yale University Press, 1996); Marianne Thalman, *The Romantic Fairy Tale* (Ann Arbor: University of Michigan, 1964); and John Pilling, *Samuel Beckett's "More Pricks than Kicks": In a Strait of Two Wills* (New York: Continuum, 2011). Also see *The Letters of Samuel Beckett: 1929–1940*, vol. I, ed. Martha D. Fehsenfeld, Lois M. Overbeck, George Craig, and Dan Gunn (Cambridge: Cambridge University Press, 2009).

7 Beckett, *Dream of Fair to Middling Women*, ed. Eoin O'Brian and Edith Fournier (Dublin: Black Cat, 1992; New York: Arcade Publishing Co., 1992), 109.

8 Beckett, "The Calmative," in *The Complete Short Prose 1929–1989*, 62.

9 See John Pilling, "The Uses of Enchantment," op. cit., 79.

10 Pilling, "The Uses of Enchantment,", 81.

11 See Beckett, *Worstward Ho*, 93.

12 See Stéphane Mallarmé, "Crise de vers," *Oeuvres complètes* (Paris: Éditions Gallimard, 1945), 368; "Crisis in Poetry," in Mary Ann Caws, ed. and trans., *Selected Poetry and Prose* (New York: New Directions, 1982), 76: "I say: a flower! And outside the oblivion to which my voice relegates any shape, insofar as it is something other than the calyx, there arises musically, as the very idea and delicate, the one absent from every bouquet [*l'absente de tous bouquets*]."

13 Mallarmé, "Crise de vers."

14 Stéphane Mallarmé, *Oeuvres complètes*, ed. Henri Mondo and G. Jean-Aubry (Paris: Bibliothèque de la Pléiade, Gallimard, 1945), 57: "L'enfant abdique son extase [. . .]"

Chapter Three

1 Martin Heidegger, Interview with Rudolf Augstein and Georg Wolff, *Der Spiegel* 30 (May 1976), 193–219.

2 Theodor W. Adorno, *Kierkegaard: Construction of the Aesthetic*, trans. Robert Hullot-Kentor (Minneapolis: University of Minnesota Press, 1989), 126.

3 Samuel Beckett, *The Unnamable*, 347. And see Martin Heidegger, "What Are Poets For?" in Albert Hofstadter, trans. and ed., *Poetry Language Thought* (New York: Harper & Row, 1971), 91: "Not only have the gods and the one God fled, but even the gleam of divinity has been extinguished in world history." For Heidegger, even traces of these traces and hints of these hints are now fading and vanishing.

4 Beckett, *Company*, in *Nohow On* (New York: Grove Press, 1996), 11.

5 Beckett, *Company*, in *Nohow On*, 18.

6 Beckett, The "Clare Street" Notebook, University of Reading MS 5003, 17r-18r, August 1936. The note was written in German.

7 Percy Bysshe Shelley, *Prometheus Unbound*, in *Shelley's Poetry and Prose*, ed. Donald H. Reiman and Neil Fraistat (New York: W. W. Norton, 2002), Act IV, lines 473–474, 286.

8 Theodor W. Adorno, *Kierkegaard: Construction of the Aesthetic*, trans. Robert Hullot-Kentor (Minneapolis: University of Minnesota Press, 1989), 126.

9 Beckett, *Endgame* (New York: Grove Press, 1958), 44.

10 Beckett, "Alba," *Echo's Bones* (London: Faber, 2014).

11 See Sara Kafatou, "An Interview with W. G. Sebald," *Harvard Review* (fall 1998), no. 15, 32. In this interview, Sebald talks about ash: "It is the most humble substance there is! It's the very last product of combustion, with no more resistance in it. [. . .] It represents the borderline between being and nothingness. Ash is a redeemed substance, like dust." And see David Farrell Krell, "Ashes, ashes, we all fall . . .," in *The Gadamer-Derrida Encounter: Texts and Commentary*, ed. Diana Michelfelder and Richard Palmer (Albany: SUNY Press, 1989), 222–232. See also Krell's essay, "Stuff. Thread. Point. Fire: Hölderlin and the Dissolution of History," in *Endings: Questions of Memory in Hegel and Heidegger*, ed. Rebecca Comay and John McCumber (Evanston: Northwestern University Press, 1999), 174–196. And see Jacques Derrida, *Cinders*, trans. Ned Lukacher (Lincoln: University of Nebraska Press, 1991). The first word of one of Celan's most haunted poems, "Ashglory," undoubtedly evoking the remains of all the people whom the Nazis reduced by fire to ash, declares the glory of this ash, implying its sacredness, its holiness. The poem ends by saying that there is no witness for the witness. The only ones who would experience the horror—the true witnesses—are no longer among the living, no longer able to testify.

12 Beckett, *Lessness*, in S. E. Gontarski, ed., *Samuel Beckett: The Complete Short Prose 1929–1989*, 197.

13 Kierkegaard, *Repetition*, in *Repetition* and *Fear and Trembling*, trans. and ed., Howard V. Hong and Edna H. Hong (Princeton: Princeton University Press, 1983), p. 152. Cited by Adorno in his study on Kierkegaard, op. cit., 45.

14 Adorno, *Kierkegaard: Construction of the Aesthetic*, 126. Italics added.

15 Adorno, *Kierkegaard*, 126. Italics added.

16 Beckett, *Worstward Ho*, 109.

17 Adorno, *Ästhetische Theorie*, 128; 82 in the English translation.

18 Beckett, *Wortward Ho,* 109.

19 Beckett, *How It Is*, Part II, 70.

20 In 1961, some ten years after the publication of *Malone Dies*, as if relating to the Director's question, Paul Celan wrote a poem, *Tübingen, Jänner*, in the third strophe of which we read what Beckett might have wanted to say by way of an answer: "If there came,/ came a man,/ came a man to the world, today, with/ the light-beard/ of the patriarchs: he could,/ if he spoke of this/ time, he/ could/ only babble and babble,/ over, over,/ againagain (lines 12–22). See the bilingual edition, Paul Celan, *The Poems of Paul Celan*, trans. Michael Hamburger (New York: Persea Books, 1972), 176–177. Translation somewhat altered.

21 See *The End*, in S. E. Gontarski, ed., *Samuel Beckett: The Complete Short Prose 1929–1989*, 78–99. The two quoted phrases come, however, from *The Unnamable*, 363, 378–379.

22 Adorno, *Ästhetische Theorie*, 200; 132 in the English translation.

23 Adorno, *Ästhetische Theorie*, 55–56 in the German, 32–33 in the English translation. Italics added.

24 Beckett, *Watt* (New York: Grove Press, 1953), 202.

25 Ralph Waldo Emerson, "Experience," *Essays and Lectures*, ed. Joel Porte (New York: Library of America, 1983), 478–479.

26 Heidegger, *Besinnung*, *Gesamtausgabe* (Frankfurt am Main: Vittorio Klostermann, 1997), vol. 66, 9. My translation.

27 Wittgenstein, *Philosophical Investigations*, trans. G. E. M. Anscombe (New York: Macmillan, 1953), 131, §445.

Chapter Four

1 Beckett, *Play*, in *Play and Two Short Pieces for Radio* (London: Faber 1964), 9.

2 See Gershom Scholem, *Walter Benjamin: Story of a Friendship*, trans. Harry Zohn (Philadelphia: The Jewish Publication Society, 1981), 144–145. The phrase appears in Benjamin's "Idea for an Arcanum," in which he imagines the setting up of a court, because the promised Messiah has not appeared. This court will hear "witnesses for the future": "the poet who senses it, the sculptor who sees it, the musician who hears it, and the philosopher who knows it."

3 Martha Dow Fehsenfeld and Lois More Overbeck, ed., *The Letters of Samuel Beckett: 1929–1940* (Cambridge: Cambridge University Press, 2009), vol. I, 446.

4 In *Austerlitz*, one of his fictional prose works, W. G. Sebald pays homage to the extraordinary word-image that Beckett has constructed. Sebald makes

his character, Jacques Austerlitz, confide his thoughts about the "mighty" clock he notices whilst sitting in the *Salle des pas perdus* of the Antwerp train station waiting for a train. The movements of the giant hand, he says, "resembled a sword of justice." Can there be any justice for the dead, victims in the march of history? This question stirs Austerlitz to reflect on our prevailing understanding of time and history and on an experience that would end its self-destructiveness: "none of what history tells us would be true, past events have not yet occurred but are waiting to do so at the moment when we think of them [. . .]" (ibid, 101). For a passing moment, Austerlitz contemplates retrieving, from a past, possibilities for justice that were not realized at that time, in order to complete now the work of justice and somehow redeem those possibilities, summoning them into the present. But he quickly breaks that desperate hope in a rewriting of history. The hope that suddenly, for an instant, flashed in the intricately tensed grammar of a counterfactual temporality was, as he feared, doomed to obliteration. And yet, does the past not return in remembrance? Does remembrance not interrupt the continuum of history, its power at least temporarily reversing the course? Is there any redeeming of past crimes, past injustices? Is there any redeeming of past opportunities to alter the future course of history, opportunities that were missed?

5 Beckett, *The Calmative*, in S. E. Gontarski, ed., *Samuel Beckett: The Complete Short Prose 1929–1989*, 72.

6 Cavell, "Ending the Waiting Game," op. cit., 150.

7 Cavell, "Ending the Waiting Game," 154.

8 Beckett, *Krapp's Last Tape*, in Richard Seaver, ed., *I Can't Go On, I'll Go On: A Samuel Beckett Reader* (New York: Grove Press, 1954), 491–492.

9 In "Dr. K. Takes the Waters at Riva," one of W. G. Sebald's short stories, obviously recalling Kafka and Benjamin's commentaries on Kafka, but also, of course, Beckett's *Waiting for Godot*, a certain Dr. K. encounters a crowd of townspeople waiting to welcome a representative of the Prague Workers' Insurance Company. But the man for whom they are waiting never comes. The description of the scene concludes with these words: "One of them is reported to have observed that those in whom we invest our hopes only ever make their appearance when they are no longer needed." These words are echoes of Kafka's paradoxical thought that "the Messiah will come only when he is no longer necessary; he will come only on the day after his arrival; he will come, not on the last day, but on the day after." What are we to make of this echo? Perhaps only that, for Beckett, there is pathos in the fact that we are still waiting, because the moral transformation of the world depends solely on us. The ending of history as a story of suffering is our task, our responsibility. As long as we are doing nothing but waiting, the messianic transformation will not happen. But, in what may seem like an ironic paradox, once we have worked to transform ourselves and have made the redeeming reconciliation of the world our task, the intervention of a Messianic figure will no longer be needed. However, since that transformation is necessary if we are ever to recognize the Messiah, the storyteller says, in what seems like another paradox, that his coming will be recognized only on the day *after* his coming—that is to say, only on the day *after* our own redemptive work, right here on earth, has been completed.

Chapter Five

1 Beckett, *Ill Seen Ill Said*, in *Nohow On* (New York: Grove Press 1996), 49–86. Hereafter, the larger or most significant quotes will be cited in the text by the letters IS.

2 The phrase "weak messianic force," "eine schwache messianische Kraft," comes from Benjamin's essay, "Theses on the Philosophy of History," in *Illuminations*, trans. Harry Zohn (New York: Schocken, 1969), 254. Benjamin's phrase echoes the phrase, "a weak ray of hope," which appears in Immanuel Kant's *Critique of Judgment*, trans. Werner Pluhar (Indianapolis: Hackett Publishing, 1987), §80, 304.

3 Beckett, "*Ill Seen Ill Said*," in *Nohow On*, 50.

4 See Badiou, *Conditions*, 269–271 and 283–284.

5 Adorno, *Minima Moralia*, §153, 333–334 in the German, 247 in the English.

6 Paul Celan, "Flower," *Poems of Paul Celan*, bilingual edition, trans. Michael Hamburger (New York: Persea Books, 1972), 114–115. I suppose it possible that Beckett was familiar with the poem. Translation altered.

7 Nietzsche, *On the Genealogy of Morals*, trans. Francis Golfing (New York: Doubleday, 1956), Third Essay, §1, 231.

8 Beckett, *Worstward Ho*, *Nohow On*, 109.

9 Beckett, *Endgame*, 69.

10 Nietzsche, *On the Genealogy of Morals*, First Essay, §14, 180–181.

11 See Benjamin, "On the Concept of History," *Selective Writings 1938–1940*, trans. Harry Zohn (Cambridge: The Belnap Press of Harvard University Press, 2003), §17, 396.

12 See John Banville, "Beckett: Storming for Beauty," *The New York Review of Books* (vol. LIX, no. 5, March 22, 2012), 24, in which he quotes from *The Letters of Samuel Beckett, 1941–1956*, vol. II (Cambridge: Cambridge University Press, 2011). In *Horse Feathers*, Groucho Marx says: "No matter what it is or who commenced it, I'm against it."

13 See J. G. Hamann, "Aesthetica in Nuce," in Jay Bernstein, ed., *Classic and Romantic German Aesthetics* (Cambridge: Cambridge University Press, 2003), 9, 15.

14 "A chance of happiness": I have taken this phrase from Beckett's play, *Krapp's Last Tape*, in *A Samuel Beckett Reader* (New York: Grove Press, 1976), 499.

15 See Derrida, *Archive Fever: A Freudian Impression*, trans. Eric Prenowitz (Chicago: The University of Chicago Press, 1995).

16 Beckett, *Play*, in *Play, and Two Short Pieces for Radio* (London: Faber, 1964), 9.

Part Three

Chapter One

1 Theodor Adorno, "Is Art Lighthearted?" in Shierry Nicolsen Weber, trans., *Notes to Literature* (New York: Columbia University Press, 1992), vol. II, 248.

2 Gottfried Benn, "Gesänge," in Kurt Pinthus (ed.), *Menschheitsdämmerung: Symphonie jüngster Dichtung* (Berlin: Rowohlt, 1920; Hamburg: Rowohlt Taschenbuch Verlag, 1959), 186. My translation.

3 Theodor W. Adorno, *Aesthetic Theory*, trans. Robert Hullot-Kentor (Minneapolis: University of Minnesota Press, 1997), 79.

4 Beckett, Text Six, *Texts for Nothing*, in *Stories and Texts for Nothing*, translated by Samuel Beckett from his French original (New York: Grove Press, 1967), 103. TN will hereafter be used to refer to this text. This Purgatory is also depicted as a realm of the most intense coldness: "I was, I was, they say in Purgatory, in Hell too, admirable singulars, admirable assurance. Plunged in ice up to the nostrils, the eyelids caked in frozen tears, to fight all your battles over again [. . .]" (TN 104). Hellish ice for those with cold hearts.

5 See Adorno's reference to a "closed immanence" in *Kierkegaard: Construction of the Aesthetic*, trans. Robert Hullot-Kentor (Minneapolis: University of Minnesota Press, 1989), 62.

6 There are many anticipations of the muddy swamp-world of *How It Is* in Beckett's earlier novel, *Molloy* (Part I, 10 and Part I, 73). There are also significant invocations of mud, dust, sand and clay, the primal elements of the biblical Creation story, in all three of the earlier novels: Malone conjures up "the silence of dust", a silence which bespeaks the inevitability of dissolution and death (MD 197). Losing track of his pencil, he sees his all efforts to write a story disintegrating, "like the crumbling away of two little heaps of finest sand, or dust, or ashes, [. . .] and leaving behind them, each in its own stead, the blessedness of absence" (MD 216). Circumstances prompt Malone to remark that he is either dying or possibly already dead, and to contemplate times when, as he puts it, his mind darkens and he becomes "like mud" (MD 218). Mud is also invoked at an earlier moment in the novel, when Malone, after concluding that he cannot continue writing without first looking at himself as he is, admits that that self-examination, which he calls a "mud-bath", is just what he wants to avoid (MD 183). Like the narrator in *How It Is*, the unnamable narrative voice in *The Unnamable*, an earlier work, says, "I'm like dust, they want me to make a man out of dust" (UN 341). See Beckett's trilogy, *Molloy* (1947), *Malone Dies* (1951), and *The Unnamable* (1953), published together in Beckett, *Three Novels: Molloy, Malone Dies, The Unnamable* (New York: Grove Press, n.d.).

7 Friedrich Nietzsche, *Twilight of the Idols*, trans. R. J. Hollingdale (New York: Penguin, 1968), Part I, §5, 38.

8 A. Alvarez, *Beckett* (London: Fontana Press, 1973, 1992), 80. These are his words.

9 W. G. Sebald's borrowings from Beckett are surprisingly numerous. One of them involves an allegorical allusion to a gleam of light coming from the world that

is "above"—above the water. See *Austerlitz*, trans. Anthea Bell (New York: Random House, 2001), 53.

10 See Sigmund Freud, *Three Essays on the Theory of Sexuality* (New York: Basic Books, 1975), 90n.

11 See Walter Benjamin, "Theses on the Philosophy of History," trans. Harry Zohn, in *Illuminations* (New York: Schocken, 1969), 257–258.

Chapter Two

1 See Dante Alighieri, *Purgatorio*, bilingual edition, trans. W. S. Merwin (New York: Alfred A. Knopf, 2000), XVII, ll. 127–129, 168–169: "Ciascun confusamente un bene apprende,/ nel qual si queti l'animo, e disira;/ per che di giugner lui ciascun contende." My translation.

2 Malcolm Bowie, *Proust Among the Stars* (New York: Columbia University Press, 1998), 65.

3 Beckett, *Molloy*, in *Three Novels: Molloy, Malone Does, The Unnamable*, 35.

4 Herbert Marcuse, "The Affirmative Character of Culture," in *Negations: Essays in Critical Theory*, ed. Jeremy J. Shapiro (Boston: Beacon Press, 1968), 111.

5 Christopher Holman, "Marcuse's Affirmation: Nietzsche and the Logos of Gratification," in *New German Critique* (no. 115, winter 2012), 107.

6 Stanley Cavell, "Between Acknowledgement and Avoidance," *The Claim of Reason* (New York: Oxford University Press, 1979), 397. And see Gerald Bruns, *On Ceasing to be Human* (Stanford: Stanford University Press, 2011), 31–34

7 Walter Benjamin, *Gesammelte Schriften* (Frankfurt am Main: Suhrkamp Verlag, 1974), vol. I, pt. 3, 1241. My translation.

8 Leo Strauss, *The Political Philosophy of Hobbes: Its Basis and Its Genesis*, trans. Elsa M. Sinclair (Chicago: University of Chicago Press, 1963), 122.

9 See Lois Gordon, "Samuel Beckett and *Waiting for Godot*," in *A Companion to Samuel Beckett*, ed. S. E. Gontarski (Malden, MA: Wiley-Blackwell, 2010), 32–47.

10 H. Porter Abbott, *Beckett Writing Beckett: The Author in the Autograph* (Ithaca: Cornell University Press, 1996), 138, 147.

11 See Emmanuel Levinas, *Autrement qu'être, ou au-delà de l'essence* (The Hague: Martinus Nijhoff, second edn., 1978), 149; *Otherwise than Being, or Beyond Essence*, trans. Alphonso Lingis (Dordrecht and Boston: Kluwer Academic Publishers, 1991), 117. And see the chapters on Levinas in my books, *Gestures of Ethical Life* (Stanford: Stanford University Press, 2005) and *Before the Voice of Reason* (New York: State University of New York Press, 2008).

12 See Merleau-Ponty, *Le visible et l'invisible*, 181; 137 in the English translation.

13 Breaking free in the 1960s of the vestiges of Cartesianism still operative in his early phenomenology, Merleau-Ponty introduced some extremely bold and radical concepts for thinking about our social and ethical existence. See Maurice Merleau-Ponty, "The Child's Relations with Others," trans.

William Cobb, in *The Primacy of Perception*, ed. James M. Edie (Evanston: Northwestern University Press, 1964), 96–155, and see *The Visible and the Invisible*, trans. Alphonso Lingis (Evanston: Northwestern University Press, 1968).

14 Jay Bernstein, "Love and Law: Hegel's Critique of Morality," *Social Research* (summer 2003), vol. 70, no. 2, 1–17.

15 Thomas Altizer, *The Call to Radical Theology*, ed. Lissa McCollough (Albany: State University of New York Press, 2012), 45.

16 Altizer, *The Call to Radical Theology*, 42.

17 Altizer, *The Call to Radical Theology*, 43.

18 Adam Sitze, "The Tragicity of the Political: A Note on Carlo Galli's Reading of Carl Schmitt's *Hamlet or Hecuba*," in Graham Hammill and Julia Reinhard Lupton, *Political Theology and Early Modernity* (Chicago: The University of Chicago Press, 2012), p. 52.

19 S. E. Gontarski, "Introduction," *Samuel Beckett: The Complete Short Stories 1929–1989* (New York: Grove Press, 1995), xxiii. On the whole, I greatly admire Gontarski's writings.

20 Richard Rorty, *Contingency, Irony, and Solidarity* (Cambridge: Cambridge University Press, 1989), xvi.

21 Theodor Adorno, *Metaphysics: Concepts and Problems*, trans. Edmund Jephcott (Stanford: Stanford University Press, 2000), 116.

22 See Paul Klee, *The Diaries of Paul Klee 1898–1918*, trans. Pierre B. Schneider, R. Y. Zachary, and Max Knight (Berkeley: University of California Press, 1964), 313.

23 *How It Is* (New York: Grove Press, 1964), here translated by Beckett himself, was first written and published in French, bearing the title, *Comment c'est* (Paris: Les Éditions de Minuit, 1961). The English title is the correct translation, but Beckett undoubtedly assumed that one would hear in the pronunciation of the French title the words "*Commencer*" and "*Commencez!*" i.e., the infinitive "to begin" and the imperative "Begin!" This text will hereafter be cited as H.

24 H. Porter Abbott, ""Beginning Again: The Post-Narrative Art of *Texts for Nothing* and *How It Is*," in John Pilling, ed., *The Cambridge Companion to Beckett* (Cambridge: Cambridge University Press, 1994), 113. Also see P. J. Murphy, "Beckett and the Philosophers," 222–240, in the same edited anthology; Leslie Hill, *Beckett's Fiction: In Different Words* (Cambridge: Cambridge University Press, 1990); and John Pilling, "How It Is," in James Knowlson and John Pilling, ed., *Frescoes of the Skull: The Later Prose and Drama of Samuel Beckett* (London: John Calder, 1979), 61–78.

25 See Jacob Taubes, *Occidental Eschatology*, trans. David Ratmoko (Stanford: Stanford University Press, 2009).

26 See Dante Alighieri, *The Inferno*, bilingual edition, trans. Robert Hollander and Jean Hollander (New York: Doubleday, 2000), VII, ll. 127–30, 126–27: "Così girammo de la lorda pozza/ grand' arco, tra la ripa secca e 'l mézzo,/ con li occhi vòlti a chi del fango ingozza." My translation.

27   This is Beckett's own phrase. See *Molloy*, in Beckett, *Three Novels: Molloy, Malone Dies, The Unnamable*, Part II, 104. The phrase evokes biblical theology: Malone recalls the words with which he spoke to his son, speaking of "a simple prophetic present, on the model of those employed by Youdi [i.e., by the Jews, or perhaps by Yahweh Himself]." Hereafter, *Molloy* will be cited as MO.

28   See the discussion of archaic justice in Walter Benjamin, "Critique of Violence," trans. Edmund Jephcott, in Peter Demetz, ed., *Reflections: Essays, Aphorisms, Autobiographical Writings* (New York: Schocken Books, 1986), 277–300. Also see Emmanuel Levinas's discussions, in his *Totality and Infinity: An Essay on Exteriority*, trans. Alphonso Lingis (Pittsburgh: Duquesne University Press, 1969), 82–101 and 240–246; *Otherwise than Being, or Beyond Essence*, trans. Alphonso Lingis (Pittsburgh: Duquesne University Press, 1998), 159–160; and "An Eye for an Eye," in *Difficult Freedom: Essays on Judaism*, trans. Sean Hand (Baltimore: Johns Hopkins University Press, 1997).

29   Regarding this very significant, but easily overlooked phrase, see Beckett's early short story, "The Calmative," in *Stories* and *Texts for Nothing* (New York: Grove Press, 1967), 40. The narrator asked a stranger for the time. The stranger answered, but later, the narrator cannot remember what was said. "He said a time, I don't remember which, a time that explained nothing, that's all I remember, and it did not calm me. But what time would have done that? Oh I know, I know, one will come that will. But in the meantime? [. . .]?" In a subtle, reticent way, Beckett's narrator was enquiring about the time of messianicity: When will it happen and how? But until that time, how can I live in the meantime? This "meantime" represents a distinctive transitional moment. See my discussion of Levinas's "*maintenant*" in my chapter, "Arrhythmia in the Messianic Epoché: Opening the Gate with Levinasian Gestures," in my book, *Gestures of Ethical Life: Reading Hölderlin's Question of Measure After Heidegger* (Stanford: Stanford University Press, 2005).

30   Friedrich Nietzsche, "On the Tarantulas," *Thus Spoke Zarathustra*, trans. Walter Kaufmann (New York: Viking Penguin, 1954), 99.

31   See the Martin Heidegger interview, "Nur noch ein Gott kann uns retten: Spiegel-Interview mit Martin Heidegger," *Der Spiegel*, no. 30 (May 1976), 193–219. There is an English translation by William Richardson in Thomas Sheehan, ed., *Heidegger: the Man and the Thinker* (Chicago: Precedent Press, 1981), 45–67.

32   See the libretto written by Hugo von Hofmannsthal for Richard Strauss's opera, *Ariadne auf Naxos*.

33   See Alain Badiou, *Beckett* (Paris: Hachette, 1955), 11–12 and 38–39. In *How It Is*, he thinks, Beckett at last succeeds in breaking out of Cartesian solipsism and also out of the "noir grise" of being. See his *Conditions*, trans. Steven Corcoran (New York: Continuum, 2008), 264. Attempts to demarcate stages, phases, and periods in the writings of a philosopher or fiction writer can be very illuminating, but invariably, such schemas miss important things they are not prepared to recognize.

34 Beckett, *How It Is* (New York: Grove Press, 1964), 7. There is a brief reference to *Comment c'est* in Adorno's *Aesthetic Theory,* 133.

35 See A. Alvarez, *Beckett* (London: Fontana, 1992), 77.

36 See Badiou, *Conditions,* 274.

37 Badiou, *Conditions,* 274.

38 In "Franz Kafka: On the Tenth Anniversary of His Death," Benjamin says that Kafka's novels are "set in a swamp world" and that it is as if Kafka's female characters emerge "from the swampy soil." See *Selected Writings 1927–1934* (Cambridge: Harvard University Press, 1999), vol. II, 808. I do not know whether or not Beckett read this essay by Benjamin, but I would conjecture that he did. Incidentally, the intertwining of limbs that Beckett describes in such detail is reminiscent of what Zarathustra says to his disciples after talking to the hunchback he encounters on his journey: "Verily, my friends, I walk among men as among the fragments and limbs of men. This is what is terrible for my eyes, that I find man in ruins, scattered as over a battlefield or a butcher-field. And when my eyes flee from the now to the past, they always find the same: fragments and limbs and dreadful accidents—but no human beings" ("On Redemption", *Thus Spoke Zarathustra,* 138). For Beckett as for Nietzsche, it is a question of the redemption, without any god, of our potential humanity as human beings: the possibility of another justice, replacing the one that, in its violence, reduces men to fragments and limbs. Nietzsche's visionary wants to see, and insofar as possible, make human beings whole, or whole once again: "I walk among men as among the fragments of the future—that future which I envision. And this is all my creating and striving, that I create and carry together into One what is fragment and riddle and dreadful accident. [. . .]" (139)

39 Adorno, "On Lyric Poetry and Society," op. cit., 53.

40 Friedrich Hölderlin, "Germanien," *Sämtliche Werke,* ed. Paul Stapf (Berlin and Darmstadt: Der Tempel-Verlag, 1960), fifth strophe, 322.

41 Beckett's biblical metaphorics draws not only on mud and slime; it also draws on the allegorical narratives associated with dust, sand, ashes, and clay. And it is always a question of a certain "justice", divine or natural. Molloy wonders: "[W]ho can say exactly when on my helpless clay the fatal seeds were sown" (MO, Part I, 50). When Malone refers to "the silence of dust," he is evoking the inevitability of dissolution and death (MD 197). And when, losing track of his pencil, Malone sees all his efforts to write a story disintegrating, he compares it to "the crumbling away of two little heaps of finest sand, dust, or ashes, [. . .] leaving behind them, each in its own stead, the blessedness of absence" (MD 216). Circumstances prompt Malone to contemplate the times when his mind darkens and he becomes "like mud" (MD 218). Mud is also invoked at an earlier moment in the novel, when Malone, after concluding that he cannot continue writing without first looking at himself as he is, acknowledges that that self-examination, which he calls a "mud-bath", is just what he wants to avoid (MD 183).

42 Merleau-Ponty, "The Child's Relations with Others", op. cit., 113–120.

43 Robert Pogue Harrison, "Dante: The Most Vivid Version," in *The New York Review of Books* (October 24, 2013), vol. LX, no. 16, 41–43.

Chapter Three

1　Samuel Beckett, *The Letters of Samuel Beckett 1929–1940*, ed. Martha Dow Fehsenfeld and Lois More Overbeck (Cambridge: Cambridge University Press, 2009), vol. I, 33. The letter was written in July, 1930. See Arthur Schopenhauer, *Essays and Aphorisms*, ed. and trans. R. J. Hollingdale (London: Penguin, 1970), 50. Perhaps Beckett would eventually want to add "love" to these four morally essential dispositions of character.

2　Gerhard Richter, *Afterness: Figures of Following in Modern Thought and Aesthetics* (New York: Columbia University Press, 2011), 157. Beckett made the claim in an interview reported by Herbert Marcuse.

3　Teju Cole, *Open City* (New York: Random House, 2011), 208.

4　Beckett, *Malone Dies*, in *Three Novels. Molloy, Malone Dies, The Unnamable* (New York: Grove Press, 1955), 270.

5　Beckett, *Texts for Nothing* (New York: Grove Press, 1967), Eighth Text, 111.

6　Beckett, *Molloy*, in *Three Novels. Molloy, Malone Dies, The Unnamable* (New York: Grove Press, 1955), 79.

7　Richard Toscan, "MacGowran on Beckett," in S. E. Gontarski, ed., *On Beckett: Essays and Criticism* (New York: Grove Press, 1986), 213–225.

8　Beckett, *Enough*, in *The Complete Short Prose 1929–1989*, 192. This story is one of the very few in which Beckett's narrator is a woman.

9　Beckett, *Worstward Ho*, in *Nohow On*, 93.

10　Beckett, *Endgame* (New York: Grove Press, 1958), 50–83.

11　Samuel Beckett, *Waiting for Godot* (New York: Grove Press, 1954), 58.

Chapter Four

1　Adorno, "On Lyric Poetry and Society," in *Notes to Literature*, vol. I, 38.

2　In *The Unnamable* (UN 342), the narrating voice, sometimes sounding like a surrogate for Beckett himself, the real author of the novel *Murphy*, confesses that *Murphy*'s story "was clumsily done, you could see the ventriloquism."

3　The "voice of Reason" is named explicitly in the fifth text of Beckett's *Texts for Nothing*, 95–96. Beckett's narrator creates here a scene that mixes Kant's notion that the critique of reason is a tribunal together with Kafka's novel about a trial, and, as if that were not enough to make it a sublime comedy, he throws in a passing reference to Heidegger's *Being and Time*, evoking "a different justice" and suggesting that, in Heidegger's conception, there is only a slight variation on the old theological doctrine of original sin, "to be is to be guilty". Beckett seems to be inviting us here to suppose that the voice his narrator hears is the voice of conscience, pronouncing him guilty; although, as with Kafka's hero K., it is never made clear what he might be guilty of, if not simply of existing. Beckett's narrator obviously is unwilling to fall for that judgment.

4 The phrase "prophetic present" is Beckett's. See *Molloy*, pt. II, 104.

5 Adorno, *Negative Dialectics*, trans. E. B. Ashton (New York: Continuum, 1973), 17–18.

Chapter Five

1 Friedrich Hölderlin, "Rousseau," *Sämtliche Werke*, ed. Paul Stapf (Berlin and Darmstadt: Der Tempel Verlag, 1960), 227: "Dem Sehnenden war/ Der Wink genug, und Winke sind/ Von alters her die Sprache der Götter." My translation.

2 Hans-Georg Gadamer, *Truth and Method*, trans. Joel Weisheimer and Donald G. Marshall (New York: Crossroad Publications, 1990), 483.

3 See Sigmund Freud, *Three Essays on the Theory of Sexuality*, trans. James Strachey (New York: Basic Books, 1975), Third Essay, 90. See Part Three above, Chapter 1, n. 10.

4 Adorno, *Aesthetic Theory*, 82.

5 Samuel Beckett, *How It Is*, 138. As before, references to this work will, in future, be cited by H.

6 See Friedrich Hölderlin, "In lovely blue," in *Hymns and Fragments*, trans. and ed. Richard Sieburth (Princeton: Princeton University Press, 1984), 248–253. Also see the first page of Novalis, *Heinrich von Ofterdingen*, trans. Palmer Hilty (Prospect Heights: Waveland Press, 1990).

7 Regarding these gleams, I would like to note that in *Austerlitz*, W. G. Sebald alludes to a "gleam of light," "a faint glimmer of light from above," recapitulating its allegorical significance as an indication of possible, eventual redemption. See *Austerlitz*, trans. Anthea Bell (New York: Random House, 2001), 53. In homage, Sebald's "borrowings" from Beckett are surprisingly numerous—and bear a similarly desperate hope.

8 Dante Alighieri, *The Inferno*, trans. Robert Hollander and Jean Hollander (New York: Doubleday, 2000), 42–43.

Chapter Six

1 See Dante Alighieri, *Purgatorio*, op. cit., XIX, ll. 118–120, 188–189: "Se come l'occhio nostro non s'aderse/ in alto, fisso a le cose terrene,/ così giustizia qui a terra il merse." My translation.

2 Max Horkheimer and Theodor Adorno, *Dialectic of Enlightenment*, trans. Edmund Jephcott, ed. Gunzelin Schmid Noerr (Stanford: Stanford University Press, 2002), 32.

3 Georg Wilhelm Friedrich Hegel, "Introduction," *The Philosophy of History*, trans. Leo Rauch (Indianapolis: Hackett Publishing Company, 1988), 24. The Hegelian influence on Beckett appears not only with regard to the dialectic of lordship and bondage in *How It Is*, but also with regard to Hegel's powerfully

evocative "*Schriftbild*" for comprehending the course of history—and the extent of human cruelty. Slaughterhouse images appear in each of the novels in Beckett's great trilogy. Slaughterhouses are never far from scenes where Beckett's characters try to survive. Wandering into regions with which he was not familiar, Molloy remarks that slaughterhouses "are everywhere, the country is full of them" (*Malloy*, Part I, 40). In *Malone Dies*, Beckett tells a story about a family of animal slaughterers (*Malone Dies*, 193–200, 206ff.). And Beckett's unnamable narrator-voice lives in a jar opposite a restaurant on the way to an abattoir (UN 321–322).

4 Susan Buck-Morss, *Hegel, Haiti, and Universal History* (Pitttsburgh: University of Pittsburgh Press, 2009), 16. In Beckett's *The Unnamable* (343), the narrator reflects that he may be "a tenth-rate Toussaint L'Ouverture." He is referring to the leader of the Haitian revolution that freed the slaves from European rule, set up a constitution, and made the island a republic. With this allusion, the narrator is clearly invoking a struggle for *social and civil* justice. At stake is not the metaphysical, cosmological, or ontological dimensions of justice. In Beckett's *How It Is*, we can find the "concrete exemplification" that is needed. But as regards Hegel's system, Beckett clearly would agree with Buck-Morss. In *The Unnamable* (UN 286), one of his narrative voices says: "The thing to avoid, I don't know why, is the spirit of the system."

5 Buck-Morss, *Hegel*, 21.

6 Buck-Morss, *Hegel*, 250.

7 Ralph Waldo Emerson, "Fate," in *Essays and Lectures*, ed. Joel Porte (New York: The Library of America, 1983), 953.

8 See Franz Kafka's fragment, "Before the Law," which appears in a different version in his novel *The Trial*. In this fragment, a "man from the country" waits at the entrance to the Law, hoping to be admitted. He dies there without ever attempting to pass the first of the innumerable gates.

9 Cited in Buck-Morss, op. cit., 49. Her source is Karl Rosenkranz, *Georg Wilhelm Friedrich Hegels Leben* (Darmstadt: Wissenschaftliche Buchgesellschaft, 1977), 543.

10 See Adorno, *Kierkegaard: Construction of the Aesthetic*, trans. Robert Hullot-Kentor (Minneapolis: University of Minnesota Press, 1989), 29.

11 I am borrowing the quoted words from Stanley Cavell, *Emerson's Transcendental Etudes* (Stanford: Stanford University Press, 2003). The phrase strikes me as a fitting question about Beckett's ending to the tale, although Cavell is not referring to Beckett, but to Descartes's melodrama of the cogito.

12 See "Break from the Material," in Adorno, *Philosophy of Modern Music*, trans. Anne Mitchell and Wesley Blomster (New York: Seabury Press, 1973).

13 See, in this regard, the essays in David S. Stern, ed., *Essays on Hegel's Philosophy of Subjective Spirit* (Albany: State University of New York Press, 2013), 121–137, 139–154, and 155–179.

14 Robert Hullot-Kentor, *Things beyond Resemblance: Collected Essays on Theodor W. Adorno* (New York: Columbia University Press, 2006), 60.

15 See my essay on "*The Lost Ones*: A Tale for Holocaust Remembrance," forthcoming in the journal *Philosophy and Literature*.

16 Buck-Morss, op. cit., 75.

17 Catherine Chalier, *What Ought I to Do? Morality in Kant and Levinas*, trans. Jane M. Todd (Ithaca: Cornell University Press, 2002), 1–3.

18 See Sandra Wynands, *Iconic Spaces: The Dark Theology of Samuel Beckett* (Notre Dame: University of Notre Dame Press, 2007), 136.

19 See Walter Benjamin, "Theses on the Philosophy of History," in *Illuminations*, trans. Harry Zohn (New York: Schocken, 1969), 256.

20 See Dante, *Purgatorio*, bilingual edition, trans. W. S. Merwin (New York: Alfred A. Knopf, 2000), III, ll. 58–60, 24–25: "da man sinistra m'appari una gente/ d'anime, che movieno i piè ver' noi,/ e non pareva, si venian lente." My translation.

21 Concerning Beckett's numerology, see Brett Stevens, "A Purgatorial Calculus: Beckett's Mathematics in 'Quad'," in S. E. Gontarski, ed., *A Companion to Samuel Beckett* (Malden, MA: Wiley-Blackwell, 2010), 164–181.

22 Thomas Hobbes, *De Corpore*, published in 1655. See Philip Pettit, *Made with Words: Hobbes on Language, Mind, and Politics* (Princeton: Princeton University Press, 2008), 43–44.

23 Buck-Morss, op. cit., 88.

24 Levinas, *Otherwise than Being, or Beyond Essence*, trans. Alphonso Lingis (Pittsburgh: Duquesne University Press, 1998), 159.

25 This is Kant's phrase, in "Idea for a Universal History with a Cosmopolitan Purpose," in *Kant's Political Writings*, ed. Hans Reiss (Cambridge: Cambridge University Press, 1970).

26 See C. J. Ackerly, "Samuel Beckett and Science," in S. E. Gontarski, ed., *A Companion to Samuel Beckett*, 143–165.

27 See Maurice Blanchot, *The Infinite Conversation* (Minneapolis: University of Minnesota Press, 1993), 314.

28 Adorno, "On Lyric Poetry and Society," *Notes to Literature*, trans. Shierry Weber Nicholsen (New York: Columbia University Press, 1991), vol. I, 54.

29 See Hullot-Kentor, op. cit., 190–192. In "Apple Criticizes Tree of Knowledge," he speculates on how dialogue according to Jürgen Habermas's theory of communicative action might intervene to "rectify" the relation between Pozzo and Lucky. Hullot-Kentor quotes Karl-Otto Apel's argument for this theory, which Apel formulates in a mouthful of extremely long, highly abstract philosophical terminology: a Germanic sentence that, if inserted into a performance of Beckett's play and spoken by one of his characters, would certainly have evoked much audience laughter, its "quaquaqua" sounding like an ironic parody of philosophical solemnity. So much for "messianic hopes"!

30 See Beckett, *Waiting for Godot* (New York: Grove Press, 1954), 28–30. And see Hullot-Kentor, op. cit., 190–192.

31 Benjamin, "Theologico-Political Fragment," op. cit., 312.

32 Levinas, "The Ego and the Totality," in Alphonso Lingis (ed.), *Collected Philosophical Papers* (Pittsburgh: Duquesne University Press, 1998), 40.

33 On waiting in hope, for the moment to realize utopia by means of an apocalyptic intervention in history signifying the time of redemption, see Siegfried Kracauer's essay, "The Ones Who Are Waiting," in *The Mass Ornament: Weimar Essays*, trans. Thomas Y. Levin (Cambridge: Harvard University Press, 1995).

34 Blanchot, *The Infinite Conversation* (Minneapolis: University of Minnesota Press, 1993), 314. In "Words Must Travel Far" (op. cit., 329–331), Blanchot discusses Beckett's *How It Is*.

35 Adorno, *Aesthetic Theory*, 117.

36 Franz Rosenzweig, *Star of Redemption*, trans. William H. Hallo (Notre Dame: Notre Dame Press, 1985), 194.

37 G. W. F. Hegel, *Phenomenology of Spirit*, trans. A. V. Miller (Oxford: Clarendon Press, 1977), §671, 409.

38 Rebecca Comay, *Mourning Sickness: Hegel and the French Revolution* (Stanford: Stanford University Press, 2011), 131.

39 Comay, *Mourning Sickness*, 131.

40 Comay, *Mourning Sickness*, 132.

41 Adorno, *Aesthetic* Theory, 117.

42 Beckett, *Proust and Three Dialogues with Georges Duthuit* (London: John Calder, 1965), 11.

43 There is, in Beckett, an agitated dialectical oscillation, a certain "*Schweben*," between positions important in the literature of German Romanticism and positions strongly associated with contemporary anti-Romanticism and the existential literature of disenchantment. On Romanticism, see Jean-Luc Nancy and Philippe Lacoue-Labarthe, *The Literary Absolute: The Theory of Literature in German Romanticism*, trans. P. Barnard and C. Lester. Albany: State University of New York Press, 1987.

44 Hannah Arendt, *The Origins of Totalitarianism* (New York: Harcourt Brace Jovanovich, 1973), 479. And see Augustine, *The City of God Against the Pagans*, trans. R. W. Dyson (Cambridge: Cambridge University Press, 1998), bk. XXII, ch. 21, 532.

45 Gottfried Benn, "Gesänge," in Kurt Pinthus (ed.), *Menschheitsdämmerung: Symphonie jüngster Dichtung* (Berlin: Rowohlt, 1920; Hamburg: Rowohlt Taschenbuch Verlag, 1959), 186. My translation.

46 Paul Celan, "Breathturn", *Selected Poems and Prose of Paul Celan*, trans. John Felstiner (New York: W.W. Norton, 2001), 135. My translation.

47 Benjamin, "Goethe's Elective Affinities," trans. Stanley Corngold, in *Selected Writings 1913–1926* (Cambridge: Harvard University Press, 1996), 356.

48 Paul Celan, *Fadensonnen, Gesammelte Werke* (Frankfurt am Main: Suhrkamp Verlag, 1983), vol. II, 152. Translation altered.

49 Beckett, *The Unnamable*, 406, 380.

BIBLIOGRAPHY

Abbott, H. Porter. *The Fiction of Samuel Beckett: Form and Effect*. Berkeley: University of California Press, 1973.

Abbott, H. Porter. "Beginning Again: The Post-Narrative Art of *Texts for Nothing* and *How It Is*," in John Pilling, ed., *The Cambridge Companion to Beckett*. Cambridge: Cambridge University Press, 1994.

Adorno, Theodor W. *Negative Dialectics*. Trans. E. B. Ashton. New York: Continuum Publishing Co., 1973.

Adorno, Theodor W. *Minima Moralia: Reflections from Damaged Life*. Trans. Edmund Jephcott. London: Verso Editions, 1978.

Adorno, Theodor W. "On Lyric Poetry and Society," *Notes to Literature*, vol. I. Trans. Shierry Weber Nicholsen. New York: Columbia University Press, 1991.

Adorno, Theodor W. *Aesthetic Theory*. Trans. Robert Hullot-Kentor. Minneapolis: University of Minnesota Press, 1997.

Agamben, Giorgio. *The Time That Remains: A Commentary on the Letter to the Romans*. Trans. Patricia Dailey. Stanford: Stanford University Press, 2005.

Agamben, Giorgio. *The Sacrament of Language: An Archaeology of the Oath*. Trans. Adam Kotsko. Stanford: Stanford University Press, 2011.

Albright, Daniel. *Beckett and Aesthetics*. New York: Cambridge University Press, 2003.

Altizer, Thomas. *The Call to Radical Theology*. Ed. Lissa McCollough. Albany: State University of New York Press, 2012.

Alvarez, A., *Beckett*. London: Fontana Press, 1973, 1992.

Arendt, Hannah. *The Origins of Totalitarianism*. New York: Harcourt Brace Jovanovich, 1973.

Atik, Anne. *How It Was: A Memoir of Samuel Beckett*. London: Faber, 2001; Shoemaker & Hoard, 2005.

Auster, Paul. *The Art of Hunger and Other Essays*. London: Menard Press, 1982.

Badiou, Alain. *Beckett*. Paris: Hachette, 1955.

Badiou, Alain. *L'Etre et l'événement*. Paris: Seuil, 1988.

Badiou, Alain. "On Subtraction," in Ray Brassier and Alberto Toscano, ed., *Theoretical Writings*. London: Continuum, 2006.

Badiou, Alain. *Conditions*. Trans. Steven Corcoran. New York: Continuum, 2008.

Banham, Gary. "Cinders: Derrida with Beckett," in Richard Lane, ed., *Beckett and Philosophy*. New York: Palgrave Macmillan, 2002.

Banville, John. "Beckett: Storming for Beauty," *The New York Review of Books*, vol. LIX, no. 5, March 22, 2012.

Bataille, Georges. *The Absence of Myth: Writings on Surrealism*. Trans. Michael Richardson. New York: Verso, 1994.

Beckett, Samuel. *Whoroscope*. Paris: Hours Press, 1930.

Beckett, Samuel. *Echo's Bones and Other Precipitates*. Paris: Europa, 1935.
Beckett, Samuel. *Waiting For Godot*. New York: Grove Press, 1954.
Beckett, Samuel. *Endgame*. New York: Grove Press, 1958.
Beckett, Samuel. *Three Novels: Molloy, Malone Dies, The Unnamable*. New York:
    Grove Press, 1958.
Beckett, Samuel. *Watt*. Paris: Olympia Press, 1953; New York: Grove Press, 1953.
Beckett, Samuel. *How It Is*. New York: Grove Press, 1964.
Beckett, Samuel. *Play*, in *Play, and Two Short Pieces for Radio*. London: Faber &
    Faber, 1964.
Beckett, Samuel. *Stories and Texts for Nothing*. New York: Grove Press, 1967.
Beckett, Samuel. *More Pricks than Kicks*. London: Calder and Boyars, 1970.
Beckett, Samuel. *I Can't Go On, I'll Go On: A Samuel Beckett Reader*, ed. Richard
    Seaver. New York: Grove Press, 1976.
Beckett, Samuel. *Disjecta: Miscellaneous Writings and a Dramatic Fragment*.
    London: John Calder, 1983; New York: Grove Press, 1984.
Beckett, Samuel. *Proust and Three Dialogues with Georges Duthuit*. London: John
    Calder, 1987.
Beckett, Samuel. *Dream of Fair to Middling Women*, ed. Eoin O'Brian and Edith
    Fournier New York: Arcade Publishing Co., 1992.
Beckett, Samuel. *The Complete Short Prose 1929–1989*. New York: Grove Press,
    1995.
Beckett, Samuel. *Nohow On*. New York: Grove Press, 1996.
Beckett, Samuel. *The Letters of Samuel Beckett 1929–1949*. Ed. Martha D.
    Fehsenfeld, Lois M. Overbeck, George Craig, and Daniel Gunn. Cambridge:
    Cambridge University Press, 2009.
Beckett, Samuel. *A Companion to Samuel Beckett*, ed. S. E. Gontarski. Malden:
    Wiley-Blackwell, 2010.
Beckett, Samuel. *Manuscripts*. Department of Special Collections, Beckett
    International Foundation, The University of Reading
Begam, Robert. *Samuel Beckett and the End of Modernity*. Stanford: Stanford
    University Press, 1996.
Benjamin, Walter. *Illuminations*. Trans. Harry Zohn. New York: Schocken,
    1969.
Benjamin, Walter. *Reflections: Essays, Aphorisms, Autobiographical Writings*.
    Trans. Edmund Jephcott. New York: Schocken, 1986.
Benjamin, Walter. *Selected Writings 1913–1926*, vol. I. Cambridge: Harvard
    University Press, 1996.
Benjamin, Walter. *The Origin of the German Tragic Drama*. Trans. John Osborne.
    London: New Left Books, 1998.
Benjamin, Walter. *Selected Writings, 1927–1934*, vol. II. Cambridge: Harvard
    University Press, 1999.
Benn, Gottfried, "Gesänge," in Kurt Pinthus, ed., *Menschheitsdämmerung:
    Symphonie jüngster Dichtung*. Hamburg: Rowohlt Taschenbuch Verlag, 1959.
Ben-Zvi, Linda. "Samuel Beckett, Fritz Mauthner, and the Limits of Language,"
    PMLA, vol. 95 (March 1980), 183–200.
Bernstein, Jay M. *The Philosophy of the Novel: Lukács, Marxism, and the Dialectic
    of Form*. Minneapolis: The University of Minnesota Press, 1984.
Bernstein, Jay M. "Philosophy's Refuge: Adorno in Beckett," in David Wood, ed.,
    Philosophers' Poets. New York: Routledge, 1990.

Bernstein, Jay M. *The Fate of Art: Aesthetic Alienation from Kant to Derrida and Adorno*. University Park: The Pennsylvania State University Press, 1992.

Bernstein, Jay M., ed., *Classic and Romantic German Aesthetics*. Cambridge: Cambridge University Press, 2003.

Bernstein, Jay M. *Against Voluptuous Bodies: Late Modernism and the Meaning of Painting*. Stanford: Stanford University Press, 2006.

Bersani, Leo. *The Culture of Redemption*. Cambridge: Harvard University Press, 1990.

Bersani, Leo and Ulysse Dutoit. *Arts of Impoverishment: Beckett, Rothko, Resnais*. Cambridge: Harvard University Press, 1993.

Blanchot, Maurice. *L'Entretien Infini*. Paris: Gallimard, 1969.

Blanchot, Maurice. *Après Coup, précédé par "Le Ressassement éternel."* Paris: Les Éditions de Minuit, 1983.

Brater, Enoch. *Beyond Minimalism: Beckett's Late Style in the Theater*. Oxford and New York: Oxford University Press, 1987.

Brater, Enoch. *Drama in the Text: Beckett's Late Fiction*. Oxford and New York: Oxford University Press, 1994.

Bruns, Gerald L. *Tragic Thoughts at the End of Philosophy: Language, Literature, and Ethical Theory*. Evanston: Northwestern University Press, 1999.

Bruns, Gerald L. *On the Anarchy of Poetry and Philosophy: A Guide for the Unruly*. New York: Fordham University Press, 2006.

Bruns, Gerald L. *On Ceasing to Be Human*. Stanford: Stanford University Press, 2011.

Bryden, Mary. *Samuel Beckett and the Idea of God*. New York: St. Martin's Press, 1998.

Buck-Morss, Susan. *Hegel, Haiti, and Universal History*. Pitttsburgh: University of Pittsburgh Press, 2009.

Calder, John. *The Philosophy of Samuel Beckett*. London: John Calder, 2001.

Cavell, Stanley. *Must We Mean What We Say?* New York: Charles Scribner's Sons, 1969.

Cavell, Stanley. *The Claim of Reason: Wittgenstein, Skepticism, Morality, and Tragedy*. New York: Oxford University Press, 1979.

Cavell, Stanley. *In Quest of the Ordinary: Lines of Skepticism and Romanticism*. Chicago: University of Chicago, 1988.

Celan, Paul. *Poems of Paul Celan*. Trans. Michael Hamburger. New York: Persea Books, 1972.

Celan, Paul. *Selected Poems and Prose of Paul Celan*. Trans. John Felstiner. New York: Norton, 2001.

Chesney, Duncan M. *Silence Nowhen: Late Modernism, Minimalism, and Silence in the Work of Samuel Beckett*. New York: Peter Lang, 2013.

Ciaran, Ross. *Beckett's Art of Absence*. New York: Palgrave Macmillan, 2011.

Comay, Rebecca, *Mourning Sickness: Hegel and the French Revolution*. Stanford: Stanford University Press, 2011.

Connor, Steven. *Samuel Beckett: Repetition, Theory, and Text*. Oxford: Blackwell, 1988.

Critchley, Simon. *Very Little . . . Almost Nothing: Death, Philosophy, Literature*. New York: Routledge, 1997.

Critchley, Simon. *The Faith of the Faithless: Experiments in Political Theology*. London and New York: Verso, New Left Books, 2012.

Dante Alighieri. *Purgatorio*, bilingual edition. Trans. W. S. Merwin. New York: Alfred A. Knopf, 2000.

Dante Alighieri. *The Inferno*, bilingual edition. Trans. Robert Hollander and Jean Hollander. New York: Doubleday, 2000.

Derrida, Jacques. *Writing and Difference*. Trans. Alan Bates. Chicago: University of Chicago Press, 1978.

Derrida, Jacques. "How to Avoid Speaking: Denials," in *Derrida and Negative Theology*. Ed. Harold Coward and Toby Foshay. Albany: State University of New York Press, 1992.

Derrida, Jacques. *Arts of Literature*. Trans. and ed. Derek Altridge. New York and London: Routledge, 1992.

Derrida, Jacques. *Monolingualisme de l'autre*. Paris: Galilée, 1996.

Derrida, Jacques. *A Taste for the Secret*. Trans. Giacomo Donis. Cambridge: Polity Press, 2001; Malden, MA: Blackwell Publishers, 2001.

Derrida, Jacques. *Futures: Of Derrida*. Richard Rand, ed., Stanford: Stanford University Press, 2001.

Derrida, Jacques. "Faith and Knowledge: The Two Sources of 'Religion' at the Limits of Reason Alone," trans. Samuel Weber, in Gil Anidjar, ed., *Acts of Religion*. New York: Routledge, 2002.

Derrida, Jacques. "Language Is Never Owned," Interview with Evelyne Grossman, June 29, 2000, in Derrida, *Rogues: Two Essays on Reason*. Trans. Pascale-Anne Brault and Michael Naas. Stanford: Stanford University Press, 2005.

Emerson, Ralph Waldo. *Essays and Lectures*, ed. Joel Porte. New York: Library of America, 1983.

Federman, Raymond and Fletcher, John. *Samuel Beckett, His Works and His Critics: An Essay in Bibliography*. Berkeley: University of California Press, 1970.

Feldman, Matthew. *Beckett's Books: A Cultural History of the Interwar Notes*. London and New York: Continuum, 2006.

Feldman, Matthew and Maude, Ulrike, ed., *Beckett and Phenomenology*. New York: Continuum, 2009.

Fenves, Peter. *The Messianic Reduction: Walter Benjamin and the Shape of Time*. Stanford: Stanford University Press, 2011.

Fifield, Peter. *Late Modernist Style in Samuel Beckett and Emmanuel Levinas*. New York and London: Palgrave Macmillan, 2013.

Fort, Jeff. *The Imperative to Write: Destitutions of the Sublime in Kafka, Blanchot, and Beckett*. New York: Fordham University Press, 2014.

Gibson, Andrew. *Beckett and Badiou: The Pathos of Indeterminacy*. Oxford and New York: Oxford University Press, 2006.

Gontarski, S. E. "Introduction," *Samuel Beckett: The Complete Short Stories 1929–1989*. New York: Grove Press, 1995.

Gontarski, S. E. "Introduction," "The Conjuring of Something Out of Nothing: Samuel Beckett's 'Closed Space' Novels," *Nohow On: Company, Ill Seen Ill Said, Worstward Ho*. New York: Grove Press, 1996.

Gontarski, S. E. *Beckett's Happy Days: A Manuscript Study*. Columbus: Ohio State University Libraries, 1997.

Gontarski, S. E. and Uhlmann, Anthony, ed. *Beckett After Beckett*. Gainesville, Florida: University of Florida Press, 2006.

Gontarski, S. E., ed. *A Companion to Samuel Beckett*. Malden, MA: Wiley-Blackwell, 2010.

Gontarski, S. E., ed. *On Beckett: Essays and Criticism*. New York: Grove Press, 1986, revised edition 2012.

Hägglund, Martin. *Radical Atheism: Derrida and the Time of Life*. Stanford: Stanford University Press, 2008.

Hägglund, Martin. *Dying for Time: Proust, Woolf, Nabokov*. Cambridge: Harvard University Press, 2012.

Hamann, Johann G. "Aesthetica in Nuce," trans. Joyce P. Crick, in Jay Bernstein, ed., *Classic and Romantic German Aesthetics*. Cambridge: Cambridge University Press, 2003.

Harvey, Lawrence. *Samuel Beckett, Poet and Critic*. Princeton: Princeton University Press, 1970.

Hegel, G. W. F. *Phenomenology of Spirit*. Trans. A. V. Miller. Oxford: Clarendon Press, 1977.

Hegel, G. W. F. *Faith and Knowledge*. Trans. Walter Cerf and H. S. Harris. Albany: State University of New York, 1977.

Hegel, G. W. F. *The Philosophy of History*. Trans. Leo Rauch. Indianapolis: Hackett Publishing Co., 1988.

Hegel, G. W. F. *Lectures on the Philosophy of Spirit*. Trans. and intro. Robert R. Williams. New York: Oxford University Press, 2007.

Heidegger, Martin. *Being and Time*. Trans. John Macquarrie and Edward Robinson. New York: Harper & Row, 1962.

Heidegger, Martin. *On the Way to Language*. Trans. Peter D. Hertz. New York: Harper & Row, 1971.

Heidegger, Martin. Martin Heidegger, "Interview with Rudolf Augstein and Georg Wolff," *Der Spiegel* 30 (May 1976), 193–219.

Hill, Leslie. *Beckett's Fiction: In Different Words*. Cambridge: Cambridge University Press, 1990.

Hofmannsthal, Hugo von. "The Lord Chandos Letter." Trans. Joel Rotenberg. *New York Review of Books*, 2005, 121.

Hölderlin, Friedrich. *Sämtliche Werke* [*Grosse Stuttgarter Ausgabe*], 7 vols. Ed. Friedrich Beissner *et al*. Stuttgart: W. Kohlhammer, 1943–1985.

Hölderlin, Friedrich. "In lovely blue. . ." in Richard Sieburth, ed., *Friedrich Hölderlin: Hymns and Fragments*. Princeton: Princeton University Press, 1984.

Hölderlin, Friedrich. "Becoming in Dissolution," *Essays and Letters on Theory*. Trans. and ed. Thomas Pfau. Albany: State University of New York Press, 1988.

Hullot-Kentor, Robert. *Things beyond Resemblance: Collected Essays on Theodor W. Adorno*. New York: Columbia University Press, 2006.

Hume, David. *Enquiries Concerning Human Understanding and Enquiries Concerning the Principles of Morals*. L. A. Selby-Bigge, 3rd edn. revised, ed. P. H. Niddich. Oxford: Oxford University Press, 1975.

Hunkehr, Thomas. "The Role of the Dead Man in the Game of Writing: Beckett and Foucault," in Richard Lane, ed. *Beckett and Philosophy*. New York: Palgrave, 2002.

Husserl, Edmund. *Ideas: General Introduction to Pure Phenomenology*. Trans. W. R. Boyce-Gibson. New York: Collier-Macmillan, 1963.

Husserl, Edmund. *The Crisis of European Sciences and Transcendental Phenomenology*. Trans. David Carr. Evanston: Northwestern University Press, 1970.

Iser, Wolfgang. "The Pattern of Negativity in Beckett's Prose." *The Georgia Review*, vol. 29, no. 3 (1974), 1–9.

Iser, Wolfgang. "When Is the End Not the End? The Idea of Fiction in Beckett," in S. E. Gontarski, ed., *On Beckett: Essays and Criticism*. New York: Grove Press, 1986.

Iser, Wolfgang and Sanford Budick. *Languages of the Unsayable*. New York: Columbia University Press, 1989.

Janvier, Ludovic. *Beckett par lui-même*. Paris: Seuil, 1979.

Jay, Martin. "Is Experience Still in Crisis?" in Tom Huhn, ed., *The Cambridge Companion to Adorno*. Cambridge: Cambridge University Press, 2004.

Jones, David Houston. *Samuel Beckett and Testimony*. New York: Palgrave Macmillan, 2011.

Kaelin, Eugene. *The Unhappy Consciousness: The Poetic Plight of Samuel Beckett*. Boston: D. Reidel, Kluwer, 1981.

Kant, Immanuel. *Critique of Practical Reason*. Trans. Lewis White Beck. New York: The Liberal Arts Press, 1956.

Kant, Immanuel. *Religion Within the Bounds of Reason Alone*. Trans. Theodore M. Greene and Hoyt H. Hudson. New York: Harper & Row, 1960.

Kant, Immanuel. *Critique of Judgment*. Trans. Werner Pluhar. Indianapolis: Hackett Publishing, 1987.

Kennedy, Seán and Weiss, Katherine, eds. *Samuel Beckett: History, Memory, Archive*. New York: Palgrave Macmillan, 2009.

Kenner, Hugh. *Samuel Beckett: A Critical Study*. New York: Grove Press, 1961.

Kierkegaard, Søren. *Stages on Life's Way*. Trans. Walter Lowrie. Princeton: Princeton University Press, 1940.

Kierkegaard, Søren. *Either/Or*, vol. I. Trans. David F. Swenson and Lillian M. Swenson, with revisions by Howard A. Johnson. Princeton: Princeton University Press, 1971.

Kierkegaard, Søren. *Either/Or*, Vol. II. Trans. Walter Lowrie, with revisions by Howard A. Johnson. Princeton: Princeton University Press, 1971.

Kierkegaard, Søren. *Repetition and Fear and Trembling*. Trans. and ed., Howard V. Hong and Edna H. Hong. Princeton: Princeton University Press, 1983.

Kleinberg-Levin, David Michael. *Before the Voice of Reason*. Albany: State University of New York Press, 2008.

Kleinberg-Levin, David Michael. *Redeeming Words and the Promise of Happiness: A Critical Theory Approach to Wallace Stevens and Vladimir Nabokov*. New York: Lexington Books, Rowman & Littlefield, 2012.

Kleinberg-Levin, David Michael. *Redeeming Words: Language and the Promise of Happiness in the Stories of Döblin and Sebald*. Albany: State University of New York Press, 2013.

Knowlson, James. *Damned to Fame: The Life of Samuel Beckett*. London: Bloomsbury; New York: Grove Press, 1996.

Kracauer, Siegfried, "The Ones Who Are Waiting," in *The Mass Ornament: Weimar Essays*. Trans. Thomas Y. Levin. Cambridge: Harvard University Press, 1995.

Lane, Richard, ed. *Beckett and Philosophy*. New York: Palgrave Macmillan, 2002.

Levin, David Michael. "Civilized Cruelty: Nietzsche on the Disciplinary Practices of Western Culture," *New Nietzsche Studies*, vol. 5, nos. 1–2 (summer 2002), 72–94.

Loevlie, Elizabeth M. *Literary Silences in Pascal, Rousseau, and Beckett*. New York: Clarendon, 2003.

Lukács, Georg. *Theory of the Novel*, trans. Anna Bostock. Cambridge: The MIT Press, 1971.

Mallarmé, Stéphane. *Oeuvres complètes*, ed. Henri Mondor and G. Jean-Aubry. Paris: Bibliothèque de la Pléiade, Gallimard, 1945.

Marcuse, Herbert. *Negations: Essays in Critical Theory*, trans. Jeremy J. Shapiro. Boston: Beacon Press, 1968.

Maude, Ulrike and Feldman, Matthew, ed. *Beckett and Phenomenology*. New York: Continuum, 2009.

Menke, Christoph. "Der Stand des Streits: Samuel Beckett, *Endspiel*," in *Die Gegenwart der Tragödie: Versuch über Urteil und Spiel*. Frankfurt am Main: Suhrkamp Verlag, 2005.

Menke, Christoph. *Tragic Play: Irony and Theater from Sophocles to Beckett*. Trans. James Phillips. New York: Columbia University Press, 2009.

Moran, Dermot. "Beckett and Philosophy," in C. Murray, ed., *Samuel Beckett: One Hundred Years*. Dublin: New Island Press, 2006.

Murphy P. J. "Beckett and the Philosophers," in John Pilling, ed., *The Cambridge Companion to Beckett* Cambridge: Cambridge University Press, 1994.

Naas, Michael. *Miracle and Machine: Jacques Derrida and the Two Sources of Religion, Science and the Media*. New York: Fordham University Press, 2012.

Nabokov, Vladimir. *Strong Opinions*. New York: Vintage International, 1990.

Nancy, Jean-Luc. *Hegel: L'inquiétude du negatif*. Paris: Hachette, 1977.

Nancy, Jean-Luc and Philippe Lacoue-Labarthe. Trans. P. Barnard and C. Lester. *The Literary Absolute: The Theory of Literature in German Romanticism*. Albany: State University of New York Press, 1987.

Nietzsche, Friedrich. *Thus Spoke Zarathustra*, trans. Walter Kaufmann. New York: Viking Penguin, 1954.

Nietzsche, Friedrich. *The Will to Power*. Trans. Walter Kaufmann. New York: Random House Vintage Books, 1967.

Nietzsche, Friedrich. "On Truth and Lies in a Nonmoral Sense," in Daniel Breazeale, ed. and trans., *Philosophy and Truth: Selections from Nietzsche's Notebooks of the Early 1870s*. New Jersey and London: Humanities Press International, 1979.

Nixon, Mark. *Samuel Beckett's German Diaries 1936–1937*. New York and London: Continuum International Publishing, 2011.

Nixon, Mark and Dirk Van Hulle. *Samuel Beckett's Library*. Cambridge: Cambridge University Press, 2013.

Novalis, Friedrich von Hardenberg. *Heinrich von Ofterdingen*. Trans. Palmer Hilty. Prospect Heights: Waveland Press, 1990; New York: Continuum Publishing Co., 1992.

Pettit, Philip. *Made with Words: Hobbes on Language, Mind, and Politics*. Princeton: Princeton University Press, 2008.

Piette, Adam. *Remembering and the Sound of Words: Mallarmé, Proust, Joyce, Beckett*. New York: Clarendon, 1996.

Pilling, John. "How It Is," in James Knowlson and John Pilling, ed., *Frescoes of the Skull: The Later Prose and Drama of Samuel Beckett*. London: John Calder, 1979.

Pilling, John, ed. *The Cambridge Companion to Beckett*. Cambridge: Cambridge University Press, 1994.

Pilling, John. "Beckett and Mauthner Revisited," in S. E. Gontarski and Anthony Uhlmann, ed., *Beckett After Beckett*. Gainesville, Florida: University of Florida Press, 2006.

Rabaté, Jean-Michel. "Philosophizing with Beckett: Adorno and Badiou," in S. E. Gontarski, ed., *A Companion to Samuel Beckett*. Malden, Massachusetts: Wiley-Blackwell, 2010.

Rabinovitz, Rubin. *The Development of Samuel Beckett's Fiction*. Chicago: The University of Illinois Press, 1984.

Ricks, Christopher. *Beckett's Dying Words. The Clarendon Lectures 1990*. New York: Oxford University Press, 1993.

Rilke, Rainer Maria. *Sämtliche Werke in zwölf Bänden*, ed. Rilke-Archiv, Ruth Sieber-Rilke and Ernst Zinn. Frankfurt am Main: Insel Verlag Werkausgabe, 1976.

Robinson, Michael. *The Long Sonata of the Dead*. New York: Grove Press, 1969.

Rorty, Richard. *Contingency, Irony, and Solidarity*. Cambridge: Cambridge University Press, 1989.

Sabin, Margery. "Signs of Life and Death in Beckett's Trilogy." In *The Dialect of the Tribe: Speech and Community in Modern Fiction*, 241–291. Oxford: Oxford University Press, 1987.

Santner, Eric. *On the Psychotheology of Everyday Life: Reflections on Freud and Rosenzweig*. Chicago: University of Chicago Press, 2001.

Santner, Eric. *On Creaturely Life: Rilke Benjamin Sebald*. Chicago: University of Chicago Press, 2006.

Smith, Joseph E., ed. *The World of Samuel Beckett*. Baltimore: The Johns Hopkins University Press, 1991.

Smith, Russell. *Beckett and Ethics*. New York: Continuum, 2008.

Szafraniec, Asja. *Beckett, Derrida, and the Event of Literature*. Stanford: Stanford University Press, 2007.

Taubes, Jacob. *Occidental Eschatology*. Trans. David Ratmoko. Stanford: Stanford University Press, 2009.

Trezise, Thomas. *Into the Breach: Samuel Beckett and the Ends of Literature*. Princeton: Princeton University Press, 1990.

Trezise, Thomas. *Witnessing Witnessing: On the Reception of Holocaust Survivor Testimony*. New York: Fordham University Press, 2013.

Ullman, Anthony. *Beckett and Poststructuralism*. Cambridge: Cambridge University Press, 1999.

Ullman, Anthony. *Samuel Beckett and the Philosophical Image*. Cambridge: Cambridge University Press, 2007.

Ullman, Anthony. "Beckett and Philosophy," in S. E. Gontarski, ed., *A Companion to Samuel Beckett*. Malden, Massachusetts: Wiley-Blackwell, 2010.

Van Hulle, Dirk and Mark Nixon. *Samuel Beckett's Library*. Cambridge: Cambridge University Press, 2013.

Weller, Shane. *A Taste for the Negative: Beckett and Nihilism*. London: Legenda, 2005.

Weller, Shane. *Beckett, Literature and the Ethics of Alterity*. New York: Palgrave Macmillan 2006.

Weller, Shane. *Literature, Philosophy, Nihilism: The Uncanniest of Guests*. New York: Palgrave Macmillan, 2008.

Weller, Shane. "Beckett and Ethics," in S. E. Gontarski, ed., *A Companion to Samuel Beckett*. Malden, Massachusetts: Wiley-Blackwell, 2010.

Wittgenstein, Ludwig. *Philosophical Investigations*. Trans. G. E. M. Anscombe. New York: Macmillan, 1953.

Wittgenstein, Ludwig "Lecture on Ethics," in *Philosophical Occasions: 1912–1951*. Indianapolis and Cambridge: Hackett Publishing Co., 1983.

Wynands, Sandra. *Iconic Spaces: The Dark Theology of Samuel Beckett*. Notre Dame: University of Notre Dame, 2007.

Wolosky, Shira. *Language Mysticism: The Negative Way of Language in Beckett, Eliot, and Celan*. Stanford: Stanford University Press, 1995.

Ziarek, Ewa Plonowska. *The Rhetoric of Failure: Deconstruction of Skepticism, Reinvention of Modernism*. New York: The State University of New York Press, 1995.

PERMISSIONS

INDEX

Abbott, H. Porter, 188, 195

Adorno, Theodor W., on art and reconciliation, 2–4 *passim*, 21, 25, 62, 84, 199, 129, 175, 196; on art and tears, 263n90, 275n244; on authentic art, 95, 231, 257n6, 275n244; on beauty and the promise of happiness, 9, 129, 221; on Beckett's closed immanence, 176; on *Endgame*, 66; on the Enlightenment, 196; on a Gnostic reading of Beckett, 20; on *Waiting for Godot*, 87, 124; on a humanness that does not yet exist, 25, 247–52 *passim*; on justice for victims, 235; on language as bearing the promise of happiness, 10; on language in damaged life, 65, 240; on longing and utopia, 62–9 *passim*, 149–52 *passim*, 175, 201; on meaning and absurdity, 46, 66; on melancholy, longing and happiness in Kierkegaard, 149, 233; on negative dialectics, 87, 90, 170; on nihilism, 20–1, 51, 89; on poetry after Auschwitz, 89; on remembrance in art, 151, 196; on the idea of salvation, 129; on the lyrical, 43, 88, 131, 217; on the promise of happiness, 1–27 *passim*, 37, 170, 196, 221, 259n28; on the standpoint of redemption, 161; on the theological, 265n111; on the torturable body, 194; on traces of hope, 145; on truth in the voice of suffering, 219, 229, 247–9 *passim*; on the word and reconciliation, 84

Agamben, Giorgio, 23, 25, 73

Altizer, Thomas, 47–50, 98, 120, 191–2

Alvarez, Albert, 9, 200, 268n143

Anselm, 54, 281n3

Apostle Paul, 50, 77, 116, 145, 159, 209, 272n205, 274n226, 283n14

Arendt, Hannah, 14, 248, 253, 260n42, 280n22

Aristotle, 11, 233

Auster, Paul, 272n212

Benjamin, Walter, against progress, 183, 239; on art as past, 3; on a history of the vanquished, 187, 235; on a "weak messianic force," 58, 65, 288n2; on bare life ("bloßes Leben"), 239; on dialectic at a standstill, 77–87 *passim*, 124; on guilt, 97, 100; on his relation to theology, 107; on historical memory and redemption, 283n14; on hope and hopelessness, 254; on justice and the figure of the Messiah, 248–9; on justice and the promise of happiness, 6, 80–3; on Klee's "angel of history," 183, 239; on language and the promise of happiness, 15–16, 79–83; on language in relation to justice, 79–83; on meaning lost in the abyss of language, 72, 77–9; on redemption; 3, 6, 79–83, 235, 282n13, 282n14; on tales for children, 139, 142–3; on the art of storytelling, 34–5, 90; on the difference between *Erlebnis* and *Erfahrung*, 34–5; on the German Baroque *Trauerspiel* (Mourning-Play), 37, 54, 77–9, 97, 148, 159;